WRITING IN LIGHT

*The Silent Scenario and the
Japanese Pure Film Movement*

JOANNE BERNARDI

D0924792

WAYNE STATE UNIVERSITY PRESS

DETROIT

Grateful acknowledgment is made to the Japan Foundation for its
generous support of the publication of this volume.

Library of Congress Cataloging-in-Publication Data

Bernardi, Joanne.
Writing in light : the silent scenario and the Japanese pure film
movement / Joanne Bernardi.
p. cm.
Includes bibliographical references and index.
"Notes 000 Select Bibliography 000 Index."
ISBN 0-8143-2926-8 (alk. paper)—ISBN 0-8143-2961-6 (pbk: alk. paper)
1. Motion pictures—Japan—History. 2. Silent films—Japan—History
and criticism. I. Title.
PN1993.5.J3 B47 2001
791.43′0952—dc21

00-011103

WRITING IN LIGHT

In memory of
YODA YOSHIKATA

CONTENTS

ACKNOWLEDGMENTS

THIS BOOK BEGAN in the spring of 1985 with a series of discussions, over a period of five years, with the late screenwriter Yoda Yoshikata. In memory of his patience (as he pointed out, some questions were better than others), and out of gratitude to his family, I dedicate it to him. Many others shared their knowledge and offered generous guidance and assistance early on. Donald Keene was a constant source of knowledge, support, and inspiration as I worked on the first version of this manuscript as my doctoral dissertation at Columbia University. I also thank the members of my committee, Paul Anderer, Richard Peña, Andrew Sarris, and David Wang.

I gratefully acknowledge the following individuals and organizations for granting permission to draw from earlier versions of portions of this book: Amsterdam University Press ("The Pure Film Movement and the Contemporary Drama Genre in Japan" in *Film and the First World War*); Columbia University Press ("Tanizaki Jun'ichirō's 'The Present and Future of the Moving Pictures'" in *Currents in Japanese Culture: Translations and Transformations*, ed. Amy Vladeck Heinrich, 1997); the Center for Japanese Studies at the University of Michigan ("The Literary Link: Tanizaki and the Pure Film Movement" in *A Tanizaki Feast: The International Symposium in Venice*); Richard Koszarski ("Norimasa Kaeriyama and *The Glory of Life*" in *Film History* 9:4 [1997]); and Leonardo Quaresima ("Genre Distinctions in the Japanese Contemporary Drama Film" in *The Birth of Film Genres*).

Among friends in Japan, I am grateful to Ōta Yoneo, not only for his assistance in helping me with sources, but for sharing with me, over the years, his tremendous knowledge of and enthusiasm for the history of Japanese cinema. Thanks, too, to the late Miyagawa Kazuo and Takizawa Osamu,

9

and Yamada Kōhei and other faculty members of the Osaka University of Arts, all of whom gave me a foundation on which to build. Makino Mamoru was, as always, generous with his time and his expertise. This book would not have been possible without his warm hospitality and kind assistance in allowing me to peruse his invaluable collection. Special thanks are due to Mr. Makino for also allowing me to reproduce illustrations from reprint editions of *Katsudō shashinkai, Katsudō shashin zasshi, Katsudō no sekai, Katsudō gahō, Kinema Record,* and *Kinema junpō.* Other illustrations were obtained through the kind intervention of Ted Fowler and Abe Shūjirō. Fujita Mitsuo kindly granted permission to reprint photographs from Tanizaki Jun'ichirō. *Shinchō Nihon bungaku arubamu,* vol. 7 (Tokyo: Shinchōsha, 1985). Hayashi Kanako, formerly of the Kawakita Memorial Film Institute, her successor, Sakano Yuka, and the Kawakita staff enthusiastically provided me with much-needed help in the form of illustrations and screenings.

My former colleagues at Ibaraki University, particularly Shimaoka Susumu and Suzuki Yoshio, were ever supportive and helped me over more than a few hurdles during the difficult early stages of research. At the National Film Center of the Museum of Modern Art in Tokyo, I thank Okajima Hisashi, Curator of Film, Saiki Tomonori, Sazaki Yoriaki, and the staff of the research study center for accommodating my tight schedule during a brief, intense flurry of research, screening, and copying during the summer of 1995. Professor Iwamoto Kenji at Waseda University kindly assisted me with library access. Mizuguchi Kaoru, formerly of the Museum of Kyoto, was very helpful in the early stages of my research, and Moriwaki Kiyotaka, Emma Michitaka, and Arita Yoshio of the Museum of Kyoto selflessly took time from their busy schedules to provide invaluable visual and print materials and refuge from the merciless Kyoto summer. Donald Richie, who is responsible for so many people's earliest opportunities to see Japanese films, was a continuous source of encouragement throughout my research. I would be remiss not to mention here those scholars who helped make my work easier by painstakingly collecting, preserving, and making accessible important material from the period: Iwamoto Kenji, Makino Mamoru, and their colleagues on the "fukkokuban" front, Komatsu Hiroshi and Ogasawara Takeo. Finally, I would have accomplished nothing in Japan without Yamazaki Hiroko, Tobita Junko, Makino Naoko, and the Nakamura and Togasaki families, who graciously shared both their friendship and their hospitality.

On this side of the world, I must first thank my colleague Sharon Willis for sharing her time and valuable insight on a draft of the manuscript and coming up with a wonderful title. Together with Sue Gustafson, she was a major source of support throughout. Colleagues Mariko Tamate and Fumino Shino helped keep me out of many a linguistic loop. The Japan–United

States Friendship Committee and the Social Science Research Council, the Susan B. Anthony Institute for Gender Studies at the University of Rochester, and the NEAC (Near East Asia Council) of the Association of Asian Studies helped finance various stages of my research in Japan. I am grateful for their interest in my work. I am especially indebted to Mrs. Miyo Wagner, the late Sachiko Murakami, who guided me through my first reading of Tanizaki's scripts many years ago, and the late Ichiro Shirato and his wife, Masa. David Bordwell and Tom Gunning offered insightful comments on versions of my manuscript, as did Leslie Midkiff Debauche, Frederick Dickenson, Ronald Grant, Kristine Harris, and my readers at Wayne State University Press, David Desser and Peter Grilli. At the George Eastman House, Ed Stratman and Paolo Cherchi Usai helped in many ways with both materials and screenings. At the critical stage when I had the first opportunities to present my work outside of Japan, Carol Morley at Wellesley College provided me with a home base, Kristin Thompson offered encouragement and generous comments, and Cobi Bordewijk renewed my interest in intertitles and encouraged me to attend the International Film Studies Conference on titles in silent cinema at the University of Udine. A postdoctoral fellowship at the Edwin O. Reischauer Institute for Japanese Studies, Harvard University, provided an intellectually stimulating environment and a much-needed year off from teaching duties to gather my thoughts, as well as important resources, from 1993 to 1994. Becky Copeland at Washington University in St. Louis, Kyoko Hirano at the New York Japan Society, Adriana Boscaro at the University of Venice, and Leonardo Quaresima and Francesco Pitassio at the University of Udine provided me with welcome opportunities and venues for feedback on my research in progress.

The staff at Wayne State University Press were a pleasure to work with. I especially thank Danielle DeLucia, Robin DuBlanc, Arthur Evans, Kristin Harpster, Jane Hoehner, and Alison Reeves for their assistance, interest, and support. I gratefully acknowledge the Japan Foundation for publication assistance.

As always, friends and family helped me at every point along the way. Thanks to Dale, my best film companion; my brother, my best grammarian; and my parents, who lived the silent period—they were all integral to the making of this book. (Thanks, Dad, for Hoot Gibson, Harry Carey, Douglas Fairbanks, Tom Mix, Wm. S. Hart, and Roy Rogers, Trigger, and Lassie, even if these three do not count.)

Finally, I join the ranks of many others in thanking the Pordenone Silent Film Festival just for being, and for making it possible for me to indulge in the wonder that is silent film.

INTRODUCTION

GENERALLY REFERRED TO as the *jun'eigageki undō* (pure film movement), efforts to change the production and exhibition practices of the Japanese film industry during the 1910s gained momentum throughout the decade. Operating on a discursive level and focusing on a contemporary recognition of film as a unique and culturally respectable form of art (a trend visible on an international level during this decade), pure film advocates sought to radically alter or eliminate such standard industry practices as the dependence on preexisting stage repertories, a continuing preference for the *benshi* lecturer instead of intertitles, and the use of *oyama* or *onnagata* (female impersonators). At the same time, the industry was internally adjusting to the demands of increasingly large-scale and systematic production. The debate over the artistic legitimacy and cultural role of film, closely linked to the growth of a new market for articles and books on films and filmmaking, raised issues of authorship, screenwriting practice, gender representation, genre and, at least rhetorically, the attainment of an internationally viable level of narrational clarity for films also endowed with a comprehensible and distinct national and cultural identity. *Writing in Light* is an analysis of this discursive network of issues, the social fluctuations conditioning it, and the *jun'eigageki* productions that were its result.

Culturally, the first two decades of the century were a complex period in Japan, one not easily characterized. The literary world, which shared a close proximity with film, embraced an expanding market for translations and the importation in turn of romanticism, naturalism, and realism, together with the first attempts to write in the colloquial language. Stage drama, arguably an even more important practical and theoretical influence on film at the

13

time, was complicated by the rise and fall, during this short period, of the modernist or protomodern forms of the *shinpa* and *shingeki* theaters.

To best approach this period of intense creative activity, I isolate the threads of discourse in contemporary written work (including criticism, practical information on filmmaking, and scripts) associated with the pure film movement, and the points at which these discussions intersect with what might be interpreted as changing international trends in attitudes toward film. One example would be the pure film supporters' advocacy of preproduction planning at the level of the film script as it was carried out in Hollywood. (The feasibility of duplicating the Hollywood continuity script and screenwriting system on a similar scale in Japan was a significant issue in pure film debate, just as it was, at various times, in Europe.) Another example is the degree to which pure film advocates decried the assumption that film was inextricably related, as if by blood, to theater and theatrical practices, either of the legitimate stage or the "lesser" forms of vaudeville entertainment. This too was an issue elsewhere in the world but in Japan, in the context of the pure film movement, it had a special urgency. A variety of factors allowed such onstage fixtures as the *benshi* lecturer and female impersonator a unique, continuous currency—continuous domestic marketability—throughout the 1910s and into the early 1920s (the female impersonator) or beyond (the *benshi*).

Pure film enthusiasts made screenwriting practice prominent in the practical application of pure film theory, and because of this, as well as the tradition of interest in the publication of screenplays in Japan, I give priority to extant scripts that for the most part appeared in contemporary publications. These scripts are also the only known surviving remains of pure film production apart from a reconstructed partial print of the Shōchiku kinema production *Rojō no reikon* (*Souls on the Road,* Murata Minoru, 1921) and two partial prints (they are slightly different versions) of the Kokusai katsudō kabushiki kaisha (Kokkatsu) production *Kantsubaki* (*Winter Camellia,* Hatanaka Ryōha, 1921). Translations of *Sei no kagayaki* (*The Glory of Life,* Kaeriyama Norimasa, 1918–1919),[1] written by Kaeriyama at Tennenshoku katsudō shashin (Tenkatsu) under the pseudonym Mizusawa Takehiko, and the Taishō katsuei (Taikatsu) production *Amachua kurabu* (*Amateur Club,* Thomas Kurihara, attributed to Tanizaki Jun'ichirō, 1920), are included in the appendix. Also included are excerpts from another Taikatsu pure film script, *Jasei no in* (*The Lust of the White Serpent,* Thomas Kurihara, 1921), by Tanizaki and the Nihon katsudō shashin (Nikkatsu) *shinpa* film *Chichi no namida* (*A Father's Tears,* Tanaka Eizō, 1918), by Masumoto Kiyoshi.

Approaching Japanese film history with an interest in screenwriting practice provides an opportunity to consider this history from a perspective that has not been taken in other literature on the period. This is one of the

The popular female impersonator Tachibana Teijirō in the *shinpa* film *Suteobune* (*The Abandoned One*). *Katsudō gahō,* July 1917. From Makino, ed., *Nihon eiga shoki shiryō shūsei* (*A Collection of Research Material from the Early Days of Japanese Film*).

Tachibana Teijirō and Sekine Tappatsu in the *shinpa* film *Kachūsha* (1914), based on the *shingeki* stage adaptation of Leo Tolstoy's *Resurrection.* Courtesy of Kawakita Memorial Film Institute.

Rojō no reikon (*Souls on the Road*), directed by Murata Minoru, 1921. (*Left to right*) Hisamatsu Mieko, Suzuki Denmei, Sawamura Haruko. Courtesy Kawakita Memorial Film Institute.

Kantsubaki (*Winter Camellia*), directed by Hatanaka Ryōha, 1921. Inoue Masao and Mizutani Yaeko. Courtesy Kawakita Memorial Film Institute.

ways in which this study differs from others describing the pure film movement. There is a marked absence of full-length studies of silent Japanese cinema, and traditional histories of Japanese film that do address the period—those by Tanaka Jun'ichirō, Iijima Tadashi, Hazumi Tsuneo, and (more cursorily in English), Joseph L. Anderson and Donald Richie, for example—treat the pure film movement subjectively within the context of its presumed technical achievements. The pure film movement has received more detailed attention in the work of Peter High, Noël Burch, Hiroshi Komatsu, and, more recently, Aaron Gerow, who sees the actual pure films as irrelevant to his focus on censorship and the ways in which he believes the pure film movement allied with certain legislation defining discourse on film. Whereas Peter High closely follows the perspective of Japanese historians such as Tanaka and Iijima, Noël Burch, in *To the Distant Observer,* made a significant impact on the study of silent Japanese film in the 1980s with a revisionist view of the importance of the movement. In adhering to the concept of an aesthetically idealized Japanese cultural self, however, and lacking recourse to surviving contemporary sources in print, he offers a limited interpretation. In his earlier references to the pure film movement, Hiroshi Komatsu generally shares Burch's admiration for a resilient, lingering influence of "archaic forms of Japanese art and culture" on silent Japanese film, and an essential Japanese cinema that might have existed before the emergence of pure film discourse. This stance is less marked in his more recent and provocative introductions to the facsimile reprints of the contemporary film publications *Katsudō shashinkai* and *Kinema Record.*[2]

A large part of the challenge in understanding the nature of the silent Japanese film industry lies in learning how to work within the boundaries of what is feasible. Film is fragile and the potential benefits of its preservation (let alone archival preservation) were not self-evident from the start anywhere in the world, but the survival rate is particularly bad in Japan. Although the Japanese film industry was extremely active in its early years, for various reasons (for example, copyright procedures that in the United States ensured a legacy for certain material were not standard practice in Japan) only 4 percent or less of its products before 1945 is known to have survived.[3] Some material related to production and exhibition exists, but printed records, photographs or frame reproductions in contemporary sources, and conventional histories are our most likely sources of information.

Such printed or written records are useful, but they cannot be used to re-create or even simulate the viewing experience, and they often reveal little about film style. Photographs are a valuable visual aid, but can be deceptive. As Susan Sontag has pointed out, photographs are "an invitation to sentimentality. . . . [They] turn the past into an object of tender regard, scrambling moral distinctions and disarming historical judgments by the generalized pathos of looking at the past."[4] Histories of the period are susceptible to being colored by contemporary aesthetic and ideological criteria as well as personal bias, leading to problems in understanding and visualizing very basic aspects of genre and form.[5]

A study of early conceptions of screenwriting, screenwriting practice, and extant "screen texts"[6] (photoplays, film scripts, scenarios, or screen-plays—all alternate terms used, sometimes interchangeably, during this period) provides a fruitful approach to understanding the way in which a national film industry works as a system, and helps define that system within an appropriately international context. This is not to suggest that the scripts for *The Glory of Life* and *Amateur Club* be studied as replacements for lost films, but they are useful in that they are a record of the conceptualization of the visual narrative for these films. As I show in the following chapters, scripts from this period also inform us of issues of genre, authorship and con-trol, and gender representation. According to the degree in which these scripts attempt to describe with some continuity and detail what the spectator will see, they are also important keys to understanding the variety of approaches taken and experiments made during this period of the narrative feature film's development in Japan.[7] Finally, they help us to understand Japan's place in relation to the international market of the 1910s, when con-tinuity devices in particular spread beyond national boundaries.

This study began as a dissertation exploring the origins of the Japanese screenplay and that specific interdependence between silent filmmakers and the written word that it represents. Finding myself involved in a period of filmmaking that had left little in terms of a visual record, and curious to know, if not what these lost films had looked like then at least what they had been about, I was particularly drawn to those screen texts that did survive. This narrowed my focus to material dating primarily from the 1910s, and my interest in drawing attention to this material led to subsequent questions that arose, as the popular saying goes, like bamboo shoots after the rain. Who had written these texts; how, why, when, and where had they been written; and perhaps most important, what can they tell us about a period of filmmaking that, at least until recently, has been sadly neglected?

Although working in this period means contending with a lost body of work, it is worth noting that in general, the relative dearth of circulating, sub-titled prints of Japanese films outside Japan has not prevented a recognition of their importance, nor hindered a steady increase in interest. Over the past twenty years, Japanese cinema has hardly been relegated to the shadows in either film or area studies. In the academic curriculum in the United States, it is arguably the leading subject in non-Western cinema in spite of the vexing impossibility of procuring a wide variety of prints from different genres and

18

periods. College courses in Japanese cinema have become common, if not necessarily required, and it is notable that such courses are not exclusively taught by area specialists. Just as the lack of circulating prints of Japanese films has not automatically precluded interest in the subject, or the possibility of studying it and appreciating its significance, the poor survival rate of silent Japanese cinema should not impede our appreciation of this formative and fascinating period.

The histories of European and American cinema have a relatively long tradition of scholarship that allows those working in these fields to take for granted a considerable body of assumed general knowledge. In comparison, half lost and half dispersed, historiographically, across a complex layering of space and time, silent Japanese cinema poses considerable challenges to the researcher. In chapter 1, I address those that proved most pertinent in the context of my own interests. I provide a clarification of basic terminology and draw attention to a number of relevant issues concerning source material, genre systems, and aspects of researching Japanese cinema that have influenced prior scholarship of this period. In defining the parameters of my study, I also introduce the basic concerns that are developed throughout the following chapters.

My focus on extant silent screen texts led to creative efforts that did not always neatly fit the definition (however ambiguous that might be, as I will demonstrate,) of the commercial product between 1908 and 1921. Simultaneously, my concern with the larger picture of an evolution of an industry (a necessary prerequisite to situating Japanese cinema in a global context) takes for granted a community of individuals whose associations, both personal and professional, were important to that evolution. This study, then, accepts on a preliminary, working basis the canon of films that are generally understood to have defined the pure film movement, and draws attention to the individuals involved in their creation.[8] Chapter 2 introduces the circumstances leading up to the first of these pure films, Kaeriyama Norimasa's *The Glory of Life,* beginning with a description of the writing department established at the Yoshizawa studio in Meguro in 1908. I then describe early discourse on the emergence of the concept of pure film, focusing on Kaeriyama's preoccupation, as the main theorist of the movement, with screenwriting. I conclude with an analysis of Kaeriyama's work, in particular his script for *The Glory of Life* in comparison to the contemporaneous chain drama script *A Father's Tears* by Masumoto Kiyoshi, who began writing for the screen as a staff writer for the Yoshizawa company.

In chapter 3 I consider different factors that contributed to the founding, in 1920, of two new studios (Shōchiku kinema and Taikatsu) that were established with the sole intention of producing pure films. These factors fall into two general categories: the cultural, social, and political factors at work as the pure film movement took shape and the ways in which these elements in turn determined the subsequent path of pure film; and those elements of the production and exhibition of the commercial product that were the key targets of pure film "reform." In the remainder of the chapter, I discuss Mori Iwao's *Katsudō shashin taikan* (*A Survey of the Moving Pictures*), which provides a good picture of the above factors at work in the late 1910s, particularly within the context of Mori's contention that the Japanese film industry (like other national industries during this period) might profit from expanding its market overseas. An analysis of Mori's work provides a segue into a description of Tōyō Films and its successor, Taikatsu. My consideration of Taikatsu's prospectus, written in 1920, prepares the reader for chapters 4–6, which focus on Tanizaki Jun'ichirō's involvement in film production at the Taikatsu studio.

The popular writer Tanizaki Jun'ichirō was arguably the most prominent literary figure to take up the cause of pure film and become active in pure film production. The Taikatsu prospectus named Tanizaki as the resident studio screen author, acknowledging a familiarity with trends of literary involvement in silent screenwriting in the United States. Chapter 4 considers Tanizaki's long-term fascination with film, as evidenced in novels, plays, essays, and short stories, and concludes with a description of the scripts Tanizaki wrote at Taikatsu, and a consideration of his influence on both screenwriting and the pure film movement. Chapter 5 continues this focus on Tanizaki with a consideration of the manner in which journalism, particularly after 1913, contributed to the gradual popularization of the pure film concept, and an analysis of Tanizaki's own 1917 article, "Katsudō shashin no genzai to shōrai" ("The Present and Future of the Moving Pictures"). Chapter 6 provides a description of the production and reception of Tanizaki and Thomas Kurihara's first collaboration at Taikatsu, *Amateur Club,* and a detailed analysis of the script, which is translated in full in the appendix.

The scripts that provided the motivation for this book, translated (partially or in full) in the appendix, help fill important gaps in our historical perception of Japanese silent cinema. Within the context of this study, they also reveal the extent to which developments within the Japanese cinema corresponded to such contemporary concerns in Europe and the United States as the concept of cinema as art, cinema as the site of resistance and negotiation between preexisting forms of popular entertainment and other forms of art, and cinema as a product with a national identity. I especially hope these translations will provoke further interest in silent Japanese cinema, and will be revisited now and again as new materials from this extraordinary period continue to come to our attention.

1

Developing Images, Defining Words

TRADITIONAL HISTORIES OF Japanese cinema provide a colorful anecdote that describes a cultural confusion presumed inherent to early encounters between Japanese and foreign (specifically, in the 1910s and 1920s, European and American) film production practices. It is worth noting as one of the more conspicuous references to the presence (or lack thereof) of the screenplay at this time. In 1920 the director and company executive Taguchi Ōson went to the United States to tour famous American studios. As the story goes, when he returned to Japan, he was chosen to direct the first film to be released by the newly established Shōhiku Cinema Company. As Shōchiku was determined to follow only the most modern production techniques, Taguchi duly set about putting into practice the expertise he had acquired during his study abroad. First, he ordered the script to be typed in the roman alphabet. Then he explained that in Hollywood, actors merely did what the director told them, and therefore did not need to read the script. Suffering from technical complications, this production was abruptly discontinued. Taguchi, undaunted, persisted in his mission to modernize Japanese films. He directed his next attempt shot by shot with neither story nor continuity script, and instructed the actors to laugh or cry without the slightest hint at motivation. Another colleague just back from Hollywood employed similar methods. According to one report, in order to elicit fear from an actor he would simply shout that a lion was coming and they should be afraid, though the story being filmed had absolutely nothing to do with a lion.[1]

We know that by 1930, when Japan was on the verge of producing its first sound feature, novices at Nikkatsu's branch studio in Kyoto—the screenwriter Yoda Yoshikata (later famous for his collaborative work with

21

the director Mizoguchi Kenji) is an example—learned basic steps in writing continuity from their seniors in the screenwriting department. They formed groups in order to study and analyze their own handwritten transcriptions of such popular imported films as F. W. Murnau's *Sunrise* (1927) and Josef von Sternberg's *The Docks of New York* (1928). The minute analyses they carried out based on their transcriptions included breaking them down scene by scene, then learning how to identify the narrative function of each scene.[2] They also compiled charts comparing the ratio of titles to cuts per scene and did exhaustive comparative studies based on their findings. There was little question of the legitimacy of the screenplay, nor had there been for some time. The concepts of screenwriter and screenplay had been part of the production process in Japan to some degree by 1910, since the establishment of the earliest production companies, and written, comparative analyses of narrative structure were already being carried out by the mid-1910s.

In Europe and the United States, the early decades of this century were marked by discursive efforts to establish the uniqueness of the silent "photoplay" as opposed to stage drama. Together with related discussions arguing for the recognition of the new medium as an art form, this debate had repercussions in Japan, particularly between 1914 and 1923, where such efforts emerged as the *jun'eigageki undō* (pure film movement).

A capsule description of the pure film movement is that it was a loosely defined discourse-based "movement" comprised of diverse paths leading to a single destination. Generally speaking, the single destination, or common cause, was the realization of a culturally respectable film, endowed with both aesthetic legitimacy and contemporary realism, that theoretically would challenge a mainstream commercial product that had theatrical origins: the *shinpageki* (*shinpa*, or "new school" film), the prototype of the *gendaigeki* (contemporary life film) genre; the *kyūha* or *kyūgeki* (period film) genre; and the mixed-media *rensageki* ("chain drama"), a production combining film projection and live performance.

I define pure film "in general," because it is entirely unclear to me that the term was universally applied or understood at the time.[3] Although the term was prevalent enough throughout the 1910s to generate the expression "pure film movement," that this "movement" existed entirely on a discursive level (at least until the production of the first pure films after 1918) prevented it from becoming formally organized or well defined. The starting point for all discussion of pure film was that it was something other than the mainstream commercial *shinpa* film or *kyūgeki*. The term implied that such a film would be independent of certain practices associated with theater entertainment. These included practices present at the levels of both exhibition and production: *benshi* accompaniment, stage sets and proscenium framing,

Publicity montage of scenes from the *shinpa* film *Oboroyo* (*Misty Night*). *Katsudō gahō,* April 1917. From Makino, ed., *Nihon eiga shoki shiryō shūsei* (*A Collection of Research Material from the Early Days of Japanese Film*).

Scenes from "Two Classical Drama [period films] (Tennenshoku Katsudoshashin Co.) with Sawamura Shirogoro, Famous Japanese Actor." *Katsudō hyōron,* August 1919. From Makino, ed., *Nihon eiga shoki shiryō shūsei* (*A Collection of Research Material from the Early Days of Japanese Film*).

Inoue Masao (*second from left*) in the chain drama *Shōfū murasame* (*Pine Breeze, Passing Shower*). Double page (foldout) glossy illustration, *Katsudō gahō,* March 1917. From Makino, ed., *Nihon eiga shoki shiryō shūsei* (*A Collection of Research Material from the Early Days of Japanese Film*).

heavily coded histrionics, and the prevalence of female impersonators in place of women actors.[4]

The pure film movement was largely defined by the work of a young studio employee, Kaeriyama Norimasa (1893–1964). The director of the first two major pure film productions, *The Glory of Life* and *Miyama no otome* (*The Girl in the Mountain,* 1918–1919), and author of one of the earliest technical books on film in Japan, Kaeriyama emphasized the need to recognize the importance of the silent film script and, in the manner of the imported film publications with which he was familiar, the ways in which it differed from a play written for the stage. In his own words, he regarded a detailed and well-written script as the "foundation of a film."[5] Although the several films Kaeriyama directed between 1918 and 1924 are believed lost, surviving accounts indicate that he applied his theories to their production. In making *The Glory of Life,* for example, he held a script reading for the entire cast and crew that achieved legendary status as an unprecedented event in the history of the industry.[6]

25

Kaeriyama's work inspired subsequent efforts to produce films with intertitles, cinematic frame composition and editing, naturalistic (verisimilar) acting, and a woman actor in place of a female impersonator: the standard "female" presence in the industry until the early 1920s. It was not required that a pure film be a contemporary drama (Kaeriyama's third production, a period film made in Kyoto, is a case in point), but the concept of a truly "contemporary" (even modern) contemporary drama film was a key issue in pure film debate. Such films were made with the intention of portraying contemporary Japanese life, often in imitation of the small-scale American features—films with simple stories shot on location, such as Universal's Bluebird productions—that were popular with the intellectual audience in Japan at the time.

Kaeriyama's work was also influential in the founding of the Taikatsu and Shōchiku studios in 1920 for the explicit purpose of producing pure films, specifically, modern "action comedies" or "artistic" films to rival the *shinpa* film (influenced by the *shinpa* theater) and *kyūgeki* (influenced by the period pieces of the kabuki theater). Kaeriyama admittedly modeled his work on his studies of imported films and film-related publications, but a major feature of Shōchiku and Taikatsu was the presence of a number of actors and technicians who had been trained in Hollywood. Thomas Kurihara (1885–1926) at Taikatsu and Henry Kotani (1887–1972) at Shōchiku, for example, both contributed to the transformation of the contemporary drama form, although this transitional period posed difficulties in adapting Hollywood production practices to the Japanese studio system. Kurihara in particular helped forge a place for the director as the central figure of authority, and he drew attention to the use of a continuity-style film script during the production of several pure films at Taikatsu. Surviving continuity-style scripts used at Taikatsu resemble those used in the United States at the time in that they feature a cast of characters, action broken down (scenes dissected) into numbered interior and exterior shots, locations, indications for camera angles and camera movement, inserts, and expository and dialogue titles.

The participation of two prominent members of the literary community, Tanizaki Jun'ichirō (1886–1965) at Taikatsu and Osanai Kaoru (1881–1928) at Shōchiku, marked a turning point in the "film as art" argument. Tanizaki and Osanai were involved in the production of a number of films, notably the Taikatsu production *Amateur Club*, inspired by American slapstick, and Shōchiku's *Souls on the Road*, a film with closer ties to European literature and theater, and one of only two surviving examples of all early pure film efforts.[7]

The preoccupation with pure film debate was enough to concern the most established production company at the time, the Nikkatsu Company. In 1917 the company hired Tanaka Eizō, a young drama student with an interest in the modernization movement then taking place in the theater. It is interesting to note that the historiographical tendency is to refer to "progressive" *shinpa* films like those of Tanaka Eizō and Oguchi Tadashi, many of which were written by the *shinpa* and *shingeki* theater playwright Masumoto Kiyoshi, as "reform(ed)" films (*kakushin eiga*), while films that overtly laid claim to being inspired by films of "the West" are classified as pure films. The films Tanaka directed in the late 1910s were highly regarded by pure film enthusiasts. By the time he completed his most ambitious project, *Kyōya eriten* (*The Kyōya Collar Shop,* 1922), the industry was on the verge of the major upheaval caused by the Great Kanto Earthquake of 1923. *The Kyōya Collar Shop* marked the final screen appearance of the female impersonator, but it took several more years for directors and writers to supersede the authorial status of the popular and powerful *benshi* lecturers.

The Great Kanto Earthquake is generally regarded as the final catalyst in this transitional period characterized by such attempts to "modernize" Japanese film during the silent period (at the time and in this context, "modernization" implied, in part, bringing the industry "up to" international standards). The damage suffered by the head studios in Tokyo provided the opportunity for a major restructuring of the industry and the consequent elimination of what were then regarded as timeworn theatrical practices. A vigorous popular culture arose in the wake of the disaster, and the moviegoing public barely paused long enough for new theaters to be built. In 1922 there were 112 movie theaters in Tokyo and adjoining areas, and attendance stood at 17,400,000 a year. By 1926, the theaters that had been destroyed in the earthquake had been replaced, the total number of theaters jumped to 178, and attendance had increased to 24,879,000.[8] This spurt of growth had special meaning, because it reflected a sudden flourish of interest in the Japanese film: only one year after the earthquake the number of domestic productions exceeded the number of films imported to Japan for the first time.

By this time several filmmakers who had entered the industry in the midst of the pure film debate were now well on their way toward successful careers. The director who best responded to the new spirit of the times was a colleague of Kaeriyama, Murata Minoru (1894–1937). Murata, who first pursued a stage career, had by 1912 formed his own acting company (at the age of eighteen) and was an active supporter of the movement to modernize Japanese theater. His film career began in the early days of the pure film movement when, beginning with *The Glory of Life,* he acted in several of Kaeriyama's pure films. Murata continued to be an important presence in the contemporary drama film throughout his regrettably short career. Together with Kaeriyama, he sponsored study groups and screenings of amateur films, and with the director Ushihara Kiyohiko, then working at the Kamata Shōchiku studios, he supervised the publication of the quarterly *Eiga kagaku*

27

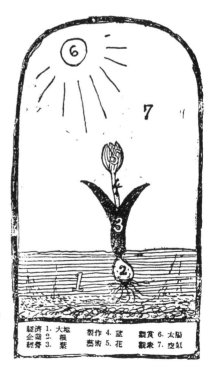

7　6　5　4　3　2　1
←

觀　觀　藝　製　經　企　經
衆　賞　術　作　營　業　濟

映畫科學研究とは何か

村田實

Title page of an article by Murata Minoru in the first issue of *Eiga kagaku kenkyū* (*Scientific Film Research*), June 1928, edited by Murata Minoru and Ushihara Kiyohiko. A schematic diagram of the essentials of film creation: finance (1); enterprise (2); management (3); production (4); art (5); audience appreciation (6); audience (7, the ramp leading from the top of the tower back down to the economic base of production). Author's collection.

From the first issue of *Eiga kagaku kenkyū* (*Scientific Film Research*), June 1928. An alternative depiction of the essentials of film creation: finance (1, "soil"); enterprise (2, "roots"); management (3, "leaves"); production (4, "stem"); art (5, "flower"); audience appreciation (6, "sun"); audience (7, "air"). Author's collection.

經濟　1. 大地　　製作 4. 莖　　觀賞 6. 太陽
企業　2. 根　　　藝術 5. 花　　觀衆 7. 空氣
經營　3. 葉

kenkyū (*Scientific Film Research*), started in 1928. Polished transcriptions of handwritten continuities of popular films currently being imported from Europe and the United States were a special feature of this quarterly. They regularly appeared with either a foreword by Murata highlighting the qualities of each script or a note on writing for the screen in general. By the 1920s the contemporary drama form had achieved a high level of generic diversity. The term *gendaigeki* ("contemporary drama" or "modern life drama") had completely eclipsed the term "*shinpa* film" within the production system by 1927.

"FIRST, THE STORY"

In 1896 Edison's individual "peepshow" Kinetoscope was imported to Japan. This was followed by the Vitascope and Lumière's Cinematograph, which enabled the first public screenings, and within a few years domestic films were being shown together with films from Europe and the United States. The earliest domestic productions, like their foreign counterparts, were only one or two reels in length. According to conventional histories, typical subjects included street scenes, highlights from kabuki plays, and dances performed by geisha. Such descriptions suggest most of these films were actualities. Possibly, a few were improvised; some might have originated from random ideas written down on paper.

The first film studios began to appear around 1904, and at one of these an enterprising *shōgekijō* ("small theater") manager, Makino Shōzō (1878–1929), started directing occasional one-reelers in 1907. Within two years he had created Japan's earliest screen star persona, Onoe Matsunosuke, and together they made a total of 168 films between 1909 and 1912. It has been pointed out that in his early career Makino's role was really little more than that of a theater company manager, which was his job prior to entering films.[9] History has nevertheless bestowed him with the title of "the father of Japanese film" and, in English language literature, the distinction of being the first Japanese director "in the Western sense of the word."[10]

Most of the films Makino made with his star were only one reel long, but at the rate of some fifty films a year he was working at a rapid pace, often under pressure to complete a film a day. (For the sake of comparison, D. W. Griffith often completed a film in a day, with his average being fewer than three days.[11]) This was before it was customary to make extra prints for circulation, and Makino and his crew shot the same film several times in order to fulfill distribution demand. As a result, they were steadily working on the set, conceivably with little time left to write out even the simplest form of continuity for each film. No extant scripts from this period are available, and

29

Onoe Matsunosuke in action.
Katsudō gahō, March 1917. From
Makino, ed., *Nihon eiga shoki
shiryō shūsei* (*A Collection of
Research Material from the Early
Days of Japanese Film*).

Onoe Matsunosuke (*foreground, third from left*) and Makino Shōzō (*foreground,
third from right*) pose on the set in Kyoto. *Katsudō shashin zasshi,* July 1915. From
Makino, ed., *Nihon eiga shoki shiryō shūsei* (*A Collection of Research Material from
the Early Days of Japanese Film*).

it is generally believed that Makino instead carried the plot in his head, improvising lines for the actors to repeat while the camera was running.[12] In Yoda Yoshikata's opinion, Makino's method of delivering lines in this way, called *kuchidate,* would have resembled the *jōruri* narration of the bunraku puppet drama.[13]

It would appear that after a few years of such work, Makino learned to appreciate a well-prepared script. When he eventually established his own production company in the 1920s, he promoted an important generation of *jidaigeki* ("period film") screenwriters. In his early days he had stressed the importance of a story that was accessible to the general audience,[14] but the scripts written for him by these writers were particularly detailed with a strong element of psychological realism. Makino's period film screenwriters were well rewarded for their work. At his peak of popularity Onoe Matsuno-suke had earned an unprecedented salary that corresponded with his tremendous success, but the salary Makino later allotted to his main writers exceeded the earnings of his most popular stars.[15] Makino summed up his production philosophy with the famous words: "First, the story; second, a clear negative; third, the action."[16] Even the "father of Japanese film," it seems, was apprised of the benefits of a film script.

Not only were the majority of the earliest domestic films stage presentations of scenes from kabuki or the new and increasingly popular nontraditional *shinpa* ("new school") plays with contemporary settings, but often the purpose of a filmed version of a kabuki play was solely to preserve the performance of popular actors. In addition, the majority of individuals involved in film production came from theatrical backgrounds, like Makino and Onoe. This was not unlike the situation in the United States and Europe, but in Japan the relationship between the Japanese theater and film was complex and more enduring.

The *film d'art,* along with Italian historical epics and the work of D. W. Griffith, helped set the precedent for longer films in Europe and the United States after 1910. Japanese filmmakers soon followed this trend, but at this point the development of the screenplay in Japan and abroad diverged. Longer films abroad required detailed and developed scripts that contained a description of the action as well as lines of dialogue. This dialogue was mimed during the shooting and summarized on titlecards referred to as "leaders" or "subtitles," now referred to as intertitles. These leaders or subtitles were inserted between the appropriate scenes. In addition to presenting the dialogue, they often explained action occurring offscreen. The use of intertitles in Europe and the United States has been traced at least as far back as 1903–1904,[17] but throughout the 1910s and 1920s there were periods when writers tended to move away from their use. In Hollywood such a trend was particularly noticeable from 1913 to 1916.[18] After 1917, the Hollywood film featured fewer expository intertitles, but a greater number of dialogue intertitles.[19] In Europe, the most notable example of an inclination to rely less on intertitles and more on what could be communicated by the image was the German *kammerspielfilm* of the 1920s, later an important influence on the contemporary drama filmmakers at Nikkatsu's Kyoto studio. In Germany the filmmakers working in this genre believed that fewer titles brought the viewer closer to understanding the psychology of the characters, forcing the viewer to guess their thoughts, and these somber German "chamber dramas"—described as "silent dialogues of the soul"—often had no titles at all.[20]

Fewer titles, it was believed, would also relieve the viewer from the strain of constantly shifting between visual images and verbal information flashed on the screen "at awkward moments" for "as long as the less literate required to spell out the words."[21] Throughout the 1910s, the volume of publications in English on film technique and the virtue of the medium as art increased steadily, and many of these early treatises stressed the need to grasp the visual necessities of the silent film script with as few titles as possible. Such comments arguing against an onslaught of verbalism often refer to the need to distinguish between the "photodrama" (or "photoplay") and the stage drama. As one author writes: "Dialogue is of the *essence* of drama. Its analogue in the photodrama—the 'caption' or 'leader'—is only an *adjunct*. This distinction is fundamental."[22]

Such opinions make it clear that in Europe and the United States at various points in the 1910s it was the less talented writer who failed to "cultivate the 'picture eye,'" and visualize the story at hand in terms of the screen, resorting instead to using titles, "a much more crude way of expressing his ideas."[23] The truly talented writer was a "cinema-composer" intent on achieving "the delineation of human character." With the notable exception of writers specializing in witty intertitles (Anita Loos, for example) or the creation of a screen persona for individual stars (Loos, Frances Marion, and C. Gardner Sullivan),[24] titles were often regarded as something to be avoided. They were justified when used to explain dramatic action that could not be depicted on screen "either because it is mechanically impossible to do so or because propriety forbids."[25] The emphasis was, for the most part, on mastering the technique of writing in a visually expressive manner.

In Japan the formal development of the silent film script moved in a different direction. Complaints about actors' theatrical mannerisms and the heavy dependence on stage material for source material was something shared, to an extent, with the more critically inclined segment of audiences elsewhere. The presence of the *benshi* and the use of female impersonators, however, were lingering theatrical devices particular to Japan.

Portrait collage of two *benshi. Katsudō shashin zasshi,* July 1915. From Makino, ed., *Nihon eiga shoki shiryō shūsei (A Collection of Research Material from the Early Days of Japanese Film).*

THE *BENSHI* INTERVENES

The institution of the *benshi,* while undergoing continual stylistic changes throughout the 1910s, discouraged early experimentation with systematic approaches to film titling. Even brief one-reelers were accompanied by the *benshi* lecturer, whose role has been compared to that of his or her counterpart in the bunraku theater. Even in a relatively early (1909) reference to *benshi* practice it is possible to find evidence of a concern for being attentive to the nature of the film at hand, but the *benshi* differed from the narrators of the bunraku theater in that they were under no formal compulsion to strictly follow the text of a play.[26]

33

Publicity collage of the *benshi* Nishimura Rakuten. *Katsudō gahō,* March 1917. From Makino, ed., *Nihon eiga shoki shiryō shūsei* (*A Collection of Research Material from the Early Days of Japanese Film*).

Foreign films arriving in Japan did not come with fully developed scripts for the *benshi* to follow, although after 1910 the *benshi* were given rough translations of the dialogue, or, in the case of domestic films, simple scripts.[27] Even in such cases, the *benshi* routinely elaborated on these narrative outlines in addition to providing the dialogue. That was the attraction of the *benshi*'s performance, a "continually shifting commentary, at times objective and at times subjective."[28] Instead of strictly following the text, these "poets of darkness" (as they often referred to themselves) entertained the audience with their observations and opinions, and often prepared their own texts based on their personal interpretation of the stories.[29] Many of the earliest domestic scripts were in fact written for the *benshi* rather than the director and cast involved in the actual production of the film.[30]

It has been pointed out that the *benshi*'s presence delayed the innovations in camera movement and editing techniques being explored abroad, because Japanese filmmakers relied on the *benshi* to provide the necessary narrative continuity.[31] In the same manner, although longer, more complex stories required written scripts prepared in advance, there was less demand for these scripts to be detailed or elaborately constructed due to the nature of the *benshi*'s performance. In short, regardless of the manner in which the *benshi*'s presence affected changes in cinematic language in Japan, the importance given to *bensetsu* (*benshi* delivery) tended to deflect attention from the scriptwriter, the preproduction film script, and the role of such a film script during production.

During his presentation the *benshi* narrated the dialogue, called *kagezerifu* ("lines in the dark"), changing the pitch of his or her voice (some were in practice women) to portray the various characters, including those of the opposite gender, in an attempt to simulate their emotions. This technique, *kowairo,* dated back to the Genroku period (1688–1703), when the term was used for the custom of imitating an actor's rendition of his most memorable lines. In the beginning, this *kowairo* was performed by a group of several narrators, and sometimes even the actors themselves sat behind the screen and delivered their lines alongside the *benshi,* who provided the expository narration. Gradually, the presence of a single narrator performing both functions became more common, and their popularity grew to the extent that their billing often upstaged that of the film's star. Neither the director nor the screenwriter had much presence or authority.

It was commonly believed that one effective way to override the *benshi*'s performance would be to use titles more frequently to advance the story. As a result, actual experiments with titles by early writers in Japan could have conceivably taken place around the same time that writers abroad were often devising means to eliminate them. With more existing evidence this generalization could be qualified by making a distinction between the use of expository titles (often referred to as *togaki*) and dialogue titles or "spoken titles" (*supōken taitoru*). Spoken titles began to be used more frequently in Europe and the United States after 1908, at least four or five years before the marked interest in experimentation with titles in Japan.[32] At that point, there was virtually no precedent for either type of title in Japan. The type of title believed to be commonly used in the *shinpa* film is now more accurately regarded as a subtitle rather than an intertitle, as it more closely resembled the chapter title of a book.[33] The distinction among types of titles (expository or dialogue) was not systematically made clear in general references to their use except in discussions related to pure film.

When titles did become a concern in Japan, this interest brought about a change in the presumed functions of the prepared script. Narrative clarity was no longer the privilege of the *benshi*. Writers began to concern themselves with maintaining a balance between the verbal and visual elements of the story. Then they began to devise rhythmic patterns with the frequency of titles, or, for example, to use them for emphasis at dramatic moments.[34] The first step had been taken toward achieving a cinematic script with firm dramatic structure, realistic characterization, and dialogue that formed an integral part of the plot.

Ironically, by challenging practitioners of the more histrionic *kowairo,* Kaeriyama and the pure film platform actually strengthened the position of the solo *benshi*, and after 1917 they enjoyed a more distinguished reputation.[35] In spite of what was usually a scanty formal education, the *benshi* began to pepper their narrative with literary phrases, and their delivery became increasingly rhythmical.[36] Their authority went unquestioned in the major studios like Nikkatsu, where they even dictated the maximum number of shots per reel in order to insure there would be no complications caused by intricate cutting.[37] And by the early 1920s the *benshi* were not only reciting narration and acting out the dialogue—they had assumed responsibility for interpreting and analyzing the film as well.[38] In view of the importance given to the *benshi*'s presence, it is not surprising that the authority of the director and role of the scriptwriter were largely overlooked. In 1918, a year before the opening of *The Glory of Life,* the Nikkatsu director Tanaka Eizō made an attempt to change this situation when he credited himself as director (along with the other members of his production crew) in the title cards of *Ikeru shikabane* (*The Living Corpse,* 1918).

In terms of the development of the film script, the institution of the *benshi* represented more a phase of development than a stubborn obstacle to overcome. As the narrative systems of films developed in complexity, the *benshi*'s performance changed too, and popular performers like Tokugawa Musei gradually replaced histrionic *kowairo* with a more subdued, thought-

Ikeru shikabane (*The Living Corpse*), directed by Tanaka Eizō, 1918. Yamamoto Kiichi (*left*), Kinugasa Teinosuke. Courtesy Kawakita Memorial Film Institute.

ful style of commentary. At least one old-timer who remembers the opening of *The Cabinet of Dr. Caligari* in 1921, for example, has said that he cannot recall the film without remembering the realistic and thoughtful narration of the great Tokugawa Musei as well.[39] It was the artistry of such *benshi* that enabled the institution to endure, though just barely, the onslaught of sound (an alternative orality) in the 1930s.[40]

   The *benshi*'s presence was only one aspect of the commercial theater's influence on the early development of the film industry. The proximity of the theater was a crucial factor in the founding of the first studios, and assured the solvency of the industry in its infancy; in one way or another, it continued to influence the subject matter of films being made throughout the first three decades of domestic film production.

A WORD ABOUT GENRE

Any consideration of pure film is complicated by the absence of a complete understanding of an "impure" film to which we can compare it.[41] Except for a scant amount of mostly fragments and reconstructions from the 1910s, the bulk of the actual films made during this period are believed lost. Today the people who worked on these films and the studios where they made them are identifiable by name only. Other than in the pictures in print materials, whole genres exist solely in our imagination, colored by what we read about them, contemporary with the time or otherwise. Because of this, Japanese cinema of the 1910s is more than anything else a cinema defined by loss. At this point a word about early conceptions of genre in Japan is in order.

The customary division of Japanese cinema into "contemporary" (*gendai*) and "period" (*jidai*) "genres" is an ambiguously motivated and at times seemingly arbitrary system of classification with its own logic and historical justification. It is well known that from its earliest period Japanese cinema retained this basic generic division, which characterizes the Japanese theater. The customary split between "contemporary" and "period" has broad implications, because in the Japanese film industry it also encompassed distinctions of place and practice. This suggests a variegated industry loosely divided along generic and geographical lines: historical Kyoto and its environs was favored for period films, and in general the Tokyo area became the bastion of the *shinpa* film after that genre's inception. This was a transitional period marked by changing technology and a trend toward longer films, and subsequent shifts in genre definitions and cinematic practices were even further complicated by regional differences in these definitions and practices.[42] The popularity of the *shinpa* melodrama films made at the Nikkatsu Mukōjima studio in Tokyo, the historical resources that endow the Kyoto area with ready-made sets for period films, and the exploding cosmopolitan culture of Tokyo between 1900 and 1920 are a few of the factors that converged to make Tokyo the center of contemporary drama production. The issue of regionalism (regional cultural identities—here, particularly those of Tokyo and Kyoto/Osaka) can confuse or mislead us in our understanding of this time, but it is important to note that contemporary drama films were not exclusive to Tokyo-based production. The relatively little attention that has been given to "provincial" contemporary genre production prior to the 1923 Kanto earthquake enables only a partial understanding of this particular form. Because the contemporary drama posed special considerations for pure film enthusiasts, my purpose here is to propose some points of departure for a more thorough reconsideration of the long-standing tendencies and assumptions of generic classification in Japanese film, with a focus on the contemporary drama form.

A formal consideration of specific contemporary drama films made before 1920 would be very short indeed. When dealing with this genre at this particular point in time, we are faced with not just a "blank screen of reception," such as that described by Richard Abel in the context of French cinema,[43] but quite literally, a blank screen. The earliest productions of films that fall under the rubric "*shinpa* film" (the blanket term for the contemporary drama genre up to 1917–1918) can be traced back to at least 1908, but as is well known, the earliest extant examples of the contemporary drama genre are the reconstructed print of Murata Minoru's pure film, *Souls on the Road* (1921) and the *shinpa* film *Futari Shizuka*, (*Love and Sacrifice/The Two Shizukas*, 1922). The earliest productions in the contemporary drama genre considered to be of note are adaptations of popular plays in the *shinpa* theater repertory: *Ono ga tsumi* (*One's Own Sin*) was first filmed by the Yokota studio in 1907, by the Yoshizawa Company in 1908, and adapted for the screen at least twenty times between 1907 and 1936; and *Hototogisu* (*The Cuckoo,* which appeared in five different versions between 1909 and 1911 alone). Other *shinpa* dramas that were consistently mined for the screen include *Nasanu nakama* (*Not Blood Relations,* the first version by M. Pathe, 1909), *Kyōenroku* (*A Record of Gallantry and Charm,* 1910), and *Biwa uta* (*Lute Song,* two Yoshizawa versions in 1910 and two Fukuhōdō versions in 1911).[44]

Parenthetically, the term "*shinpa* film" is confusing. It is loosely used to denote theater-derived dramatic productions such as those mentioned above as well as comedies and any other type of story with a setting later than the 1880s that was made during this period. But by 1908—late in the *shinpa* theater's development—melodrama had become representative of the theater, and the *shinpa* melodrama (*shinpa daihigeki*) dominated the film industry as well. As I have already mentioned, as an active means of classification, the term "*shinpa* film" seems to have been compromised by the appearance of pure film productions after 1918, and was finally retired in favor of the term "contemporary" (or "modern") drama (*gendaigeki*) after the mid-1920s. Because I am more concerned here with the conception of certain genre classifications (and issues of expectations and assumptions) rather than the variety and multiplicity of genres present in the industry at the time, this limited interpretation of the term "*shinpa* film" and its life span corresponds to my temporal framework of the 1910s. Despite the lack of extant films, print materials dating from 1909 are relatively accessible, and I briefly describe below the degree and nature of genre classification in film periodicals up to 1922–1923. I should add that to an extent, the custom of transcribing the film viewing experience for reading enjoyment opens a window to the popular *shinpa* melodrama in particular. Such transcriptions would be a logical point of entry for a study that focuses on this genre.

Scene from *Nasanu naka* (*Not Blood Relations*), with Inoue Masao (*right*) as Atsumi Shunsaku and Akimoto Kikuya as his wife, Masako. *Katsudō no sekai,* December 1916. From Makino, ed., *Nihon eiga shoki shiryō shūsei* (*A Collection of Research Material from the Early Days of Japanese Film*).

Scene from one of the many film versions of the *shinpa* staple *Ono ga tsumi* (*One's Own Sin*). Tachibana Teijirō (*far right*). *Katsudō gahō,* June 1917. From Makino, ed., *Nihon eiga shoki shiryō shūsei* (*A Collection of Research Material from the Early Days of Japanese Film*).

One of the many silent versions of *Hototogisu* (*The Cuckoo*). Courtesy Kawakita Memorial Film Institute.

The period genre in film is older but better documented in terms of extant film prints, and its origins are arguably richer in variety as it was less confined to the theater for source material. The Japanese theater has a long tradition of privileging the period (which is equated with "classic") over the contemporary,[45] as is evident from a comparison of the contemporary drama plays (*sewamono*) and period plays of the kabuki theater alone. In short, in terms of both pedigree and spectacle, the contemporary genre has always been the period genre's poor relation. In the cinema, on the other hand, the contemporary drama during the 1910s is a provocatively elusive shadow of a form. Although it was mainly but not exclusively dependent on theatrical source material (significantly, this source material was both imported and domestic), this material itself underwent rapid and consistent change between the late 1900s and 1920. The genesis of the *shinpa* film ironically coincided with the virtual stagnation of the *shinpa* theater repertory and a

41

rising intellectual interest in the more recent *shingeki* ("new drama") theater. As a result, the contemporary drama genre in film contained tensions generated by the rival status of its sources and the changing configurations of these sources as they experienced spurts of development, transition, and uncertainty.

The complex theatrical genealogy of the *shinpa* film helps explain why the early contemporary drama genre in film embraced varied and at times conflicting concepts of contemporary representation. For this reason it is important to approach the contemporary drama film with the understanding that at the point of conception and production, even the *shinpa* film was not exclusively the progeny of the *shinpa* theater. It follows that more sensitivity to the connections between the *shingeki* theater and film during the 1910s, both in terms of source material and personnel, as well as a sorting through of the incestuous relationship between the *shinpa* and *shingeki* theater movements (again, in terms of source material and personnel) could be helpful. This relationship between the contemporary genre and theater will be addressed in more detail in the following chapter.

At the risk of sounding obvious, much of the appeal of researching the contemporary drama film during the 1910s is in the challenge created by the constantly fluctuating nature of the "contemporary" at this time. David Bordwell has addressed the rapid transformation in the social and cultural climate of Tokyo already underway by the 1920s, most recently in his study of visual style in Japanese cinema between 1925 and 1945.[46] In fact, much of this transformation, which took place during a period roughly corresponding with the Meiji and Taishō reigns (1868–1924), complements and corresponds to the phenomenal acceleration brought about by changes in technology and culture in Europe and the United States.[47]

The world was getting smaller and, particularly after the Sino and Russian Japanese wars, Japan had set a course toward defining its place in it. In an article in an early issue of the film periodical *Katsudō shashinkai* (alternatively titled *The Cinematograph*), even before World War I swept the country into the context of world history, the head of the Yoshizawa Company story department made an appeal for more cultural sensitivity (more cultural specificity) on the part of readers who responded to a solicitation of original scripts. "What is interesting to Westerners," he complains, "is not necessarily interesting to Japanese."[48] But just a line or two later he remarks how fortunate the Japanese are to have access to Western works, commenting that the film version of *Othello* was much better than the domestic *shingeki* version that had already been presented on stage. It was a complicated period, one not easily characterized, embracing an expanding market for literary translations and the importation, in turn, of romanticism, naturalism, and realism—together with the first attempts to write in the colloquial

Cover of *Katsudō shashinkai* (*The Cinematograph*), no. 4 (December 1909, New Year's issue). From Makino, ed., *Fukkokuban Katsudō shashinkai.*

Cover of *Katsudō shashinkai* (*The Cinematograph*), no. 21 (May–June 1911). From Makino, ed., *Fukkokuban Katsudō shashinkai.*

language. As David Pollack describes it, Japan at the turn of the century was the site of a cultural feeding frenzy:

> It was during the Meiji period (1868–1912) that the Japanese encountered for the first time, as part and parcel of all the other sorts of "modern" ideas suddenly being imported from Europe and America, the notion of an autonomous individual "self" and realized, not without misgivings, that they were going to have to have one of these, too. The urgency of this realization has returned especially in periods of conflict or crisis . . . to take the form of a question only the terms of which have changed in succeeding historical periods: *what does it mean to be Japanese with respect to what is foreign?*[49]

DRAWING A MAP

In 1909 the debut issue of *Katsudō shashinkai,* a fan-oriented publication[50] associated with the Yoshizawa Company that was available to patrons of the studio-owned Denkikan theater, explained that the publication would be useful to the moviegoer as an aid in his or her comprehension of all the wonderful new information that film appreciation would bring:

> even the offerings of a single entertainment hall fall into various categories concerning astronomy, geography, history, science, literature, and the like. Because these are shown one after another in the course of two or three hours, there is no time to sufficiently explain them. Nor is there time to become absorbed in a picture as there is only an instant to admire it before it is replaced with another, and yet another. Therefore, whether or not you are familiar with a film's plot beforehand (or even afterwards) probably makes a difference in the depth of your interest in moving pictures. For this reason, this magazine is necessary in order to compensate for a lack of explanation and to make the moving pictures more enjoyable to watch.[51]

This idea that such publications would help educate the viewer and thus indirectly enhance the viewing experience continued to influence the nature of film periodicals throughout the 1910s. An important aspect of this process of edification involved the introduction and explanation of imported films, which often included a classification of these films according to different types. *Katsudō shashinkai,* which was published between 1909 and 1912, lacks any systematic classification, but an article in the January–February 1911 issue (no. 17) suggests awe of and appreciation for the variety of pictures arriving to Japanese screens:

The growing popularity of films has been accompanied by a rapid expansion of the range of source material for film manufacturing. From Tragic, Historical, Educational, and Comic plays, to the manners and customs and scenery of foreign countries, magic, even animals in motion or special world events—nowadays nearly everything is made into a film.

Most of these are foreign films. Of course, when it comes to drama, there are many excellent films that are Japanese productions—that is to say, Yoshizawa productions. But other than these such [Japanese] films are few and far between.[52]

In *Katsudō shashinkai,* classification (and, by extension, genre variation) in the domestic film is not completely absent, as seen by a page advertising films imported or produced by the Yoshizawa Company. Here Japanese productions are labeled as either comedies (*kigeki*) or tragedies (*higeki*). *Soldiers Work on the Embankment of Mukōjima,* which appears to be a topical film and is not labeled, is an exception.[53] It is interesting that although two of the films being promoted could be categorized as *shinpa* films (they are called tragedies here) there is no reference to the classifications *shin* ("new" or contemporary, an abbreviation for *shinpa*) or *kyū* ("old" or period, an abbreviation for *kyūha*), which are standard in later publications.

The publication *Kinema Record* (1913–1917) picked up where *Katsudō shashinkai* left off, and regularly indicated the type (*shurui*) of an imported film in title listings and plot synopses, regular features of the publication. Japanese productions were also classified, but in a manner that foreshadows the tendency prevalent today. In *Kinema Record,* Japanese films fall almost entirely into one of two categories: *shinpa* or *kyūha*. A cursory comparison of the categorization of imported and domestic films gives the impression that the imported films were more varied, but the custom of relegating domestic films to one of these two monolithic classifications camouflages the variations that are there, such as topical and news films.[54] My readings of such later journals as *Kinema junpō* and *Katsudō kurabu* suggest that the "new" and "old" terms faded away after the mid-1910s as the all-encompassing and more versatile term "film drama" (*eigageki*), or even simply the word "work" (*sakuhin*) became more common. This might be interpreted as a loosening up of the traditional framework of categorization after the appearance of the first so-called pure film dramas around 1919.[55] *Kinema junpō,* considered the heir to publications in the tradition of *Katsudō shashinkai,* avoided genre designation beginning with its 1919 debut issue. Again, the February 1923 issue of *Katsudō kurabu* features a novelization of Tanaka Eizō's *The Kyōya Collar Shop,* usually described as the last significant production to feature female impersonators. In the mid-1910s this Nikkatsu Mukōjima film would more

45

likely have been designated a Mukōjima *shinpa* drama, but here it is referred to as a Nikkatsu Mukōjima *sakuhin*.[56]

The problem with relying on *Kinema Record* for information about domestic productions during this period is its inherent bias toward the idea of pure film. As with the traditional Japanese language histories from the 1950s and 1960s (particularly those written by former pure film enthusiasts), glimpses of the mainstream commercial *shinpa* film and popular *rensageki* ("chain dramas," productions combining film and live performance), both staples of the industry in the mid-1910s,[57] are accessible in *Kinema Record* mainly through a symptomatic reading. As I have explained, the general conception of the pure film was that of a film unencumbered by those very same elements that could be considered essential to the *shinpa* film's generic identity: the female impersonator; the familiarity of a text that had passed through several generic transformations (the antecedents of the most popular *shinpa* plays were popular bestsellers that originally appeared as newspaper serializations); marketability as mass audience-oriented entertainment; and a thematic preoccupation with the impossibility of romantic love. This conceptualization of an "anti-*shinpa*" pure film ideal was more often than not accompanied by a zealous admiration of European and American films. These films had been marketed since the earliest days as "windows to the world," and even if they didn't represent a *Japanese* reality, at least they had women as women.

In addition to considering this period in the context of the relationship between the regional identities of the Tokyo and Kyoto/Osaka areas and their respective film industries, and a historical perspective that has favored a monolithic framework when it comes to making generic distinctions, the pure film, the *shinpa* melodrama, and the chain drama need to be considered in the context of a contemporary literary and aesthetic tradition that privileged "the pure" (high art) over the popular, and the influence of a "translation culture" that flourished early in the century. This translation culture included both the *shinpa* theater, which began in the 1880s as a mixture of plays about contemporary political events and an attempt to compensate for the increasingly "classical" status of the kabuki *sewamono,* and the Ibsen-inspired *shingeki* theater movement that staged its first production, Ibsen's *John Gabriel Borkman,* in 1909. Further adding to this already tangled mix is the existence of what Pollack has described as "the intimately related twin projects of discovering the self and building the nation."[58]

In this respect it may be surprising that the concept of pure film was not limited to the contemporary drama genre. For example, Kaeriyama Norimasa's second production, the lost *The Girl in the Mountain,* moved back and forth between the present and past (according to anecdotal evidence and an early version of the script). Also, observations concerning the pure film's

Interior and exterior scenes from a *shinpa* film: a café in Shanghai (*top*) and a suicide attempt. *Katsudō gahō,* August 1917. From Makino, ed., *Nihon eiga shoki shiryō shūsei (A Collection of Research Material from the Early Days of Japanese Film).*

Shinpa in Western dress: scene from *Pari no adauchi* (*Revenge in Paris*). *Katsudō gahō,* September 1917. From Makino, ed., *Nihon eiga shoki shiryō shūsei* (*A Collection of Research Material from the Early Days of Japanese Film*).

Scene from the *shinpa* film *Onnagokoro* (*A Woman's Heart*). Double page (foldout) glossy illustration, *Katsudō gahō,* November 1917. From Makino, ed., *Nihon eiga shoki shiryō shūsei* (*A Collection of Research Material from the Early Days of Japanese Film*).

Scenes from four "new *shinpa* films." *Katsudō kurabu,* January 1920. From Makino, ed., *Nihon eiga shoki shiryō shūsei* (*A Collection of Research Material from the Early Days of Japanese Film*).

potential for use in exploring new generic forms, including the mining of Japan's rich tradition of literature and folklore, were familiar and integral parts of pure film discourse. Judging from the early tendency toward contemporary life narratives, however, it appears that the contemporary drama was generally considered a good place to start in exploring new themes and the preoccupations of the era. An analogy between the pure film movement and the *shingeki* theater movement is helpful at this point, not only because both shared personnel, a preoccupation with Western texts, and mixed feelings about the pros and cons of imitation. When the pure film, like *shingeki*, is understood as an attempt "to confront the modern world"[59] (only with film instead of theater), its narrative idiosyncrasies—for example, the quasi-Ruritanian setting of Edamasa Yoshirō's *Aware no kyoku* (*Song of Sadness,* 1918–1919) and the Christian choir, inspirational smoke from a factory chimney, and improbable triangulation of an aristocrat, a chemist, and the daughter of a botanist in *The Glory of Life*—are less ridiculous than revealing.

The lack of extant prints of the *shinpa* film and the ephemeral presentational nature of the chain drama, compounded by problems of historiography, complicate considerations of these two forms. In particular, what did the *shinpa* melodrama, a major part of the market and a potential component of the chain drama, look like?[60]

With no known surviving examples of significance from the 1910s to defend it, the *shinpa* film has been either villainized for its insistence on theatrical conventions, a feudalistic, misogynist ideology, and/or trivializing melodrama, or it has been described as part of a "traditional" mode of expression that represents an aesthetically idealized cultural self.[61] The newly published filmography of Japanese films made between 1896 and 1945, *Nihon eiga sakuhin jiten senzenhen* (the first published filmography of this magnitude to cover the silent period), does make it tempting to interpret some aspect of national character from a body of films that survives primarily in print. The phonetically based reference system that replaces alphabetization in the Japanese language yields pages of titles that begin with the character "mother," as well as columns of titles beginning with "flower," "heaven," or "spring," a combination that is reminiscent of the now infamously quaint rendering of the 1878 Japanese adaptation of Bulwer-Lytton's *Ernest Maltravers* (1837) into "The Spring Tale of Flowers and Willows." This is eerily similar to the kind of interpretation done in wartime studies like that of the 1944 Institute for Intercultural Studies: "An Analysis of Japanese Character Structure Based on Japanese Film Plots and Thematic Apperception Tests on Japanese Americans."[62]

The repeated appearance of certain titles like *One's Own Sin* and *Konjiki yasha* (*Demon Gold,* based on Izumi Kyōka's last unfinished novel) are nevertheless an undeniable indication of the mythical proportions acquired by these stories. The persistent popularity of such stories becomes all the more evident when the *shinpa* stage melodrama is traced back to its own antecedent, the literary genre called the *katei shōsetsu* ("family novel"). At that time, this genre exemplified (among other things) the conflict between old and new views on the importance of conjugal love and tragedies about women oppressed by a male upper class. This knowledge in turn raises new questions: how legitimate are later interpretations of *shinpa* melodrama's ideologically subversive nature or to what extent did the film versions of *The Cuckoo, One's Own Sin,* and *Chikyōdai (Foster Sisters,* first version in 1909, the Yoshizawa Company) retain the Christian spirituality of Tokutomi Roka and Kikuchi Yūhō's turn-of-the-century novels?[63] It is possible these questions ultimately cannot be answered, and although this was not an issue for contemporary audiences, in hindsight, the complex nature of the *shinpa* melodrama's own background alone suggests that to compare the *shinpa* melodrama to the pure film is like comparing apples to oranges. Ultimately, the intent of a pure film plot was subordinate to stylistic preoccupations. Within this context, the pure film reflects, above all, a very specific confrontation with the modern. The poetic dimension of what allegedly inspired Tanaka Eizō's *The Kyōya Collar Shop,* described here by Kishi Matsuo, could not be more different: "In the autumn of 1922, while Tanaka Eizō was browsing about Ginza, he passed a store selling quality collars for kimono . . . and the many beautiful variously colored collars caught his eye. The pallid light of a shaded gas lantern streamed into the shop. He thought how beautiful it would be if the collars were to whirl up in the rays of light. He wanted to make that into a film. As a result, he wrote *The Kyōya Collar Shop.*"[64]

In addition to providing Mizoguchi Kenji with one of his earliest experiences in the industry (he was an assistant director, a term used fairly loosely at the time), *The Kyōya Collar Shop* is generally considered the last major feature film to use the female impersonator. Another important personality to be adopted from existing stage tradition, the impersonator, together with the *benshi*, appears only in a dim outline in references that appear in pure film rhetoric of the 1910s. Like the *benshi,* the impersonator takes shape as another worrisome barrier to experimentation with new narrative systems and genres: just as the *benshi* precluded the use of titles, the impersonator displaced women actors.

It is interesting to note, however, that contrary to what might be gleaned from contemporary film periodicals at first glance, women were in fact present on screen before the first pure film productions, most notably in the hybrid chain drama form. By 1916, at the peak of the chain drama's popularity (and the eve of its demise, irrevocably affected by new censorship regulations), discussions of the potential of women actors vis-à-vis the art of the

51

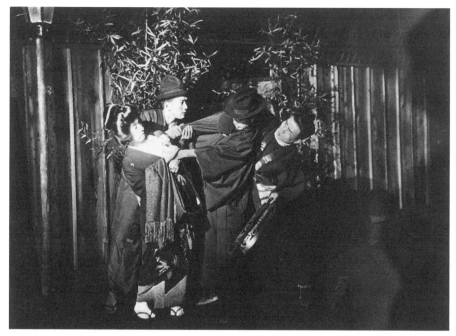

Kyōya eriten (*The Kyōya Collar Shop*), directed by Tanaka Eizō, 1922 (assistant director, Mizoguchi Kenji). Generally acknowledged as the last appearance of the female impersonator on screen. Courtesy Kawakita Memorial Film Institute.

popular female impersonator were common. Even so, it was not until the 1920s, after the first pure film productions, that women actors became standard throughout the industry.

WOMEN IN THE CHAIN DRAMA

One of the hallmarks of pure film discourse was the importance of introducing women actors to the screen, and it could be argued that it was the presence of the female impersonator that ensured the *shinpa* melodrama's demise. In kabuki, the impersonator is an icon that has long been regarded as intrinsic to this art, and she also has a practical justification: kabuki performance is physically demanding. Neither rationale really translates to the *shinpa* film. Women were already performing alongside impersonators in the *shinpa* theater, and a repertory specializing in family relationships, forced marriages, and star-crossed lovers is presumably less physically strenuous.

52

Publicity collage of an *oyama* (Ichikawa Kyūzō). *Katsudō gahō,* September 1917. From Makino, ed., *Nihon eiga shoki shiryō shūsei* (*A Collection of Research Material from the Early Days of Japanese Film*).

Scenes from three *shinpa* films produced at the Nikkatsu Mukōjima (Tokyo) studio. *Katsudō hyōron,* August 1919. The director Kinugasa Teinosuke began his career in film as a female impersonator. He appears at left in the top scene. From Makino, ed., *Nihon eiga shoki shiryō shūsei* (*A Collection of Research Material from the Early Days of Japanese Film*).

Tachibana Teijirō in *Wakaki onna no hansei* (*A Young Woman's Half Life*). Double page (foldout) glossy illustration, *Katsudō gahō,* April 1917. From Makino, ed., *Nihon eiga shoki shiryō shūsei* (*A Collection of Research Material from the Early Days of Japanese Film*).

Tachibana Teijirō as the geisha Fujimaru in *Yaegasumi* (*Boundless Mist*). Double page (foldout) glossy illustration, *Katsudō gahō,* September 1917. From Makino, ed., *Nihon eiga shoki shiryō shūsei* (*A Collection of Research Material from the Early Days of Japanese Film*).

Tachibana Teijirō in *Osanaki haha* (*Young Mother*). *Katsudō gahō,* May 1917. From Makino, ed., *Nihon eiga shoki shiryō shūsei* (*A Collection of Research Material from the Early Days of Japanese Film*).

Kinoshita Yaoko and Inoue Masao *(right)* in the Tenkatsu production *Hanashigure* (*Blossom Shower*). *Katsudō no sekai,* May 1916. From Makino, ed., *Nihon eiga shoki shiryō shūsei* (*A Collection of Research Material from the Early Days of Japanese Film*).

Characters and a scene from the chain drama *Shōfū murasame* (*Pine Breeze, Passing Shower*), Kinoshita Yaoko (*bottom right*). *Katsudō gahō,* June 1917. From Makino, ed., *Nihon eiga shoki shiryō shūsei* (*A Collection of Research Material from the Early Days of Japanese Film*).

Hazumi Tsuneo points out that at its origins, *shinpa* theater was not synony-mous with melodrama, and its purpose was not, as it later became, to bring on the tears. Rather, the rising popularity of the female impersonator imposed this limitation.[65] A look at the women who were performing in the chain drama helps illustrate how a gradual reallocation of the rights to gender representation facilitated more genre diversity within the broad classification of the contemporary drama.[66]

Nakamura Kasen's performances for the M. Pathe company beginning in 1908 are considered the earliest instances of a female performance on screen.[67] Not coincidentally, her appearances paralleled the popularity of all-female kabuki that same year. European and American film actresses were being paid considerable attention in publications like *Kinema Record* in the early 1910s, and by 1916 articles debating the relative merits of women actors and the female impersonator were common. The September 1916 issue of the film periodical *Katsudō no sekai,* which appeared shortly after the opening of *The Broken Coin* (Francis Ford, 1915), featured a special sec-tion titled "Studies for Miss Grace Cunard." Topics in this special Cunard corner range from "All about Miss Cunard," to "The Art of Grace Cunard," "The Psychological Explanation for Cunard's Expression," and "Compari-son of Grace Cunard and Pearl White," as well as an article on Cunard by Suzuki Yuriko, the editor's wife.[68]

How does coverage of Japanese women actors—or even the female impersonator—fare in comparison? In the ample glossies of *shinpa* films and chain dramas, the impersonators outnumber women. This may simply reflect the smaller number of women in the acting profession, but it could also be because women's association with the newer, more innovative studios that produced chain dramas was of a more casual nature. The resident actors at major studios like Nikkatsu were all men. Nikkatsu was the major supplier of *shinpa* films, and its resident star impersonator, Tachibana Teijirō, was by far the most prominently featured actor up until 1917. In these same issues of *Katsudō gahō,* full-page portrait stills of Nakamura Kasen, Nakayama Utako, and Kinoshita Yaoko finally make an appearance alongside those of European and Hollywood stars.

In *Katsudō no sekai,* articles about Japanese women actors occur with increasing frequency in 1916, its first year of publication, but certain articles that appear in the film periodical *Katsudō gahō* a year later are of special interest. Written by the chain drama actress Kinoshita Yaoko, they represent a rare example of women's writing in such publications, and they give an idea of what it might have been like for a woman to have aspired to screen acting at the time.

Performing in chain dramas was a grueling experience: it is hard to describe as glamorous a day that started early with location shooting, after

Publicity montage: Nikkatsu Mukōjima studio. Stage set (*top right*) and exterior (*bottom*), the studio head Kubo Hidehiko (*top left*) and resident actors. *Katsudō gahō*, May 1917. From Makino, ed., *Nihon eiga shoki shiryō shūsei* (*A Collection of Research Material from the Early Days of Japanese Film*).

Nakamura Kasen, *Katsudō gahō,* December 1917. From Makino, ed., *Nihon eiga shoki shiryō shūsei* (*A Collection of Research Material from the Early Days of Japanese Film*).

Nakayama Utako, *Katsudō gahō,* November 1917. From Makino, ed., *Nihon eiga shoki shiryō shūsei* (*A Collection of Research Material from the Early Days of Japanese Film*).

Kinoshita Yaoko. A biographical caption refers to Kinoshita as "our country's only film actress." *Katsudō gahō,* October 1917. From Makino, ed., *Nihon eiga shoki shiryō shūsei (A Collection of Research Material from the Early Days of Japanese Film).*

which the actor rushed to the theater in order to perform onstage and supply a voice for the filmed part of the presentation. Such a schedule caused one working actress, Ichikawa Shizue, to remark, "It is said that 'if you are to be born, do not be a woman. You will have one hundred years of suffering and pleasure at the hands of others.' I say, if you are born a woman, do not be an actor, because you will experience in one day the suffering of a hundred years."[69] In spite of such difficulties, Kinoshita Yaoko appears to have been eager to establish a reputation as a serious and hardworking *firumu joyū* ("film actress"), the appellation she preferred. This apparently entailed a certain amount of publicity savoir faire, as she responded to some unusual opportunities to advance her career. For example, when films featuring Marguerita Fisher handling a twenty-eight-foot snake received an inordinate amount of press, Kinoshita accepted a proposal for a Japanese remake, *Majinai no hebi (The Enchanted Snake,* 1917). (This was not without some

61

リアム・デスモンド氏とブルドッグ

（上より）ファニー・ワード嬢と白猫、マーガリッタ・フィッシャー嬢と二丈八尺の大蛇

Marguerita Fisher and snake (*in circle at right*, Fanny Ward and kitten). *Katsudō gahō*, June 1917. From Makino, ed., *Nihon eiga shoki shiryō shūsei* (*A Collection of Research Material from the Early Days of Japanese Film*).

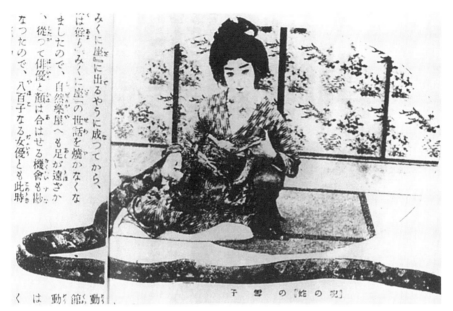

Kinoshita Yaoko in *Majinai no hebi* (*The Enchanted Snake*), 1917. *Katsudō gahō*, June 1917. From Makino, ed., *Nihon eiga shoki shiryō shūsei* (*A Collection of Research Material from the Early Days of Japanese Film*).

hesitation, as she later admitted in her first *Katsudō gahō* article, "Yaoko kara mōshiage sōrō" ("A Word from Yaoko").[70]

"Rakuba no hanashi" ("The Story of My Falling off My Horse"), in the April 1917 issue of *Katsudō gahō*, details Kinoshita's attempt to become Japan's first serial queen. Approached with the offer to star in a forty- to fifty-reel serial that would be "a Japanese version of a picture like *The Broken Coin*," Kinoshita began taking horseback riding lessons at the studio's request. In her own words, "In order to prepare for filming the picture, I would need to practice riding a horse, motor boating, driving a car, piloting an airplane, and riding a bicycle, and I began with cars and horses."[71] As can be guessed by the title of Kinoshita's article, the project ended when she fell from her horse and suffered a head injury that kept her from appearing on stage. The real end to such projects came with the sudden decline in chain drama production just a few months later, but Kinoshita's case indicates a heightened awareness of the marketability of women on screen. In this light, the highly acclaimed 1918 performance of Hanayagi Harumi in *The Glory of Life* seems less of a project sprung from the head of Zeus.

Helen Holmes, action serial queen. *Katsudō no sekai,* October 1916. From Makino, ed., *Nihon eiga shoki shiryō shūsei* (*A Collection of Research Material from the Early Days of Japanese Film*).

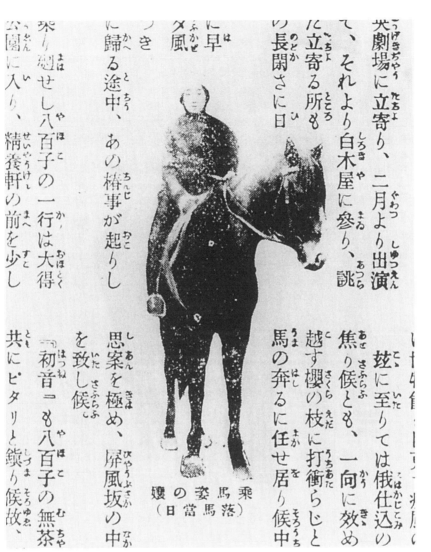

演劇場に立寄り、二月より出演して、それより白木屋に参り、誂立寄る所も長閑さに日は早夕風つきに帰る途中、あの椿事が起りし思案を極め、屏風坂の中を致し候。『初音』も八百子の無茶共にピタリと鎮り候故、架り劇せし八百子の一行は大得公園に入り、精養軒の前を少し

兹に至りては俄仕込の焦り候とも、一向に効め越す櫻の枝に打衝らじと馬の奔るに任せ居り候中

嬢の姿馬乗
（日常馬落）

Kinoshita Yaoko, illustration from the article "Rakuba no hanashi" ("Falling off My Horse"). *Katsudō gahō,* April 1917. From Makino, ed., *Nihon eiga shoki shiryō shūsei* (*A Collection of Research Material from the Early Days of Japanese Film*).

In retrospect, it is clear that from the point of view of traditional histories, the chain dramas that featured a smattering of stage actresses like Kinoshita Yaoko were a regressive form of entertainment outside the realm of their consideration and interests. In their view, these stage productions, punctuated by intermittent segments of filmed exterior location scenes, were at best plays that aspired to be moving pictures. At worst, they were poor substitutes for the real thing, and the fact that they might have featured women on screen was not considered a significant breakthrough for the industry during the 1910s. By taking a closer look at print materials from this period, it is evident that some of the influences that helped establish a permanent place for women within the industry were already at work.

By the 1920s, the modernization of Japanese film was being approached from several directions. The reforms promoted by the intellectuals who led the *shingeki* movement included the introduction of psychological realism to replace *shinpa*'s stylized romanticism with a modern, colloquial style of writing dialogue, a natural acting style, and the exclusive use of women in female roles. When such members of the movement as Osanai Kaoru and Murata Minoru moved into the film world, they continued to push for these changes there as well. At the same time, young intellectuals not directly involved with the theater, like Kaeriyama Norimasa, supported the application of similar reforms; Kaeriyama in particular proposed techniques gleaned from the imported American and European film literature he was reading at the time. Finally, the American film industry's sudden boom in production after the First World War prompted a number of filmmakers and producers to tour the studios of Hollywood, and they brought home news of the latest production techniques. They were joined by men like Thomas Kurihara and Henry Kotani, who had received training on the sets of internationally renowned Hollywood directors like D. W. Griffith and Cecil B. DeMille. The Japanese industry transformed quickly between 1917, when Kaeriyama began preparations for his first pure films, and the years immediately following the Great Kanto Earthquake. In 1925, Murata Minoru described this rapid change in the Japanese film as a reflection of the new trends of Japanese society. "The *shinpa* film that thrived on misery is in ruins," he wrote, "and the geisha films with their flavor of Edo no longer draws crowds. . . . Now it is Delirium. Power. Speed. Science. Thrill. It is sensual pleasure, Western clothes, Western buildings, automobiles. It is airplanes, dance, nudity, fist fights, blood."[72] Although the *shinpa* film laid a foundation for the modern melodrama and influenced important directors like Mizoguchi Kenji, by 1925 these stylized, romantic tragedies were being crowded out by the demand for a much greater variety of contemporary life narratives onscreen.

2

Kaeriyama Norimasa and
The Glory of Life

THE EARLIEST ACCOUNT of a scriptwriter's name appearing in the titles of a Japanese film is in 1911. The movie industry was fifteen years old, and Onoe Matsunosuke was at the peak of his popularity in theatrical swordfight films. *Shinpa* films featuring female impersonators still dominated contemporary screen drama, but onstage the *shingeki* actress Matsui Sumako was captivating audiences with her performance as Nora in *The Doll House.* Imported films (at this point, particularly European films) were a great attraction, and in this year the theaters specializing in foreign films were offering *Anna Karenina, Hamlet,* and documentary footage of Tolstoy's funeral. *Zigomar,* the enormously popular French detective film, came under fire for supposedly inspiring an outbreak of criminal behavior among Japanese youths, and in the secluded garden of a remote country villa, the Meiji Emperor experienced his first moving picture.[1]

THE FIRST WRITERS

Screenwriting as a craft actually had appeared on the horizon two years earlier, in 1909. There is record of writers providing scripts for individual actors, and even some *benshi* writing scripts before this time, but in 1909, Kawaura Kenichi, the head of the Yoshizawa Company in Tokyo, set up a separate story department at the company headquarters in Shinbashi.[2] Built only a year earlier, the glassed-in Yoshizawa studio in Meguro, unusual for that time in Japan (Kawaura had visited Edison's studio in the Bronx), had been producing films at an increasingly rapid pace, and the story department,

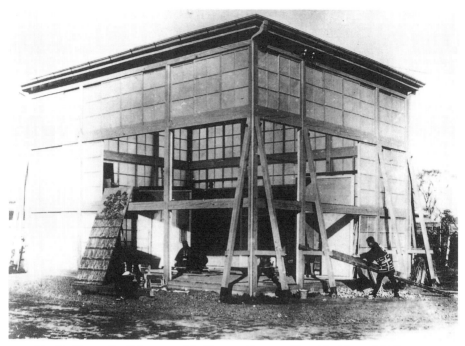

The Yoshizawa Co. "glass stage" in Meguro. Courtesy Kawakita Memorial Film Institute.

called the "*kōan-bu*" ("idea" or "plan" department), was conceived in an effort to meet the growing demand for scripts. Satō Kōroku, a *shinpa* playwright and producer, was appointed head of the department. He soon had five writers working under him, including his acquaintance, Masumoto Kiyoshi, a member of the Bungei kyōkai (Literary Society, 1905), which was responsible, together with the Ibsen kai (Ibsen Society, 1907), for promoting and staging the earliest *shingeki* stage productions. Masumoto was also an experienced *shinpa* dramatist, and became one of the more notable *shinpa* film scriptwriters of this early period (he later wrote the script for Tanaka Eizō's *Ikeru shikabane* (*The Living Corpse,* 1918). According to Kawaura's original plan, the job of the *kōan-bu* department would have been twofold: to solicit scripts from the general public through special screenwriting competitions, and to oversee the administration of an acting school on the studio premises. According to an article by Satō Kōroku in the May 1910 issue of *Katsudō shashinkai,* plans to expand the *kōan-bu* were coupled with plans formulated the previous year for the establishment of an acting school. The person in charge of the school, according to Satō, the actor Sekine Tappatsu, was unable to keep up with the demands of his heavy schedule and this part of the plan shortly, it seems, ended in failure.[3] Still, even at this early stage, original story material and well-trained actors were understood to be two essential, intrinsically related requirements for successful film production, and in this sense the conception of the Yoshizawa *kōan-bu* set a precedent for all subsequent efforts to transform the domestic film.

As I mentioned in chapter 1, although *Katsudō shashinkai* is commonly referred to in secondary source material as the house organ for the Yoshizawa studio, it was generous in its coverage of the films by rival production companies. There is some question of the extent to which it was sponsored directly by the Yoshizawa Company, as it was issued by a publishing entity called Nihon katsudōsha, and articles critical of Yoshizawa but favorably inclined toward rival studios are common. According to one such article in the May 1911 issue, the magazine regarded its responsibility to be that of a mediating force between spectators and management for the betterment of the trade in general.[4] Even so, Yoshizawa productions receive sufficient exposure in the pages of illustrations toward the front of most issues to give the latter-day reader an idea of the company's turnout. The number of comedies is intriguing considering complaints in film magazines later in the 1910s that the Japanese industry had yet to establish a solid tradition in this genre; of notice too are illustrations with a caption identifying them as a "Yoshizawa *kōan-bu* product."

The most conspicuous production based on a winning entry in the Yoshizawa competition was *Matsu no midori* (*The Green of the Pines*), adapted by Masumoto Kiyoshi. The film opened in January 1911 at the Denkikan, a movie theater—Japan's first—in Asakusa that was managed by the Yoshizawa Company. According to a critique of the film in *Katsudō shashinkai,* (which begins with a reference to the film as a "pure" moving picture [*junsui no katsudō shashingeki*]), the central character was a poor country girl, Ohana, who leaves home against her parents' wishes in order to find work in Tokyo. Before leaving home, she receives a letter from her fiancé, who is fighting in the Russo-Japanese war. In the letter he confesses his fear that he might die on the battlefield, and urges her to be prudent and accept any promising proposal for marriage that she receives in his absence. After arriving in the city, the girl works in a beer factory and spends her free time at the moving picture theater. Then one day, while watching a picture (at the Denkikan) she sees the face of her fiancé in a newsreel from the front. But just as she jumps onto the stage, the film ends. His image vanishes from the screen, and she weeps uncontrollably. Suddenly, the girl's parents and her fiancé appear in the theater, and they are all joyously reunited.

The Green of the Pines is the one Yoshizawa *kōan-bu* production to be

Advertisement for the Yoshizawa Co. in *Katsudō shashinkai*, no. 16 (December 1910–January 1911, New Year's issue). From Makino, ed., *Fukkokuban Katsudō shashinkai*.

Advertisement for the first dedicated movie theater, the Denki-kan. *Kinema Record,*
10 April 1916. The Denki-kan was one of many theaters to advertise regularly in
Kinema Record. From Makino, ed., *Fukkoku-ban Kinema rekōdo.*

commonly referenced in secondary source material, and although the film
does not survive, it is apparent from a review in the February–March 1911
issue (no. 18) of *Katsudō shashinkai* that it had many of the elements that
later would be deemed desirable by pure film advocates. For one, the central
character, Ohana, was played by a woman in place of a female impersonator.
According to the review, the actress (referred to as "the woman") playing
Ohana did not appear especially skilled, but was appealingly natural. This
review of *The Green of the Pines* is striking in its detail, divided as it is into
separate sections on the script, staging, cast, landscape, and lighting, and
ending with "Zasshi no chûi," what could be interpreted as a few minor
objections and words of advice "on behalf of the magazine" (or the uncred-

71

ited writer). The gist of the review is that the plot overall is clever, contemporary (the writer notes how common it is for spectators to think they recognize an acquaintance or relative in a film on screen), and even slightly comic. Although admitting that some viewers no doubt found the film a bit dull, the writer claims to have had the opportunity, through the film, to become familiar with the sentiments of the average young Japanese girl. Locality, another highly valued element of pure film, was amply represented, according to the review, in the film's six separate scenes, particularly the final scene that takes place in the Denkikan itself. In fact, the harshest criticism of the film is that an exterior shot outside the theater is spoiled by bystanders who are obviously aware of the camera, a clear sign that Japanese actors and technicians had yet to master this aspect of location shooting.[5]

It is doubtful there was a standard format for the material handled by the early members of the *kōan-bu* staff.[6] Even so, it was the first time a unit of its kind appeared within the production system, and the staff members, like their counterparts in the American studios, were responsible for both original material and rewrites of scenarios submitted by the general public. Kawaura's innovative move to set up a permanent story department was remarkable for several reasons. To begin with, in Kyoto around 1909, Makino Shōzō was still narrating film dialogue from behind the camera. This *kuchidate* narration (a familiar technique for his actors, many of whom were members of traveling troupes where it was used for last-minute changes in the program) was then jotted down by an actor or Makino's assistant, and this became the script for the *benshi*'s narration.[7] This procedure, in which the film script was written after the film was shot, was an interesting departure from the growing tendency in the United States and Europe to treat the silent film script as a plan for shooting the film.

Of particular interest was the Yoshizawa Company's practice of soliciting scenarios (or stories) from outside the studios. In the United States this had become commonplace at least as early as 1907. The first staff writers were for the most part former journalists or popular fiction writers drawn to the trade by the rumor of very large payments for very short stories, but within a few years the rapid increase in the length of films outdistanced the output of the story departments' staff. The studios were forced to accept material from among the "ten thousand people" who were hastily writing scenarios.[8] A direct result of this was a flood of "how-to" literature for the budding silent scenarist as well as books and articles debating the qualities of the silent film script. Much of this material crossed the ocean and was avidly read by Japanese movie fans (later such material appeared in translation). Epes Winthrop Sargent's pioneering articles in *Moving Picture World,* for example, were compiled in book form and published in 1912 as *Technique of the Photoplay,* which became one of the references Kaeriyama used five years later for his own "how-to" book, *Katsudō shashingeki no sōsaku to satsuei hō* (hereafter referred to as *The Production and Photography of Moving Picture Drama*).

In the United States this period of "scenario fever," when the opportunities for the amateur scenarist seemed limitless, lasted only a few years, from around 1907 to 1914, but it has been pointed out that this was an important period of development in the structure of the narrative film. At the very least, the bulk of literature created by the growing popularity of the craft helped to standardize the format of silent film scripts. As early as 1909 a magazine article laid out the ground rules to this format for freelance hopefuls, and it was no coincidence that sometime between 1911 and 1915 the use of a continuity script became standard practice on American sets, allowing, for example, an increase in film length, more freedom in location shooting, and the development of more complex, psychologically developed narratives.[9] At this point it is significant to note that such transformations in screenwriting practice in the United States (and subsequent developments throughout the 1910s) were increasingly familiar throughout Europe as well as in Japan.[10] In this sense, the growing awareness of and interest in aspects of the preproduction script in Japan, closely linked to the concept of pure film, challenge any assumption that the Japanese industry was conspicuously isolated from the rest of the filmmaking world during this period.

In the story departments of the American studios, a scenario (or story) editor reviewed submitted manuscripts and reworked any material that showed possibilities for production. At least as early as 1912, newspapers and magazines in the United States also promoted competitions in order to recruit scripts from the general public, and this practice was soon taken up by major studios as well.[11] At the Yoshizawa Company, original scenarios (short synopses or stories) were submitted to regularly held competitions, and the winning material was reworked and filmed. In addition, these original ideas were published in *Katsudō shashinkai*. This practice of collecting and circulating original story material is perhaps the earliest evidence in Japan of a popular interest in writing for the screen. The scenario competitions sponsored by the Yoshizawa Company, however, were relatively short-lived. Whatever interest they aroused for the craft of screenwriting, it scarcely had the chance to develop into the "scenario fever" that broke out in the United States. But because the magazine was strongly fan-oriented, it would have been enough to draw interest to this aspect of the production process, and it can be considered a precedent for the competitions providing a foothold into the industry for aspiring screenwriters to this day. The degree of awe and wonder that comes across in the frequent description of the movies as a marvel of modern technology (subject matter could range from "astronomy, geography, history, biography, science, social conditions, human nature and customs")[12] is particular to *Katsudō shashinkai,* but the exposure given to story material and the way the magazine provided a venue for more general debate on this relatively new form of entertainment was continued in subsequent film periodicals, most notably *Kinema junpō.*

In the April 1910 issue of *Katsudō shashinkai,* Satō Kōroku wrote an article expressing his disappointment in stories submitted to the *kōan-bu* staff. He comments on problems that would continue to complicate the formulation of the contemporary drama film over the next two decades. In Europe and the United States, the people involved in this great shuffling of paper complained of practical problems—incompetent editors and amateurs with little knowledge of the basic requirements of "plot, cohesion, and technique"[13]—but the lack of knowledge Satō laments concerns the less tangible problem of expressing cultural identity. He complained that first of all, amateur scenarios were too artificial, too much like imitations of "Western pictures" *(seiyō no shashin).* In his opinion, first they should instead advocate a Japanese manner of living for Japanese people (he cites as an example that even the manner of dress for a magician is different in Japan than in the West), and he suggests that writers look to Japan's own traditions and past as a foundation for their stories. Second, he criticizes Japanese screen acting as deplorable. Third, the recognition of the ways in which plays for the stage and scripts for moving pictures differ was necessary in overcoming the above problems. It is interesting to note that although Satō acknowledges that a recent Russian visitor to the Yoshizawa studio seemed impressed with the technical quality of the studio's work, in his own opinion the studio still had a long way to go before it could make films comparable to those of France, England, Italy, and the United States.[14]

Two years later the Yoshizawa Company merged with the Yokota, M. Pathe, and Fukuhōdō companies to form Nikkatsu, and a story department was organized under Masumoto Kiyoshi. From then on the story department was an essential unit within the production system.[15] The merger also resulted in the discontinuation of *Katsudō shashinkai* (the last surviving issue, no. 26, is dated November 1911; issues 22–25 are no longer extant). To compensate for the loss, a small group of its young former contributors, including Kaeriyama Norimasa (who published in *Katsudō shashinkai* under a pen name that reflected his alleged fondness for the mountains in summer), published the first issue of *Katsudō no tomo (Moving Picture Companion)* in January 1913.[16] This publication is believed to have survived only through the fourth issue, dated 30 June 1913. This was followed in October of that year with *Kinema Record* (titled *Film Record* through the first three issues).

74

Kinema Record became Japan's (self-proclaimed, in English) "illustrated leading cinema trade journal," but shortly after Kaeriyama, then editor, entered the Tennenshoku katsudō shashin kabushiki kaisha (Natural Color Moving Picture Company), or Tenkatsu, in 1917 the *Kinema Record* staff quietly disbanded. *Kinema junpō,* founded in 1919, followed in the tradition of *Kinema Record,* and it has continued to circulate since then. *Kinema Record* is generally regarded as the point of departure for serious film criticism in Japan, but the influence of *Katsudō shashinkai* lingers in much of its format and orientation.

"OBSERVE TO LEARN"

Kaeriyama Norimasa did not officially enter the film industry until 1914, when he joined the short-lived Kinetophone Company, and it wasn't until 1918, after having been employed for one year in the import division of the Tenkatsu Company, that he had the opportunity to direct. By then he presumably had a fairly clear idea of the manner of films he wanted to make as he had been developing his ideas over several years in numerous magazine articles written since his early youth.

By the time Kaeriyama and his colleagues started *Kinema Record* in 1913 (under the title *Film Record*), he had been collecting imported film-related publications for a few years and was familiar with the increasing volume of literature stressing a distinction between the screen and the stage. These imported publications also allowed him to keep up with the latest developments in filmmaking apparatus, and his familiarity with imported films from the United States and Europe lent authority to his comments on the transitions taking place in film technique abroad.

The material covered in *Kinema Record* reveals the extent of Kaeriyama and his colleagues' enthusiasm for foreign films. It was an enthusiasm close to reverence.[17] The staff called themselves the *Katsusha kōyūkai* ("Friends of Moving Pictures") and consisted of about a dozen members. They published *Kinema Record* twice a month, and the responsibilities of each staff member changed every two weeks. Each member was assigned a theater, and beginning with basic information—the title, subject, cast—he would give a detailed report on the film being shown.[18] In this way, the magazine functioned as a kind of contemporary guide to imported films, with an emphasis on film criticism. It reflected an attitude toward films from Europe and the United States that continued to play an essential role throughout the silent period, reaching a high point with the detailed transcriptions and analyses published in Murata's quarterly *Eiga kagaku kenkyū* (*Scientific Film*

Cover (Francesca Bertini), *"Kinema Record:* The Illustrated Leading Cine. Journal." *Kinema Record,* 10 October 1916. From Makino, ed., *Fukkokuban Kinema rekōdo.*

Research) in the late 1920s. "Observe to learn" appears to have been the guiding principle among the members of the Friends of Moving Pictures. This was common advice found abroad in virtually every "how-to" book of the period ("'Study the screen.' There, in three words is contained the one big secret of success in the picture field"),[19] but for these young intellectuals the advice applied most specifically to imported pictures.

In July 1917, Kaeriyama published *The Production and Photography of Moving Picture Drama,* combining some of his major articles from *Kinema Record* with material culled from imported film books and magazines. In it he plotted a course for the future of domestic film drama by stressing the need for his ideal motion picture, "pure film drama" (*jun'eigageki*), as opposed to *katsudōgeki* ("moving picture drama") or *katsudō shashin* ("moving pictures"), terms that were often used to insinuate that all other films were, in comparison, a lesser form of entertainment.[20] In addition to the use of women actors in place of female impersonators, and "spoken titles" (dialogue intertitles) that would eliminate the need for a *benshi,* Kaeriyama advocated location shooting, more complex and varied camera work (in particular, close-up shots and moving camera techniques) and editing, and a more "natural" style of acting. In this book Kaeriyama also expressed the opinion that only a well-developed film script could guarantee the successful implementation of such an approach. *The Production and Photography of Moving Picture Drama* underwent no fewer than ten printings in seven years, from 1917 to 1924.[21] Priced at a little over one yen, the book was intended for the amateur fan.[22] This focus on the amateur, clearly stated in the preface, and the careful introduction of foreign criticism and production methods, allow us a glimpse of Kaeriyama's vision for the future of Japanese films.[23] Most notable, however, is the systematic treatment of the proper elements of a film script and the inclusion of several samples (all written by Kaeriyama under the pen name Mizusawa Takehiko) that are the earliest surviving examples of a continuity-style format. One of these, *Ai to hana* (*Love and the Flower*) was to become the model for Kaeriyama's second film, *The Girl in the Mountain,* made in 1918 and released the following year.

Kaeriyama had a decent command of English, and parts of his book are apparently translations of material selected from the copious foreign-language references listed at the beginning of the book. These include Sargent's *Technique of the Photoplay* (1912), Hugo Münsterberg's *The Photoplay: A Psychological Study* (1916), Vachel Lindsay's *The Art of the Moving Picture* (1915), and in the 1924 edition, Victor Freeburg's *The Art of Photoplay Making* (1918).[24] In view of this list, it is not surprising that Kaeriyama advises the novice writer of the necessity for titles, but titles that are as "simple and few as possible," for example, or of the importance of "harmony between picture and subtitles [expository intertitles]," and thinking in terms of the screen ("the silent voices must be communicated by the screen").[25]

The foreword to the chapter "Scenario Technique and the Scenario Writer" includes the following passage: "The scenario is the foundation of motion picture drama. The value of the drama depends on the scenario a great deal because the director decides the actions of the actor and all aspects of the film according to it . . . it is very different from the script for stage drama. . . ."[26] Here Kaeriyama not only states the importance of the film script, but he also introduces the idea of a movie as the creation of someone (a director) with a definite plan in hand (the film script). This was an entirely new concept at a time when audiences were still fascinated by adaptations of *shinpa* plays and the acrobatic feats of Onoe Matsunosuke, and would greet the *benshi*'s entrance with the same fan calls reserved for a popular kabuki actor.[27] Kaeriyama's conception of a pure film in *The Production and Photography of Moving Picture Drama* strongly suggests one narratively explicit (and engaging) enough to be coherent and enjoyable without a *benshi's* explanation, interpretation, or embellishment. The best way for a director to realize such a well-rounded narrative, in his opinion, was to make the film according to a plan, the script, which would give him greater control over the finished product.

In the previous chapter I explored some of the difficulties involved in chasing down a single interpretation or definition for the meaning of the term "pure film" as it was used and understood during this period. Kaeriyama's own formulation of the term evolved over time as the result of a number of influences. In his contributions to *Katsudō shashinkai* early in his critical career, he wrote fairly extensively on the nature of film as art, and these articles are of interest considering the degree to which film as art becomes a prominent motif in his later references to "pure film" attributes summed up in *The Production and Photography of Moving Picture Drama*.[28] In "Katsudō shashin geijutsuron," a contribution to the final extant issue of *Katsudō shashinkai* (no. 26, November 1911), Kaeriyama raises some points concerning possibilities to improve the film trade that he would later repeat periodically throughout his career in production. For example, he blames both "the authorities" (*tōkyokusha,* a vague reference to "management") and the undiscriminating tastes of spectators unable to distinguish a difference between "*shinpa* love stories [*shinpa ren'ai mono*] and Pathé romances and dramas" as responsible for inferior films. Equally familiar is his suggestion that the production of better pictures would in turn raise audience expectations. His musings on film as art in both this article and the earlier "Geijutsu toshite no katsudō shashin" (no. 19, March–April 1911) lend themselves to less straightforward interpretation, and have been offered as evidence that, at least at this point, Kaeriyama's film ideal privileged the visual over the narrative.

Komatsu Hiroshi suggests that in "Geijutsu toshite no katsudō shashin," Kaeriyama equates the art of film with a certain conception of pictorial beauty, a position he suggests is reflective of a late-Meiji period sensibility that placed a higher priority on the visual rather than narrative (in terms of story or plot) dimension of the medium. Komatsu sees the admiration Kaeriyama expresses in this article for the 1910 Pathé Frères production, *Les Assiettes artistiques* (in Japan, *Meiga no sara*), a stencil-colored hybrid trick film and scenic picture without a dramatic plot, as comparable to an interpretation of the art of film in which art is incumbent in the changing visual images. This perception of the art of film, he points out, is quite different from the view that forms the foundation for the more story-oriented classical system of narrative (made dominant by Hollywood).[29] But Kaeriyama's critique of *Les Assiettes artistiques* comprises only a part of his argument in both articles. In "Geijutsu toshite no katsudō shashin," he also writes that while the art or beauty of film is not limited to the drama or narrative (something he reiterates in "Katsudō shashin geijutsuron"), neither is it restricted to that which is purely visual, in the sense of a landscape or scenic picture, for example. Kaeriyama also describes how pictorial beauty can also be generated through the synergetic reaction that takes place at moments when the visual (something visually perceived) enhances the drama, be it human emotion or comedy. As a case in point, he cites a picture recently featured at the Denkikan, during which he was struck by an old man's betrayal of a smile as a child struggles at his practice on the violin.[30] Komatsu also suggests this sort of dynamic (between the visual and the dramatic narrative) in an elaboration of Kaeriyama's appreciation of visual beauty, the appreciation of narrative diegesis as it is expressed within the visual.[31] Seen in this light, both articles in *Katsudō shashinkai* suggest Kaeriyama at this point was considering a more inclusive interpretation of the artistic dimension of film, one in which "Art" can in fact permeate all aspects of film—something he says in so many words in both articles.

ASPECTS OF PURE FILM

Kaeriyama's first job in the Tenkatsu Company was in the photography department, but because of his knowledge of English he was quickly moved to the import division. He continued to be interested in film production, and eventually approached the managing director with the idea of making a film for export that would help promote Japanese pictures abroad. Apparently, the company had little confidence in the financial potential of his plan, but Kaeriyama's offer to make two films for the price of one proved persuasive; in addition, although *shinpa* films were still popular, the Tokyo Nikkatsu studio had just hired the young director Tanaka Eizō to revamp and revitalize their *shinpa* dramas, and it is possible that Tenkatsu anticipated an increase in competition.

The Glory of Life has a poignantly privileged place in the traditional histories of Japanese cinema. Tanaka Jun'ichirō describes it as a "brilliantly shining beam of white light" piercing through what he evidently perceived to be a gloomy future for the Japanese film.[32] Its release was delayed for a year after its completion, which might account for some of the sensation when it opened. Because *The Glory of Life* was by no means an unqualified success, it is tempting to argue that Kaeriyama's reputation or, more specifically, that of his theoretical platform, was the single major factor behind the critical attention the film received both when it was made, and ever since. Its celebrity exceeds that of Kaeriyama's subsequent works, reputedly better made and more favorably received. Perhaps these films have faded into the background because nothing of them, other than one other unpublished scenario, remains. The script for *The Glory of Life* has been published at least three times, and is the first work encountered in the six-volume collection of Japanese screenplays edited by the Nihon shinario kyōkai (Japanese Association of Screenwriters.[33] When it was first published in an addendum to an "epoch-making" multivolume screenplay collection commemorating the fortieth year of *Kinema junpō* (heir apparent to *Kinema Record*), its inclusion, along with that of *Souls on the Road,* was likened to "gilding the lily."[34]

This kind of hyperbole is put into perspective by a recognition of the loyalties of historians like Tanaka with a (lifelong, apparently) bias toward the concept of pure film. As Kaeriyama's debut film, *The Glory of Life* holds the position in the trajectory of these histories as that of the first pure film and, by implication, the first indication—that beacon of white light shining in the darkness—that the Japanese film had finally come into its own. When *The Glory of Life* and *The Girl in the Mountain* were released on the same day, reviews and comments were enthusiastic about Kaeriyama's attempt to try something new, but expressed disappointment in the films themselves.

Some commented that his efforts were premature, but at least admitted the films were an indication of hope for the future. The actors were praised for their good intentions, but their acting itself was criticized as "bland," laughable, or even "more Western than Japanese." Kaeriyama was criticized for not being more daring, and more than one viewer felt "betrayed."[35] To some extent, it was as if Kaeriyama were being taken to task for making what were merely *shinpa* films with Western titles. The director Yamamoto Kajirō, enrolled in preparatory courses at Keiō University when the films were released, later wrote of his experience seeing the first run of *The Glory of Life*:

It was around the time I entered the preparatory course at Keiō University. . . . One spring afternoon, after skipping my last class as usual, I took my habitual stroll through the Ginza . . . I thought about having a cup of coffee at the Café Paulista and was leisurely walking down Mita slope when I saw a young man passing out handbills. They were made of cheap pink paper (probably the most inferior type) about the size of a postcard, but the printed message caught my eye: "The first film [*eiga*] made in Japan!" This catchphrase announced the opening of *The Glory of Life,* the first production of the Film Art Association and [the director and the actors] were all active in the vanguard of the *shingeki* theater movement. . . . Ah, film! Just seeing that word made my heart race. A film had been made in Japan for the first time. Although there had been moving pictures [*katsudō shashin*] of *shinpa* melodramas and trick [*ninjutsu*] pictures, there

*Miyama no otom*e (*The Girl in the Mountain*), directed by Kaeriyama Norimasa, 1918–1919. (*Left to right*), Kondō Iyokichi, Hanayagi Harumi, Aoyama Sugisaku. Courtesy Kawakita Memorial Film Institute.

were as yet no films. But now, Japan had given birth to the long-awaited "film" that was just like that of America. . . .

I immediately headed for the theater. This film, the greatest epoch-making event in the history of Japanese cinema, was opening in a small moving picture hall (movie theater) called the Toyotama theater. . . . About two hundred people could fit in the narrow seats, but less than 10 percent of the spaces were taken by patrons scattered here and there.

It was the first Japanese film I had ever seen! Japanese titles of a modern design . . . close-ups and moving camera work, the actors' faces untouched by elaborate stage makeup, the plain, unaffected presence of a real woman ["female flesh"], and the slightly awkward yet straightforward and sincere acting. This was a genuine film. I cried like a baby in the darkness.

Yet somehow something was missing. The film was rooted in literature, and the acting lapsed into mannerisms from the stage. A true film would not be so crude. Surely film has a more pure, invulnerable, isolated beauty. I was impressed, but at the same time I burned with frustration and anger."[36]

Toyotama theater in Kyōbashi (Tokyo). *Katsudō shashin zasshi* (June 1915), the first issue. Caption attributes the photograph to a staff member of the magazine. From Makino, ed., *Nihon eiga shoki shiryō shūsei* (*A Collection of Research Material from the Early Days of Japanese Film*).

There is some question whether Yamamoto's recollections actually were of *The Glory of Life* or *The Girl in the Mountain,* but his comments are interesting in that they correspond, point by point, to most written accounts of these first two pure films in both contemporary reviews and even more recent references: these were "films," not just "moving pictures" (the words *eigageki* and *katsudō shashingeki* were both used throughout the 1910s), with all the prerequisites of a pure film.

In the previous chapter, in describing the various forms of film prevalent in the 1910s, I briefly acknowledged three factors involved in the definition of pure film: the inherent geographical (Tokyo and Kyoto/Osaka areas) and genre (contemporary drama film and period film) divisions that continued to characterize the Japanese film world; the symbiotic relationship between formulations of a contemporary drama genre in film (still classified as "*shinpa* film") and developments in the *shingeki* theater movement; and the influence of European and American films, film-related print materials, and film practice. These last two aspects of pure film are particularly pertinent to a consideration of *The Glory of Life*.

During this transitional period, developments in the contemporary drama film and the period film were not always parallel. To an extent, "reform" within each genre depended on the nature of the parent theatrical form. In the case of the contemporary drama film, the *shinpa* melodrama was still popular in the 1910s, but like any form of popular entertainment, it was not immune to senectitude. Not all pure films belonged to the contemporary drama form, but it is important to keep in mind the particular situation Kaeriyama was faced with in choosing to situate *The Glory of Life* as a contemporary drama film.

Onstage, the contemporary drama could not always accommodate the rapid cultural reconfiguration that took place in Japan after national seclusion ended in the nineteenth century. Kabuki has always been a major form of entertainment, but it stopped being contemporary late in the decade. In some ways *shinpa* theater complemented Meiji (1868–1911) culture with its populist appeal and eclectic mix of Western and Japanese elements. In 1910, shortly after the repertory (now predominantly domestic melodrama) was established within the film industry, it was still popular but on the verge of the same fate as kabuki.[37] Throughout the 1910s, the borders between the film world and the *shingeki* movement (Japan's response to Ibsen and his contemporaries' realist reforms in Europe) blurred as *shingeki* writers and actors (among them Murata Minoru and the other actors Kaeriyama engaged for *The Glory of Life*) moved into film production. *Shingeki* contributed another important ingredient to *The Glory of Life:* a woman actor (in this case, the *shingeki*-trained Hanayagi Harumi) in place of a female impersonator.

But *shingeki* did not solve the problem of contemporary representation. Instead it raised new problems by bringing an unprecedented rhetoric to dramatic discourse, as well as the new dimension of a concern for intellectual respectability. Although the *shingeki* repertory began with original plays influenced by European drama, its success was based on translations of plays by the likes of Shakespeare, Ibsen, Tolstoy, Chekhov, and Gorky. Drama was elevated to literature, and imitation to an art. In this sense, in addition to encouraging the study of films onscreen, the admonition "observe to learn" can be seen as a password to culture throughout the decade. For the intellectuals behind the *shingeki* movement, the *shinpa* drama fell out of date. As Thomas Rimer notes in his study of Kishida Kunio, a major figure in the *shingeki* movement:

In a lecture in 1909 on Ibsen's contribution to the world theatre, [Tsubouchi] Shōyō lamented the fact that, although the Japanese had been able to create successful novels in the international style, the low level of the contemporary Japanese theatre represented the greatest shortcoming in all the Japanese arts. Japan, Shōyō insisted, lagged forty years behind the west and had not even been able to imitate, let alone create, western-style drama. Ibsen had led the modernization of the European stage and Ibsen must therefore be studied.[38]

The intricate relationship between pure film theoretical debate and a familiarity with both imported print materials and discussions and observations of film and film practice in the United States and Europe (as is evident in Yamamoto Kajirō's recollections of Kaeriyama's debut) was also part of a larger trend in Japanese culture during the 1910s. As Edward Seidensticker has remarked, this was a period when "popular entertainments went resolutely international."[39] *The Glory of Life* and *The Girl in the Mountain* opened on 13 September 1919, and issues of the English-language *Japan Times Weekly and Mail* that summer reveal a culture cosmopolitan enough to entertain the average émigré. There are the expected headlines with news of the demobilization of Europe, and those that suggest a relatively eventful summer on the domestic front ("Hailstorm Spoils Osaka Festival," "Whale Meat Will be Sold Cheaper than Beef at Public Market"). But in addition there are several announcements of visits to Japan by foreign entertainers ("Russian Operatic Stars Coming to the Imperial"), and advertisements for the upscale Odeon Theatre in Yokohama featuring Italian dramas, Christie Brothers comedies, a generous amount of Mabel Normand, and *The Triumph of Venus* ("Breezy! Airy! Cool!").[40]

Another feature of the *Japan Times Weekly and Mail* was a column called "New Books," a weekly report of recent arrivals at the Maruzen foreign bookstore in Tokyo. Maruzen was a common source for the foreign-language publications and books (including "how-to" books) included in the bibliography of Kaeriyama's *The Production and Photography of Motion Picture Drama.* Lists of publications from Europe and the United States were another feature of *Kinema Record,* and articles from them were sometimes translated and published in Japanese. Kaeriyama wrote some of his articles in *Kinema Record* in English, and much of his first book is heavily indebted to English-language sources.

Going abroad to tour foreign production sites was also common, beginning at least as early as Kawaura Ken'ichi's trip to the United States before he built a glass stage at the Yoshizawa studio in 1908. This practice culminated at the end of the decade in the "field trips" taken before the establishment of studios like Kokkatsu (Kokusai eiga kabushiki kaisha) and Shōchiku, both of which identified with pure film rhetoric (Taikatsu was established with the help of Thomas Kurihara after he left an acting career behind in Hollywood). Such trips abroad for "research" were not exclusive to members of the film world, although it is interesting to note that other art practices (theater, painting) tended to steer toward Europe.

As we shall see in chapter 5, domestic film periodicals featured articles on film industries in both Europe and the United States. As the market for Hollywood films expanded after the mid-1910s, articles describing production methods in Hollywood were common. The influence of Hollywood screenwriting practice in particular is visible in articles like "Katsudōgeki no kyakuhon no kakikata" ("How to Write a Script for Moving Picture Drama," in the February 1916 issue of *Katsudō no sekai*), which described the characteristics and features of the continuity format.[41] Detailed synopses and even transcriptions of films from Europe and the United States were featured in magazines like *Kinema Record, Katsudō no sekai,* and *Katsudō gahō*. Industry professionals have admitted to reading them for more than just pleasure.[42] But attention was also directed to the potentialities of screenwriting with the 1916 Japanese release of *Cabiria* (1914), which was widely and favorably noted by the intelligentsia.[43]

One result of the focus on industry practices abroad was the interesting mix of nationalist rhetoric and entrepreneurial spirit that emerged over the Japanese film's potential and viability as an international product. There were several aspects to this phenomenon. Racial discrimination toward the Japanese abroad was a factor. Economics was another: the Hollywood market put pressure on the home front, as revealed, for example, in several cartoons published in *Kinema Record* throughout 1917.[44]

The interest in export made not only the female impersonator problematic. It also exacerbated pure film enthusiasts' impatience with production and exhibition practices favoring the *benshi,* and subsequently boosted the interest in debating the mechanics of writing for the screen. Criticism of the mainstream *serifugeki* ("line play," a commercial script or film made with *benshi* accompaniment in mind)[45] was directed toward several aspects of the commercial industry: an ignorance of the importance of a continuity script as a blueprint for production; the prevalence of on-set narration by the director that undermined preproduction preparation; and the authorial weight given to *benshi* accompaniment, which precluded the use of intertitles.

Smoke and Mirrors?

Kaeriyama has been credited with achieving many "firsts," and *The Glory of Life* is where he is said to have achieved them. No doubt his reputation in terms of stylistic accomplishments was, and perhaps remains, influenced by

活動寫眞漫畫第八
Cinema Caricature No. 8.

米國活動界の勢力

世界のフイルム界を一手に引きうけたアンクル・サ
ム爺の喜び顔。日本も一寸首を出してゐる。（飛仙畫）

Cartoon lampooning Hollywood's monopoly of the international market, *Kinema Record,* 10 November 1916. Uncle Sam sits on a pile of films, surrounded by profits from the South Seas, Japan, and Europe. The banners behind him (*left to right*) represent France, England, and Japan (the latter is the figure exchanging a bag of cash for a reel of film). The caption reads, "The cheerful face of Uncle Sam, who controls the film world all over the world. Japan also makes a minor appearance." From Makino, ed., *Fukkokuban Kinema rekōdo.*

the knowledge of and interest in film technology evident in the wide range of technical articles he wrote in *Kinema Record* (*The Production and Photography of Moving Picture Drama* brought together many of these articles). An affinity for the hard sciences evidently ran in the family: Kaeriyama's father was a chemistry teacher at a secondary school (in the downtown Tokyo district of Kanda), and his own background was in engineering. It is not likely to have been a coincidence that Kaeriyama first worked for the short-lived Nippon Kinetophone Company and moved from there to Tenkatsu, the company that owned the rights to G. A. Smith and Charles Urban's Kinemacolor process. *The Glory of Life* was financed by Tenkatsu while he was employed there.[46] After directing his last film in 1924, Kaeriyama remained involved in promoting amateur filmmaking, and published film manuals directed at the nonprofessional reader. His fascination with the technology of film is generally blamed for his short-lived career as an "artistic" auteur.

It is said that Kaeriyama's greatest achievement was in writing Japan's first continuity script with detailed terminology suggesting a stylistic approach unconventional for the time. The extent and nature of stylistic decisions made during the film's production is unclear, although the cameraman, Ōmori Masaru (who used the name Shibata Masaru at the time) had the habit of keeping a daily work diary, some of which he has published, and he has said (albeit rather off-handedly) that the film was basically the same as the published version of the scenario.[47] Anecdotal evidence points to few alterations, although this is impossible to substantiate. Ōmori mainly remembers having to give up the idea of using actual yachts in the opening scene because "there weren't any" (presumably, smaller boats were used instead).[48] Because none of Kaeriyama's works survives, what *The Glory of Life* (or any of his other films) actually looked like is uncertain. As in the case of reviews, the film's absence limits the kind of information the scripts can provide. Publications of collected screenplays in Japan customarily feature the version of a screenplay that can be identified most closely with the "vision" of the writer as if it were a finished work (a finite text) in and of itself (independent of the film). Many synopses of the film *The Glory of Life* available in reference books, however, seem to correspond to the published version of Kaeriyama's scenario. In his history of Japanese cinema, Tanaka Jun'ichirō's synopsis of the film is quite different from the published version of Kaeriyama's scenario, and his synopsis is accompanied by an excerpt of a version of the script that also appears to be different from the version I have translated here.[49]

In secondary sources, the history of screenwriting in Japan begins in 1908 with the establishment of the Yoshizawa studio's planning department, but there appear to be just as few extant early scripts as there are films. An excerpt from Masumoto Kiyoshi's script for a Nikkatsu (Mukōjima studio)

Frontispiece advertisement (for the Kodascope Model B 16mm projector) and title page of the first edition of *Kaériyama's Ciné-Handbook* (Tokyo: Nippon Amateur Cinema League, 1930), one of Kaeriyama's manuals for amateur filmmakers. Author's collection.

shinpa film *Chichi no namida* (*A Father's Tears*, 1918) has some of the same details for which Kaeriyama's scenario is known: for example, the term *ōutsushi* ("close shot") and descriptions of frame composition and acting.[50] Masumoto's work is not necessarily representative of the contemporary *shinpa* film standard, as he had been one of the original members of the Yoshizawa planning department, was involved in the *shingeki* movement, and collaborated with Tanaka Eizō on the so-called *kakushin eiga* ("reform(ed)" films) that are considered the *shinpa* film's equivalent to Kaeriyama's pure film. *A Father's Tears* opened the year before the delayed release of *The Glory of Life,* which suggests that some practices in the *shinpa* film might have paralleled what was considered innovative in the work of Kaeriyama.

Masumoto's scenario is different from *The Glory of Life* in many respects. For one, the scenes in *A Father's Tears* are much longer (neither scenario reveals the extent to which the individual scenes might have been broken down into shots). As was the custom in the *shinpa* film, the titles are short headings (or subtitles) more closely resembling the chapter titles in a novel. *A Father's Tears* has extensive dialogue, but no dialogue titles explicitly identified as such, resulting in the particular loquacity implied by the term *serifugeki,* or "line plays." In a brief commentary accompanying the excerpt from *A Father's Tears,* Tanaka Jun'ichirō describes the excerpt as analogous to the *benshi daihon* ("*benshi*'s script").

In circumventing *benshi* accompaniment, intertitles were indispensable to *The Glory of Life.* In *The Production and Photography of Moving Picture Drama,* Kaeriyama promoted the use of intertitles but advised using them sparingly. In language resembling that of many "how-to" books on scenario writing contemporary to the time, he emphasized the importance of thinking in terms of the screen.[51] In terms of innovation, Kaeriyama's inclusion of dialogue intertitles appears genuine. Compared to the intertitles, or more correctly, the subtitles that seem to have characterized the commercial *shinpa* film, the variety and range of functions identifiable in Kaeriyama's expository titles are of interest.[52] So is their brevity, particularly when compared to some of the longer, more "literary" titles of Murata Minoru's *Souls on the Road,* the most important surviving pure film. Although it is not possible to comment with authority on the actual positioning of the intertitles and their relation to adjacent shots, at least in the scenario they appear to have been placed with a conscious effort to "dovetail." The noninformational aspect of the title "Two fluttering butterflies" suggests a degree of expressivity that, according to certain reviews of other films, seems to have been complemented by Kaeriyama's visual composition.[53] A frame reproduction of the expository title in scene no. 38 included in a review in *Kinema junpō* reveals it to be an art title (the artist is credited in the scenario along with the rest of the cast and crew).[54] Kaeriyama was evidently not successful in having the film open without *benshi* accompaniment, but given the nature of the intertitles it is understandable that he requested a *benshi* skilled in accompanying foreign films.

The nondiegetic title in the final scene of the script strikes at the heart of what was judged one of Kaeriyama's great failings. He later wrote that his intention at the time was to make something that resembled a foreign film as closely as possible. To do this, he says, he needed to use foreign films as a model in every respect, and began by writing a continuity "in a foreign manner." He writes that he included technical terms (he specifically mentions "close up," "insert," "bust," "full shot," "fade in," "fade out," and "iris") following examples he found in imported handbooks, and explains his choice of subject matter in the following manner: "It was a youthful script entitled *The Glory of Life.* I had high hopes for the plot, but as a technician with a poor appreciation of literature, I wrote something that could be called a scenario in

問題劇「深山の乙女」姉妹篇「生の輝き」優秀場面。

Sei no kagayaki (*The Glory of Life*), directed by Kaeriyama Norimasa, 1918–1919. Frame reproductions of an art title for expository title (scene 38) and Hanayagi Harumi as Teruko. *Kinema junpō,* 11 October 1919. From Makino, ed., *Fukkokuban Kinema junpō.*

form only. I was trying to express on film the idea that 'life is effort,' and it ended up having a crude, scholarly air, but I thought the plot was substantial for breaking the dull monotony of the *shinpa* film."[55] According to Kondō Iyokichi, who played the role of the young chemist Yamashita, Universal's Bluebird films were a major influence on the scenario. The moral message, the trope of "bucolic haven versus the urban den of iniquity," and the happy ending could be singled out to invoke the kind of sentimental melodrama that is said to have characterized the Bluebird photoplays that seem to have been popular in Japan at the time.[56] Both Kondō and Ōmori have indicated that Murata Minoru, who played opposite Kondō as the young aristocrat Yanagisawa, had a hand in rewriting the scenario, and it is interesting to speculate on the degree and nature of Murata's input. Murata and Kaeriyama had been classmates as boys. Either by Kaeriyama's own choice, or because of some antagonism toward him on the part of the regular Tenkatsu production staff (or a mixture of both),[57] Kaeriyama looked outside the studio when he cast the film, and Murata was a fairly well-known member of the *shingeki* movement at the time. He had organized a small acting troupe, the Tōrōsha, that was receiving favorable reviews for its staging of such *shingeki* staples as Wedekind's *Spring's Awakening* and Ibsen's *Ghosts*. The rest of the cast were primarily *shingeki* actors, including Hanayagi Harumi, who played the role of Teruko, the third member of the somewhat unlikely love triangle. The insert shots of written text in the script are a possible *shingeki* touch—they do enhance the sense of arid bourgeois respectability—but such epistolary flourishes were not necessarily foreign to the mainstream *shinpa* or period film. The hint of Turgenev, however, is pure *shingeki*.

Kaeriyama wrote about what he knew. The "glory of life" that he had in mind was none other than the sparks given off in an experiment with "radioactive carbonium" and the black smoke rising from a factory chimney. In 1918 radioactivity was about twenty years old; Marie Curie had received her Nobel prize seven years earlier. Around 1912 to 1916 the term "carbonium" was used to describe the mechanism of some chemical reactions. There is a class of pigments in plants, called anthocyanins, that was being studied between 1910 and 1920. There was controversy as to whether the pigments are oxonium or carbonium salts. But there is no radioactivity associated with these compounds. There is such a thing as "radiocarbon," and Kaeriyama may have taken some literary liberties with the term because radioactivity and "carbonium carbon" were being discussed at the time.

In Tanaka Jun'ichirō's synopsis of the film, possibly based on his recollections, the plot is somewhat more elaborate than that of the scenario translated here. Teruko and Yanagisawa have a child, who is born after Yanagisawa deserts her and marries the daughter of a wealthy banker in Tokyo. Yamashita rescues Teruko just as she is about to fling herself off a seaside cliff. Yamashita tells Teruko that it is only the weak who give up the will to live. Teruko becomes his assistant and helps him research radio-carbonium. The child born to Yanagisawa and Teruko becomes ill and dies. Five years pass. In the meantime, Yamashita builds a splendid factory thanks to the success of his experiments. Yanagisawa returns, but by now Teruko is happily married to Yamashita. She scorns his life of leisure and tells him that although she is but a commoner, she has found the happiness of a full life. Rejected, Yanagisawa leaves and Teruko and Yamashita open their upstairs window to the view of smoke rising from the factory chimney. They rejoice in the glory of life.[58]

This synopsis has all the earmarks of a *shinpa* melodrama, but the reviews suggest that at least one aspect was new and exciting. Comments on Hanayagi Harumi's performance were generous. The issue of women on screen as opposed to the female impersonator was another key feature of pure film debate, as evidenced in numerous articles in fan magazines and periodicals. As I mentioned in the previous chapter, a focus on screen actresses from Europe and the United States was apparent in Japanese film culture throughout the 1910s. Women were not completely absent from the screen, as they were appearing in chain drama productions (a Tenkatsu specialty), but as we have seen it was a far from glamorous way to make a living. The relative lack of genre variety was another limiting factor, as witnessed by the interesting career of the chain drama actress Kinoshita Yaoko. Although her attempt to become the Japanese Grace Cunard was not successful, it is an informative example of the shifting parameters of concepts of female beauty and femininity. The September 1919 issue of *Katsudō kurabu* was a special issue on *bijin* ("beauties"). Hanayagi appears at the end of a collection of bromides that starts off with such stars as Pearl White, Norma Talmadge, Theda Bara, Dorothy Phillips, and a scantily dressed Annette Kellermann in *The Daughter of the Gods* (1916).

Anecdotal accounts of the production of *The Glory of Life* are plentiful. Kaeriyama claims to have started with a script reading of the love scene between Murata and Hanayagi, but the two ended it abruptly in a fit of embarrassed laughter. The actual filming, all done on location, began with the scene of the rainstorm. Locations included the Tokyo YMCA in Kanda, Tokyo station, the lobby of the Kinkikan movie theater, and the Mitsukoshi department store. The scenes in Ginza were shot from an open car. (Ginza was an urban zone on the ascendancy, and Mitsukoshi the most popular store.) Additional shooting was done in Hakone, a resort town near Tokyo. Kondō Iyokichi later wrote that in spite of the dialogue written for the actors, there were many instances when they were only moving their lips.[59]

It took one month to shoot all four reels of *The Glory of Life*. Kaeriyama

Publicity shot of Hanayagi Harumi. *Katsudō kurabu,* September 1919. From Makino, ed., *Nihon eiga shoki shiryō shūsei* (*A Collection of Research Material from the Early Days of Japanese Film*).

and the cameraman, Ōmori, processed the film, and they continued to work together on the editing. Reviews suggest the film was both tinted and toned. Kaeriyama wanted his first two films to open in theaters for foreign films in the popular Asakusa entertainment district, but they eventually opened at two of the better theaters located elsewhere in the city. Opposition from the company *benshi* is reported to have been the cause of the one-year delay.[60]

Critics were finally satisfied with Kaeriyama's third release (his fourth production), *The Girl in His Dreams,* calling it the first Japanese film that could compare favorably with those of the West. By then Kaeriyama and his colleagues had left Tenkatsu, and with the assistance of the former founder and head of Tenkatsu, Kobayashi Kisaburō, they were producing films under

"A. A. C. Kaeriyama and company on location" filming *Gen'ei no onna* (*The Girl in his Dream*), *Kinema junpō*, 11 June 1920. In the picture at left, Kaeriyama is the first figure seated on the left, holding the megaphone. Center (*left to right*): Azuma Teru, Kondō Iyokichi, Aoyama Sugisaku. From Makino, ed., *Fukkokuban Kinema junpō*.

the official title of the Film Art Association (Eiga geijutsu kyōkai, referred to in *Kinema junpō* as L'Association des Artistes Cinematographiques) at Kobayashi's new company, Kokkatsu. When Kobayashi's influence in his own company waned, the group moved to Shōchiku at the invitation of Taguchi Ōson. For a few months they were managed by Shōchiku in the hope that they would provide competition for Osanai Kaoru's newly formed Shōchiku Cinema Institute, but on the second film Kaeriyama broke the conditions of their contract by refusing to submit his scripts for approval. The original staff members soon drifted apart (Murata was one of the first to leave, joining Osanai's institute, where he directed *Souls on the Road* the following year), and the group disbanded in July 1921. Kaeriyama managed to keep the name of the Film Art Association alive for a few more years, supporting himself by making commercial films for soap and toothpaste. His last film was a commercial failure, ending his career as a director in 1924. After that he turned his full attention to noncommercial amateur film, and conducted seminars in 9.5 mm filmmaking. He also continued to publish small manuals for the general reader, taught at the university level, and became an honorary member of the Japanese Society of Motion Picture Engineers.

Miss Teru-ko Azuma

Leading Lady of A. A. C.

NEW EPOCH WILL BE MADE

in the Japanese Filmplay Circle

by A. A. C. KAERIYAMA

Productions

It was last year that Mr. Kaériyama, formed L' Association des Artistes Cinématographiques. Mr. Kaériyama, director himself, has produced four pictures. Though the first two productions, "The Girl in the Mountain" and "The Glory of Life" were unsuccessful owing to the inexperience before the camera on the players part and the insufficient study on the producer's side, but the fourth one, "The Girl in His Dream", did surely assure that the future production will prove a great success. The third one, "Shiragiku's Romance" was produced at the request of an Italian company. The fourth picture which deals with the problem of love, will receive the great applause owing to its surprising advancement in Japanese photoplay manufacturing. This picture is by no means inferior to any foreign production.

「幻影の女」の二
上、郊外散歩　下、長濱

りよ塲影撮マネキ竹松

田村 。氏薫内山小りょ右 。すで中影撮 ∟傳優女⌐ で同合露日
・一 ₁テキ 。(樂音)氏一キツラベ 。(師技)氏谷水。(督監)氏實
。氏新津根 。環ナ₁ヴラス

Publicity still of Osanai Kaoru (*far right*) and Murata Minoru (with megaphone) on the set of *Joyūden* (*Story of an Actress,* also known as *Mikari ni tatsu onna*), a Shōchiku Russo-Japanese coproduction directed by Murata. *Kinema junpō,* 11 November 1920. From Makino, ed., *Fukkokuban Kinema junpō.*

The same month that his first two films opened, Kaeriyama published a diatribe against the "management" of the film industry, claiming that the only way the Japanese film industry would be "reformed" was if films were made in a new place (new companies) by new people.[61] Within a year this was on the verge of happening with the establishment of Shōchiku and Taikatsu.

3

Reformation in Transition:
Tōyō Films and the Founding of Taikatsu

ACCORDING TO KAERIYAMA's cameraman, Ōmori Masaru, a large part of the audience of *The Glory of Life* and *The Girl in the Mountain* were invited guests, proof that these films had only a limited commercial appeal.[1] Even if they were not successful commercial endeavors in themselves, Kaeriyama's productions encouraged further experimentation in circumventing industry standards regarded as uncinematic theatrical legacies at the time. It is clear that the general audience continued to patronize *shinpa* and *kyūha* films, but conscious efforts to broaden the parameters of these forms became more conspicuous over the next few years. Kaeriyama's attempts to apply European and American conceptions of "artistic" films and foreign filmmaking techniques to his productions in the late 1910s and early 1920s contributed to this trend.

Kaeriyama's influence, which ultimately reached only a limited audience, was not the only factor contributing to the significant changes in the industry during these years. Many issues had left an imprint on developments in filmmaking by the mid-1920s. A look at the more major influences will provide a background for a discussion of the establishment of Taikatsu, inspired by the pure film movement and Kaeriyama's work at Tenkatsu, and the contemporary genre films Thomas Kurihara and Tanizaki Jun'ichirō made at Taikatsu between 1920 and 1923.

URBANIZATION, FOREIGN INFLUENCE, POLITICAL CHANGE

The rise of popular culture that began early in the century gained momentum after World War I, and peaked during the years following the earthquake of

1923. Among the new cultural phenomena to appear during these years was the mass consumption of newspapers, magazines, and popular fiction. I have already described how the rapid rebuilding of Tokyo after the earthquake (two-thirds of the city was leveled by the disaster) further encouraged a cosmopolitan urban environment, and foreign movies, dance halls, and jazz became fashionable forms of leisure for the new urban class. In addition, imported magazines and books, foreign visitors, and Japanese travelers contributed to the blurring of cultural boundaries along national borders. Further developments in the formation of a modern theater, the avant-garde film movement, dada, expressionism, and other innovations in modern art had all made their way to Japan by the mid-1920s.

This movement toward a new urban culture influenced the modernization of Japanese film during this period in several ways. In the contemporary drama film, it encouraged the gradual replacement of *shinpa* story material with adaptations of Japanese novels and adaptations (or actual remakes) of foreign films. Later in the 1920s, period film writers in particular began to turn more frequently to popular fiction for their sources, and the original film script adaptations of Susukita Rokuhei and the work of Itō Daisuke represented this genre's most important contributions to the process of narrative transformation. More rigorously psychological films, such as Futagawa Buntarō's *Kagebōshi* (*Shadow Figure,* 1925, written by Susukita) and Itō's partially recuperated, three-part *Chūji tabi nikki* (*A Diary of Chūji's Travels, I–III,* 1927), for example, challenged Matsunosuke's virtual monopoly on the period film market. For a brief period after Matsunosuke's death in 1926, the genre gained the attention and esteem of critics and intellectuals who had generally favored what was perceived as the less formulaic (and therefore more sophisticated) contemporary drama form.[2] In fact, the increasingly ideological dimension of period films in the later 1920s became an additional influence on changes in the contemporary drama film.

As in many of the European and American films that were being imported at the time, the subject of urbanization itself soon became a common theme in the Japanese contemporary drama film. The contrast between the bucolic haven and the inherent dangers of urban life, already portrayed in *The Glory of Life,* remained a popular motif throughout the transition into the 1920s. There is a hint of it at least as early as *The Green of the Pines,* and public preference for such subject matter is further suggested by the overwhelming popularity of Universal's Bluebird films around 1916 to 1919. Only fragments of these films are known to survive today, but they were reportedly for the most part sentimental stories of innocent youths who abandon their country sweethearts for the fortunes they believe await them in the city.[3] They were considered minor films in the United States but were highly praised by Kaeriyama and others involved in the pure film movement.

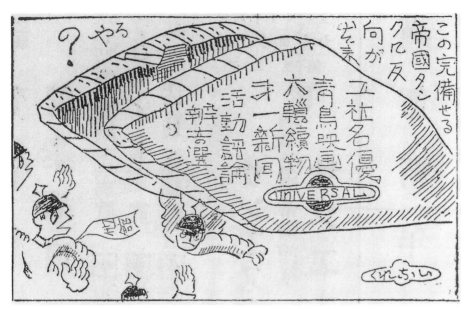

Cartoon illustrating the enormous popularity of Universal's Bluebird photoplays. The characters above the tank read, "Can you oppose this fully equipped imperial tank?" *Katsudō hyōron,* December 1918. From Makino, ed., *Nihon eiga shoki shiryō shūsei* (*A Collection of Research Material from the Early Days of Japanese Film*).

The steady stream of foreign films being imported into Japan was another important influence on the contemporary drama film. Judging from contemporary film publications, the Japanese market in the 1910s appears to have been quite cosmopolitan, though films continued to be segregated according to origin (domestic or foreign) at the point of exhibition.[4] European films— particularly Italian historical spectacles (notably, Enrico Guazzoni's *Quo Vadis?* in 1913 and Giovanni Pastrone's *Cabiria* in 1916) and French detective serials (Louis Feuillade's *Fantomas* in 1913, for example, and *Judex* in 1918)—were popular throughout the 1910s, but the role played by American films after the mid-1910s is particularly significant. After the war devastated the major European film industries, the United States replaced France as the world's leading producer of films, and in 1916 Universal became the first American studio to establish its own branch office in Tokyo.

In addition to Universal's Bluebird films, American serials (particularly cliff-hangers featuring serial queens like Helen Holmes and Pearl White) and

99

Thomas H. Ince's westerns (such as *Hell's Hinges,* in 1919) and his epic *Civ-ilization* (in 1917) were also popular. Imported comedies were a perennial favorite: Mack Sennett's Keystone Bathing Beauties and Keystone Kops pic-tures enjoyed a long run at the Asakusa Denkikan in 1916, and Chaplin films drew immense crowds, particularly after 1916. The popularity of Chaplin—affectionately known as *Arukōru sensei* ("Professor Alcohol," in reference to his precarious gait)—was so great that it encouraged a crop of Japanese imi-tators.[5] Chaplin was also a critical favorite. In 1924 his *A Woman of Paris* (1923) was voted the best film of the year in the first *Kinema junpō* "Best Films" listing.

Perhaps the single most influential American film seen in Japan at the time was D. W. Griffith's epic, *Intolerance* (1916). The film's initial run in 1919 was at Tokyo's first Western-style theater, the fashionable Teikoku the-ater. Murata Minoru's *Souls on the Road,* directed two years later, featured a similar, if less narratively complex, dependence on parallel editing. *Intoler-ance* also has been credited with inspiring a more frequent use of close-ups in the early Japanese film. More generally, it also hastened the perception of the movies as a form of "art" at a time when they tended still to be regarded as an alternative to the popular vaudeville halls that were now declining in their shadow. This was partly due to the entertainment entrepreneur Kobayashi Kisaburō's unusual distribution of the film, which resembled the skillful marketing of *Quo Vadis?* in the United States and Europe several years earlier.[6]

The former director of one of the member companies of the original Nikkatsu Trust and the founder of Tenkatsu, Kobayashi had quit Tenkatsu and was in desperate need of a film that would replenish his dwindling funds. Scraping together what little money he had left—including his wife's sav-ings—he sent an employee to the United States to fetch whatever film hap-pened to be most popular at the time. The employee chose *Intolerance,* with its scores of extras and impressive battle scenes. With the help of an affiliate of the Shōchiku theater chain, Kobayashi managed to reserve the exclusive Teikoku theater for the film's opening. He set the admission price at an unprecedented ten yen, nearly fifty times the average price of twenty to thirty sen and far more expensive than any kabuki performance had ever been; as a finishing touch, he sent telegrams containing a single word, "Intolerance," to important families and the social elite throughout the city a few days before the opening. People came in spite (or because) of the exorbitant price, and the film was a huge commercial success.[7]

In addition to the favorable reception of imported films, interest in imported film publications created a sustainable market in the latter half of the 1910s and early 1920s. Some filmmakers who began their careers during this period have said that going to see the films themselves was a more effec-

東京淺草電氣館 "チャップリン大會" を
十一月十九日(日曜日)より催ふせり

The first Chaplin-days were held the 19-30th Nov.
and Our first imitated Chaplin appeared on the
Stage of the Denki-Kan Theatre.

チャップリンに扮せる杉浦市郎君.

Mr. I. Sugiura
as made up Chaplin.

電氣館ではエッセネー會社のチャップリン劇のみを以
てチャップリン大會を十月十九日から催ふした。所

The *benshi* Sugiura Ichirō dressed as Charlie Chaplin for his performances at the
Denki-kan Chaplin film screenings. *Kinema Record,* 10 December 1916. From
Makino, ed., *Fukkokuban Kinema rekōdo.*

tive way of studying foreign technique, but even so they often cite the transcribed (recorded by hand) continuities of films of foreign origin that appeared in these magazines as useful models for their own work.[8] From as early as 1916–1917 at least one Japanese film magazine, *Katsudō no sekai,* was printing transcriptions of foreign films for reference on a fairly regular basis, together with comparisons of the shot ratios per reel in foreign and domestic films.[9]

It is not surprising that filmmakers with a vested interest in writing their own film scripts turned to the stories and transcriptions of foreign films, particularly American films, for helpful ideas or suggestions. In Hollywood, the craft of screenwriting had developed rapidly throughout the 1910s to become, by the end of the decade, what has been described as a "swollen public fantasy."[10] There is evidence that at least as early as 1912 nationwide advertisement campaigns were used to solicit both stories and talent from the general public. Scenario writing contests, schools, and courses to teach the craft multiplied (by 1915 there were sixty-one screenwriting schools throughout the United States), and the industry's courtship of major playwrights and novelists, particularly later in the 1910s, imparted a certain prestige to the craft.[11] The standardization of the detailed continuity script around 1914 helped guarantee standards of quality for the medium, and by the end of the decade screenwriting had reached a complex level of development.

Throughout the 1920s, another manifestation of the Japanese industry's focus on the West was the frequent practice of going abroad for a firsthand look at developments there in production methods. In addition to men who began careers in Hollywood, like Thomas Kurihara and Henry Kotani,[12] there were others who visited the United States and Europe to observe Western techniques at early stages in their careers. This group included the directors Abe Yutaka (Jack "Jackie" Abbe), "Frank" Tokunaga, and Ushihara Kiyohiko.[13] Even executives not directly involved in production traveled abroad. With his profits from *Intolerance,* Kobayashi, for example, contributed to the establishment of a new studio, Kokusai katsuei kabushiki kaisha (International Motion Picture Company), or Kokkatsu, and sent the actor and director Inoue Masao and the scriptwriter Masumoto Kiyoshi to Hollywood to observe American production methods. Shortly after the two returned from their four-month stay abroad, they collaborated on the first Kokkatsu contribution to pure film, *Winter Camellia.* Released in 1921, it was one of the earliest films featuring an actress in place of a female impersonator in the leading role.[14] In a similar manner the establishment of the Shōchiku Cinema Company was based on information gleaned during a tour of the theaters of Europe as well as the Hollywood studios.[15] In this way many Western production methods were brought back to Japan and incorporated into the domestic studio system in the early 1920s.

"Taisho Film Star Mr. Thomas Kurihara." *Katsudō kurabu,* June 1920. Taikatsu's prospectus appears in the same issue. From Makino, ed., *Nihon eiga shoki shiryō shūsei* (*A Collection of Research Material from the Early Days of Japanese Film*).

The foreign influence on the industry in Japan during this period was part of the attraction of film for the popular writer Tanizaki Jun'ichirō, and other prominent literary figures and members of the intellectual elite (Kawabata Yasunari, for example) were attracted by the potential of the new medium. Tanizaki was particularly interested in screenwriting as a craft. The newly established Taikatsu Company in Yokohama engaged Tanizaki as a "literary consultant" in April 1920, not long after Shōchiku commissioned Osanai Kaoru, a leading figure in the movement to modernize Japanese theater, to head its new school for film actors. In view of their contract requesting Tanizaki's presence at the Yokohama studio once a month, the Taikatsu executives were apparently most interested in using his name and literary reputation to endorse the studio. It is well known, however, that Tanizaki

Advertisement for Henry Kotani Productions ("Henrii eiga seisakujō"). *Kinema junpō,* 21 May 1922. From Makino, ed., *Fukkokuban Kinema junpō.*

井
上
正
夫
外
遊
記
念（其の二）

ゴールドウイン撮影所にて……ゴールドウイン社客廻

(*Back row, left to right*) Masumoto Kiyoshi, Aoki Tsuru (Mrs. Sessue Hayakawa), Mabel Normand, and Inoue Masao at Goldwyn, Hollywood. The figure seated in the foreground is the Kokkatsu representative to the United States. *Katsudō kurabu,* November 1920. From Makino, ed., *Nihon eiga shoki shiryō shūsei (A Collection of Research Material from the Early Days of Japanese Film).*

promptly rented a room in Yokohama not far from the studio and began writing stories for Thomas Kurihara, although he was under no formal obligation to do so.[16] After Kurihara wrote *Amateur Club,* the continuity script with numbered scenes, locations, camera angles, inserts, and intertitles based on Tanizaki's original story, Tanizaki claimed that he was determined to learn this skill himself. After admittedly apprenticing himself to Kurihara, Tanizaki wrote three scripts at Taikatsu, gradually working toward the continuity-style format he perfected with *Jasei no in (The Lust of the White Serpent/The Lasciviousness of the Viper,* 1921).[17] The evident interest of respected individuals like Tanizaki did not escape the attention of the public, and further contributed to a perception of film as art.

Finally, the overwhelming popularity of foreign films during this period underscored a preoccupation with the quality of screen acting. This aspect of the modernization movement in film closely paralleled the attempts to develop a psychologically motivated acting style on stage, and proved no less challenging an issue for filmmakers than it was for the members of the *shingeki* reformation movement in the theater. Even in 1919 the particular style of acting associated with the *shinpa* theater was popular with the general audience, and the *shingeki* actors themselves reportedly revealed traces of *shinpa*-style elocution and mannerisms.[18]

As the pure film movement moved into the 1920s, increasing importance was given to the training of actors for the screen. An acting school was envisioned as an integral part of both the Shōchiku and Taikatsu studios when they were established in 1920. The promise of these two schools was never fully realized, but the reputable Nihon eiga haiyū gakkō (Japan Academy of Screen Acting) followed in 1923. Founded by Mizuguchi Biyo, a member of Tsubouchi Shōyō's Bungei kyōkai (Literary Society), the school featured classes in "Western and Japanese film history and drama," screenwriting, and film theory in addition to general classes in acting and film technique, and the staff included pure film advocates Kaeriyama Norimasa, Tanaka Eizō, and the critic Mori Iwao.[19] This emphasis given to the education of actors in the early 1920s undermined the importance of cultivating directors and writers, but this was to change later in the decade when attention shifted to establishing a method of training studio personnel involved in these two disciplines.[20]

The enthusiastic response to the first films imported to Japan and the subsequent development of a domestic industry was a phenomenon of the Meiji era (1868–1912), a period of intense interest in the West as Japan carved out its place as a modern world power. This preoccupation with Europe and the United States affected Japan in many ways, creating an atmosphere of cultural, social, and political change that prevailed into the ensuing Taishō period (1912–1925) and beyond. In addition to the extensive urbanization and growth of popular culture characterizing these years, fluctuating trends in political thought were a formative influence on the film industry throughout the transition from silent to sound technology, which was standardized by the late 1930s. Of specific importance was the replacement of the relative liberalism of the Taishō period (dubbed "Taishō democracy") with an increasingly ultranationalistic political agenda at the government level.

Inflation and the swelling ranks of unemployed caused a weakening of the Japanese economy after World War I and general discontent among the members of the working class. With the intention of establishing a society based on justice and equal rights, intellectuals familiar with leftist ideology promoted the need to bring such thinking to the less fortunate classes. A flourishing independent press and proliferation of popular literature, two products of an expanding popular culture, provided one kind of venue for the dissemination of liberal and social thought. In addition, impromptu organizations or movements proclaiming a commitment to the liberation of the working class were formed by members of a variety of cultural disciplines, including the theater, literature, the fine arts, and film. In the Diet the bid for universal suffrage was hotly debated. In the midst of these changes, the Japanese film took on a new dimension as a medium for ideological expression.

The imperial constitution of prewar Japan had been created in 1889 for the primary purpose of guarding the emperor's sovereignty, and while it allowed a limited degree of civil liberties for the first time in modern Japanese history, it restricted freedom of ideological expression in speech, the press, and public gatherings. By the 1920s, the popular appeal of socialist and communist ideas challenged such limitations. This resulted in strict surveillance of leftist activities and purges of leftist leaders throughout the 1920s and 1930s, beginning as early as 1923 with the murder of the left-wing dramatist Hirasawa Keishichi (b. 1889).

Some form of film censorship in Japan took place from the time the first films were imported in the late Meiji period, but the only official law before 1925, the 1917 Katsudō shashin kōgyō torishimaru kisoku (Restriction on the Moving Pictures Entertainment Industry), had been a local restriction primarily enforced by the Tokyo Metropolitan Police. It required separate seating arrangements for men and women in the theaters, and licenses valid for two to three years at a time for the *benshi*.[21] The increasing surveillance of "subversive" leftist activities in the early 1920s had a major impact on the film industry, resulting in censorship directly enforced by the government, the first official attempt to curb any expression of leftist thought in the industry. In 1925 the government issued the Chianijihō (Peace Preservation Act), aimed at suppressing the rising leftist movement, and the same year the first nationally enforced censorship law, the Katsudō shashin firumu ken'etsu kisoku (Censorship Restriction on Moving Picture Films) went into effect. For the first time, the censorship requirements of film were regarded as distinct from those of other performance entertainments.[22] Besides confirming an official recognition of film's ideological potential, the imposition of this law signaled a shift from a cultural to an ideological standard of censorship. This marked the beginning of the government's move toward the more aggressive attitude it would assume in its large-scale promotion of war propaganda films in the late 1930s.[23]

The contemporary drama film, in its attempt to reflect the unstable cultural, social, and political conditions of the time, was deeply affected by the establishment of an official system of censorship. A surge in the popularity of socialist ideology in the late 1920s, in spite of increasing restrictions, had resulted in a spate of nihilistic period films, notably Itō Daisuke's *A Diary of Chūji's Travels, I–III,* and *Gerō (The Servant,* 1927). Their indictment of Tokugawa feudalism was easily interpreted as indirect criticism of

Publicity still for the tendency film *Nani ga kanojo o sō saseta ka* (*What Made Her Do It?*), directed by Suzuki Shigeyoshi, 1930. Takatsu Keiko (*right*). Courtesy Kawakita Memorial Film Institute.

contemporary society, and such trends in the period film encouraged attempts at more direct social criticism in the contemporary drama film. The new censorship restrictions made open criticism impossible, and as a result these contemporary genre films were referred to as "tendency films" (*keikō eiga*) because of their "tendency" toward leftist sympathies while avoiding explicit political commitment.

With the exception of a recently reconstructed partial print of Suzuki Shigeyoshi's major work, *Nani ga kanojo o sō saseta ka* (*What Made Her Do It?* 1930), the most influential tendency films have disappeared.[24] Scholars have suggested that in spite of similarities to the German radical theater of the 1920s and the Soviet films of Eisenstein and Pudovkin, the tendency film appears to have run its course in relative isolation,[25] and although adaptations of left-wing literature were being made as early as the mid-1920s, films expressing leftist sympathies dominated the box office for only a year or two, from roughly 1929 to 1931. It is generally acknowledged that the brief trend toward such films was curtailed by censorship measures causing the films to be cut to the point of being incomprehensible,[26] but by using the contemporary drama film as a vehicle for social criticism, the tendency film broadened the parameters of the form in a direction that would continue to be pursued in the 1930s.

In contrast to the tendency films, which were ideological films made for the mainstream commercial market (leftist critic Iwasaki Akira in 1936 dryly referred to them as films "produced at capitalist studios purely as money-making commodities"),[27] Prokino (Nihon puroretaria eiga dōmei. Japanese Proletarian Film League), which was formed in 1929, made films for the purpose of documenting developments within the Communist Party. Prokino was forced to disband when tightening government surveillance in the 1930s outlawed the various openly pro-worker organizations that had begun to appear in the previous decade. A number of the members quietly entered the Nikkatsu Uzumasa studio in Kyoto, where their ideological sympathies greatly influenced the contemporary drama films being made there.[28] Traces of this influence still lingered in some of the films made at this studio in the late 1930s, such as Tomotaka Tasaka's *Gonin no sekkōhei* (*Five Scouts,* 1938), ironically commissioned by the government as military propaganda, and Uchida Tomu's saga of the hardships of the life of a peasant farmer, *Tsuchi* (*Earth,* 1939).

For Taikatsu personnel, working in 1920–1921, such developments were still nearly a decade away. Yet even the production of the comedy *Amateur Club,* superficially a nonsensical film about a group of young college students on vacation at a seaside resort, encountered difficulties when the script was submitted to the censors for approval. And when censors blocked the opening of *Tabakoya no musume* (*The Cigarette Shop Girl,* 1921), a film starring *Amateur Club* star Hayama Michiko, it only contributed to hastening the end of the ill-fated Yokohama studio.[29]

"FOREIGN FILM" IN CLOSE-UP: MORI IWAO'S *A SURVEY OF THE MOVING PICTURES,* 1919–1920

Because the concept of pure film initially did not emerge in response to popular demand, its survival throughout the 1910s depended almost entirely on members of an intellectual class who believed that the introduction of Western technique was the most effective way to counteract the influence of the indigenous theater. Besides being well acquainted with films from the United

States and Europe, many of these intellectuals, like Kaeriyama, closely followed developments taking place abroad by studying imported handbooks and magazines. Roughly, the years 1914 to 1920 coincided with a highly productive period for film literature in Europe and the United States, and a glance at Kaeriyama's bibliography to *The Production and Photography of Moving Picture Drama* suggests that the interested reader with some knowledge of English had access to a broad range of material that included the writings of Vachel Lindsay, Hugo Münsterburg, and Victor Freeburg, critics who were influential in the development of film criticism abroad.

The founding of *Kinema junpō* in 1919 encouraged the practice of film criticism in Japan by providing the industry with its first critical magazine published on a regular basis. The profession was well established by the end of the 1920s. As many of the young supporters of pure film turned to writing their own criticism, their articles not only shed light on their perception of pure film, but also helped familiarize readers with European and American film theory and production technique.

Mori Iwao (1899–1979) was one of several film critics to appear during this period. During the first ten years of his career he not only wrote criticism, but penned film scripts, notably, *Machi no tejinashi* (*The Street Juggler*) in 1925 and *Tsubakihime* (*Camille*) in 1926 for Murata Minoru, taught Western film history at the Nihon eiga haiyū gakkō (Japan Academy of Screen Acting), and was a member of the Kinyōkai, a group formed by members of the Nikkatsu studios in 1926 to raise the quality of contemporary drama scripts.

Katsudō shashin taikan (hereafter referred to as *A Survey of the Moving Pictures*) was Mori's first work of film criticism, a manuscript he wrote over a two-year period, from 1919 to 1920, when he was twenty to twenty-one years old. Although he hoped this manuscript would serve as a springboard to a career in the industry, it was rejected because of its length—an impressive 1,200 pages of 600 characters each—and was forgotten until 1976, when the Japan Film Library Council published it as a four-part supplement to their series, "Notes on Japanese Film History."[30] It offers an engaging and often thought-provoking perspective of the Japanese film industry during the 1910s, particularly in comparison to the situation in Europe and the United States. Of particular interest is an informative section on the screenwriting departments of the various domestic studios and the problems involved in the conceptions of screenwriting technique, especially in the context of the contemporary drama film script.

Mori began writing *A Survey of the Moving Pictures* after a serious illness caused him to leave the professional school where he had just enrolled as an economics student. A year of hospitalization and the subsequent forced rest gave him a chance to reconsider his plans for the future. After he recovered he was invited back to school, but he chose instead a daily routine of baseball and attending the theater and movies, eventually deciding to give up his plans for a future in business to pursue a career in what he enjoyed the most—the moving pictures.[31]

Perhaps for this reason, and doubtless also because of his youth, Mori's *A Survey of the Moving Pictures* is an exuberant celebration of the unique qualities of the cinematic medium as well as a fervent call for reform. The exuberant tone recalls *The Art of the Moving Picture* (1915) by Vachel Lindsay, who described moving pictures as "the new weapon of men," the new art form that would "re-unite the lower class families."[32] Mori, too, was enchanted by the power of cinema to draw people together, referring to a "renowned American religious leader" who believed that if Christ himself were among us today he most certainly would use the movies to spread his message of salvation (4: 87). Mori also provides exhaustive detail on the state of the industry abroad, and his sample film scripts written under the pseudonym "Rockman Wood" (a nearly literal translation of, and therefore a play on, the characters of his name) reveal a familiarity with foreign production methods that most likely was acquired both through a careful study of imported films and film literature, and through Japanese film magazines that featured selected translations from these publications.

For all Mori's interest in foreign films, *A Survey of the Moving Pictures* reveals his greater concern with what he perceived to be the state of the Japanese film. At the time, twice as many films were being imported into Japan as were produced locally, and in view of this it is not surprising that after the mid-1910s, pure film rhetoric was increasingly associated with the desire to create a foreign market for Japanese films. It was Mori's understanding that as long as the domestic product stayed at the artistic level of the period dramas of Matsunosuke and *shinpa* melodramas, it would be no commercial match for the films pouring in from abroad (2: 29). He repeatedly pointed out that the primary importance of studying European and American films was to understand better why domestic films, in his opinion, seemed to suffer in comparison, and what might be done to improve their quality (2: 61). In his preface, Mori listed four requirements for the improvement of Japanese films: large amounts of capital, a study of Western production technique, "passionate resolve," and "serious and sympathetic scholars of Japanese films" (1: 8; 2: 52).

From his vantage point in the wake of Kaeriyama's pioneer pure film productions, Mori seemed aware that the desire to make a product that would compare favorably with foreign films and compete with them on a commercial level could too easily lead to the indiscriminate copying of foreign films. By emphasizing the importance of making films that would appeal to a general audience, he hoped to reduce the danger of imitations that lacked any semblance of contemporary Japanese life. Instead of transporting the plots of imported films to the Japanese city and countryside, he suggested (in retrospect, a bit naively) that filmmakers turn to their immediate surroundings for suitable material:

> The Japanese have always excelled in copying, but they seem to lack persistence and tenacity. They plan only for immediate results and absorb themselves in short-term goals. Today this fault is apparent in films as well. At a glance the industry presents us with grand spectacles, but upon closer inspection, this is no more than an empty dream.
>
> Is there no hope for the development of Japanese films?
>
> If you examine the nature of Japanese culture, there is much in our history and our legends that would make a splendid subject for movies, and from our unique religion, literature, and national consciousness to the topography, climate, geography, plants, and animals, from the graceful mountains and rivers to the magnificent coasts, from the steamy islands where poisonous snakes dwell to the icebergs where the penguins cry, and even in the change of seasons, from the blooming of the cherry blossoms to the withering and falling of the leaves, [Japan] overflows with an infinite wealth of treasures. (1: 7)

This problem of imitation was shared by intellectuals involved in the modernization of Japanese theater, who were also faced with the dilemma of having to depend on a set of foreign principles as the framework for dramas of contemporary Japanese life when such principles were not yet fully understood.[33] It was understandably tempting for filmmakers simply to reproduce foreign films, plot and all; the only alternative at the time was to try to fit traditional *shinpa* themes or adaptations of *shingeki* drama into a "Western" framework.[34]

For this reason, Mori, like Kaeriyama before him, was convinced that any "reformation" of the Japanese film must begin with the written script. Specifically, he felt the basic problem with scripts for the contemporary genre was that they too closely resembled stage plays. By this he meant that there was too much emphasis on the *kagezerifu* ("lines in the dark"), which he felt were far less important than the movements and expressions of the actors on screen, and actually hindered the dramatic development of the plot. Scripts written in a *kagezerifu* style, scripts that he calls *serifugeki* ("line plays"), were written in the style of *benshi* narration, with little or no indication of camera work or shooting location, and often little or no dialogue or division of the action into numbered shots or scenes. To begin with, these *serifugeki* were useless for script readings, and as long as such a style continued this important function of the script would, in Mori's opinion, never be recognized:

[The use of *serifugeki* instead of film scripts] results in a script reading that does not help the director in guiding the actors. The actors concentrate on the lines being read by the director and pay no attention to the acting.

In addition, each individual scene is too long and boring, and because *kagezerifu* impede the use of titles the way they are used in foreign films, for dialogue and explaining the action, it is impossible to express the story in a clear manner so the audience can understand the content of the film.

These problems are all due to the use of scripts that are modeled on stage plays. This discourages directors, actors, and technicians from developing [their skills], is extremely unprofitable because it reduces the possibilities for export, and greatly endangers the welfare of our industry.

The reformation of the Japanese film must begin with [the reformation of] the film script. (2: 61)

The emphasis on the need to recognize the distinct difference between a film script and a play written for the stage is reminiscent of much of the early film criticism written in Europe and the United States. In his preface Mori mentioned that it was only a matter of time until Japan produced its own Victor Freeburg, and it is very likely that he was familiar with that critic's 1918 *The Art of Photoplay Making* (1: 8).[35] One of the points Freeburg makes is that it is essential for the scriptwriter to think of his story in terms of the screen ("The cinema composer must think of visibilities, not of fragrances or bird notes"),[36] and Mori also criticized the tendency of Japanese scriptwriters to ignore this important requirement in writing for the screen: "A film script is not literature. It is only a guideline for the director, the technicians, and the actors, and is no more than a suggestion [of the finished film]. Its importance is in the artistic sense that extends beyond the page. What about the Japanese authors? They expend so much energy thinking about what goes onto the surface of the page that they have no strength left to refine and dramatize in their heads" (2: 65).

Mori's greatest objection was to the impracticality of *serifugeki,* the fact that they were inadequate blueprints for pure film drama. He points out that while European and American films seemed compact and quick paced, with the benefit of titles to communicate dialogue and the passage of time, Japanese films were characterized by long and static shots, no dialogue, and no clarification of time—all the result of overwritten scripts. While he admitted that some filmmakers were attempting to increase the number and diversity of shots and experiment with various camera locations, he points out that the use of such techniques was unsystematic and of little expressive value because of the absence of a properly written script (2: 64–65).

Mori also acknowledged a need to make changes in the story material being used for *shinpa* film. He classified *shinpa* source material into three different categories: sensational journalism, which he described as generally reflecting a lack of aspiration and competence on the part of the writer; popular *shinpa* melodramas written by hack writers, which use contemporary characters and landscapes but are in bad taste and hopelessly removed from reality; and well-known works by scholars and novelists. He added that adaptations based on material from this last category were occasionally made into successful films, giving as examples the work of Satō Kōroku and Tanaka Eizō's *The Living Corpse* (2: 63).

Here too he criticized Japanese scriptwriters for being too concerned with an excessively verbal mapping out of the narrative on the page. He condemned the lack of originality, the bland stories, and poorly described characters who were little more than stereotypes described in terms of extreme good or bad (2: 64). Again, with a characteristic sense of urgency, he urged writers to turn to their own environment for more contemporary, realistic stories to replace trite domestic tragedies and melodramatic love stories: "In films of contemporary life, sentimental romance, family disputes, and applause-seeking sensationalism should be avoided in favor of genuine people and the day-to-day occurrences of the actual world around us. We should deal with that which is most intimate to us and will arouse sympathy" (2: 65).

Who were these writers Mori criticized so severely? After a consideration of the regular staff writers employed by the various studios, Mori's observation was that with a few exceptions, most of them were hack writers with little interest in writing for the movies. He believed that the heavy production load of two to six scripts a month was partly to blame for this situation: given such a rate of production, he wrote, "it is little wonder the scripts lack a certain luster" (2: 62). Mori's conclusion was that a new kind of writer conscious of the unique requirements of his craft was needed to push for changes in the production system: "All film lovers are clamoring for the burial of those dropouts from literary circles and playwrights past their prime who call themselves screen authors. . . . The film script is fundamentally different from the stage play, and for this reason we must have genuine scriptwriters with new skills and the resolve to study" (2: 62).

As Mori saw it, one change needed in order to encourage the flow of fresh talent into the industry was the establishment of a system that would solicit scripts from the public at large. He mentioned a few cases where this had been encouraged by competitions sponsored by newspaper companies and banks, but noted that such efforts compared poorly to the wide-scale campaign being carried out in the United States (2: 62–63).

Mori did not indicate in his manuscript that he anticipated changes in the Japanese film script in the near future, partly because he believed little could be done as long as the *benshi* remained popular and the priority given to live narration continued. He also felt that fundamental improvements in the struc-

114

ture and thematic content of the film script could not be implemented until more recognition was given to the role of the writer and the director. In this respect, changes were already happening in the industry despite the *benshi*'s continuing popularity. At Nikkatsu, the young director Tanaka Eizō was gradually establishing a name for himself by attempting change within the conventional *shinpa* film. And the establishment of several new film companies in the early 1920s, most notably Taikatsu and Shōchiku, provided a foothold into the industry for young intellectuals interested in a chance to engage on a practical level the issues raised by pure film.

KURIHARA'S TŌYŌ FILMS AND THE FOUNDING OF TAIKATSU

Kobayashi Kisaburō had been the first to challenge Nikkatsu's monopoly of the domestic market when he formed the Tenkatsu Company in 1914. He eventually left Tenkatsu, but for six years it continued to be the only major production company to share the market with Nikkatsu. This situation changed abruptly when the enterprising Kobayashi became the motivating force behind the establishment of the Kokkatsu Company in December 1919, buying out his former company, Tenkatsu, in the process. Kokkatsu's official name, Kokusai katsudō shashin kabushiki kaisha, translates literally as "International Moving Picture Company," and according to Mori Iwao, the goals of this new company were not only to set new standards for the domestic industry but also to gain some sort of foothold in the market overseas. In Mori's words, it specifically proposed to "rely on the vast universal appeal of film to build a foundation of goodwill between Japan and the United States," in addition to contributing to "the education and entertainment of the masses" (2: 29–30). The appearance of Kokkatsu did indeed signal change for the contemporary drama film. Within six months three new film companies were organized in quick succession, and at least two of these encouraged important developments in the contemporary drama film.

The Shōchiku kinema gōmeigaisha (Shōchiku Cinema Company), a branch of the powerful Shōchiku theater company that managed a chain of theaters and several kabuki and *shinpa* acting troupes, was the first of the three companies established, early in 1920. It was followed by the Taishō katsudō shashin kabushiki kaisha (Taishō Moving Picture Company, later Taishō katsuei, or the Taishō Film Company), commonly referred to as Taikatsu, in April, and the Teikoku kinema engei kabushiki kaisha (Imperial Cinema and Dramatic Art Company), or Teikine, in May. Formed when the head of Tenkatsu's Osaka branch refused to merge with Kokkatsu, Teikine specialized in filmed versions of stage plays. In contrast, both the Shōchiku and Taikatsu companies set out from the very start to produce

115

exportable "artistic" films that would bear no resemblance to the indigenous theater.

In February 1920 announcements in Tokyo and Osaka newspapers confirmed the rumors that the Shōchiku theater monopoly was embarking on a new venture in film production. According to these articles, the new studio would produce "moving picture films" for both the domestic and foreign market. These would include historical dramas that would appeal to foreign audiences as well as films that would depict contemporary Japanese life in "as humorous a light as possible." Given the focus on Hollywood, particularly after 1916, and the overwhelming popularity of American films at the time, it is not surprising that Shōchiku stated it would hire a director from America who specialized in comedies and could supervise the production of such innovative contemporary drama films. He would also be responsible for coaching amateur male and female actors in screen acting technique. In exchange for pictures introducing Japanese culture to audiences abroad, Shōchiku would in turn import the latest foreign movies for Japanese viewers. In brief, not only would the new studio use the most modern production techniques to rival the widespread popularity of the *shinpa* film, it would also contribute to "international harmony" by making exportable films that "truthfully" portrayed Japanese culture.[37]

The same month that Shōchiku announced the establishment of its new film company, a former Hollywood actor and novice director, Thomas Kurihara, returned to Japan after an unsuccessful attempt to market several of his films in the United States. These films, including a five-reel comedy called *Narikin* (*Sanji Goto/The Upstart*) starring an actor (Nakajima Iwajirō) billed as the "Japanese Charlie Chaplin," had been Kurihara's bid to bring a glimpse of contemporary Japan to foreign audiences.[38] The surviving fragment of *Sanji Goto,* with copious English language intertitles (including art titles) and intricate decoupage for the time, suggests as much.[39] Kurihara's failure to carry out this plan brought his small import and part-time production company, Tōyō Film ("The Sunrise Film Manufacturing Company" in the United States) to a standstill. But within two months of Shōchiku's announcement, Kurihara's company had a new owner, the wealthy businessman Asano Yoshizō (who was an acquaintance of Kurihara and had invested heavily in the company) and a new name. In June this new company, Taishō katsudō, or Taikatsu, announced its plans for the full-scale production of a new type of Japanese film in addition to the distribution of recent foreign films.

In general, Taikatsu's announcement in the June issue of *Katsudō kurabu* echoed Shōchiku's earlier proclamation: the company proposed to import the newest foreign films and produce "comedies and historical dramas that rely primarily on action." Like Shōchiku, Taikatsu emphasized its

横濱東洋會社の日
本チャップリン事
中島好洋君

愛護者諸君に
よろしくとのこと
です

來の傑作である。

『空中王』『密計』『優しき復讐』な
どに出演した人で、今度のアリ
ュースの役に於ても感ず可き巧
妙なる表情を見せて居た。

勿論ない。筋は北歐の映畫には
極めて有り勝ちな人情もので、
新味に乏しいと云ふ缺點はある
が眞實味はある。

此の映畫徹頭徹尾である。に扮する夫人は、フェルナ出させる、此の種でもあるーセル氏に上場さした人でなくはあ缺く可らユースに

唯、残念なのは主人公の一人
に現はれるエスリル少年に扮した俳
優の不明なことである。
サブ・タイトルに原詩中の文

マグダレンはキリストの物語
に現はれる女である。彼女は罪
深く賤しい賣女であったが、一
度キリストの教へを承けてから

ウォルター
マグダレン
ジョージ・ジョ
北歐の映畫
ぜられたもの
可成熱心に演
もステラ・リ
レンは女主
いものであ
撮影が北歐
く、且つ現な
に馴らされて
は、如何に
欧洲の映畫
もないことさ
て來ることは、

『新マグダレン』
きが最も適切か

The "Japanese Chaplin" Nakajima Iwajirō (Kōyō) of Tōyō Film Co., Yokohama, introduces himself to the readers of *Katsudō hyōron*, 1919. From Makino, ed., *Nihon eiga shoki shiryō shūsei* (*A Collection of Research Material from the Early Days of Japanese Film*).

intention to make exportable films: the company claimed its product would "promote the distinctive characteristics of Japan and the Japanese to the world." The announcement also stated that Kurihara would supervise production, using "the most advanced camera technique" and providing guidance for "educated men and women who wish to act." Finally, the Taikatsu prospectus observed that "the latest trend" was to "emphasize the importance of the content of film scripts." Along with a reference to the current trend to bring famous authors into Hollywood studios and an explanation of the importance of the film script, the prospectus included the startling claim that the well-known author Tanizaki Jun'ichirō would supervise the choice of material as Taikatsu's "literary consultant."[40]

Kurihara and Tanizaki managed to produce pure films at Taikatsu for roughly one year, until the increasingly unstable financial climate that followed World War I, coupled with Kurihara's bad health, forced the company executives to abandon their commitment to the initial company prospectus in favor of the more lucrative production of *shinpa* films. During their brief collaboration at Taikatsu, Kurihara and Tanizaki both appeared to be committed to the development and implementation of a more detailed continuity script, and Tanizaki's efforts to perfect this format were greatly aided by the expertise Kurihara contributed based on his experience in Hollywood.

Kurihara, like many of the Japanese who emigrated to the United States at the turn of the century, was looking for temporary, profitable employment in order to ease financial problems back home when he arrived in Seattle in 1902.[41] He was seventeen years old when he left his homeland, and he intended to earn enough money in the United States to salvage his father's wholesale lumber business and buy back the family property. After a brief stay in Seattle, he moved to San Francisco, where he worked as a farmhand, a houseboy, and a dishwasher during the day and attended school at night.[42]

He succeeded in repaying his family's debts, but a bicycle accident while traveling to one of his numerous obligations left him with a severe chest injury and chronic pleurisy, an illness from which he never fully recovered. He moved on to Los Angeles in search of a milder, more comfortable climate. The movie studios being built along the southern California coast, particularly in the small Los Angeles suburb of Hollywood, offered new opportunities for work, and in the spring of 1912 Kurihara entered a training course in film acting.[43]

The following year, after working as a part-time extra at the Kalem, Selig Polyscope, and Universal studios, Kurihara was hired as a regular staff member by the director Thomas H. Ince.[44] Kurihara (whose first name Tōmasu, or Thomas, is said to have been suggested by Ince himself) continued to work with the director until he and his crew moved to Paramount in 1917. Although Kurihara was to work with many directors before returning to Japan, Ince, as Kurihara's first teacher and mentor, exerted the greatest influence on his namesake, and Kurihara's experience working under him played a significant role in determining the nature of his own directing career. Ince also had entered the industry as an actor (only about two years before Kurihara). His career as a director began with IMP in Cuba, but he moved on to the New York Motion Picture Company, where he was in charge of the famous Bison "101" films. As Eileen Bowser has noted, these highly successful westerns, made with the former Wild West show and rodeo by the Miller Brothers 101 Ranch, were "the most spectacular and beautiful re-creations of the Old West yet seen."[45] According to Mori Iwao, who included a section on the Japanese in Hollywood in his *A Survey of the Moving Pictures,* Ince initially hired Kurihara to do odd jobs about the studio, but before long he was casting him as a Mexican in his westerns. It was in this role, playing opposite Ince's most popular cowboy star, William S. Hart, that Kurihara was known to audiences in Japan long before he returned to that country (2: 22).

By late 1913, Ince had begun moving away from direction to production, and it is in this capacity, at his studio in the Santa Ynez Canyon—soon a sprawling complex known as Inceville—that he formulated highly efficient production systems that later earned him the reputation of having defined the production model for the Hollywood studio system. Existing records suggest that it is true Ince set up an organized system of production based on a division of labor, with writing, directing, and editing recognized as separate disciplines. Ince himself, as studio head, managed the entire process, largely through the use of continuity scripts.[46] But Bowser points out that there is evidence such a system was already being used among most producers of the Motion Picture Patents Company group.[47] Ince might not have introduced this system of production, but he did work at refining it. In addition to adding more technical, emotional, and aesthetic detail, Ince's particular method of dissecting scenes lent a conscious rhythm to his scripts. Ince's scenario department produced at least one major writer of the silent period, Charles Gardner Sullivan, whose prolific writing career bridged the transition into sound and lasted until 1940.[48]

A familiarity with the tightly written scripts being used by directors like Ince is evident in the considerable detail of Kurihara's *Amateur Club.* In Japan, Kurihara's scripts would not have been put to the same degree of organizational use as their counterparts in, for example, Ince's larger and more complex production system. Production at Taikatsu remained on a small scale throughout the studio's abbreviated existence, and Kurihara's authority as a director was severely limited by budget restrictions as well as problems with company management and changes in production policy. The fact that Kurihara himself wrote continuity scripts based on Tanizaki's original stories, however, does suggest that he regarded them as an important element of the production process, and in spite of Tanizaki's interest in screenwriting before entering the studio, his enthusiasm was significantly sustained by his fascination with the director's screenwriting expertise.[49]

Ince by no means limited himself to westerns. By 1913 he employed a significant number of Japanese actors, and he began to use them in special "Oriental productions." Several of these films, including the first venture, *The Vigil,* a two-reeler starring Sessue Hayakawa's wife, Aoki Tsuruko, as a poor fisherman's daughter, responded to a popular surge of interest and curiosity in the exotic East (2: 18–22).[50] Other productions, however, seemed more directly related to an outbreak of anti-Japanese sentiment caused by the sudden increase in Japanese emigration. The nature of such films, and the anti-Japanese mentality they conveyed, were an important influence on Kurihara and the goals he set for his work at Taikatsu.

The first of Ince's "Oriental productions" to win critical acclaim, *The Wrath of the Gods* (also known as *The Destruction of Sakurajima*), opened in 1914.[51] A relatively benign story of a heathen's conversion to Christianity, it was indebted to the appeal of many spectacular scenes inspired by the actual volcanic eruption in Japan earlier that year. Kurihara played the part of a diviner opposite Sessue Hayakawa, Aoki Tsuruko, Henry Kotani, and Abe Yutaka. Ince immediately followed this up with *The Typhoon,* a courtroom drama about a colony of Japanese in Paris who stop at nothing for the sake of their country. Hayakawa played the part of Dr. Takemora [*sic*], a spy entrusted with compiling an important and highly confidential military report. His French girlfriend, who resents his fanatical commitment to his work, goads him into an argument in which he loses his temper and kills her. A Japanese student, Kironari (Kotani), who understands the importance of Takemora's work, stands in for him and is executed in his place, but in the end, Takemora himself dies from guilt and a broken heart.

The director was not alone in his fascination with the East, and the next year Hayakawa and Kotani appeared in Cecil B. DeMille's *The Cheat.* In this film Hayakawa played a Japanese moneylender who brands his would-be lover (Fannie Ward) when she refuses to repay her debt in the agreed-upon manner. The sight of the Japanese actor ripping the clothes of his Caucasian costar and searing her shoulder with a branding iron aggravated the already tense atmosphere of anti-Japanese resentment in the United States (convincingly reflected in the quasi-lynching of Hayakawa's character in the courtroom finale). Reportedly, enraged audiences shouted anti-Japanese slogans at the screen in theaters throughout the country. When news of this reaction reached Japan, Hayakawa was accused of being a traitor, and at home his reputation among fellow members of the Japanese community was severely damaged (2: 18).[52] The protests of the Japanese Association of Southern California, combined with pressure resulting from Japan's alignment with the

Publicity photo of "Famous Japanese Screen Star, Miss Aoki Tsuru." *Katsudō kurabu,* August 1920. From Makino, ed., *Nihon eiga shoki shiryō shūsei (A Collection of Research Material from the Early Days of Japanese Film).*

Allied effort in the First World War, caused Hayakawa's Japanese character (Hishuru Tori [*sic*]) to be transformed into a "Burmese Ivory King" named Haka Arakau when the film was re-released in 1918. (This is the version that is currently in general circulation, although restoration of the original 1915 print is scheduled for completion by the end of 2000.)[53]

In Japan, the concept of using film as a vehicle for exporting Japanese culture to the West surged after the outbreak of the war. Although the war provided opportunities for Japan to expand its realm of influence in Asia, the government overestimated its allies' preoccupation with Europe. Early in 1915, Japan lost international prestige when it initiated an unreasonable and embarrassingly conspicuous diplomatic offensive against China. These were also the "yellow peril" years. In 1913 the first California Alien Land Law

121

THE MOVIE TIMES

July 1, 1922 =No. 104=

Published by

THE MOVIE TIMES PUB. CO.,

No. 35, IMAI-CHO, AZABU, TOYKO, JAPAN.

A smiling Sessue Hayakawa after his return to Japan. Cover of *Kinema junpō,* 1 July 1922. From Makino, ed., *Fukkokuban Kinema junpō.*

was passed forbidding Japanese nationals to own land, and the United States government continued to issue increasingly restrictive immigration laws against Japanese nationals. The mysterious, diabolical Japanese characters in such films as *The Typhoon* and *The Cheat* no doubt reflected the racist tension underlying this campaign against Asian immigration. A contemporary review of *The Cheat* in *Moving Picture World,* for example, commented on the "inherent Oriental beastliness" of Hayakawa's character.

Kurihara himself did not appear in all of these films, but he claimed that the sinister portrayal of Japanese in such pictures deeply disturbed him, and influenced his decision, after returning to Japan, to make exportable films that would more realistically portray Japanese and their culture for the benefit of misinformed audiences abroad.[54] Ince's westerns were in great demand in Japan, but his "Oriental productions" were not. *The Wrath of the Gods* was banned for its primitive depiction of Japanese shortly after it opened there in 1918. *The Typhoon* was not shown in Japan until 1920, and DeMille's *The Cheat* was never shown at all.[55]

While continuing to act under Ince, Kurihara worked as an extra at several other studios, gaining firsthand experience with the internal workings of the young, rapidly growing industry. Throughout the decade, the small network of studios continued to spread. In 1915 Ince joined with D. W. Griffith and Mack Sennett to form the Triangle Film Corporation. The company brought together the visions of three major figures of the American silent screen, making Kurihara a member of one of the most dynamic and influential institutions in the industry. In 1917, however, both Griffith and Sennett withdrew from the company, and Ince moved to Paramount. Kurihara struck out on his own, working as an extra for the Essanay, Lasky, Fox, and Hart studios until returning to Japan in April 1918.[56] Kurihara spent the next two years traveling between the United States and Japan, until confirmation of the plans for Taikatsu required him to return permanently to Japan in the spring of 1920.[57]

When Kurihara returned to Japan to survey the state of its industry in the spring of 1918, Kaeriyama had just begun his pioneering efforts at pure film production at Tenkatsu. *The Glory of Life,* completed a few months after Kurihara's return, would not open for more than a year, however, and the pure film movement itself, never formally organized or well defined, was even at this point no more than a kind of spiritual atmosphere created and sustained by concerned spectators.[58] American films ranked at the top of foreign imports, and Universal's idyllic Bluebird romances, Charlie Chaplin comedies, and serial pictures were popular. It was possible for the more serious fan to keep up with developments abroad by reading about them in the growing number of domestic and imported film-related publications, and Japanese audiences had long been familiar with many influential European

123

films, such as the Italian historical epics *Quo Vadis?* and *Cabiria.* But backstage the domestic industry was dominated by the *benshi,* still the major
attraction at the box office as well. Theaters specializing in the domestic
product offered a mixed bill of chain dramas, *shinpa* films, and *kyūgeki,*
especially those starring the industry's most popular icon, Onoe Matsunosuke. Discussion of the "artistic potential" of film was limited to a relatively
specialized audience.

Kurihara had returned to Japan with a specific purpose in mind. Before
leaving Ince's company, he had established a small business with Benjamin
Brodsky, an assistant to Reginald Barker. Barker had been instrumental in
diverting Ince's attention to the Far East, and had directed both *The Wrath of
the Gods* and *The Typhoon.* The origins and nature of Kurihara and Brodsky's company are unclear, although according to Kurihara himself it was
organized for the purpose of improving Japanese-American relations. The
enterprise was, at any rate, short-lived, but soon after Kurihara left Ince's
studio, he and his colleague formed another small production company, the
Sunrise Film Manufacturing Company, later called Tōyō Film in Japan.
Kurihara's primary objective in establishing this company was to make dramatic films that would introduce Japan and Japanese culture to foreign audiences, and he had returned to Japan hoping to secure financial support for
this project from prominent Japanese businessmen.[59]

In May 1918 Kurihara obtained the backing of Asano Yoshizō, the
wealthy second son of Asano Sōichirō, the founder of the Asano Cement
conglomerate. Like Kurihara, Asano had lived in the United States (he had
been educated at Harvard) and he might have been drawn to the idea of
supporting Kurihara's fledgling company based on this common experience.
It has also been pointed out that his interest in the film world coincided with
the tendency of prominent American businessmen, including his friend and
former classmate Joseph P. Kennedy, to publicly lend their support to the
American film industry; he possibly wanted to play a similar role in the
development of the industry in Japan.[60]

In addition to these possibilities, Asano clearly had more pragmatic reasons for sharing Kurihara's desire to promote culture exchange, particularly
between Japan and the United States. One of Asano's subsidiary companies,
the Tōyō Steamship Company, had been the first Japanese shipping company
to begin passage across the Pacific, a market previously dominated by the
Union Pacific Railway. It was also a member of a coalition of shipping, trad-
ing, hotel, and railroad companies, which under the sponsorship of the Japanese Foreign Ministry and the Tourist Bureau had been trying to increase the
rate of tourism to Japan since the end of the First World War.[61]

After receiving Asano's pledge of support, Kurihara returned to the

United States in November to study editing ("cutting") and art titles (*aato taitoru*).[62] The following spring he went back to Japan to continue his endeavors to produce "dramatic promotional films,"[63] such as the previously mentioned *Sanji Goto,* and *Tōyō no yume* (*A Dream of the Orient*). He had hoped his films would bring a more authentic depiction of Japan to American audiences, but he was unable to market them when he took them to the United States that December.

Asano, who had invested generously in Kurihara and Brodsky's company, inherited full ownership after Kurihara returned to Japan two months later. Although Asano's name did not actually appear on the list of executive directors for his newly adopted enterprise, now called Taikatsu, he supplied the necessary capital, marking the first foray of the *zaibatsu* (big business conglomerates) into the moving picture entertainment world.[64] Asano's initial investment was a relatively paltry 200,000 yen (99,000 U.S. dollars), and although an additional 1,500,000 yen (740,000 dollars) was added when the name of the company was changed to Taishō katsuei, the total increased amount of capital was still considerably less than the amount of money behind Taikatsu's competitors: the four companies that merged to form Nikkatsu in 1912, for example, had brought to it a combined total of 2,500,000 yen (1,200,000 dollars; in April 1920 it added 6,000,000 yen, equivalent to 3,000,000 dollars at the time, to meet the increase in competition); Kokkatsu was backed by 10,000,000 yen (5,000,000 dollars); and Teikine and Shōchiku each by 5,000,000 yen (2,500,000 dollars). Even the pioneer of Nikkatsu's rivals, Tenkatsu, had started in 1914 with a capital of 550,000 yen (270,000 dollars)—nearly three times the amount of Taikatsu's original capital.[65] In hindsight, Taikatsu's meager capital helps explain its brief existence, but it also makes the studio's accomplishments all the more impressive.

Initially, Taikatsu set out as an importer of first-rate foreign films, allowing Japanese audiences the additional privilege of being able to enjoy these films just as they were opening to their local audiences. According to Hazumi Tsuneo, at the time Nikkatsu and Tenkatsu, for example, dealt with individual brokers. These companies were known to haggle over the cheapest possible price for films that were already hopelessly outdated, importing via Shanghai—which took at least six months if not a year or more—for the sake of a discount.[66] When Asano took over ownership of Kurihara's company, foreign passengers aboard Tōyō Steamship's three trans-Pacific liners were already enjoying screenings of the latest films from New York, and he was only one short step away (it took only fourteen days to sail from California to Yokohama) from bringing these films ashore to Japan.[67] As a start, contracts were made with First National, Goldwyn, and Metro in order to import popular American pictures within days of their New York openings. But difficulties in enforcing exclusive distribution rights made the prospect of production increasingly attractive, and Kurihara was enlisted to supervise the production of modern films at the small Yokohama studio that formerly had belonged to Tōyō Film.[68] Given Kurihara's expertise and experience, the company's management was confident that he would turn out films that could rival European and American imports.

A closer look at the content of Taikatsu's prospectus in the June 1920 issue of *Katsudō kurabu* reveals a remarkable concurrence between the proclaimed goals behind the establishment of Taikatsu and Mori's vision of a reformation of the industry as described in *A Survey of the Moving Pictures:*

The Establishment of the Taishō Moving Picture Company
  I. Statement of Purpose
    At present in Japan there has been a phenomenal improvement in the audience's ability to appreciate moving pictures, yet this has not been reciprocated by a reformation of the film industry. Imported films are more than four or five years old, and the domestic industry has continued to produce the same type of *serifugeki* that they have offered us up until now. In view of these faults, this company proposes the following goals in hopes of fully satisfying all of these avid film fans.
  II. Goals
    1. We will import and distribute only the newest and best films from Europe and the United States. This will enable us to introduce the changes that have taken place in the technique of screen acting in the West over the past five years.
    2. Our company will produce and export Western-style films, using the natural beauty and picturesque landscape of our land as background. In this way we will widely promote the distinctive characteristics of Japan and the Japanese to the world.
    3. In the domestic entertainment market, we will do away with those films, resembling moving picture weeklies, that deal with current topics of interest, as well as the *serifugeki* that have been common up until now. Instead we will produce comedies and historical dramas that rely primarily on action.
  III. Company Organization
    In carrying out the above goals, a group of idealists in this field will work most earnestly and assiduously toward the realization of their ideals with the backing of businessmen influential in the financial world, bearing no resemblance to those speculative companies and manufacturers that are common these days.

IV. Execution
   1. At present in the Western film world, the days when audiences could be captivated by stars alone are over, and the latest trend is to emphasize the importance of the content of film scripts. Accordingly, individual companies are laboring over the production of film scripts, and they compete to enlist the talents of famous authors. Using one of the companies with which we have a special contract, Goldwyn, as an example, we will begin by importing this year's films, timing their opening in Japan to coincide with their opening in New York in order to introduce all these new tendencies in the moving picture world.
   2. Domestic films must also improve in order to keep up with the progressive Japanese audience described above. Accordingly, our company will produce superior films by building upon the ideas of the famous author Tanizaki Jun'ichirō, assembling a group of up-and-coming young actors and actresses under the guidance of Thomas Kurihara, and employing the most advanced camera technique. These films will be made in our Yokohama studio, where all the necessary equipment has already been installed.

   In addition to the actors mentioned above, we will accept applications for admission to a separate training school from educated men and women who wish to act. They will receive comprehensive instruction from Director Kurihara on Western screen acting. The most outstanding students in this group will be chosen for employment on a gradual basis.[69]

In *A Survey of the Moving Pictures,* Mori stated basic requirements for the improvement of the domestic industry: increased capital; the study of Western technique; and a dedicated, serious approach by spectators concerned with the state of Japanese film. The founders of Taikatsu unfortunately neglected to fulfill Mori's financial requirement, an oversight that later became a decisive factor in the company's demise. But they met his demand for "passionate resolve," both by their own account, as "earnest" and "assiduous" idealists, and by the enthusiasm and sense of purpose that comes through to us in the wording of the company's prospectus, a blueprint for nothing short of a fundamental overhaul of the industry. Finally, in line with Mori's demand for the study of Western technique (a concept that can be traced back at least as far as the inception of *Kinema Record* in 1913), the prospectus states that Taikatsu would promote the importation of "only the newest and best films from Europe and the United States" in order to "introduce the changes that have taken place in the technique of screen acting in the West." Finally, from the refutation of the *serifugeki* in the company's "Statement of Purpose"—reiterated under "Goals"—to the declaration of the

127

need to "emphasize the importance and content of film scripts," Taikatsu's prospectus specified that the importance of the film script was one current trend abroad that Japan would do well to follow.

As early as 1910 the Japanese film script had been criticized for a tendency toward verbosity. Commenting on the sorry state of amateur Japanese scriptwriters at the time, Satō Kōroku stressed the need to make a distinction between the stage play and the script for a moving picture: although a certain literary flourish might be acceptable for the stage, it was regarded as redundant in writing for the screen.[70] The perceived conflict between stage and screen drama was a transnational phenomenon during the 1910s, as the ascendancy of narrative film generated a period of transformation and exploration in formulating narrative systems for the new medium. Influenced by a familiarity with imported literature promoting the distinction of the "photoplay," Kaeriyama took the same stance toward screenwriting several years later. Two months after the publication of Taikatsu's prospectus, in an article announcing plans to open an acting school at the company's studio, Kurihara perpetuated this disposition, although he was decidedly vague about the mechanics of transforming the commercial *serifugeki* into "pure films." He wrote:

> Needless to say, film drama and stage drama are, fundamentally, two completely different things.
>
> In spite of this fact, film productions in this country have yet to rise above the level of *serifugeki*. They are of a nature that contradicts the true essence of film drama and as such they represent a step backwards in film development. I believe that as long as this situation continues, sending Japanese films to the Western market is an eternally hopeless impossibility.
>
> In view of this deficiency and the new direction of advancements in the West, this company proposes to completely do away with *serifugeki* of the kind that have been made up until now, dedicate itself to the funding of comedies and historical films that rely chiefly on action, and advertise the distinctive characteristics of Japan and the Japanese people worldwide by producing Japanese "pure films" for export. We are organizing this training school to enable us to effectively realize these goals.[71]

In *A Survey of the Moving Pictures,* Mori pointed out that the implausible plots and stereotyped characters of the melodramatic *shinpa* film in particular was another aspect of the typical *serifugeki* script (and the films that were made from them) that needed drastic improvement. At Kokkatsu in 1920, Kaeriyama had not yet found a solution to the problem of imitation. Meanwhile, a rising new class of critics clamored for contemporary realism.

One way to work toward this in the contemporary genre was to improve the quality of the acting, another aspect that made the domestic product less appealing to spectators partial to imported films. Again in 1910, in his assessment of the domestic screenwriting situation, Satō Kōroku included a comment on the acting technique (or lack thereof) of Japanese screen actors: frank and to the point, he dismissed the "poor level" of Japanese acting as "deplorable." In *The Glory of Life,* Kaeriyama set a precedent for bringing to the screen amateurs and actors that had not been trained on the traditional stage, but although Murata Minoru and his troupe won the critics' sympathy for their "bravery," they were criticized just the same for awkward gestures, unnatural posturing, and an obvious lack of training. Even Kaeriyama's *The Girl in His Dreams,* his most successful film, was hailed as the first contemporary drama film to compare favorably with imported films—in all respects but acting. Critics conceded that the acting was at least better than that of his previous films, but they felt it still left much to be desired. Had an acting school been organized on the studio grounds as promised in the Taikatsu prospectus, it might have been the first of its kind. In 1909 Satō Kōroku helped organize an acting school at the Yoshizawa studio (also the home of the first screenwriting department), but it is unclear to what extent the Yoshizawa school encouraged the participation of actresses.[72]

According to a former Taikatsu actress, Benisawa Yōko, the elaborately planned acting school, with proposed courses on makeup, costumes, movement, Western dance, and Japanese dance and singing, never actually materialized. Instead, Kurihara's actors—a group of amateurs that included three women, a former *benshi,* and a student—learned from Kurihara as they worked on his set.[73] We do know that aspiring applicants received screen tests, which were judged by both Kurihara and Tanizaki,[74] and that the lucky ones were well paid, the women receiving higher salaries than the men.[75] Screen tests were without precedent in 1920, as were high salaries, the latter indicative of a new trend to risk paying extra for individuals with certain skills (or the willingness to learn such skills) essential to the screen. The generous wages were apparently well deserved. Critics praised the acting in Taikatsu films such as *Amateur Club* and *The Lust of the White Serpent.* They applauded the actors for having an unaffected, naturalistic style that seems to have continued to elude Kaeriyama's actors, and they admired Kurihara's directing skills. Even Kaeriyama's own colleagues lamented that in comparison Kurihara was clearly the superior director.[76]

By all accounts, Kurihara's praise was well earned too. A demanding director, he ordered his actors to push themselves to honestly "feel" the emotions he wanted them to express. Often he repeatedly demonstrated a gesture or a line until they achieved the effect he was after. He was known to have reduced young actresses to tears,[77] and it is reported that in true Hollywood style he ordered one retake after another until he was completely satisfied with a scene.[78] His perfectionism on the set impressed Tanizaki, and it was

129

common knowledge that he often became so involved in his work that he laughed and cried along with the actors. One visitor to Kurihara's set went so far as to say that he was more entertained by Kurihara's expressions as they shifted with each subtle change of mood than he was by the actors themselves.[79] Script readings and rehearsals prior to shooting were not common practice at Taikatsu, and Kurihara still prompted the actors from his place beside the camera, but his technique differed from more conventional directing methods then in vogue in that he coached the actors and indicated the beginning and end of each scene. Also, Kurihara's actors were familiar with their lines before they went before the camera. According to Benisawa, she and her colleagues were expected to deliver their lines at the appropriate times, although they might not have always done so exactly as written.[80]

Taikatsu's prospectus indicates that the company's founders were inclined to believe changes in acting technique must be accompanied by a more serious attitude toward script production. In order for the contemporary drama pure film to successfully compete with popular imports and the domestic *shinpa* film, they would have to provide spectators with something that neither of these two competitors offered. Once again, Satō Kōroku had put his finger on this essential ingredient ten years earlier, in his appeal to Japanese scriptwriters to "advocate a Japanese lifestyle for Japanese people." By 1920, it had become increasingly common to link contemporary realism or contemporaneity—a quality not required of (by definition, not essential to) *shinpa* melodrama—with the desire to market Japanese films abroad. As we have seen, rhetoric promoting a systematic exportation of Japanese films played a significant role in the establishment of Taikatsu and Shōchiku that year, and the necessity to build a foreign market for Japanese films was a major theme of Mori's *A Survey of the Moving Pictures*. Whether or not this was in fact perceived as an actual possibility, a consideration of some of the issues Mori raises is important in order to understand the extent to which this attitude was associated with the conception of screenwriting at both the Taikatsu and Shōchiku studios.

CHALLENGING BORDERS

It is doubtful Kaeriyama's pure films were ever seen by foreign audiences.[81] He was purportedly granted permission to make these films under the pretext that they were for export, but the general opinion is that such a proposal helped him to bypass the production standards imposed on commercial box office attractions. It is not clear just how interested Kaeriyama was in actually exporting his work, but the premise proved to be remarkably effective, for example, in obtaining permission to photograph locations that otherwise would have been forbidden to a film intended merely for domestic consumption. When he made *The Tale of the White Chrysanthemum,* a romantic sword fight film set in the Middle Ages, the monks at the Kiyomizu temple in Kyoto repeatedly refused his requests for permission to shoot on the temple grounds. They had washed their hands of moving pictures after Onoe Matsunosuke knocked some tiles off a roof during one of his acrobatic stunts. The monks eventually granted Kaeriyama permission to use the temple when they learned that the film had been commissioned by an Italian company and was slated for export, having been persuaded by the director's argument that his film was for the purpose of introducing Japanese culture abroad.[82] By now the idea of using film as a vehicle for exporting Japanese culture to the West had become inextricably intertwined with the issue of pure film, as we can see from this review of Kaeriyama's *The Girl in His Dreams,* a contemporary drama film that opened one month before *The Tale of the White Chrysanthemum* in June 1920:

> At last the technique and expressions are not, as in [Kaeriyama's] previous films, imitations of foreign acting style, or inappropriate for Japanese people. Nevertheless, the suspicious man's action of gripping the pistol and raising it with both hands when he gets angry is more Western than Japanese. . . . If you want to introduce the true character of the Japanese to audiences abroad, you should not use such gestures. Even if the Japanese are not very expressive, there must be certain expressions and gestures that are characteristically Japanese. The skillful use of them would serve to introduce the true nature of the Japanese abroad in a meaningful way.[83]

To a large degree this new consciousness was awakened by imports that featured on-screen portrayals of "Japan" and the "Japanese." Sessue Hayakawa's films, which Japan began importing in 1918, were perhaps the most conspicuous examples, but in fact Japanese audiences had been aware of these fantastical (sometimes alarmingly so) cinematic interpretations of their country from at least as early as 1913.

In *A Survey of the Moving Pictures,* Mori included a section, "Foreign Countries and Japan," in which he offered his observations on foreign screen portrayals of Japan and the aspects of his country that he thought most attracted foreigners' interest and curiosity. In all, he listed eighteen foreign films about Japan or stories inspired by Japan (including *The Wrath of the Gods*) that opened in Japan between 1913 and 1920. He also listed the titles and synopses of at least fourteen dramatic films (including *The Vigil* and *The Cheat*) and several nonfiction films (*The Land of the Rising Sun,* made by the "American-Japan Film Company," and six Lyman Howe and Burton Holmes travelogues listed under the heading "Paramount Holmes Travel Pictures")

131

"幻影の女" の二場面
上、郊外散歩　下、長濱の最後

Two scenes from *Gen'ei no onna* (*The Girl in his Dreams*), directed by Kaeriyama Norimasa, 1920. *Kinema junpō,* 11 June 1920. From Makino, ed., *Fukkokuban Kinema junpō*.

that had not been bought for distribution in Japan (2: 1–24). Mori's commentary on such films was both detailed and reflective regarding the European and American perceptions of Japan that he felt they expressed.

Forever the observant and ardent admirer of European and American films, Mori praised their technical virtues, even noting a few films that he considered ideal models for contemporary drama pure films (for example, E. Mason Hopper's *Her American Husband,* a five-reel 1918 film starring Kurihara and "Jack" Abe [Abe Yutaka], and George Fitzmorris's *A Japanese Nightingale*) (2: 12–13). Nevertheless, his comments throughout this chapter also reveal that he was offended by the tendency to depict the Japanese as a semi-barbaric race with a propensity toward self-sacrifice—the most extreme expression of which was ritual suicide, a key ingredient in nearly all of these plots. His disappointment is also evident, particularly in his criticism of a Bluebird film by Rupert Julian, *The Door Between.* Here he sadly noted that the appearance of Japanese actors in such an outlandish portrait of Japan and the Japanese people was "a national disgrace" (2: 11–12). Rupert Julian was a favorite director of many pure film enthusiasts, and it is not hard to imagine the disillusionment of his Japanese admirers upon realizing that even this particular director was, after all, in a land that seemed very distant indeed.

Nearly all of these imports about Japan featured tales of honor, revenge, self-sacrifice, and unrequited love, the last usually in some variation or another of the Madame Butterfly theme. A number of them had been deemed so offensive that they were withdrawn from distribution soon after they opened to the public. This was the case, for example, with the first film on Mori's list, an Italian film titled, in Japanese, *Ōshoku jin* (*Yellow Man*), which opened in 1913, and the first Hayakawa import, *The Wrath of the Gods.* But Mori noted that as strange as these films were, there was still something to be learned from them not only in the area of technical expertise, but in understanding just what it was about Japan that would attract foreigners to make films about a country and culture with which they were totally unfamiliar. Reflecting on the "curiosity and admiration of foreigners for Japan," he wrote:

> All over the world, since the days of Columbus and Marco Polo, many attractive aspects of our country have been related through the countless tales of tourists and the diaries of travelers, and for this reason Japan is believed to be some sort of paradise.
>
> It is as if the entire country were buried in cherry blossoms, with young Japanese maidens and "geisha girls" strolling through them dressed in gorgeous kimonos. When night falls, crimson lanterns of all sizes beautifully adorn the darkened cities, and in the morning graceful Mount Fuji rises up, Hiroshige's deep blue sea stretches out, and white sails glide gently by. It is unbelievable the

extent to which a great number of foreigners strive to envision Japan as a land of dreams and visions, a land of poetry, and a land of beauty.

This tendency encourages those whose hearts cherish all things Japanese, who say that their esteem for Japanese works of art and such is beyond imagination. It shows that they believe Japan to be a paradise cradled in the midst of natural beauty, and will thus like anything provided it is Japanese.

On the other hand, this country of ours, a minor power that has been neither noticed nor esteemed by other nations, is suddenly attracting attention after the Sino-Japanese and Russo-Japanese campaigns. "The magnificent Mikado commands an army of unparalleled valor. Sons of samurai, they surpass even the Spartans in their respect for bushido, and once disgraced, they will commit ritual suicide after revenging themselves on all involved." This is how they see us, and from this point of view our way of thinking seems quite extraordinary. Thus they have a tremendous desire to learn about the way we think and how we feel.

In short, because the curiosity of foreigners concerns "beauty and bushido," it seems to have an intensity even greater than that of our own curiosity to learn about the West. (2: 6)

In sum, however bizarre and incoherent such films as *The Wrath of the Gods* might be as renditions of Japan, the sheer volume of such films suggested to Mori that foreigners were indeed very curious about both the nation and the people, and in fact had "strong feelings of affection" for Japan (2: 10). He did not doubt that viewers abroad would be interested in Japanese films. The problem was not whether there would be an audience for Japanese films, but perfecting a marketable product. For advocates of reform like Mori, until then the world would continue to accept the exotic fantasies offered in foreign films as the real Japan. What was needed seemed the impossible. First, there would have to be a domestic product that would draw upon the cinematic innovations of the West without lapsing into slavish imitation: the establishment of a foreign market would undoubtedly follow. At least rhetorically, these two goals were inseparable.

When Mori wrote his commentary on "Foreign Countries and Japan," the emergence of new companies like Taikatsu and Shōchiku offered the promise of change and innovation. Notwithstanding this glimmer of hope, the *shinpa* film, female impersonator, and powerful *benshi* still dominated the industry—just as popular, enduring, and unexportable as ever. Mori ended his commentary on "Foreign Countries and Japan" with a touch of regret and resignation, writing, "What anguish to think that had we been exporting Japanese films all this time, [foreign filmmakers] would not have been able to make pictures like this, full of misunderstandings and insults to our national pride" (2: 20).

Mori was apparently not far wrong in his assessment of foreign reaction to such "Oriental" productions. Only one year after *The Wrath of the Gods*

134

and *The Typhoon* opened, Vachel Lindsay noted in *The Art of the Moving Picture* that "it would be a noble thing if American experts in the Japanese principles of decoration . . . should tell stories of old Japan with the assistance of such men as Sessue Hayakawa. Such things go further than peace treaties."[84] In Lindsay's opinion, if American filmmakers insisted on filming tales of the Orient, they should at least attempt "stories of Iyeyasu and Hideyoshi, written from the ground up for the photoplay theater," or "the story of the Forty-seven Ronin, not a Japanese stage version, but a work from the source-material."[85] By making good use of Hayakawa's typically Japanese "atmosphere of pictorial romance," he observed, such films would have more appeal than ones like *The Typhoon,* in which "very little of the landscape of the nation is shown," and "the one impression of the play is that Japanese patriotism is a peculiar and fearful thing."[86]

In its 1920 prospectus, Taikatsu, like Shōchiku before it, acknowledged the necessity to make exportable films and announced plans to make both historical dramas and contemporary comedies that would "use the natural beauty and picturesque landscape" of Japan to "widely promote the distinctive characteristics of Japan and the Japanese to the world." Appearing alongside this prospectus was an article by Kurihara, "Katsudō shashin to boku" ("The Moving Pictures and I"), in which the author gave a short résumé of his accomplishments (focusing on his work in the United States) and what he hoped to achieve at Taikatsu, closing with the sincere hope that Japanese audiences would receive his films favorably, as "an important contribution to the nation." For Kurihara, just back from the United States, where anti-Japanese incidents had been steadily increasing over the last few years (a second Alien Land Law forbidding Japanese to own or rent land was passed in 1920), this "contribution to the nation" would be films that would communicate something of the beauty of his country to audiences abroad. He declared his vision of the goodwill mission he planned to carry out at Taikatsu in the article's opening paragraph:

> While living for many years in the United States, I was able to observe all the different aspects of anti-Japanese sentiment on the part of a certain class of Americans. I realized that this feeling is largely due to the fact that Japan and the Japanese are not understood, and I took it upon myself to research the various possibilities for enlightening their ignorance. As a result, I decided the moving pictures would be most useful for this purpose. Depictions of cultured and educated Japanese, time-honored Japanese morals, bushido, and the spirit of Yamato can all be arranged into film dramas against the beautiful scenery of our country as a background. . . . We have come to the conclusion that this would be most effective. In embarking on this project, which we are undertaking with great determination and aspiration, we feel it is necessary to have, first of all, a complete understanding of the task at hand.[87]

135

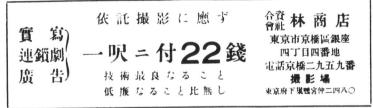
Two advertisements for topical films in *Kinema Record*: 10 November 1915 ("Enthronement Ceremony") and December 1917 ("Japanese Scenic Pictures"). From Makino, ed., *Fukkokuban Kinema rekōdo*.

According to *A Survey of Moving Pictures,* there had been earlier attempts to export Japanese films abroad, for the most part Nikkatsu *shinpa* films or short promotional films like *Tōkyō kōgai no sakura* (*Cherry Blossoms of the Tokyo Suburbs*). A version of the story of the Loyal Forty-Seven Rōnin starring Onoe Matsunosuke had been shown to a select audience in New York, but they reportedly had not been impressed with Matsunosuke's performance. Mori explained the tepid response to such attempts by claiming that no one had really taken the possibility of export seriously enough, spending as little money as possible to send only one print abroad for special screenings (2: 38–39). Kurihara determined to take a different approach, believing, as he later wrote, that "Filming Mount Fuji, Nikkō, and cherry blossoms with the intention of introducing Japan abroad is akin to our being shown films of Niagara Falls and the Alps: both are equally useless means for learning anything about native customs and manners."[88]

In his study of censorship legislation and the pure film movement, Aaron Gerow draws attention to the "profound contradiction" evident in Mori's agenda stipulating that the creation of a foreign market for Japanese films portraying a "real" Japan was contingent upon a complete reformation of the Japanese film—a reformation modeled on Western innovation, no less. From his point of view, such a desire for realism during this period was inextricably related to a "psychology of national shame," as well as the mistaken notion that "cinema was a universal, transparent language which presented one type of solution to [such seemingly contradictory problems]."[89] It is true that the logic behind Mori's assessments of such cultural intangibles as "foreign appreciation of Japan" and "the real Japan" is as potentially contradictory as it is inherently ambiguous. Handling cultural essentialisms is a slippery business, not in the least because such essentialisms are open to various interpretations. It is important to acknowledge the problems involved, in view of existing evidence, in reducing the pure film movement to a single, monolithic drive. The portrayal of cultural contemporaneity was one of many directions pure film enthusiasts suggested for the movement toward "reform," as was the attempt to achieve some degree of transformation in prevalent conceptions of film narrative that privileged the *benshi.* Besides lamenting the conditions of the domestic industry in comparison with those of Europe and the United States, Mori could also have been interested in possibilities for devising a new (different) means of achieving narrational clarity in new (different) stories, stories written specifically for the screen rather than appropriated from a preexisting theatrical repertory. However Mori might seem to emphasize the importance of these films being set in Japan in the context of their suitability for export, he does not imply that this insistence on locality was not equally important in considering these films for domestic consumption. Is it possible to flatly deny that, as David Bordwell

138

and Kristin Thompson suggest, many different criteria can be used to (relatively objectively) evaluate "quality" in a film, including those formal criteria used to assess films as artistic wholes ("coherence, intensity of effect, complexity, originality")?[90]

As Mori pondered the possibilities for transformations in the "quality" of Japanese film, Samuel Goldwyn was forging ahead with his own artistic agenda in the United States. He decided to make writers the new stars of Hollywood—he vainly hoped they might be less temperamental than actors— and within his company he had just formed a group of writers, Eminent Authors, Inc., to work at his studio. Following Goldwyn's example, and responding to the demand from pure film enthusiasts like Mori for "a burial of those dropouts from literary circles and playwrights past their prime who call themselves screen authors," Kurihara and his cofounders at Taikatsu proposed to the popular author Tanizaki Jun'ichirō that he join their ranks.

4

The Literary Link:
Screenwriter Tanizaki Jun'ichirō

THE RELATION BETWEEN the literary arts and screenwriting outside of Japan dates back to the earliest years of the industry. In 1926, pioneer film historian Terry Ramsaye observed that the first author for the screen in the United States was a playwright named Salmi Morse. Two contemporary historians of the American screenplay, Edward Azlant and Tom Stempel, are of the same opinion. By an ironic twist of fate, Morse (according to Azlant an "eccentric California dramatist") earned his place in the history of screenwriting posthumously. He had written a version of the Oberammergau passion play that was produced by David Belasco at the Grand Opera House in San Francisco in 1879, but the following year the play was banned (for religious reasons) shortly before it was to open in New York. The disappointment was more than the elderly playwright could bear. Morse never recovered from the shock and eventually took his own life years before his play was resurrected, as Ramsaye observes, as the "first motion picture scenario." The film version of the passion play, shot from Morse's script, opened in 1898 to great commercial success. As for Morse, Azlant remarks that "the current Writers Guild could do worse than mark the spot where [he] threw himself into New York's North River."[1]

In the United States the practice of hiring a special corps of well-known writers to write for the screen was pioneered by the Edison Company in 1909. Subsequently studios like Selig and Universal invested in the rights to literary works that could be adapted to the screen, but for the most part the medium continued to be scorned by "serious" writers, who still doubted its artistic value, until the late 1910s. The writers hired by the studios in the

141

meantime came from a variety of backgrounds, but a notable majority, like the first-hired writer, Roy McCardell, were journalists. Writers experienced in this field seemed more willing and better prepared to deal with film's condensed format and demanding production schedule.

The Taikatsu prospectus of 1920 singled out Goldwyn's 1919 Eminent Authors venture as a sign of a new emphasis on "quality" writing for the screen, but similar projects were undertaken at other studios toward the end of the decade. In 1918 Fox had made an arrangement with the playwright George V. Hobart for a set number of original stories, and Goldwyn's ambitious undertaking in turn inspired a rash of hiring of literary talents at Vitagraph (1919) and Metro (1920).[2] Although a few literary giants went on to achieve success in the medium, such projects were for the most part complete failures: the playwrights and novelists either displayed little interest in the special requirements of writing for the screen, or they assumed that to comply with such demands would unduly compromise their talent.

Nevertheless the association of these writers with the movies did impart a much-needed respectability to the medium and to the craft of screenwriting itself. Although it has been argued that the attention given to the well-known literary figures contracted to write scripts cast a shadow over the more deserving, hardworking "journeyman screenwriters," such attention did aid in the transition from the heyday of the amateur writer—the years of "scenario fever"—to that of the respected professional writer for the silent screen. During the golden years of the silent film in the following decade, writers' fees and the cost of screenrights rapidly increased, and by the mid-1920s the screenwriting profession was both well established and well paid.[3]

As we have seen, there was no shortage of writers with a literary background in the early Japanese film industry, and not all of them fell under the category of what Mori Iwao referred to as literary "dropouts" or "playwrights past their prime." Satō Kōroku, the head of the industry's first story department, was a *shinpa* playwright and producer and the author of numerous *shinpa* film scripts, but he was also a concerned critic of the domestic film and was respected even by intellectuals like Mori who supported the abolition of the *shinpa* film genre. The head of the first story department at Nikkatsu, Masumoto Kiyoshi, was also a member of the respectable Bungei kyōkai (Literary Society); having joined the industry at such an early date, he was already one of the more established resident writers by the end of the decade and was responsible for persuading a reluctant fellow kyōkai member, Tanaka Eizō, to enter Nikkatsu in order to improve the state of that studio's standard fare.

The presence of such writers no doubt encouraged pure film enthusiasts, but it inspired none of the elation aroused by the news that Tanizaki

Jun'ichirō and Osanai Kaoru had agreed to work at the new Taikatsu and Shōchiku studios. Like the majority of their counterparts in the West, both of these well-known writers were involved in the film industry only briefly, but they contributed to the creation of a new profile for the industry (at least on a national level) and reinforced burgeoning sympathies with the contemporary international trend toward promoting film as art. In contrast to the novelists and playwrights hired by New York and Hollywood, Tanizaki and Osanai were eager to participate in film production. Tanizaki, in particular, both through his involvement at Taikatsu and in his critical writings concerning film, drew attention to both the potentialities and requirements of writing for the screen, as well as the role of the script and the professional screenwriter in the production process.

Much of the excitement surrounding the appointments of Tanizaki and Osanai was generated by their established positions in literary circles and the popular following they both enjoyed by 1920. But it was also true that both writers had already made known their interest in film production and their support for contemporary opinion concerning changes in the industry. For Osanai, admittedly, Shōchiku's offer was timely: his theater troupe had just disbanded, and the *shingeki* movement he had helped to pioneer had suffered a setback after the death of Shimamura Hōgetsu, Osanai's former disciple, and the subsequent suicide of Shimamura's lover, the popular actress Matsui Sumako. But Shōchiku's offer also provided Osanai with an opportunity to pursue an interest in film that dated as far back as the first Cinematograph and Vitascope screenings in Tokyo early in 1897. He was only seventeen years old when he saw these films, and even then he was impressed enough to record his reactions in detail in a diary.[4] Fifteen years later, in 1912, he began a formal association with film by providing commentary at special screenings sponsored by the Bungei katsudō shashinkai (Literary Motion Picture Society) of imported film adaptations of literary works, including *Salomé, Salammbô, Parisina, The Iliad, Othello,* and *Anna Karenina.*[5]

Tanizaki also had his first experience seeing foreign films at an early age. His description of these films appears in *Yōshō jidai* (*Childhood Days,* 1957), an autobiography he wrote when he was seventy.[6] It has been pointed out that these descriptions match those of Edison and Lumière films imported primarily between 1897 and 1904.[7] If Tanizaki actually was in the audience at the time of the earliest Tokyo screenings he would have been only eleven years old. Although he attributes the clarity of his recollections after over fifty years to the fact that the films were short loops shown repeatedly,[8] his detailed account suggests the experience deeply impressed him.

Tanizaki Jun'ichirō c. 1920–1921, when he was working alongside Thomas Kurihara at Taikatsu. Courtesy of Nihon Kindai Bungaku-kan.

TANIZAKI AND THE SCREEN

In spite of his popularity, Tanizaki, like Osanai, was at a crossroads in his career when he entered the film industry at the age of thirty-five. A decade had passed since his literary debut, but as a romanticist and an aesthete, an anti-naturalist in a literary world dominated by naturalism, he was something of an anomaly among the literary elite. His personal life was also unstable: there were rumors that he was involved with his wife's younger sister, the future Taikatsu actress Hayama Michiko (her married name is Wajima Sei), and his lack of regard for his wife led to a highly publicized confrontation with his best friend, the novelist and poet Satō Haruo, in October of 1920. In view of his recent failure to complete two novels, *Nageki no mon* (*Gate of*

Sorrow) in 1918 and *Kōjin*[9] in 1920, he was evidently experiencing uncertainty in his writing as well.

He had always exhibited a strong interest in foreign cultures, and around the time he entered the film industry his fascination with the West had become extreme. This obsession with Western culture played an important role in his becoming involved in the motion pictures. He later recalled that between 1915 and 1919 in particular he regularly patronized theaters specializing in imported films, and by the time he entered Taikatsu he had become something of a connoisseur of films from the United States and Europe.[10] Charlie Chaplin and Mack Sennett comedies were particular favorites;[11] Tanizaki referred to film in his work most frequently between the years 1915 and 1925, but a comment on Charlie Chaplin appears as early as 1915 (when Chaplin films were most popular) in the story "Dokutan" ("The German Spy").[12]

Judging from various essays Tanizaki wrote between 1915 and 1925, he seems to have been interested in all kinds of films providing they were not Japanese, but he had a special reverence for Hollywood and its product. In fact, nearly half of "Jinmenso" ("The Growth with a Human Face"), a story he wrote in 1918, takes place in Hollywood. The story is about the return to Japan of a Japanese actress who has become a successful Hollywood star. In Japan she learns of the existence of a strange film, *The Growth with a Human Face,* in which she appears in the leading role: an ill-fated courtesan plagued with a growth on her knee resembling a human face. The film, a Hollywood picture featuring shocking close-ups of the growth's expressive "face" (including a final scene where, having caused the distraught heroine to kill herself, it laughs hysterically in a full-frame close-up) is tremendously popular with Japanese audiences, but the actress herself has no recollection of ever having made it.[13]

This is definitely not a comedy, but in addition to the use of Hollywood as a background, Tanizaki's choice of subject matter—characteristically unconventional for the time—and the story's unusual structure suggesting the story of a film within a film are of particular interest. More important, Tanizaki seized this opportunity to praise the evocative power of such innovative techniques as the close-up shot. "The Growth with a Human Face" also shows an early interest in two related aspects of the medium that would continue to intrigue Tanizaki even after he was no longer active in the industry: its ability to portray both realistic and imaginary (in particular, surreal or supernatural) images in an equally convincing manner, and the ways in which the medium can be used to contest the often thin line between the perception of on- and offscreen reality. In one episode a film projectionist, who has quit his job because of repeated exposure to the bizarre film, ponders the hypothetical situation of an audience of one, an actor confronted with his own image on-screen. Which is the reality and which the illusion (the projectionist muses) if, as he is drawn into his performance on the screen, the actor becomes less and less aware of his physical presence?[14]

Tanizaki pursued variations on this theme a number of times. The "dreamlike" quality of film is one aspect he mentions in his landmark 1917 article, "Katsudō shashin no genzai to shōrai" (hereafter referred to as "The Present and Future of the Moving Pictures"), and after the Japanese release of *The Cabinet of Dr. Caligari* in 1921, Tanizaki published an essay addressing the relationship between the worlds of reality and illusion as they are portrayed on film.[15] Arguably, the moving picture's affinity for subject matter that stirs the human powers of perception was, for Tanizaki, its greatest attraction. Earlier in 1921, exactly one year after he joined Taikatsu, he wrote:

> In a sense, you can even say that moving pictures are dreams that are just slightly more vivid than ordinary dreams. People want to dream not only when they are asleep, but when they are awake too. We go to moving picture theaters because we want to see dreams on the screen. We want to savor dreams even though we are wide awake. Perhaps for that reason I prefer to go to the moving pictures in the afternoon rather than at night. Spring and summer are better seasons than winter and the fall. In particular, the early summer from the end of May to June, just when one begins to perspire a bit, is the best time for stirring up all kinds of illusions. Then, even after I come home and lay my head on the pillow, those illusions travel back and forth in my mind, mingling with my dreams. In the end I can no longer distinguish between the film and the dream, and for a long time they both linger in my mind as one beautiful vision. Movies are indeed dreams men make with machines. Scientific progress and the development of the human intellect have given us various industrial products, and now we can finally also make dreams. It is said that wine and music are the greatest manmade masterpieces, but moving pictures are definitely another.[16]

Much later, in expressing his disappointment in the film adaptation of his novel *Shunkinshō* (*A Portrait of Shunkin*) in "Eiga e no kansō" ("Thoughts on Film," 1934), Tanizaki wrote that had he done the film himself he would have emphasized the contrast between reality and fantasy.[17] At Taikatsu, Tanizaki pursued his interest in the "dreamlike" quality of film in his original scenario, *Tsuki no kagayaki* (*The Radiance of the Moon*, written in 1920 but never filmed), and *Hinamatsuri no yoru* (*The Night of the Doll Festival,* 1921), a film he not only wrote the script for but partially directed.

His experimentation with this theme culminated in his most ambitious project, the script for the ten-reel *The Lust of the White Serpent* (the opening scenes of which are translated in the appendix), based on a story by Ueda

146

Thomas Kurihara, Ozaki Shōtarō, and Tanizaki working the puppets in a scene from *Hinamatsuri no yoru* (*The Night of the Doll's Festival*), 1921 at Tanizaki's Odawara residence. Courtesy of Fujita Mitsuo.

Akinari that was ultimately derived from a Chinese ghost tale.[18] The more difficult question concerning the ambiguous distinctions between the perception of reality on- and offscreen remained a concern throughout his involvement in film. In fact, he continued to be preoccupied with this aspect of the medium even after leaving Taikatsu, and in 1923 he summed up his feelings on the subject in the novel *Nikkai* (*Flesh*), which was based on his experiences at the studio:

> To exaggerate a bit, the entire universe—all the phenomena of the world around us—is something like a film. Isn't is possible, then, that even though everything changes from moment to moment, the past remains wound up somewhere? Couldn't it be that we are all nothing but shadows that disappear quickly and without a trace, while our reality lives on in the film of the universe? Even the dreams we see and the things we imagine are films of the past projecting light on our minds. For this reason they cannot be mere illusions. The things we have

147

seen once, somewhere, whether in a previous life or at some point in our childhood, project shadows. I have had this idea for some time, but seeing moving
pictures has reinforced it. Films are dreams that we see reflected on the screen
instead of visualized in our minds. And, in fact, those dreams are the real
world.[19]

As he grew increasingly absorbed with the West, Tanizaki found himself
particularly drawn to the evident contrasts between Western and Asian culture, another theme he pursued throughout his career. Although his preferences were to change, his enthusiasm for the West at the time was reflected in
his taste in films: one result of his excursions to theaters specializing in
imported films was a conviction that the domestic product suffered in comparison, but beyond the technical discrepancies he frankly preferred the
hilarity, ebullience, and contemporaneity of American comedy, for example,
to what he perceived as the drabness of *shinpa* melodrama and sword fight
features starring Matsunosuke. Moreover, imported films provided him with
a chance to escape a reality that he was finding increasingly oppressive. In
1918 he sought to temper his wanderlust by taking a trip to China; later he
wrote that if it had not been for his family and his lack of finances, he would
probably have gone to the West instead.[20] As it was, the trip only exacerbated
his loathing for Japan. Tanizaki described his feelings at the time in his 1934
essay "Tōkyō o omou" ("Thoughts on Tokyo"):

Today Japanese goods have conquered the world market, but at that time our
national industry was in a trial period when it was only a crude imitation of an
industrially advanced country. In general it seemed as if no product with a
domestic label was worth anything. I was often infuriated by matches. Most of
them would light up with a swoosh as soon as you struck them, and then immediately burn out at the tip. You needed to strike four or five matches in order to
light one cigarette. It was the same with flashlights. The contact between the bat-
tery and the light was poorly made and the switch would break while you were
still on your way home from the store. As for the Japanese moving pictures at the
time, Onoe Matsunosuke was all the rage. You could say that he symbolized the
level of culture in the country. Old Japan had been cast off, but the new Japan
had yet to come. . . .

I wondered if I was the only one who felt that way. Watching Matsunosuke's pictures, I thought Japanese drama and the Japanese face seemed
absolutely hideous, and I doubted the minds and tastes of the Japanese who
watched such things with interest. In spite of being Japanese, I hated Japan. In
those days I enjoyed nothing more than going to the Teikoku and the Odeon theaters to see Western films, and I could only think that the difference between
Matsunosuke's films and Western films was none other than the difference
between Japan and the West. Watching the perfect appearance of the cities in

Western films, I increasingly disliked Japan. My misfortune in having been born in the backwoods of Asia made me sad.[21]

Tanizaki's obsession with Western culture played an important role in his becoming involved in the motion pictures. His work at Taikatsu marked the climax of his infatuation with the West, but it also presaged its end. The shift from West to East is evident in the shift from the Hollywood-inspired comedy of *Amateur Club* to the more traditional subject matter, borrowed from the classics, of *The Lust of the White Serpent.* Tanizaki lived in a thoroughly Western style in Yokohama, where he moved in September 1921, only two months before quitting Taikatsu. He took over the fully furnished home of two foreigners, sisters who taught English in the area, and even retained their cook. He slept in a bed and (contrary to Japanese usage) wore shoes inside the house. He enjoyed cranking up his gramophone and dancing to records.[22] Yet he was never able to ignore completely his interest in and awareness of his Asian heritage. These feelings persisted despite his attraction to the distant glitter of Hollywood. One month after he quit Taikatsu, Tanizaki described these complex feelings, revealing at the same time an interest in imported film publications:

> I moved to Yokohama, and although I was working in moving pictures, living in a city redolent of Westerners and living in a Western building, the writings of Gao Qing Qiu and Wu Mei Cun lay on top of the bookshelves on each side of my desk, mixed in with American moving picture magazines. Often, when my mind and body were tired from my work and my writing, I would pick up those magazines and collections of Chinese poetry and thumb through them. When I opened *Motion Picture Magazine, Shadow Land,* or *Photo Play Magazine* my imagination would fly to that kingdom of cinema, the world of Hollywood, and I felt the blaze of boundless ambition. But then when I leafed through Gao Qing Qiu, reading just one short verse would attract me to that tranquil domain, and it was as if my ambitious thoughts and daydreams of a moment before were suddenly doused with cold water.[23]

It was while he was working on location in the western region of Kansai during the filming of *The Lust of the White Serpent* that Tanizaki became interested in that region of Japan and consequently in the traditional aesthetic atmosphere that still permeated the area.[24] He was particularly drawn to Kyoto. After the Great Kanto Earthquake, Tanizaki, like many fellow Tokyo residents, moved to the Kansai region to wait out the reconstruction of Tokyo. He lived first in Kobe, the most Westernized city in the area, but eventually moved to Kyoto.[25] He later wrote that it was after his second trip to Shanghai in 1926, after having decided to permanently make the Kansai region his home, that he "realized the time had come to say 'goodbye' to his Western habits.[26]

The decision not to return to Tokyo, a major turning point in Tanizaki's career, marked the end of his active involvement in the motion picture industry. Ironically, his move to Kyoto put him next door to Makino Shōzō's film studio in the Uzumasa district of Kyoto, where several of his former colleagues from Taikatsu were then employed. This led to the speculation that he might continue to work in the industry, but such rumors were unfounded.[27] Although Tanizaki later wrote that he would have liked to continue to work in film, and that he especially would have liked to participate in the sound revolution by writing "talkie" screenplays,[28] he became increasingly estranged from the medium after his move from Yokohama. Tanizaki's involvement in film was brief, but his prominence in the literary world, as well as his own sincere interest in his work at Taikatsu, were enough to stimulate interest in the role of the scriptwriter in the production process.

A New Voice and "a Million Allies" for Reform

The film historian Tanaka Jun'ichirō, a teenager at the time and one of many young film fans who hoped for a modernization of Japanese films, recalls that the news of Osanai and Tanizaki joining ranks with pure film enthusiasts made him and his friends feel as if they "had gained a million allies." He credits Kaeriyama and his colleagues with having supplied the motivating force behind the modernization movement through the tremendous influence their work exerted on intellectuals like these two men. According to Tanaka, journalism played a significant role in this process: journalists, though often critical of the films themselves, were enthusiastic about Kaeriyama's principles of reform, and they continued to support him far more than the businessmen who actually ran the industry. As an example of the extent to which the journalistic media amplified the impact of Kaeriyama's movement, Tanaka cites an article published in September 1918, just two months after the completion of *The Glory of Life:* "For example, the magazine *Chūō kōron* ran a special article, "Cars, Moving Pictures, and Cafés as Symbols of the New Age," in which progressive cultural figures forecast the advent of the age of the masses, and addressed the artistic qualities of film and its potential for development in the future. This in itself was cause for rejoicing."[29] Tanizaki and Osanai both contributed to this article, and Tanizaki went as far as to declare moving pictures to be the highest of all art forms. Characteristically, he expressed this novel view with a tone of utter conviction: "In my opinion, moving pictures are a true art form and the one with the greatest potential for development in the future. Moving pictures are in no way

150

inferior to the other arts—drama, of course, as well as music, literature, painting, or sculpture. The moving pictures, which have an extremely dream-like quality, are in fact superior to all other art forms because of their extensive range."[30]

Throughout his career, Tanizaki continued to make use of the forum that journalism provided for the debate of the artistic qualities of film, and in the early years of the industry in particular he was arguably the medium's most eloquent spokesman. Certainly he was the major proponent of the pure film movement to be published in literary publications. His first article on film, "The Present and Future of the Moving Pictures," for example, was published in the literary journal *Shinshōsetsu* two months after the publication of Kaeriyama's *The Production and Photography of Moving Picture Drama.* Tanizaki's seminal article introduced several themes that he would pursue in subsequent essays and articles, including the film medium's superiority over all other art forms, its ability to depict both realistic images and illusions, and the as yet largely untapped potential of classical Japanese literature as source material for film drama. In this article Tanizaki also addressed every aspect of the contemporary industry that was singled out for criticism by Kaeriyama and his colleagues. Attacking in particular the use of *benshi* and female impersonators, he called on filmmakers to experiment with new shooting techniques and stressed the importance of acknowledging the particular potentialities of screen drama.[31]

The contrast between the stage and screen was a special concern for Tanizaki, and he continued praising the newer medium at the expense of the theater even after his involvement in film had ended. After his first experience directing a stage production in 1922, he admitted that he found directing films more engaging (he had directed portions of *Hinamatsuri no yoru* [*The Night of the Doll Festival*] at Taikatsu the previous year).[32] Two years later he commented that movies were more interesting than plays and that he was even happier when he heard that his play *Honmoku yawa* (*Honmoku Nights*) was to be made into a film than when the play itself had opened on stage. This essay, "Eigaka sareta *Honmoku yawa*" ("The Film Adaptation of *Honmoku Nights*"), begins with an explanation of how he had even obtained special permission from the editor to write what was probably the first article on film to appear in the magazine *Engeki shinchō.*[33]

Tanizaki made his readers aware of his involvement in film production. When *Amateur Club* was completed in November 1920, he informed the readers of *Chūō kōron* of his decision to stop working on the novel *Kōjin,* which the journal was serializing at the time. Tanizaki stated that he had come to the realization that his participation in film required more time and effort than he had expected. He added that he firmly believed such work was more than a passing fancy and that he considered film to be just as important as literature. He even commented that someday he might make a film adaptation of *Kōjin* itself.[34] In "Eiga zakkan" ("Random Thoughts on Film"), an essay published in the March issue of *Shinshōsetsu* one year after he entered Taikatsu, Tanizaki provided his readers with a description of his first visit to the studio and his reaction to the films he saw there. And a few months after Tanizaki in turn quit Taikatsu, his short entry in the January 1922 edition of *Shinchō* implied that he would be channeling his energy back into his writing during the coming year. While admitting that he would like to continue working in film as well as literature, he acknowledged that, unlike writing, filmmaking was not a solitary endeavor, and unfortunately there did not seem to be any project that might be suitable for him to work on at the time.[35]

Of all the references Tanizaki made about his experiences at Taikatsu, "Sono yorokobi o kansha sezaru o enai" ("I Must Be Grateful for that Happiness," December 1920), published one month after the completion of *Amateur Club,* best reveals the extent of his commitment to film production at the time. In this essay Tanizaki describes how he and Kurihara developed the story for their first collaboration. Their determination to bring contemporary subject matter to the screen is evident in the following excerpt: "First we tried making an experimental five-reel comedy. In my opinion, a great number of the films that are ordinarily produced in this country are too far removed from the actual conditions and customs of present—day Japan. We made this comedy with this concern in mind. Using day-to-day life as a model, we have tried to show, as naturally as possible, the lively and cheerful milieu of a group of young men and women."[36]

It was after the completion of *Amateur Club* that Tanizaki gave himself over full-time to screenwriting, and in this essay he expressed his enthusiasm for the task. Even at this early stage in Tanizaki's involvement in film, he indicated an appreciation for the responsibilities of the screenwriter in the production process and the recognition of screenwriting as a profession:

An author to provide a story and a scenario writer to adapt it are both necessary to make a film; for me to make my own art into a film and keep it my own work as much as possible, however, I must do more than simply provide the original story. I must adapt it myself. In short, it will be of value only if I can conceive of it not as a story but as the scenes of a moving picture. I am now training as a scenario writer with Kurihara and the actors as my teachers, but in the near future I think I will be able to write by myself. If I fail to do so, my involvement in film will have been meaningless.

The second story I am now writing, *The Radiance of the Moon,* is a tragedy with mysterious overtones . . . and I am confident it will make a good film. For practice, I am dividing it up into a scenario as much as possible. I keenly feel that there is no other way to express myself than to write a scenario by myself. I confess that I put my pen to paper with a happiness that I have not felt recently. I cannot help but be grateful for becoming involved in moving pictures, which I have loved for a long time.[37]

"Sono yorokobi o kansha sezaru o enai" appeared in the moving picture magazine *Katsudō kurabu,* but all three surviving Taikatsu scripts that Tanizaki described as having been written without Kurihara's collaboration were published in magazines that were not considered film periodicals. *The Radiance of the Moon* (generally considered Tanizaki's first scenario after *Amateur Club*), was serialized in *Gendai* beginning in January 1921. The first thirty-eight scenes of his second script, *The Night of the Doll Festival,* appeared in *Shinengei* in 1923, and the magazine published a longer version (seventy-nine scenes) in September 1924. *The Lust of the White Serpent,* his third and final Taikatsu script, appeared in *Suzu no oto* in April 1922, with a preface by Tanizaki describing his role as scriptwriter in the production of the film.[38]

This was an unusual practice at a time when film scripts were just on the verge of being recognized as an important part of the production process, but very few members of the industry (including the writers themselves) yet considered them significant enough to preserve once they had fulfilled their function. In addition to lending importance to the concept of writing for the screen, the appearance of Tanizaki's film scripts in such general interest magazines saved them from the fate suffered by countless other silent scripts, which disappeared in the tumult of postproduction. They survive as enjoyable reading and as rare documents of an important moment in the history of Japanese cinema.

Itō Daisuke, who began his screenwriting career at Osanai Kaoru's Shōchiku Cinema Institute, has given us a detailed description of the more common fate of the silent film script. Itō's account of the manner in which film scripts were written and distributed for use during the silent era suggests that there was a relatively standard procedure similar to the method introduced by Kaeriyama. According to Itō, silent scripts were handwritten on sheets of lined paper, and five carbon copies (the number of copies increased to ten by the end of the decade) were made for distribution to the director, assistant director, chief cameraman, lead actor or actress, and the production department. The director usually wrote in the continuity on his copy of the script and used it as a shooting script. After shooting the film, the director and cameraman used a copy of the script once again when they edited the negative and separated sequences according to color for the toning process.[39]

Itō relates that at the time it was not customary to keep a ledger during the editing process, and the instructions for dying the scenes (blue for night, amber for evening, and pink for love scenes) were marked in colored pencil on the script. The director also jotted down on the script any other pertinent

153

directions he had for the processing laboratory, and the pieces of negative, together with the corresponding segments of script, would be sent to the lab to be tinted in separate batches according to color. The processed print eventually returned from the lab; the script, which by this point had been reduced to scattered fragments, did not.[40] In light of this, we are indeed fortunate to be able to compare Tanizaki's three Taikatsu film scripts, which reveal his development as a screenwriter in the course of only one year.

TANIZAKI'S TAIKATSU FILM SCRIPTS

A discussion of Tanizaki's first published scenario, *The Radiance of the Moon,* must begin with a disclaimer. In his essay "I Must Be Grateful for that Happiness," Tanizaki refers to *The Radiance of the Moon* as if it were his first independent effort at screenwriting after collaborating with Kurihara on *Amateur Club,* for which his primary contribution was the original story.

Actually, Tanizaki is often credited with having written the lost script for *Katsushika sunago* (*The Sands of Katsushika,* 1920), a three-reel film based on Izumi Kyōka's novel of the same name, which opened a month and a half after *Amateur Club.*[41] In a tribute to Kurihara written shortly after the director's death, however, Tanizaki attributed the work to Kurihara. He claimed that he wrote only a hasty first draft after having read the original work.[42] Several factors suggest this is true, but it is not possible to assess the extent of Tanizaki's contribution as both the script and the film itself are believed lost. Tanizaki wrote that Izumi Kyōka, who rarely went to the movies, liked the film,[43] and Tanaka Eizō was so impressed that he could still vividly describe one sequence (including an intertitle) over twenty years later.[44] Other than such anecdotes we know very little about the work.

Several features of *The Radiance of the Moon* do suggest it was a transitional piece. Particularly in comparison with Tanizaki's subsequent scripts, this appears to have been the work in which the writer first wrestled with the transition from literary prose to writing for the screen. In Tanizaki's collected works a distinction is made between *The Radiance of the Moon,* a "film drama" and *The Lust of the White Serpent,* a "film script," and the former has been described as more of a pantomime than a screenplay.[45] Although Tanizaki included a number of dialogue intertitles in *The Radiance of the Moon,* its overall structure and style bear little resemblance to a continuity-style film script. Tanizaki did use technical terms such as "C.U." (close-up),[46] "L.S." (long shot), "B.G." (background), "F.G." (foreground), "overlap" (overlap dissolve), "dissolve in," and "dissolve out" throughout and included an explanation of most of these terms, and he occasionally distinguished between interior and exterior action. He also included thirty-two intertitles:

154

Katsushika sunago (*The Sands of Katsushika*), directed by Thomas Kurihara in 1920 from a script attributed to Tanizaki. Courtesy Kawakita Memorial Film Institute.

eleven expository titles, labeled *taitoru* ("title" in phonetic script) and twenty-one dialogue titles, labeled *kotoba sōnyū* ("dialogue inserts"), both terms introduced by Kurihara in *Amateur Club*. Tanizaki stopped short of dissecting the scenes of *The Radiance of the Moon* into numbered shots, and as a result it lacks the clarity and coherence desirable for practical use. It was never made into a film.

Tanizaki's apparent preoccupation with the narrative passages in *The Radiance of the Moon* hampered the development of effective dialogue, and detracted from the overall balance of the work. On the other hand, precisely because of these carefully written passages, it is possible to regard the style of language in *The Radiance of the Moon* as more sophisticated, in terms of being more literary, than the telegraphic tenor of *The Glory of Life*. Criticizing the tendency of screenwriters even today to take the need for conciseness to Spartan extremes, the screenwriter Yasumi Toshio has implied that Tanizaki was the first to realize the importance of well-written exposition with *The Radiance of the Moon*.[47] Yasumi contends that there is no such thing as a screenplay that is "too literary" because a screenplay is not a "musical score" written with only one "instrument (the dialogue)" in mind.[48]

155

For this reason he defends *The Radiance of the Moon*'s abundant descriptive passages, and calls upon present-day screenwriters to follow Tanizaki's example in recognizing the value of words:

> A screenwriter must have the artistic technique of both a playwright (dialogue) and a writer of prose (narration), and in both the dialogue and the narration, the writer's weapon is the Word. With words, the writer unsparingly writes out the entire content and visual appearance of the film. This obviously has nothing to do with the tempo of the film itself.
>
> No doubt there are diverse opinions concerning the value of the words Tanizaki used in *The Radiance of the Moon,* whether the reader likes them or does not like them, or whether they are well-chosen or not. Yet even so, Tanizaki's words are rich, and we can well understand how much importance he placed in them.[49]

In fact, Tanizaki's opulent narration contains details that reveal he was writing with both the camera and the final projected screen image in mind. There are, for example, specific instructions for frame composition, such as a medium shot that "should include the kneecaps,"[50] a "door left wide open,"[51] and a view down a mountain road that includes "five or six houses in the distance,"[52] as well as simple instructions concerning the position of the camera in relation to the subject. All these passages are set off from the rest of the text by parentheses. Of even greater interest are the frequent and detailed references to lighting. Such references recur throughout Tanizaki's subsequent scripts and reveal his interest in this aspect of production.

Just as the title *The Radiance of the Moon* implies, light plays a notably important role in this script. The main character is a woman for whom moonlight holds fatal consequences: bathed in it she becomes so excited that she turns murderous and strangles men with her gold necklace before she is herself consumed by her own excessive ecstasy. In addition to evocative descriptions of the woman's moonlit transformation (one particularly striking passage calls for a shot of the woman's wet kimono shimmering in the moonlight),[53] Tanizaki again includes detailed instructions set off from the rest of the text in parentheses. In one instance, for example, he specifically calls for the use of natural lighting ("The lamp should be off, with the morning light dimly filtering through the openings between the shutters"),[54] while elsewhere he notes, "a dull lamp that gives off a rustic light glows in only one corner of the room," adding, "Be sure to include the lampshade in the shot."[55]

The Night of the Doll Festival, Tanizaki's second script and the first to be made into a film, contrasts sharply with *The Radiance of the Moon* both formally and thematically. This time Tanizaki broke the narrative down into numbered shots, resulting in something that more closely resembles Kuri-hara's continuity-style script for *Amateur Club*. A fairy tale about a child's toys coming to life, *The Night of the Doll Festival* is sparsely written. The shot descriptions, lines of dialogue, and titles consist of only one or two lines at most. The film itself was four reels long, and the surviving version of the script, which appears to be incomplete, consists of only seventy-nine shots and eighteen intertitles. Thirteen of these are expository titles; the remaining five are dialogue titles, most of which appear during the final scenes of the extant version of the script, a dream sequence in which the child's toys move about and talk to each other as she sleeps. Again, Tanizaki's use of the terms "title" and "dialogue insert" for the intertitles is identical to the format Kuri-hara used in *Amateur Club,* as are the lines of dialogue that did not appear as titles but were included for the actors' benefit, a common practice in writing silent film scripts. In addition, Tanizaki followed Kurihara's example by indicating the location for each shot, as well as classifying all the shots as "interior" or "exterior."

The directions for camera angles in *The Night of the Doll Festival* include close-ups, "overlap" shots (overlap dissolves), fade transitions, inserts, and iris shots. Here too Tanizaki incorporated directions for camera position and frame composition (for example, "shoot in the direction of the sitting room,"[56] "Aiko [the child] need not be included in the frame"[57]). The most conspicuous reference to lighting is a request for a gradual dimming of the sleeping child's room shortly before the climactic dream sequence (according to Tanizaki's directions, the dream sequence itself was to begin with the room slowly growing bright again, "emphasizing the transition from reality to dream").[58] Nor did Tanizaki overlook set details: a description of the contents of the child's toy box, for example, specifically calls for the inclusion of a toy car (in the film itself the car apparently reappeared during the child's dream as the vehicle that carried her to an imaginary land deep within some mountains).[59]

Tanizaki might have felt it necessary to pay such close attention to detail under the circumstances. Although Kurihara is listed as the director, Tanizaki admitted that he directed much of the film,[60] which was shot in his own home and starred his young daughter, Ayuko. He also played an active role in the arrangement of the props,[61] and was reportedly even in charge of handling the toys during the scenes in which they became animated.[62]

The Lust of the White Serpent, Tanizaki's third and final script at Taikatsu, was his most successful attempt at a continuity-style format in the manner of Kurihara's *Amateur Club.* In general, Tanizaki's approach in this script is more consciously systematic and detailed: there are detailed set and character descriptions and directions for camera angles (including a high angle point-of-view shot that calls for a composition resembling a painting of

The cast and crew of *Hinamatsuri no yoru* (*The Night of the Doll's Festival*) on location at Tanizaki's Odawara residence. Seated in the foreground (*left to right*), cameraman Inami, Ozaki Shōtaro, Kurihara (holding a copy of the script), Hayama Michiko, Tanizaki, Okada Tokihiko, Tanizaki's wife Chiyo and daughter Ayu, and Chiyo's grandmother (*far right*). Courtesy of Fujita Mitsuo.

the Tosa school,[63] a "panoramic view" pan,[64] and a "double exposure"[65]). Close-ups are used consistently to introduce the various characters, and there is even a request for real fishermen to be used in the opening scene. Tanizaki used art titles, but he used them selectively. They appear only twice: in a brief expository title later in the film,[66] and in a poem from the *Man'yōshū* (the eighth-century anthology of poetry), which appears in the story by Ueda Akinari that was used as source material.[67] Appearing early in the script (between shots 13 and 14), the title establishes the mood for the mysterious tale about to unfold.

In this script Tanizaki perfected the shot numbering style that he first attempted in *The Night of the Doll Festival.* As in the script for *Amateur Club,* each shot number is followed by "exterior" or "interior" according to the location, which appears last. In addition, the number of scenes and intertitles conspicuously resembles that of *Amateur Club.* In comparison to the 265 shots in *Amateur Club, The Lust of the White Serpent* is divided into 283

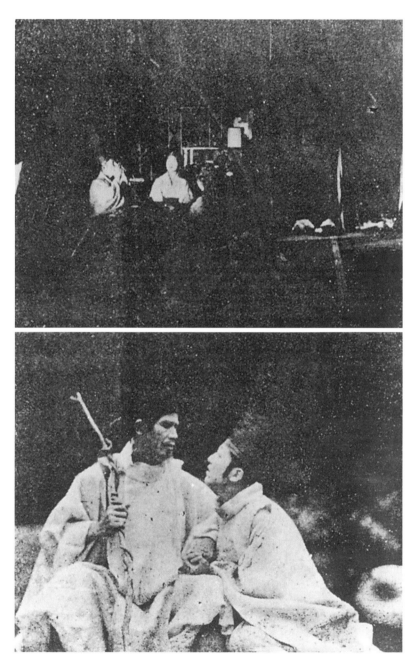

Two scenes from *Jasei no in* (*The Lust of the White Serpent*), directed by Thomas Kurihara, 1921 from a script by Tanizaki. *Kinema junpō,* 21 September 1921. From Makino, ed., *Fukkokuban Kinema junpō.*

shots. It features twenty-five expository titles and forty-one dialogue titles, a ratio that is nearly identical to the twenty-five expository titles and forty-four dialogue titles in *Amateur Club.*

The Lust of the White Serpent was not an unqualified success, and it has been credited with accelerating Taikatsu's decision to abandon its experimental pure film agenda. Perhaps the problem with the completed film had something to do with the fact that at ten reels—twice the length of *Amateur Club* and the most ambitious attempt at pure film to date—it had a script with approximately the same number of scenes. In Japan at the time, two hundred-odd scenes was considered to be an exceptional number for a five-reel film like *Amateur Club,* but even the pace of this relatively innovative and popularly acclaimed film was criticized by some as too sluggish.[68] The script for *The Lust of the White Serpent* suggests a considerably slower tempo, and the film fared no better in this respect. Tanizaki had succeeded in perfecting a consistent continuity-style technique, and with its profusion of slow transitions (irises and fades, a characteristic of Tanizaki's scripts), compact yet suggestive narrative passages, and atmospheric landscape the script is the most pleasurable to read. However impressive the magnificent sets and costumes might have been, critics found the individual scenes too long, the pace too slow, and the camera too static.[69] Tanaka Jun'ichirō has suggested the film adhered too closely to the original source material, which gave it a lumbering quality accentuated by the awkward positioning of several of the intertitles. (The segment translated in the appendix roughly corresponds to the first few pages of the original story, and the resemblance is striking in both narrative situation and tone.) Tanaka adds that he found the acting impeccable, however (no matter what else might be wrong with a Kurihara film, the acting was usually praised), and concludes that Kurihara's failing health might have been to blame for the film's weaknesses.[70]

When *The Lust of the White Serpent* was published in *Suzu no oto* in April 1922, Tanizaki wrote a short introduction in which he explained his role as the scenario writer and, more generally, the function of the silent scenario in the production process. We know from the reminiscences of actors who worked with Tanizaki and Kurihara that the working relationship among all the members of the Taikatsu staff was close,[71] and Tanizaki's introduction provides a glimpse of this. It also reveals the importance he placed on his role as the writer and an important member of the production crew. Apparently feeling that his responsibility as the author of the script did not end with the completion of a final working draft, he continued to participate on the set even when doing so involved traveling to various locations.[72] In his introduction, Tanizaki even expresses a desire to make readers more familiar with the medium and the scenario-writing process in particular. It was in fact this desire that had prompted him to publish the script:

> This script is a dramatization of Ueda Akinari's *Ugetsu monogatari* [*Tales of Moonlight and Rain*] written for the Taishō film company. We set out in April in order to film the script, traveling to Kyoto, Nara, Hatsuse, and Hakone. We then returned to the studio in Yokohama to film the interior scenes. The shooting was finally completed four months later, in July of that year. During that time I was continuously in the company of the actors working under the director, Kurihara Tōmasu, and I often recall the many experiences and pleasant times I had with them on location.
>
> Since its premiere at the Yūrakuza in September of last year, *The Lust of the White Serpent* has been traveling the circuit of movie theaters in major cities throughout Japan, and many of you may already have had the opportunity to see the film. Although many aspects of the film naturally remain unsatisfactory, it is the first attempt in Japan to adapt classical literature into pure film drama, and for this reason alone I feel great satisfaction at having played a part in its completion. Film scripts by nature are not very suitable as reading material, in comparison with theatrical plays, but if those of you who have read Akinari's original work or have seen the film—or plan to see it, for it will certainly be shown again in Tokyo in the near future—read this script with Akinari's original story or the film in mind, you will notice that it has its own interesting qualities.
>
> I am often asked how one writes a film script. Just now the moving pictures are very popular, and many people would like to know more about them. In the hope that it might contribute to the appreciation of film in general, I have decided to use this opportunity to publish this scenario in *Suzu no oto*. Recently even the film world has been affected by the economic depression, and it shows signs of stagnating. I will be grateful if my work provides even the slightest stimulus.
>
> May I remind you that this script is slightly different from the finished film. No matter what provisions are made beforehand in the script, it is common for even better ideas to come to mind while shooting the film. When limited by natural topography or certain buildings on location, one must inevitably choose alternatives. Such changes occur frequently. Perhaps it would be interesting to compare such differences.[73]

Tanizaki did more than comment on the distinct characteristics of a film script in his introduction to *The Lust of the White Serpent.* For "cinema fans," he included at the end a list with definitions of the technical terms (C.U., L.S., dissolve in, dissolve out, iris in, iris out, double exposure, overlap, background, foreground) that he had carefully and systematically used throughout the script.[74] (A similar, although not identical, list of terms had appeared on the front page of the first installment of *Amateur Club* when it was serialized in *Katsudō zasshi* a year earlier.) Although Tanizaki left

Taikatsu several months before the script was published, it was obvious that before leaving the studio he had become acquainted with some fundamental camera work. His preoccupation with such details as the explanation of technical jargon no doubt gladdened the hearts of the "cinema fans" to whom his explanations were addressed. Iijima Tadashi, for example, a young university student at the time, has pointed out that the film diary he kept in those days consisted mostly of notations on every occurrence of a new technique that he came across during his visits to the movie theaters.[75] Although Tanizaki had already left Taikatsu, the preface to *The Lust of the White Serpent* suggests a lingering interest in the course of pure film.

AFTER TAIKATSU

It was perhaps precisely because all three of Tanizaki's Taikatsu scripts relied so greatly on the quality of the medium that most fascinated him—its technical capability to present dreams or illusions on screen—that the results were never completely satisfactory. Even *The Lust of the White Serpent,* the most successful of the three, fell short of Tanizaki's expectations, and it has been suggested that he ultimately lost interest in production largely because of the gap between his vision and the completed films.[76] We can only begin to speculate how different Tanizaki's experience at Taikatsu might have been had film technology been as complex as it is today.

Before leaving Yokohama for the Kansai region, Tanizaki wrote at least one more script for a production that was apparently not associated with Taikatsu, *Shitakiri suzume (The Sparrow Who Lost His Tongue).* Tanizaki vaguely remembered the film as having been made a year after *Amateur Club.*[77] It opened at the Asakusa Dai Tokyo theater on 1 February 1923. Henry Kotani produced, shot, and directed the film, a three-reel version of a well-known children's story starring Kurihara and Tanizaki's daughter, by now a veteran after having appeared in both *Amateur Club* and *The Night of the Doll Festival.* There is also a record of Tanizaki's participation in *Zoku Amachua kurabu (Amateur Club, Part Two,* 1923), which was described in *Kinema junpō* as a collaborative effort with Kotani and Kurihara.[78]

There were in fact several factors behind Tanizaki's retirement from Taikatsu in November 1921, including Kurihara's deteriorating health and Taikatsu's decision, one month earlier, to forego support of the financially risky pure film in favor of *shinpa* film production. In later years his own explanation was that he just drifted away "naturally" as Kurihara's health declined and the studio began having difficulties.[79]

Even after he left Taikatsu, Tanizaki never entirely lost interest in film. In 1935, musing that perhaps he had finally lost all enthusiasm for film because lately he rarely went to see even foreign films anymore, he concluded that he did not truly believe he ever could lose his interest in films.[80] He remained a critic of the Japanese industry, however, attributing his reluctance to return to screenwriting to the poor state of the industry as much as to his having discontinued his "studies" before the introduction of sound technology.[81] Yasumi Toshio recalls visiting Tanizaki repeatedly when he was working on an adaptation of one of Tanizaki's works. According to Yasumi, Tanizaki modestly declined to make any suggestions, saying only, "I'll leave it to you. Please do a good job."[82] Tanizaki continued to write about film at least until the 1950s (he died in 1965). He went through periods of profound disillusionment with the Japanese film industry, but his articles, written twenty to thirty years after his tenure at Taikatsu, reveal that just as he never lost his fascination with film, he never entirely lost the critical interest (and loyalties) he had adopted during his involvement in production.

A good example is his review of Taniguchi Senkichi's newly released *Akatsuki no dassō* (*Escape at Dawn,* with a script by Kurosawa Akira), published in the *Tōkyō shinbun* in March 1950. After confessing that he happened to see this Japanese film only because there were no theaters specializing in imported films in Atami, where he lived during the winter months, he praised the tense atmosphere and tempo of the film, singling out the final scene, which he describes in detail, as being particularly well made. Of even greater interest is his observation that although the plot, the story of "a flare of passion on the battlefield," resembled that of *Morocco* and *Dishonored,* the director skillfully avoided turning the film into a mere remake of such films:[83]

> Although the plot is not unusual, the structure of the story and the manner in which the incidents are arranged, the scenes are cut, and the actors are used are outstanding. In sum, the director and production staff put forth their very best. If this film had been entrusted to a mediocre director and staff, they probably would have made it into the kind of rubbish that has been made until now. I have secretly thought that the uninteresting nature of Japanese films was primarily the responsibility of directors. I am glad this film proves this to be true.[84]

Even his conviction that a film must speak to a contemporary audience—an important motivation behind the creation of *Amateur Club*—is still apparent: "the most favorable aspect of this film is that although even we [intellectuals] can sympathize with it, it does not assume smug, artistic airs and has a popular appeal that makes it understandable to anyone who sees it. At any rate, on behalf of our film industry, we should be grateful for the appearance of people with minds capable of making such a film."[85]

In his study of Tanizaki's association with film, Chiba Nobuo suggests that the writer's brief involvement in production can be interpreted as either an expression of energy in the prime of life, or as his only recourse during a severe literary slump. Chiba concludes that in either case, it was clearly both an extension of his interest in the West, and an experiment to try to achieve something that could not be done in literature.[86] Regardless what the experience meant to Tanizaki, it was of great consequence to film fans. At the very least, it raised the medium's cultural cachet, as did Osanai Kaoru's presence at Shōchiku. Tanizaki also contributed to forging new genres. *Amateur Club* was an attempt to caricature Keystone comedies, and the subsequent Taikatsu films based on Tanizaki's scripts brought further developments to the literary genre, first introduced by Kaeriyama, that became a hallmark of the silent Japanese film and one of the strongest foundations of Japanese film tradition.[87]

Unfortunately, Tanizaki's reputation as a screenwriter and an important figure in the pure film movement has not stood the test of time. To begin with, the scripts he completed at Taikatsu represent only a meager output in comparison with his vast literary oeuvre. The accomplishments of Tanizaki and Kurihara at Taikatsu also tend to be overshadowed by the concurrent developments at Shōchiku. A branch of an established theatrical company, the Shōchiku film studio quickly outdistanced and eventually absorbed Taikatsu; Asano, the industrial entrepreneur who financed Taikatsu, was no doubt imaginative and adventurous, but he was still a mere dilettante in the entertainment field. And although Osanai (who clashed with the Shōchiku management from the start) vacated his prestigious post even more swiftly than Tanizaki, it was Shōchiku, by virtue of outlasting its smaller rival, that swelled its ranks in the early 1920s. Shōchiku has been increasingly beset by financial difficulties since the 1980s, but as the studio that fostered directors like Ozu Yasujirō and Yamada Yōji, its name has been synonymous with the contemporary drama genre since the silent period.[88] Finally, whereas none of the films produced at the Taikatsu studio has survived, *Souls on the Road,* produced under Osanai's supervision, can still be viewed today.

By 1920 an increasing number of literary figures were expressing an interest in the moving pictures, and when Tanizaki and Osanai went one step further by taking an active part in production, others decided to do the same. Thus Osanai, for example, was able to assemble at his acting school an impressive group that included the novelist, poet, and playwright Kume Masao and the playwright Matsui Shōyō, both considerably successful writers at the time. To an extent, Tanizaki also set a precedent for established writers to write for the screen in later years. The Shinkankaku-ha (New Sensationalist School) writer Yokomitsu Riichi enlisted three colleagues (Kawabata Yasunari, Kataoka Teppei, and Iketani Shinzaburō) to collaborate with Kinugasa Teinosuke on his script for *Kurutta ippeiji* (*A Page of Madness/A Page out of Order*), produced in 1926 by the Shinkankakuha eiga renmei

(The New Sensationalist School Film League). It was one of the most extraordinary productions at the time: when it opened at a Tokyo theater specializing in foreign films, the intellectual audience responded enthusiastically to the startling flashbacks and unusual editing. Both the film's macabre mise-en-scène and loosely drawn story were reminiscent of *The Cabinet of Dr. Caligari,* which had enjoyed great success in Japan five years earlier.[89] Writers in Japan have continued to contribute to filmmaking; the more celebrated cases are Satomi Ton's collaboration with Ozu Yasujirō (*Higanbana [Equinox Flower]*), Shiina Rinzō's screenplays for Gosho Heinosuke's *Ai to shi no tanima* (*The Valley between Love and Death*) and *Niwatori wa futatabi naku* (*The Cock Crows Again*), and Abe Kōbō's screenplays for Kobayashi Masaki and Teshigahara Hiroshi, *Kabe atsuki heya* (*The Thick-Walled Room*), *Otoshi ana* (*The Trap*), *Suna no onna* (*Woman in the Dunes*), and *Tanin no kao* (*The Face of Another*).

It is uncertain to what extent Tanizaki himself recognized the significance of his contribution to the development of pure film at Taikatsu, but he at least acknowledged that his familiarity with foreign films, a result of his countless excursions to the film theaters that specialized in screening them, was an important consideration. Years after he retired from the industry, for example, he commented that although Kaeriyama shared the same aspirations—to rival the ubiquitous popularity of Matsunosuke and the *shinpa* film—he failed because he did not know American films well enough.[90] For the most part, however, in his own recollections of his Taikatsu experience he modestly gave most of the credit for the studio's accomplishments to Kurihara who, he claimed, supervised every aspect of production from the script, direction, and camera work to the editing and tinting of the final print.[91]

But it would be a mistake to assume Tanizaki's legacy goes no further than the recognition that went with his name. When Kurihara returned to Japan to embark on the production of a new kind of Japanese film, he found a powerful ally in Tanizaki. Following Kaeriyama's lead, the writer had already published a blueprint for the modernization of the native film in his 1917 article, "The Present and Future of the Moving Pictures." In this article Tanizaki focused on the most urgent concerns of the reform movement. He discussed the importance of introducing innovative camera technique and more realistic stories, and the need to develop a naturalistic style of acting. Above all, he stressed the artistic virtues of the medium, and demanded the replacement of irresponsible managers—who were generally perceived in most pure film discourse to be pandering to the demands of the *benshi*—with managers who recognized this attribute. Many of these concerns, mutually acknowledged by Kurihara, were later addressed in the Taikatsu prospectus and, beginning with the production of *Amateur Club,* reappeared as important factors in the production of Taikatsu pure film.

5

Journalistic Discourse and Tanizaki's "The Present and Future of the Moving Pictures"

WHEN TANIZAKI'S "THE Present and Future of the Moving Pictures" appeared in the pages of *Shinshōsetsu* in September 1917, discussion of the artistic potential of the Japanese film and recognition of the new medium as distinct from its theatrical antecedents—two basic themes of Kaeriyama's *The Production and Photography of Moving Picture Drama* published that July—had reached a peak among advocates of reform. It is therefore not surprising that in this article, his first and most comprehensive consideration of the new medium, Tanizaki also addressed these two fundamental concerns of the pure film movement while elaborating on his perception of those attributes of film that would continue to fascinate him in the years ahead. In addition to promoting the basic principles mentioned above, (both of which later provided the motivation for pure film production at Taikatsu), the article introduced the readers of general magazines like *Shinshōsetsu* to other pertinent issues, equally relevant to the efforts of Kurihara and Tanizaki at Taikatsu, that had been under debate in the pages of domestic film magazines since the early 1910s. A comparison of the first year of publication of *Katsudō shashin zasshi* (*Moving Picture Magazine*), *Katsudō no sekai* (*Movie World*), and *Katsudō gahō* (*Movie Magazine*), three representative film magazines that first appeared between 1915 and 1917, will make clear the importance of Tanizaki's article, and help illustrate developments in the pure film movement shortly before Kurihara returned to Japan to promote his plans for a new kind of Japanese film.[1]

FILM JOURNALISM AND THE PURE FILM MOVEMENT, 1913–1917

According to Iijima Tadashi, the earliest public venues for pure film debate were the free theater handbills or programs distributed by individual movie theaters throughout the country. These programs varied from theater to theater, but they were generally about four pages long and the size of a small pamphlet.[2] The custom of selling larger programs in the theater lobby for individual features is still popular in Japan, but the contemporary version contains a synopsis of the story, interviews, an explanation of the production of the film, and commercial advertisements; an impressive publication with glossy, full-page color photographs, it can cost more than the price of admission itself. In contrast, the programs during the early years of the industry were smaller, and they were distributed for free by the attendant collecting tickets at the entrance to the theater. Although they carried a synopsis of the film being featured, their main attraction for moving picture fans like Iijima were contributions from fellow viewers commenting on newly released pictures and the management policies of the entertainment industry. These programs (*puro* or *chirashi*) were collected, traded, and even sold secondhand at special *eiga zakka* ("film notions") stores. Readers also contributed comments on articles featured in earlier programs. These small publications, according to Iijima, were a "battleground for debate by fans throughout Japan,[3] and contributed to the gradual popularization of the pure film concept and the general debate over the relative virtues or deficiencies of imported and domestic films.

These free programs were a phenomenon that appeared after 1903, when the first movie theater, the Asakusa Denkikan, was established.[4] Publications that dealt with information related to the new medium, however, predated the beginning of film production in Japan. The film historian Makino Mamoru points out that even before the Kinetoscope and Cinematograph were imported to Japan, the Japanese had been aware of these discoveries—together with many other technical developments taking place abroad toward the end of the century—through magazines; thus, the content of the earliest trade-related publications retained an instructional nature, serving to enlighten the reader of the innovative advancements of Western technology. The publication of studio-sponsored fan magazines, originating with the start of domestic production, can be traced back to the magic lantern product catalogues of import companies like Yoshizawa (according to Makino, film products outnumbered magic lantern products for the first time in the Yoshizawa Company catalogue in 1907). These were joined by small-scale publications by individuals or study groups (for example, the Katsusha kōyūkai, or "Friends of Moving Pictures," to which Kaeriyama belonged) and privately owned magazines intended for general readership.[5]

Studio-sponsored publications such as *Katsudō shashin* (*Moving Pictures*, M. Pathe Co., 1909), *Katsudō shashinkai* (*The Cinematograph*, Yoshizawa Co., 1909), and *Katsudō taimusu* (*Movie Times*, Yokota Co., 1910) are generally regarded as the earliest film publications in Japan. Only *Katsudō shashinkai* survives as an example of such publications today. First issued in June 1909, is became a monthly with the second issue (published in October). Komatsu Hiroshi makes the point that the magazine sustained the appearance of a link to the overseas market (it featured the English title *The Cinematograph* from the first issue on, and the subscription price and information appears in English at the back of the magazine beginning with the May 1910 issue), and considers the possibility of its having been shipped overseas.[6] *Katsudō shashinkai* featured articles from a wide variety of contributors, including journalists, company employees, literary and cultural figures and fans—a distinctively eclectic mix that continued to be a characteristic of subsequent film publications. For Komatsu, the degree to which *Katsudō shashinkai* was clearly oriented to spectators rather than to producers or distributors (based on the number of articles reflecting the opinions of the individual contributors) is evidence of a fan basis for early film literature that can be considered unique to Japan.[7] In comparison, contemporary publications appearing in the United States—*Variety* and *Moving Picture World,* for example—were trade publications. This raises an issue of terminology of the nature discussed in chapter 1. As Komatsu points out, fan-oriented literature does seem to have been dominant at least from this period on, but the particular mix of contributors complicates attempts to classify these publications. Established in 1913 by a group of former *Katsudō shashinkai* contributors, *Kinema Record,* for example, was clearly fan-motivated, and yet it classified itself, in English, as Japan's only (or alternatively, "foremost") trade publication. Using advertisements as a clue to classification only complicates the issue: for example, ancillary industry services are conspicuous in *Kinema Record,* but they also appear in *Katsudō shashinkai.*

An important supplement to such early publications as *Katsudō shashinkai* were contemporary newspaper articles. Most notably, Yoshiyama Kyokkō, considered a pioneer film critic, was writing a weekly column on moving pictures in the *Miyako shinbun* as early as 1911. In 1913, after the demise of *Katsudō shashinkai* when the Yoshizawa Company became part of the Nikkatsu merger, a chain of minor publications led to the first issue of *Kinema Record,* generally considered the first significant collective attempt at serious film criticism in Japan. Debate concerning the reformation of the Japanese film industry appeared primarily in its pages, but it is interesting to note its resemblance to *Katsudō shashinkai.* It retained the appearance of an attempt to stay connected to the foreign market, taking this aspect even

Copy of the cover of the first issue of *Katsudō shashinkai* (*The Cinematograph*), June 1909. From Makino, ed., *Fukkokuban Katsudō shashinkai*.

Ugo Masulli & Co, located in Yokohama, were one of many film distribution concerns to advertise regularly in *Kinema Record*. From *Kinema Record,* 10 September 1914. From Makino, ed., *Fukkokuban Kinema rekōdo.*

further with ads appealing to the local branch representatives of foreign distribution companies and articles appearing in English. Even the tenor of the contributions bears a similarity to those of its predecessor, although, as Iwamoto Kenji points out, one marked difference between the two publications is *Kinema Record*'s more negative view of Japanese films.[8] In fact, *Kinema Record* evolved from Kaeriyama Norimasa's habit, beginning in 1911, of keeping a notebook of the films he saw, and then as a kind of index to foreign films.[9]

The magazine was discontinued when Kaeriyama entered Tenkatsu in 1917, but it exerted a strong influence on several subsequent publications. *Katsudō shashin zasshi* (1915), *Katsudō no sekai* (1916), and *Katsudō gahō* (1917) were among the film magazines that appeared during the six years between the founding of *Kinema Record* and the debut in 1919 of its successor, *Kinema junpō,* the first successful publication of its kind and still a major publication today. These publications catered to a broader audience, but the first year of each publication reveals *Kinema Record*'s influence in both format and tone. Features of these publications illuminate audience preferences and inclinations, and provide a view of contemporary film culture and its incongruities during this transitional period.

Like *Kinema Record,* all three magazines contained transcriptions or synopses of imported and Japanese films playing in Tokyo theaters (these transcriptions were the main features of *Katsudō shashin zasshi*). *Katsudō no sekai* and the early issues of *Katsudō gahō* feature transcriptions of Japanese films including *shinpa* films, period films, and chain dramas. The titles of the foreign films—detective films, comedies, French and English dramas, Italian historical epics—also reflect the popular preferences of the time. Transcriptions of serials are conspicuous in the wake of the immense popularity in the fall of 1915 of the first imported American serials, *The Master Key* (Robert Z. Leonard, 1914), and *The Broken Coin* (Francis Ford, 1914).

The practice of transcribing the continuity of films for study was initiated by young film fans (usually students in their middle to late teens) who regularly contributed to the small-scale publications that predated *Kinema Record.* Many of these contributors became members of the "Friends of Moving Pictures," and submitted their work to *Kinema Record.* The practice endured into the late 1920s and early 1930s, when novice writers submitted transcriptions of foreign films (together with a detailed analysis of their structure) to the publication *Eiga kagaku kenkyū* (*Scientific Film Research,* first published in 1928). These transcriptions had a special significance for the pure film enthusiasts, who admittedly used these postproduction continuities as blueprints for their own experimental work. The transcription itself was a tedious process, involving repeated viewing of a film in order to write

へ、さア源さん、失禮ですけど受けて下さいよ。えッ、私ですか。どうかそれだけは勘忍してお

へ、えッ、私ですか。全く
・調法なんですか
・んなせえ。
……。

へ、そんな事を言
はないで御生だか
受けて下さい。

へ、どうかそれだ
は……。

へ、ちや妾の盃
や氣に入らない
だね。い～えさ
、お氣に召さな
んでせう。

、い～え、決してさういふ譯ちやねえんです。
それちや、恥をか～せずに清く受けて下さいな

源吉（大分酔ひたるこなし）いや、もう駄、駄
いけません。（此の時、女中が師匠に何事かを

ねえな。そしてそのお流れを俺にくんねえな
詮方なく思ひ切つてそれを受ける。お梅、心
な顔をしな
い波々とつぐ

源吉、ちやア
頂きます。

紫女、源さん
いねえ。久

字紫女はそ
く顔を見合
む。お梅は
ちらりと見

紫女、よう／＼
事々々。何
一つ重ねな

活動見る尾〃人々

美澤〃

An example of the illustrations characteristic of *Katsudō shashin zasshi*: a variety of "people watching the moving pictures." *Katsudō shashin zasshi*, July 1915. From Makino, ed., *Nihon eiga shoki shiryō shūsei* (*A Collection of Research Material from the Early Days of Japanese Film*).

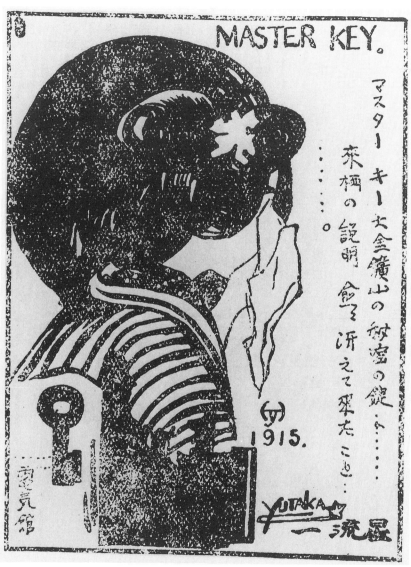

This illustration of a spectator attending *The Master Key* at the Denkikan pays tribute to the emotive power of skillful benshi narration. *Katsudō shashin zasshi*, November 1915. From Makino, ed., *Nihon eiga shoki shiryō shūsei* (*A Collection of Research Material from the Early Days of Japanese Film*).

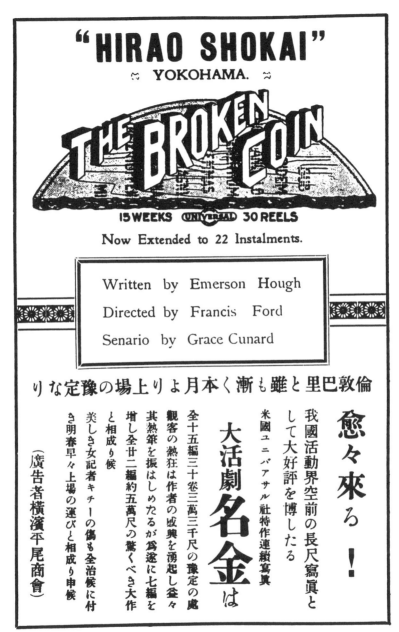

Advertisement for *The Broken Coin* in *Kinema Record,* 10 December 1915. From Makino, ed., *Fukkokuban Kinema rekōdo.*

＝＝ 曖く降る日の渚汀の砂の上に人魚のやすらひ ＝＝

神祕劇 海神の娘

ユ社ブルーバード映畫
東京帝國館上場

ウィリアム王…………ウィリアム・イ・シー氏
オルガ皇女……………リー・ベーアト孃
海神（ネプチューン）……ウィリアム・ウエルシム氏
アンネット（海神の娘）……アンネット・ケラーマン孃
アンゼラ（同）…………カ　ザ　リ　ン　リ　孃
ボリス太公……………エドマンド・モーチマー氏

○○ ボリス大公の陰謀 ○○

太右或る國にウィリアムと言ふ王様がありました。王様は今日
が恰度自分の御誕生日に當りますので、皇女のオルガ様や、從兄
弟のボリス太公など、御相談の上、今迄禁止されてあつた領海の
漁獵を臣民に御許しになりました。そして續々御愛しみのあつた
オルガ皇女と御結婚遊ばしまして、夫れからと言ふものは、毎日
のやうに海岸に出て漁民の娘々として漁撈して居るのを御覧せら

Transcribed synopsis for *Neptune's Daughter* at the Teikoku-kan. *Katsudō gahō*, April 1917. From Makino, ed., *Nihon eiga shoki shiryō shūsei* (*A Collection of Research Material from the Early Days of Japanese Film*).

新派悲劇 己が罪

日活東京派作
東京オペラ館上場

割役

楔戸歴弘 ……………………… 大村正雄
妻 環 ………………………… 立花貞二郎
塚口虔三 ……………………… 藤川三之助
玉太耶 ………………………… 市川徳子
正弘 …………………………… 市川菊久丸

一、苦肉の策

猿輪環と云へば、校内で誰一人知らぬものもない美人であつた。三人寄れば何かと人の噂をしたがる女學校で、この頃環が懐姫してゐると云ふともなく云ひ廣められ、今日しも費の休みの時にお友達に素見かされたので、彼女は身に覺えのあることは云へ、穴にも入り度い氣持で下宿へ歸つて來た。そして一人で淋しい思ひに耽つたり、または身の振方を考へたりした。

「元はと云へば先生に執持つて貰つた仲だけど、私今更怎うしたら

Transcribed synopsis for the *shinpa* film *Ono ga tsumi* (*One's Own Sin*) at the Tokyo Opera-kan. *Katsudo gahō,* June 1917. From Makino, ed., *Nihon eiga shoki shiryō shūsei* (*A Collection of Research Material from the Early Days of Japanese Film*).

out both an accurate description of the action on screen and, during the silent period, the dialogue supplied by the *benshi*'s narration.[10]

The illustrated transcriptions and synopses in *Katsudō zasshi, Katsudō no sekai,* and *Katsudō gahō* were intended as much for reading pleasure as for study. According to a promotional ad in the first issue of *Katsudō gahō,* its synopses were meant to give the impression of watching the film.[11] The transcriptions in *Katsudō zasshi* most clearly resemble *benshi* narration, and today might be our most accurate record of what it was like to attend a moving picture performance in Japan in the mid-1910s.[12] Some early scripts of many *shinpa* films and *kyūgeki* were actually written for the *benshi*'s use, and it is also conceivable that at least some of these transcriptions resemble the scripts that were used on the set during production.

Other prominent features of these magazines reflect the inclinations of the general audience: *benshi* popularity polls, interviews with popular *benshi,* and articles by *benshi,* all of which vied with behind-the-scene accounts of the ever-popular Onoe Matsunosuke and fan mail debating the pros and cons of his latest performance. Full-page advertisements for Nikkatsu, Tenkatsu and, after 1916, Kobayashi shōkai (Kobayashi Kisaburō's import company), and Universal, all emphasizing the capacity of these companies to import European and American films, also underscore the popular demand for imported films, and a great deal of space was given to commentary on the professional and private lives of foreign performers as well. Not surprisingly, foreign actresses received special attention, for Japanese women had yet to appear on screen on a regular basis. It is interesting to note that although all three magazines included photographs of *benshi* and Japanese actors and production stills of popular domestic pictures (*Katsudō gahō*'s glossy foldouts are particularly impressive), portraits of both Hollywood and European actresses often graced their front pages, and each issue of the first volume of *Katsudō gahō* featured a different foreign actress on its cover. Additional offerings of interest included readers' columns, space reserved for fan mail addressed to particular performers, backstage gossip, various types of poetry (including tanka, haiku and senryū, comic haiku poems), cartoons, and "news from our provinces," columns that reported news of performances in movie theaters outside of Tokyo.[13]

Alongside these features were articles concerned with themes made popular by the staff of *Kinema Record.* These were written by anonymous writers, members of the film community, journalists, aspiring critics (including Mori Iwao, Iijima Tadashi, and Tanaka Jun'ichirō), and a handful of prominent members of the literary world. The most common targets for complaint were the "oppressive popularity" of the *benshi,* the "anachronistic" female impersonator, and the incompatibility of stage actors with the screen. Possibilities for the domestic film received special attention. These included

THE GUILT OF SILENCE
=Bluebird=

雲中情話
無言の罪
——ブルーバート映覧——
——帝國館上場——
——よしのすけゐがく——

北郊アメリカ――　そこは純白なる金と君の宇宙の総となる家志を試けるといふ。暗雲低く垂れて、陽の光は薄いけれど、白金の輝くやうに、そのやうに光り輝く皚雪の地、實に。アラスカは銀の世界よ。

暗く、そして、冷い中空に雪は飛び飲み雪の中に、人は黄金を漁る可く、身を切る窓さし眠りなく。吹雪と聞ふその膂みユーコン河の遥に、焔のやうの往來の直さよ。

ここにマッシューと云ふ青年……君は、よい金鑛脉を得た爲に、充分黄金を蓄へ得て、アラスカを後に、この雪國を出立す可く、明日の歸鄉を悦ぶのであつた。

今宵一夜は名残の夜、假初に去るギターの音に、懐しい故鄉の人を憶ひ廻れて、追憶と悦びと、二つながら墟邊の火にはもやしも盡されず……明日は故鄉へ歸る人。幽ふ綿も身のさかへ。

歸國を思ふマッシュー、悦びに満ちたマッシュー、君が黄金の夢を抱いてゐる瞬間に、君が身柄の束縛を謝美してゐる瞬間に、薄幸アミイと、その情夫してあるフレッドとの間に、君の黄でた。

君が再度盛めた時明け渡ひに返つたその時、君が身柄の束縛は君の宇献は君の火にくれて居った。

結ばれて居つたことなれば少しも知らなかつた故に、自らの仇である人の爲に、温い慈惠を垂れてやつた。つまり君は、君を狙ふ遊蜂に甘い蜜を與へてやつたのだ。

マッシューよ、君の下に殺しを求めに來た二人の男女こそ、君の乗引幸福を家去る惡魔であつたのだ。それを、君は知らなかつた故に、自らの仇である人の爲に、温い慈惠を垂れてやつた。

けれども、勇敢なるマッシュー。黄金の夢は一夕の興。不幸なる君、黄金の夢は一夕の興。

けれども、勇敢なるマッシュー、君は、君の不幸を歎く可きではない。君の不幸を歎く可きではない。無念と云ふ感情にひきとられて魔人を遠くやるな。憎む可き盜賊こらせ。

魔人の逃歩、それは走矢の如く捷くも、君が復讐の矢羽根はそれを追ひ越すであらう。

勇敢なるマッシューは橇の用意も素早く、愛犬を従へて盜賊の跡を追つた。見渡す限り、白雪地を穿つて人跡稀なアラスカの曠野、ユーコン河の遥の島の暗き犀しなく、窓烈しく吹き荒む、狂は巴にふりしきる……

旅人の如く裝うて君の不和の小屋に数ひを求めに來た若い男と女。その若い女にはかられ、君は毒を盛られて卒倒した。狡猾な二人の男女は、君が失神の間に、冷い橇の上に苦めた苦痛と努力との結晶であるところの、そして、君の愛める故鄉への飾りでるところの、その重い黄金の總を奪ひ去つて仕舞つた。

走つた。追うた。狂奔した。けれども……不怖な青年よ。

Advertisement for Universal's Tokyo branch. *Katsudō no sekai,* October 1916. From Makino, ed., *Nihon eiga shoki shiryō shūsei* (*A Collection of Research Material from the Early Days of Japanese Film*).

"To my friends of Japan I send best wishes." Publicity photo of Ruth Roland. *Katsudō kurabu,* August 1920. From Makino, ed., *Nihon eiga shoki shiryō shūsei* (*A Collection of Research Material from the Early Days of Japanese Film*).

Publicity photo of Universal "Bluebird star" Juanita Hansen, signed in Japanese. *Katsudō hyōron,* March 1919. From Makino, ed., *Nihon eiga shoki shiryō shūsei* (*A Collection of Research Material from the Early Days of Japanese Film*).

Publicity photo, Helen Holmes. *Kinema Record,* 10 February 1917. English caption reads "exclusive in Japan to the *Kinema Record.*" From Makino, ed., *Fukkokuban Kinema rekōdo.*

Publicity photo, "Metro Star Miss Ruth Stonehouse looking at July issue" of *Katsudō hyōron* [later *Katsudō kurabu*]. *Katsudō kurabu,* November 1919. From Makino, ed., *Nihon eiga shoki shiryō shūsei* (*A Collection of Research Material from the Early Days of Japanese Film*).

FILM-RECORD
AND CINEMATOGRAPHY
VOL. I. NOV. II. 1913. NO. 4.

Mlle. Suzanne Grandais

嬢ーデンラ・グヌンザス

Frontispiece (Suzanne Grandais). *Film Record,* 11 November 1913. The frontispiece and later the covers of *Kinema Record* were regularly illustrated with portraits of American and European actresses. This was a tradition continued by magazines such as *Katsudō gahō* and *Kinema kurabu.* From Makino, ed., *Fukkokuban Kinema rekōdo.*

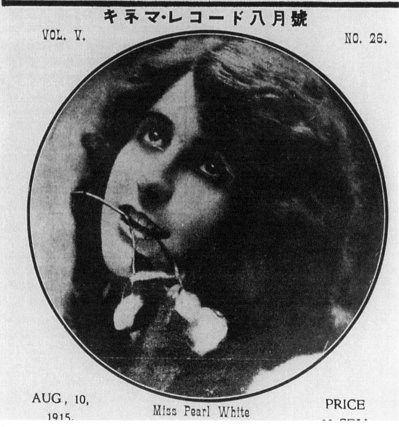

No. 26. VOL. V.   TOKIO.   10 August, 1915.

THE KINEMA-RECORD

ILLUSTRATED LEADING CINE. JOURNAL

キネマ・レコード八月號

VOL. V.   NO. 26.

AUG, 10,
1915.   Miss Pearl White   PRICE

Cover (Pearl White). *Kinema Record,* 10 August 1915. From Makino, ed.,
Fukkokuban Kinema rekōdo.

Cover (Mary Pickford). *Kinema Record,* "American Number," 10 November 1916.
From Makino, ed., *Fukkokuban Kinema rekōdo*.

Cover of *Katsudō gahō*, July 1917. From Makino, ed., *Nihon eiga shoki shiryō shūsei* (*A Collection of Research Material from the Early Days of Japanese Film*).

the adaptation of classical Japanese literature and traditional legends for the screen, a more contemporary depiction of Japan, and the development of screen comedy genres. Evidence that some contributors envisioned changes of a more idealistic nature surfaces in suggestions that the Japanese film be used as a vehicle for the affirmation of national identity and the promotion of Japanese culture abroad, and as a tool in the edification of the general audience.

THE GAP WIDENS: FOREIGN IMPORTS AND THE DOMESTIC FILM DEBATE

In view of the range of films available to audiences, comparisons between domestic productions and the European and American imports were inevitable in these articles, and their authors praised the superior storytelling skills of the European directors, the advanced camera and editing techniques of Hollywood, and the superior acting of foreign screen actors (male and female) in general. Such comparisons occasionally led to the reiteration of the need to counter the challenge of foreign imports by developing an exportable domestic product. Judging from Mori Iwao's *A Survey of the Moving Pictures,* this concept gained an increasing number of followers toward the end of the decade. The Japanese industry management—by implication, studio executives who pandered to the demands of the general audience for the sake of quick and sure profits—is repeatedly singled out for criticism, although in *Katsudō no sekai* (February 1916) the respected novelist and poet Kōda Rohan remarked that the intelligentsia was as much to blame for failing to generate change.[14]

The articles Rohan occasionally submitted to *Katsudō no sekai* were unusual because they attempted to offer solutions. In this case, the remedy he suggested was actually realized, with the founding of Taikatsu, in the near future. Observing that it was no wonder Japanese films were so inferior to Western films considering their meager budgets, he called on the leaders of the business community by name—Asano appears along with Mitsui, Mitsubishi, and others—to invest in the film industry. Carrying this idea one step further, he also suggested they provide backing for a trust organized by the leading production companies.[15] Eight months later, again in *Katsudō no sekai* (October 1916), he restated his belief that money was a major cause of the inferiority of Japanese films and, criticizing the practice of paying the highest salaries to actors—for the most part regarded by pure film enthusiasts as incompetent before a camera—he advised studio management to grant more funds instead to capable scriptwriters.[16]

Praise for imported films was often accompanied by the observation that

European films tended to be better than their American counterparts, an opinion more common among the literary elite. Rohan, for example, wrote that he preferred German and Italian pictures. He singled out the historical films of Giovanni Pastrone (*Cabiria,* 1914) and Mario Caserini (*Otello,* 1907, *Gli Ultimi Giorni di Pompeii,* 1913), adding that although the United States produced more films, very few were worth watching.[17] The attraction of Japanese intellectuals to the prosperous Italian cinema of the early 1910s is better understood when we consider the influence in that industry of cultivated aristocrats favoring adaptations of dramatic works and literature, particularly historical works and the classics. Japanese intellectuals did not overlook the conspicuous presence of literary authors at the Italian studios. The poet and novelist Gabriele D'Annunzio, who was credited with the film script for *Cabiria* when the film was released and who was something of a film enthusiast, was perhaps the most prominent among them, having sold the rights to all of his literary works to the Ambrosio company (in addition to accepting a flat rate for any future works the company might be interested in) in 1911.[18] A special supplement of *Katsudō no sekai* (June 1916) is dedicated to the Japanese opening of *Cabiria,* which was imported by the enterprising Kobayashi, and the contributors' admiration for its lavish sets, models (particularly in the sequence depicting the burning of the Roman fleet with mirrors, executed in miniature), traveling camera work, and close-ups continued throughout subsequent issues. Most of the response was to the film's technical achievements and the acting, but D'Annunzio's alleged participation was noted with enthusiasm.[19]

When it came to matters of management, studio organization, and technical details concerning the production process, interest was directed almost exclusively toward Hollywood. *Katsudō no sekai* and *Katsudō gahō,* in particular, featured articles on popular American stars and detailed descriptions of the "Studios of Southern California," and "What's New in America." The November 1917 issue of *Katsudō gahō* even had a short history of the development of the California film industry.[20] The role of scriptwriting in the Hollywood production process was a subject of particular interest. The second issue of *Katsudō no sekai* (February 1916) featured an article describing the format for a Hollywood-style continuity script comprised of a title, list of characters, synopsis, a list of shots and their locations, and the main text. Each element was described in careful detail: the title should aptly describe the picture's content and attract the potential viewer's attention and curiosity; the list of characters should include a short profile for each character, and state the approximate number of extras that would be needed; the synopsis should be concise, but interesting, and written with the buyer who would be reading it in mind; the list of scenes should be numbered and designated as either interior or exterior shots; the main text should include

Publicity montage for Cabiria, directed by Giovanni Pastrone. Sketch of the author Gabriele D'Annunzio is featured at right. *Katsudō no sekai,* May 1916. From Makino, ed., *Nihon eiga shoki shiryō shūsei* (*A Collection of Research Material from the Early Days of Japanese Film*).

props and descriptions of the background, and should be executed with careful consideration given to maintaining a sense of continuity. In general, writers were advised to beware, above all, of the dangers of overwriting, and the facile assumption that writing for the screen did not require special skills or training.[21]

The May 1916 issue of *Katsudō no sekai* included a special segment, "Katsudōgeki kyakuhon ni tsuite" ("On Scripts for Moving Picture Drama"), consisting of three articles that suggested various possibilities for improving the Japanese script.[22] The first article, "Kyakuhonka no kushin subeki ten" ("Issues of Concern for Scriptwriters"), was by the playwright and critic Tsubouchi Shikō, a nephew (and adopted son) of Tsubouchi Shōyō and a frequent contributor to the magazine.[23] Tsubouchi believed that training actors for the screen was the most important requirement for the development of Japanese film and advocated the establishment of special schools for this purpose (p. 48). He also advised the film industry to follow the Western practice of recruiting scripts from the general public, as this would increase the chances of obtaining suitable material (p. 49; advertisements for scripts do appear in earlier issues of *Katsudō no sekai*). At a time when intertitles were still relatively unusual in Japan because of the prevalence of *benshi* narration, he suggested basic tips for writing good intertitles (here referred to as "mark"): the writer should avoid describing something that has already happened, or revealing anything of interest about to occur (p. 49).

Tsubouchi concluded that the producer was essentially more important to the realization of a satisfactory film than the scriptwriter (p. 50), but in the following article, "Katsudō shashin to Chikamatsu no fukkatsu" ("The Moving Pictures and the Revival of Chikamatsu"), the author stressed that the reformation of the Japanese film must begin with the script.[24] This article is significant as an early acknowledgment of the trend toward making distinctions between a moving picture script and a drama written for the stage. Although the author suggested it would be interesting to try to adapt the works of the kabuki and *jōruri* playwright Chikamatsu Monzaemon (1653–1725), he also emphasized the importance of recognizing the difference between writing for the stage and for the screen (pp. 53–54).

The final contribution to this special selection, "Tensai no shutsugen o matsu" ("Waiting for the Emergence of Genius"), is worth noting both for the amusingly unorthodox views of the author, the playwright Matsui Shōō (here he appeared under his former name, Matsui Shōyō), and as an example of how abstract and uninformed many of the suggestions for change in the domestic industry were at this time.[25] The popular and prolific Matsui had been associated with Tsubouchi Shōyō's Bungei kyōkai, and later became a resident playwright for the Shōchiku Theater Company and an instructor at the acting school Osanai Kaoru organized for the company's film studio; in

Tsubouchi Shikō's article, he suggested that Matsui would make an excellent scriptwriter (p. 51). Matsui, who elsewhere confessed to knowing very little about film, here confined his remarks to the curious observation that Japan was at least six or seven years ahead of the West in the development of chain dramas, and recommended that the intertitles be removed from foreign films because even the few members of the audience who could manage to read English could not possibly do so quickly enough (pp. 54, 56). It was probably just as well that Matsui never attempted to write for the screen. Although he had a few interesting ideas, such as writing scripts based on Japanese legends and tales, or on the lives of such figures as the virtuous warrior Miyamoto Musashi (1584?–1645) and the Kamakura period priest Nichiren (1222–1282)—both later became popular subjects for period genre films— he concluded that, at least for the time being, it would be better for aspiring scriptwriters to limit themselves to translations of English novels and detective stories (p. 55).

One of the strongest affirmations of the value of the scriptwriter, however, is Kōda Rohan's article in the October 1916 issue of *Katsudō no sekai* concerning the need to pay writers a higher salary. Such a salary would be entirely appropriate, wrote Rohan, because "no matter how well equipped you are, you cannot hope to complete a satisfactory moving picture unless you have a good writer." The writer was the "foundation" of a good film, he continued, and the dearth of skilled writers was the main reason why the Japanese industry lagged so far behind that of the Europe and the United States.[26] The budgets of Hollywood productions, overwhelmingly generous in comparison to the money allotted to a production in Japan, were often cited as the reason for the superior technical quality of American films, together with the efficiency and organization of the Hollywood production system. In the September 1917 issue of *Katsudō gahō,* for example, a thorough analysis of the cost involved in the various stages of producing a serial picture in Hollywood begins with the observation that the first payments in the production process are for the script. The average amounts paid for a plot summary (here described as preferred over a longer, more detailed script resembling that of a stage drama, usually approximately 3,000 words [*sic;* a more accurate figure, gleaned from recommendations in English-language screenwriting handbooks of the time, would be 200–300 pages]) are described in detail, as well as the responsibilities and average salaries of a studio writer, the studio director (who is described as the person who must decide whether the script is ready for shooting or whether it needs to be rewritten), and the director of the film (who "studies the script and divides it into interior and exterior scenes"). After estimating the itemized cost of the rest of the staff's salaries, and costumes, sets, and location shooting, the writer observed that it was little wonder the Americans could afford to spend such grand amounts, considering the average number of viewers there in one day totaled "2,900,000 people, or one-fourth the entire population.[27]

Katsudō gahō was published by the same company that published Kaeriyama's *The Production and Photography of Moving Picture Drama,* and the author of the above article included a note recommending this book for further reading.[28] Two articles by Kaeriyama also appeared in this same issue of *Katsudō gahō.* One of these, an excerpt from his book including a description of the "brief" but "well-organized" American style of scriptwriting, had a postscript promoting the book as the "only professional study of the moving pictures available.[29] When the following issue of *Katsudō gahō* carried a two-page advertisement soliciting scripts for a studio-sponsored competition, it also referred the novice writer to Kaeriyama's book. Ironically, the competition was sponsored by Nikkatsu, and the scripts desired were for "*shinpa higeki* without scenes requiring a great deal of money, such as scenes of battles or exploding trains."[30]

Kaeriyama's second article in the September 1917 issue of *Katsudō gahō* was a reworking of an earlier article that had appeared in *Kinema Record.*[31] It dealt with another issue crucial to the reformation movement, one that had concerned Satō Kōroku as he surveyed the state of amateur film scripts back in 1910. Gonda Yasunosuke's pioneering general study of the moving pictures, *Katsudō shashin no genri oyobi ōyō* (*The Theory and Practical Application of the Moving Pictures*), published in 1914, had attempted to define the new medium in terms of its place in Japanese society, and the writers in *Kinema Record* were considerably influenced by Gonda's work. Emphasizing both the medium's power to record and its artistic potential, Gonda suggested it be used as an educational tool both in the classroom and for the general public, as a way of recording history, for judging competitions, and for scientific study and military use, and in addition he proposed that it be considered as a form of art.[32] In his article in *Katsudō gahō,* Kaeriyama elaborated on the concept of using film as an educational tool, and proposed that it be used not only for the edification and betterment of the individual, but also as a means of awakening the Japanese to a sense of national identity.[33] Judging from the frequency with which this theme recurs throughout the first volume of *Katsudō no sekai* and *Katsudō gahō,* it had become increasingly popular during the interval between the publication of Gonda's book and the production of the first pure films.

Several articles in *Katsudō gahō,* in particular, stress the urgent need to find solutions to the many problems involved in making films that could be considered uniquely Japanese, films that, as one writer put it, expressed a "pure Japanese spirit" (*yamato damashii*) and a sense of Japanese individuality and culture.[34] Such articles as "Mo me no sameru toki darō, Nihon no katsudō shashin jūgyōsha ni nozomu" ("The Time for Awareness Has Come: A Plea to the Employees of the Moving Picture Industry," February 1917), "Nihonsei firumu ketten to sono jissaiteki kenkyū" ("A Practical Study of the Japanese Film and Its Shortcomings," March 1917), and "Nihon eiga no shinro" ("The Course for Japanese Films," November 1917) suggest that criticism of the domestic product was becoming increasingly focused on this issue by the time Kaeriyama started directing films at Tenkatsu. These articles demanded that the director be given more authority, a practice more commonly observed at the studios in the United States, and they requested filmmakers in turn to make an increased effort to learn more about the technical developments taking place in foreign industries.[35]

Many of these articles also include the usual comparisons between Japanese and foreign films made with the sole intention of criticizing the "backward practices" of the domestic industry. One writer, for example, observed that a French crew that came to film Mt. Fuji was equipped with "twelve or thirteen lenses," while Japanese filmmakers probably would have used only three or four lenses for the task.[36] But not all the articles comparing Japanese, European, and American films do so with the sole intention of criticizing the domestic industry. Several writers contended that most American films being imported were worthwhile only for their technical achievements, and even suggested that Japanese films could surpass them in quality if the domestic industry had more financial backing, better writers, better actors, and could rid itself of the female impersonator and the *benshi* (although what exactly the Japanese film would excel at, after eliminating these constitutive elements, is unclear).[37] These writers considered the plots of American pictures to be less sophisticated than those of European films, but advised Japanese directors to emulate the ability of directors in the United States to exploit the full potential of the new medium. One writer, for example, concluded that the American film failed to impress some viewers because it had no tragedy, no unhappy endings. Yet even though he criticized Ince's *Civilization* (1916), which opened in Japan in 1917, for being little more than a showcase for impressive battle scenes, he praised the individual style of the director (still an unfamiliar concept in Japan at the time) and his perseverance in experimenting with new technique.[38] Comedy was the one genre of American films given unqualified praise. In fact, Sennett's Keystone comedies enjoyed unprecedented popularity in 1916, and their influence is apparent in several articles concerning the nature of Japanese humor.[39] Citing a dearth of comedy among Japanese productions, these articles urged filmmakers to turn their attention to developing a homegrown version of this popular genre.

193

THE INTELLECTUAL CONTRIBUTION

Perhaps the most interesting articles in these early magazines are those few submitted by well-known members of the literary community, proof that the intellectual class was becoming increasingly aware of the domestic film.[40] As in *Kinema Record,* many of the contributors to *Katsudō shashin zasshi, Katsudō no sekai,* and *Katsudō gahō* used pen names, and many of the articles were unsigned. There were occasional contributions by prominent intellectuals, however, primarily in *Katsudō no sekai,* which featured articles by Kōda Rohan, Tsubouchi Shōyō, and Shimamura Hōgetsu, among others. *Katsudō no sekai* initially had been intended as a general interest magazine, and the title, here translated as *Movie World,* originally referred not to the world (*sekai*) of "moving" (*katsudō*) pictures, but rather to the "active" (*katsudō*) world (*sekai*) of contemporary Japanese society.[41] The editor, Ide Shōichi, was a composer of Chinese- style poetry with a special interest in moving pictures, and the first issue (which opened with an essay by Kōda Rohan, "Ganbō no hyōjun" ("Standards of Ambition") contained an assortment of articles followed by a special supplement on moving pictures. About 40 percent of the articles in the first issue concerned film, however, and by the third issue the publication had clearly become a film magazine.[42]

Even so, all subsequent issues of *Katsudō no sekai* continued to carry at least one article on issues related to either art or general social values, and a preoccupation with culture was visible in many of the articles on film as well. A contribution by the educator and politician Takata Sanae (then serving as minister of education) in the third issue, for example, praised the versatility of film in the education of the general public through the depiction of the culture and people of foreign countries, and called for more involvement in the industry by respected members of the upper class. He concluded by suggesting a collaboration between an author specializing in children's stories and a writer of school textbooks in order to produce films suitable for children.[43]

Kōda Rohan and Tsubouchi Shikō's observations in *Katsudō no sekai* on the state of the domestic industry have already been mentioned, but they were not the only ones in this magazine to contribute to the rhetoric of the pure film movement. The April issue, for example, featured an article signed by Tsubouchi Shōyō, "Katsudō shashin to kusazōshi" ("The Moving Pictures and *kusazōshi*"), which was apparently an interview with the writer conducted by Ide's wife and coeditor, Suzuki Yuriko. After observing that the moving pictures could be interpreted as a modern-day form of *kusazōshi,* Edo-period pictures books of different colors intended primarily for women and children, he urged the industry to concentrate on developing well-equipped movie studios, selecting writers with a wide range of talents, and training better actors. He concluded with the observation that it would be necessary to raise the status of film in Japan before the quality of Japanese films could be improved.[44]

Shimamura Hōgetsu continued this pure film-oriented criticism in "Katsudō shashin no shin ni sakan na jidai" ("When Moving Pictures Become Truly Popular," May 1916), commenting on the need to abolish the female impersonator and *benshi* and improve musical accompaniment before moving pictures could be considered a true form of art, or even compete with the foreign imports. Of particular interest is his observation that although the moving pictures had yet to become popular with all classes of viewers, while touring the provinces he could not help but notice the increasing number of shōgekijō (small theaters featuring various forms of entertainment) that were being converted into movie theaters.[45] Shimazaki Tōson's "Pari kara kaette kite" ("Returning Home from Paris," November 1916) most vividly captures the disenfranchised attitude many members of the intelligentsia had toward the domestic industry at the time: "Not being able to see a Japanese moving picture [in Paris] was most disappointing. A single scene or newsreel would have sufficed, but it was unbearable not to be able to see a film from my native land. How depressing to think that films from countries all over the world are being shown in over forty theaters in Paris every day, but Japanese films alone are nowhere to be found."[46]

Reading through the numerous articles concerning the state of the domestic industry in these publications, there is a sense that the intellectual audience, at least, was impatient for a Japanese film that could compare favorably with the foreign films that were attracting so much enthusiasm at the box office. As one writer put it, Japanese audiences in the past went to the theaters for an experience that would satisfy their ears (the *benshi*'s delivery and musical accompaniment) and mouths (refreshments) as well as their eyes, but this was changing.[47] In the midst of this atmosphere of transition, the admirers of imported films began to take action. For Kaeriyama, this meant the publication of the first practical handbook of filmmaking in Japan, and plans for the production of *The Glory of Life*. For Tanizaki Jun'ichirō, it meant writing his first critical observation of the Japanese film, a provocative summation of many of the pertinent issues being debated in the pages of contemporary film periodicals.

"THE PRESENT AND FUTURE OF THE MOVING PICTURES"

In the opening paragraphs of "The Present and Future of the Moving Pictures," Tanizaki, like Kurihara two months earlier, made clear his desire to participate actively in the production of a new and modern Japanese film.[48] Frank in admitting both his enthusiasm for moving pictures and his

195

disapproval of certain aspects of the domestic industry, he argued, first, for recognition of the moving pictures as art:

> I have never made a special effort to attempt a thorough study of the moving pic-
> tures, nor do I have a great deal of knowledge about them. But I have been their
> ardent fan for some time now, and I have even thought that given the chance, I
> would like to try my hand at writing a Photoplay. To this end I have read two or
> three foreign reference books and I have visited the Nikkatsu studio. As a result,
> although I am a layman, I have much to say in general concerning the future of
> the motion pictures and, in particular, my displeasure and dissatisfaction with
> the managers of the entertainment industry in Japan.
>
> If I were asked whether there is a chance for the moving pictures to develop
> in the future as a true art—as an art that could be ranked with the theater and
> painting, for example—I would answer most emphatically that there is. I also
> believe that just as the theater and painting will never perish, the moving pic-
> tures, too, will last forever. Frankly, I far prefer the moving pictures to the plays
> of any theater troupe or any theater in Tokyo today, and in some of them I detect
> an artistic quality not easily achieved in kabuki or *shinpa* plays. Perhaps this is a
> slight exaggeration, but I actually think that however short or mindless it might
> be, any film, providing it has been made in the West, is much more interesting
> than the Japanese plays of today. (p. 13)[49]

Tanizaki's enthusiasm, which he acknowledged was a result of watching imported films and reading imported Western-language film literature, reveals his affinity with the majority of intellectuals contributing to domestic periodicals. His unconditional admiration for Western films and disdain for the domestic product were also in accord with contemporary intellectual tastes, although for Tanizaki such sentiments were probably influenced by his infatuation with Western culture at the time. It is evident that at this point at least, his preferences precluded a positive appreciation of traditional Japanese drama. Much of the humor in his plot for *Amateur Club,* in fact, centers on a playful parody of two well-known kabuki plays.[50] Accordingly, Tanizaki's argument for recognizing the artistic qualities of film, developed through a comparison between stage and screen drama, began with the conjecture that soon such established forms of entertainment in Japan might have to yield their favored position to the insurgent import from the West:

> Even if we assume that we cannot discriminate among the arts, those forms of art
> that suit the times will continue to develop while those that go against the times
> will naturally cease to improve. Although the content of nō and *kyōgen* drama is
> not inferior to that of kabuki drama, nō and *kyōgen* are not as popular as kabuki
> for this reason. This is the age of Democracy, and the sphere of the arts catering
> to aristocratic tastes will gradually be pared down. In this respect, the moving
> pictures, which are even more plebeian than the theater, are an art more suited to

the times, with great potential for improvement. Or rather, just as the theater outdistanced nō and *kyōgen,* there may come a time when the moving pictures become a respectable, high-class art and in turn outdistance the theater. (pp. 13–14)

Specifically, Tanizaki gave three reasons that he felt moving pictures were superior to stage drama. First, whereas each stage performance could be seen only once by a single audience, a moving picture could be shown repeatedly to different audiences in various locations; also, thanks to the durability of celluloid, a moving picture could continue to entertain audiences for many years to come. Second, as a photographic medium, moving pictures were better suited to the portrayal of both realistic and fantastic (*mugen*) subject matter, proving they were a more versatile form of art than stage drama. Third, the moving pictures allowed the writer more freedom: liberated from the physical constraints of the stage, the writer could manipulate the order and location of scenes as well as the composition of the subject matter projected on screen.

That Tanizaki opened his argument for the artistic merits of film by pointing out the durability of celluloid, revealed his fascination—perhaps influenced by his familiarity with imported trade and fan magazines and "how-to" books—with even the most basic technical attributes of the medium. Keeping in mind his concern with the future potential of moving pictures, he commented that this was one technical attribute that surely would be developed even further with time. Although in this essay Tanizaki was concerned primarily with how moving pictures surpassed the limitations of stage drama, he also pointed out ways in which the moving pictures compared favorably with other forms of art, such as literature and painting. Equating the difference between stage and screen drama with the difference between a handwritten and printed manuscript, he noted that screen drama was also more directly accessible to a larger audience than painting, which could be circulated only through the relatively indirect method of reproduction, or literature, which needed to be translated before it could be appreciated by foreign readers. He added that the moving pictures, because of their durability and universality, provided special benefits for both audiences and actors. For audiences, the moving pictures brought the art of actors far and wide to their doorstep; for actors, the moving pictures made the entire world their audience, immortalizing their art for future generations "just like the poems of Goethe . . . or the works of Michelangelo" (p. 14).

In suggesting that screen drama could accommodate a wider range of subject matter than stage plays, Tanizaki introduced the attribute of the new medium that intrigued him the most: its ability to portray both realistic and imaginary images in an equally convincing manner. Here he attributed film's

197

affinity for subject matter that stirs the human powers of perception to the fact that screen drama is "less artificial" than stage drama. He again referred to shifting trends in the popularity of established, traditional forms of drama in order to illustrate how this quality made the moving pictures better suited to the times and therefore, in his opinion, the more desirable type of entertainment:

> The nō and *kyōgen* plays, admired today as symbolic productions, seemed realistic to the people of the Ashikaga period. Could it be that just as the nō and *kyōgen* plays were followed by the more realistic kabuki theater, the moving pictures, which are even more realistic, will dominate the world in the future? I have a feeling this will indeed happen.
>   The fact that photoplays are more real in all respects proves at the same time that they are appropriate for stories that are much more realistic than stage plays and stories that are much more fantastical than stage plays. Although there is no need to explain why photoplays suit realistic stories, I think works that cannot possibly be adapted to the stage, for example, Dante's *Divine Comedy, Journey to the West* and some of Poe's short stories, or works like Izumi Kyōka's *Kōya Hijiri* [*The Saint of Kōya*] and *Fūryūsen* [*The Elegant Gang's Railroad*] (although both of these were already staged as *shinpa* plays, they were a disgrace to the originals) definitely would make interesting pictures. Poe's stories in particular—"The Black Cat," "William Wilson," or "The Mask of the Red Death," for example—would be even more effective as photoplays (p. 15).[51]

The examples of literature that Tanizaki considered particularly suitable for screen adaptation are worth noting. Izumi Kyōka's work, often about romantically tragic heroines of the pleasure quarters, or ghosts, spirits, demons, and other inhabitants of the supernatural world, was to become a favorite source for Japanese filmmakers. Several stories and novels, such as the supernatural "Uta andon" ("A Song under Lanterns"), and *Nihonbashi* (the name of a geisha district in Tokyo) and *Onna keizu* (*A Woman's Pedigree*), have been adapted many times over the years. There have been no fewer than five adaptations of *Taki no Shiraito* (the heroine's name as a performer), a *shinpa* play derived from the story "Giketsu kyōketsu" (*Noble Blood, Heroic Blood*).[52]

Thomas Kurihara was also an avid reader of both Izumi Kyōka and Poe (Tanizaki later wrote that when visiting the bedridden Kurihara, he noticed a collection of Poe's stories by his bedside), and Kurihara and Tanizaki's mutual fondness for Kyōka's work no doubt resulted in their collaboration, after *Amateur Club,* on an adaptation of the writer's *Katsushika sunago* (*The Sands of Katsushika*).[53]

In accordance with the then-progressive opinion that an understanding of the nature and function of the script was crucial to generating changes in the domestic industry, Tanizaki focused on those technical attributes of the moving pictures that offered special challenges to writers like himself. He maintained that the photographic nature of the medium not only offered writers a wider range of material to choose from but also allowed them greater control over their material, two prospects he found appealing. Tanizaki's confidence in perceiving moving pictures as a writer's medium is more understandable when we remember that during the 1910s, the director's role in the production process was still generally unrecognized in Japan. At any rate, Tanizaki did not seem very concerned—as were many of his American counterparts then being courted by Hollywood—that writing for the screen might compromise the writer's art:

> The third merit [of moving pictures] is that the manner of handling scenes is free and unrestricted as well as rich in diversity. How convenient this must be for the scriptwriter, too. He is unencumbered by bothersome conventions, unlike the process involved in constructing a story for a stage play. Moreover, rather than having to build [a set] on a stage with a limited amount of floor space, he can use any manner of magnificent background or grand-scale building in any way he wishes, and he can even shorten an incident that occurs over a long period of time in a distant land into a short drama of one or two hours. This is yet another reason why the possibilities for source material are so numerous. (pp. 15–16)

Elaborating on the technical advantages of the moving pictures, Tanizaki drew a parallel with painting, pointing out that film provided the option of composing each shot individually, an advantage that could not be achieved on stage. He observed that the newer medium of film also made it possible to control the distance between the performers and the camera—in effect, the distance between the performers and the audience. As a result, each member of a film audience had a better chance of fully appreciating the movements and expressions of the performers on screen. In this respect, Tanizaki paid particular attention to the close-up shot (one year later it became a prominent feature of "The Growth with a Human Face") noting that "cutting out a part of a scene and enlarging it—in other words, showing a detail—greatly increases the effect of the drama and adds variety." He was quick to add that although the close-up shot enhanced the dramatic impact of a moving picture, it also encouraged greater respect for realistic detail. He explained that for this reason it was customary in the United States and Europe, for example, for a beautiful actress to play the part of a beautiful woman and for older performers to play older parts. Because an actor's or actress's face appears larger than life in a close-up, screen actors cannot deceive the audience with the garish makeup used on stage. Thus, Tanizaki concluded, screen actors had more opportunities to explore the full potential of their acting ability, and so their performances were less artificial (p. 16).

Tanizaki's lengthy discussion of the merits of the close-up shot led him to a consideration of color and sound for moving pictures. Like many of his contemporaries both in Japan and abroad, he contended that such additions were both unnecessary and undesirable, as they would only weaken the unique visual intensity of moving pictures. He also believed that the absence of such techniques enhanced the medium's affinity with the "spirit" of painting, sculpture, and music—more proof of the superior artistic quality of the moving pictures in comparison with stage drama:

> The human face—even an ugly face—is such that if you stare at it intently, it seems to conceal a mysterious, solemn, and eternal beauty. When I look at a "close-up" of a face in a moving picture, this feeling is especially strong. Every individual part of the face or body of a person who ordinarily would escape notice possesses an indescribable energy, and I can feel its compelling force all the more keenly. Perhaps this is not only because film is a magnification of the real object, but also because it lacks the sound and color of the real object. Perhaps the lack of color or sound in moving pictures is an asset rather than a limitation. Just as painting has no sound and poems have no shape, the moving pictures too, because of their limitations, manifest the purification—Crystallization—of nature that is necessary to art. I believe this aspect of the moving pictures will enable them to develop into a more advanced form of art than the theater. (pp. 16–17)[54]

After discussing the merits of moving pictures, Tanizaki launched into a critique of what he observed to be the domestic industry's major deficiencies. He began by pointing an accusing finger at the businessmen in control, siding with the pure film advocates who criticized the industry management for exploiting the medium for the sake of instant profit. Stressing the need to replace present management policies with ones that both complemented the special properties of film and allowed more fluidity in the introduction of new techniques, Tanizaki wrote:

> Everyone is already fully aware of most of the advantages of the moving pictures that I have described above, and it is not necessary for me to explain them once more. I am reiterating these well-known points only because I particularly want the moving picture management to read them. To say the least, [I am writing this] because I believe they do not sufficiently acknowledge these merits—or, even if they do acknowledge them, they do not put them to good use. (p. 17)

Tanizaki was particularly critical of the staging in period films, in which actors assembled on a stage delivered their lines from stationary positions. He argued that because the managers, "stage directors," and actors involved in such productions perceived everything in terms of the theatrical stage, they failed to do justice to the medium at hand (pp. 17–18).

But his main concern was that greater attention in general be given to achieving more realism. He deplored the Japanese custom of having men play female roles, pointing out the absurdity of this "ridiculous" practice, compared with the zealous pursuit of authenticity everywhere else. In Europe and the United States, he wrote, actors occasionally were given real liquor before drunk scenes and, in some cases, were told the plot only a scene at a time so that their emotions would appear more genuine.

In contrast, Japanese screen actors, particularly the female impersonator, appeared on screen in the same costumes and makeup that they wore on stage, "apparently with the impression that they can thus delude the audience." He lamented the custom of using layers of white paint to simulate a woman's fair complexion, and drawing thick black lines for wrinkles in order to appear aged. "Women should play female parts and elderly actors should play elderly roles," he wrote, warning that "as long as the moving pictures remain imitations of the theater, they will never be able to surpass it. . . . Actors in moving pictures today have not realized that they have their own characteristics and purpose, and it is not surprising that these actors are scorned by their colleagues" (p. 18).

Tanizaki concluded, however, that the actors themselves were not solely responsible for their shortcomings. In fact, he believed that their acting gradually would improve as they became more aware of the special requirements of their art. Once again, he put the burden of blame on managers, who chose to produce scripts that were tailored more to the needs of the *benshi* than to those of the performers (pp. 18–19). Above all, he urged filmmakers to improve the content of their work by "returning to nature." There was no need for huge spectacles involving "train crashes" and "exploding railway bridges." Simple stories expressing "Japanese customs and human sentiment" would suffice. The simpler and more natural the content was, the better, for it would be unreasonable "to begin immediately with literary pictures of high quality" (p. 19).

Tanizaki noted that several popular foreign pictures with negligible plots (he specifically mentions *The Broken Coin*) were immensely successful in Japan, thanks to the skillful use of location shooting and the firsthand glimpses they provided of local life—both qualities literature could not offer. For this reason, he surmised, Japanese novels such as *Ono ga tsumi* (*One's Own Sin*) and *Konjiki yasha* (*The Demon Gold*), which were not, in his opinion, very interesting as literature, would make good moving pictures "if they were made in the manner of a Western picture and included ample shots of Japanese landscapes and native customs" (p. 19).[55] Tanizaki concluded that once the technique of adaptation was perfected, Japan's rich wealth of literary classics could be used to make pictures that would fascinate foreign audiences as much as foreign pictures enthralled the Japanese:

Going one step further, however, if great managers, great directors, and great actors were to emerge in Japan and if they used the famous and time-honored novels of our country as material for moving pictures, what magnificent films they could make! Just thinking about it makes me take heart. For example, if they filmed *Heike monogatari* [*The Tale of the Heike*] using the actual settings of Kyoto, Ichinotani, and Dannoura and dressing the actors in the armor and costumes of that time, they could make a film on a par with even *Quo Vadis?* or *Anthony and Cleopatra*. Something like the Heian-period *Taketori monogatari* [*The Bamboo Princess*] would be first-rate material for a fairy drama using trick effects.

If we made many films of this kind, we could check the importation of foreign-made films, and even export large quantities of films from Japan. Moving pictures that depict the history and human compassion of the Far East would surely capture the fancy of Westerners. (pp. 19–20)

Tanizaki also pointed out the benefits such a production policy would offer screen performers, again emphasizing the medium's advantage over all other arts in crossing international borders: "It is difficult for Japanese artists in the field of music, literature, and theater to be recognized by the West, but moving picture actors do not face such obstacles. If the name of a Japanese actor were to resound far and wide throughout the world, just like Charles Chaplin, wouldn't it be a wonderful thing for him as a Japanese? Those who seek fame would do well to become moving picture actors" (p. 20).

Tanizaki saved his criticism of the *benshi* for the end. Although his earlier comments suggested that he blamed the powerful *benshi,* together with the profit-hungry managers, for the industry's weaknesses, his closing observations were surprisingly pragmatic. Rather than call for the immediate and total abolition of the *benshi,* as did many other intellectual observers at the time, he simply recommended that their narrative skills be used in moderation. He even went so far as to praise Somei Saburō, the resident narrator of the Asakusa Teikokukan (a movie theater specializing in American serials and the popular Universal Bluebird films), as perhaps the only intelligent man in the entire industry (pp. 20–21). It is clear, however, that Tanizaki was emphatically against the *benshi* tampering with plots, or interlarding their performances with what he perceived as irrelevant, distracting, and often misleading comments. Apart form using the *benshi* to translate the foreign-language intertitles (subtitles in Japanese were experimented with in the 1920s, but became standard only with the introduction of sound), he regarded the narrators as dispensable accessories, little more than substitutes for more sophisticated background music, the preferable accompaniment:

Finally, I would like to comment on the pros and cons of the *benshi.* I would favor completely abolishing *benshi* commentary if we had suitable musical accompaniment for films in Japan, but under the present conditions I wish the *benshi* would at least limit their comments as much as possible. Their presence should be limited to situations in which Western music cannot be used, and they need only narrate the plot in a simple and brief manner without ruining the effect of the film.

In the case of Western films, it is enough to translate the English phrases into Japanese, and to play Western background music in the shadows offstage. The quiet, delicate timbre of the piano could be used for a wide range of Japanese pictures and perhaps might be appropriate even for a historical film. If *benshi* commentary is absolutely necessary, I would prefer the *benshi* do no more than deliver the commentary following the phrases that appear in the film as faithfully and skillfully as possible. Breaking up the entire plot right from the start or bantering the lines of dialogue back and forth between each other should be absolutely forbidden. (p. 20).

In May 1920, three years after the publication of "The Present and Future of Moving Pictures," Taikatsu officially appointed Tanizaki as their "literary consultant"; that same month Tanizaki published an article in the *Yomiuri shinbun* reiterating several of the views he had expressed in 1917. If anything, the three intervening years had only served to strengthen his convictions. He again admitted that, apart from his great love of films, he was "a complete amateur regarding the technical aspects" of the medium, but had been drawn to the idea of working at Taikatsu in order to help improve the "unbearably low quality of Japanese pictures." This time he singled out the *benshi*'s presence, which hindered the perfection of "the film script and location shooting, which are the foundations of film," as the primary obstacle to reform, and consequently to the development of an exportable Japanese film. He urged both authors and technicians to concentrate more on the skillful use of locations and scene changes rather than the demands of the actors; in doing so they would make films that could be understood by means of intertitles instead of *benshi* narration.[56]

Tanizaki also observed that more serious consideration needed to be given to the content of moving pictures, and he suggested that authors turn to "conventional *kōdan* and *kibyōshi*," two popular forms of literature that he believed would make interesting films "provided the scenes were skillfully rearranged." Furthermore, by "borrowing from the works of gifted authors" (here he cited Izumi Kyōka's *Fūryūsen* and his own "The Growth with a Human Face"), higher-quality films could be made "regardless of the arrangement of scenes." He stated that by making pictures that were both popular and artistic, he himself hoped to contribute to the popularization abroad of Japanese "art and national sentiment." And finally, regarding the need for improvement in the quality of screen acting, he recommended the use of amateurs who had no previous relation to the traditional Japanese theater.[57]

Perhaps the most significant difference between "The Present and Future of the Moving Pictures" and the 1920 *Yomiuri shinbun* article is that by the time Tanizaki wrote the latter, he had already committed himself to assisting Kurihara in the production of pure films at Taikatsu. In "The Present and Future of the Moving Pictures," Tanizaki revealed an impressive amount of awareness and foresight in his appraisal of both the potential of the new medium and the immediate problems facing the emergent modernization movement. Tanizaki's apparent knowledge of issues being discussed in domestic film periodicals was undoubtedly of great value to Kurihara when he returned, after a prolonged sojourn abroad, to seek financing for the production of new, exportable Japanese films. The two already had in common a familiarity with and appreciation of foreign films, but Tanizaki provided an important link between Kurihara and the domestic pure film debate.

6

Mayhem, Mischief, and a
Certain Esprit de Corps: *Amateur Club*

TODAY ALL THAT remains of the Taikatsu studio is a stone marker in a corner of Yokohama's Motomachi Park, not far from the main commercial street that runs through the heart of the city. The location was once well known for its spring water, which was delivered to the boats in the harbor by a Frenchman who owned a tile factory on the land where the park now stands. The tiles were for the Western-style homes that once graced the neighborhood.[1] The entire area, known as the Yamate Bluff, looks out over the port, and was a favorite location for the foreign residents of the city. Adjacent to the park is the Foreign Cemetery, where some of Japan's earliest and most illustrious foreign residents are buried.

Very little of the city of Yokohama survived the Great Kanto Earthquake; much less remained after the destruction of the Second World War. It is hard to imagine what this quiet, residential neighborhood was like in March 1920 when Tanizaki first visited the Taikatsu studio. Descriptions in accounts by former employees indicate that the studio itself was in fact quite small.[2] Tanizaki's own recollection of the experience, written one year later, suggests that on that day he was drawn to the exotic, cosmopolitan atmosphere of the city, to which he moved in the following year. But even more significant to him was his arrival at Taikatsu and his exhilarated response to what he found there; his detailed description reveals a fascination with moving pictures that made the prospect of creating them irresistible. He arrived at the studio office accompanied by Kurihara:

As I recall it was last spring, sometime around March, that I had an appointment in Yokohama to meet Thomas Kurihara of the Taishō Moving Picture Studio. I

205

left Odawara around noon and arrived at Sakuragi station a little after two o'clock. Kurihara had come to the railway station to meet me, and the two of us got in a taxi and headed for his office at 12 Yamashita Street. It was very fine weather that day, warm, glistening, and bright. As I was jostled about in the car, I gazed out the window at the city of Yokohama, where I had not been for many years, at Bashamishi Street, with its somewhat foreign character, and the manners and dress of the Chinese and Westerners passing by. We arrived at the office, a small building across the street from the old brick Japan Gazette Company building, on the street before Kaigan Road. For some reason the area reminded me of Shanghai. Kurihara opened the door of the building and led me inside. There was only an old man of about sixty, called "Jimmy," and I couldn't see anyone in the small room downstairs. But as soon as I entered I could detect that uniquely sweet odor of film. "The developing room must be somewhere back here," I thought, and discarded the cigarette I was holding, putting it out with care. "Please come upstairs," Kurihara said, leading the way. Upstairs there was a small room facing the back streets, not too wide, but tidy and bright, with a window on both sides. A large desk that seemed to be where Kurihara worked was placed against one wall. Inami, the technician, came and greeted me, and said, "We would like you to take a look at two or three films made by our company." Then he and Kurihara immediately began setting everything up. They put a household-model Acme projector on the desk. They attached an electrical cord to the projector, and closed the blinds of each window. The room that had been so full of sunlight from the clear, blue sky suddenly became pitch dark. The films appeared as a small image projected from one wall of this narrow room to the other. I watched two films there. One was of the cherry blossoms of Sankei Park, and one was about the silk industry, from the silk being made by the silkworm, to its appearance in a draper's shop, made into an exquisite fabric, and ending with its transformation into the fancy attire of a city woman. Needless to say these were extremely ordinary pictures, but the inside of that bright room suddenly becoming dark and, most of all, that very small, brilliantly distinct reflection of a moving object projected like a glittering jewel on the wall, gradually lured me into a strange trance. A world that was less than a mere three or four square feet of light cutting through the darkness, where the silkworm's figure wriggled silently—as I watched that I forgot that there was a reality apart from this small world. Outside this room was the city of Yokohama, the Sakuragi train station, and the train, and the fact that if I got on the train I could return to my house in Odawara, the fact that I even had a house in Odawara, all seemed unreal. After the projection was over, we left the office to go to the shooting studio at 77 Yamate Street. The air outside suddenly restored me to my senses. Then, as if I couldn't believe my own eyes, I gazed at what was around me as if it were all rare and unusual.[3]

It is uncertain whether Tanizaki was aware of Kurihara and Brodsky's work before his first visit to the studio.[4] (Indeed, it is difficult to determine whether or not supporters of the pure film movement were familiar with the two's efforts at Tōyō Film before Asano assumed ownership of the studio, although mention of "film dramas by the American Brodsky featuring the natural landscapes of Japan" can be found in the November 1917 issue of *Katsudō gahō*.) According to Tanizaki, the invitation to become affiliated with the Taikatsu studio occurred through the fortuitous intervention of a close friend, the actor Kamiyama Sōjin and his family. Then living in Odawara, Tanizaki often stayed at the Kamiyama home in Tokyo, and it was there that he was introduced to Shimo Nariyasu, a friend of Kamiyama and an executive of the Tōyō Steamship Company. When plans were being final-ized for the organization of the Taikatsu Company, Shimo (who had been appointed the studio's management director) and Kurihara stopped by the Kamiyama home one day when Tanizaki was visiting. After Tanizaki and Kurihara were introduced, it was suggested that Tanizaki join the studio as "literary consultant."[5]

Everything about the timing of subsequent events suggests that it was a race from start to finish between the small Taikatsu studio and its rival, Shōchiku, which had already hired Osanai and published its prospectus in February. Taikatsu took over management of the Chiyoda theater, along with four resident *benshi,* in April; Tanizaki officially assumed his position in May; and the company prospectus was released in June. In November 1920, the two companies released their debut productions, Shōchiku's three-reel *Shima no onna* (*Island Woman*), shot by Kurihara's former Hollywood col-league, Henry Kotani, and a little over two weeks later, Kurihara and Tanizaki's first collaborative effort, *Amateur Club.*

THE "VITALITY AND VIGOR OF YOUTH"

Unlike Kaeriyama's *The Glory of Life, Amateur Club* had the benefit of opening at the centrally located Yūrakuza theater, but the Taikatsu manage-ment took the additional precaution of presenting it featured together with two foreign offerings.[6] Tanizaki, who favored musical accompaniment rather than *benshi* narration, fought hard to have the film open without narration. Two *benshi* from the Chiyoda theater appeared in the film, and it has been suggested that they received their roles as a means of currying favor with the theater, which ran the film one month after its opening at the Yūrakuza.[7] However, it is unclear whether *benshi* were present at either theater. Tanizaki may have been successful in blocking their appearance in Tokyo, but the director Yoshimura Kōzaburō recalls *benshi* commentary when he saw the film in Kyoto a month later.[8] At any rate, *Amateur Club* was not released as a mainstream commercial attraction, and many viewers no doubt were drawn to the film mainly because of the novelty of Tanizaki's participation. It is probable that it was seen by a larger—and possibly more diverse—audience than viewed *The Glory of Life* and *The Girl in the Mountain,* but according to the recollections of viewers, its playful iconoclasm was best appreciated by members of the intellectual class, who welcomed any attempt to bypass overt theatrical influences. Presumably, this select audience would also be most familiar with the American comedies that had inspired the film.[9]

Writing about *Amateur Club* thirty years later, Tanizaki recalled that he and Kurihara were not averse to using a European film as a model for their first collaboration, but decided on American slapstick comedies—in particular, Mack Sennett's Bathing Beauties and Keystone Kops pictures—because of Tanizaki's familiarity with American films, Kurihara's Hollywood experience, and the ties between the United States and their patron, the Tōyō Steamship Company. He recalled that although at the time they thought of Hollywood films as being technically superior to European pictures, they considered European films to be more sophisticated.[10] This distinction was common among intellectuals writing about film toward the end of the decade (Kōda Rohan is one example), but Tanizaki apparently admired more than merely the technical qualities of American comedies. In "I Must be Grateful for that Happiness," he explained that in the original story for *Amateur Club* he had sought to capture the "lively and cheerful milieu of a group of young men and women," and in this respect he had clearly been inspired by the American comedies that were enjoying great success in Japan at the time.[11] For example, in a much-quoted passage in this article he pointed out that although American comedies had flimsy, absurd plots, their humor had a certain "musical" rhythm that he greatly admired. This was particularly true, he said, of Chaplin's comedies, which made him feel as if he could understand "the spirit of the American people, overflowing with the vitality and vigor of youth."[12]

Tanizaki's fascination with this "vitality" that he associated with American culture is also visible in *Kōjin,* the novel he was in the process of writing when he joined Taikatsu. Asakusa, a hub of music halls, movie theaters, vaudeville houses, and theaters—Tokyo's main entertainment district and the breeding ground for the new forms of popular entertainment that flourished after the war—provides the background for the novel; Tanizaki's descriptions of it are so vivid that the area takes on the presence of an additional character in the novel.[13] Two years earlier, in his contribution to the article "Cars, Moving Pictures, and Cafes as Symbols of the New Age," Tanizaki had described his affection for the area, a center of excitement that constantly generated "new" and "youthful" entertainments that "left old customs behind." He wrote: "Just as the United States of America is a 'melting pot' for various cultures from all over the world, Asakusa, I believe, is a 'melting pot' of the arts and entertainments of the new age."[14]

208

町動活草淺ぶ呼を氣人

The popular movie theater district of Asakusa. From the first issue of *Katsudō shashin zasshi,* June 1915. From Makino, ed., *Nihon eiga shoki shiryō shūsei (A Collection of Research Material from the Early Days of Japanese Film).*

"Asakusa opera" was one of these new forms of popular diversion. This term referred to the wide variety of musical entertainment that thrived in the Asakusa music halls from around 1915 until the early 1920s, including hybrid Western and domestic forms of light opera, operetta, and chorus-line revue.[15] Dating back to the legitimate efforts of an Italian, G. V. Rossi, to import opera to Japan in 1912, Asakusa opera is credited with having laid the foundation for a popular appreciation of Western music. It also introduced a new dimension of eroticism to the world of popular entertainment: as Tanizaki himself observed in *Kōjin,* the Asakusa opera "made us look toward the beauty of the new [Japanese] woman and away from that of the old."[16]

Tanizaki's preoccupation with women in his writing is well known, and it was not likely that he would ignore these transformations taking place in the traditional concept of beauty. In "Thoughts on Tokyo," for example, written a decade after the Great Kanto Earthquake, he described his excitement at the time as he imagined a thorough modernization (or, as he envisioned it, Westernization) of Japanese women in the modern city that would arise from the rubble of destruction.[17] In 1920 the average Japanese woman, unlike the average male, still wore traditional dress, but even then it was possible to catch glimpses of an occasional *moga, (modan gaaru,* or "modern girl") in Western finery. These audacious young women defied both conventional attire and traditional ways, and it was such a woman that Tanizaki and Kurihara chose for the leading role in *Amateur Club.*[18] According to Satō Haruo, Tanizaki's primary motive for writing the original story for *Amateur Club*— and for becoming involved in moving pictures at all—was the prospect of having his sister-in-law, Hayama Michiko (her professional name), appear in a bathing suit.[19]

The very first scene of the film ended with Hayama nonchalantly walking home in a bathing suit after her clothes have been stolen at the beach, and Tanizaki himself later commented on the novelty of the scene at a time when women were seldom even seen in Western dress.[20] Hayama, who then was studying voice at a Western-style music school, recalls that she took a screen test, during which Kurihara was very strict.[21] But Tanizaki himself later admitted that he chose her for the role (he also chose her professional name), and it is clear that he wrote the film with Hayama in mind.[22] She was a "modern girl," quite the opposite of her older sister, Tanizaki's wife, a quiet, more reserved woman. (Tanizaki's wife also appeared briefly in the film along with her daughter, as mother and child, in the audience of the Amateur Club performance.) It is commonly believed that it was precisely the un-Japanese characteristics of both Hayama's personality and physical appearance that Tanizaki found so attractive.[23]

These characteristics resurfaced in Naomi, the "modern girl" depicted in *Chijin no ai* (*A Fool's Love,* 1925).[24] Tanizaki wrote this novel after moving to Kansai, but it was inspired in part by his previous two years in Yokohama, and is among the last works written while he was still obsessed with Western culture. It is the story of mild-mannered Jōji, the "fool" of the title, who is hopelessly infatuated with the willful, demanding Naomi, a waitress with features and a physique that are exotically un-Japanese. Often in the course of the novel, Jōji compares Naomi to Mary Pickford and Mack Sennett's Bathing Beauties.[25] He takes her to Asakusa to see *Neptune's Daughter* (1914, released in Japan in 1917), and when the film is over, begs her to imitate a pose taken by its star, Annette Kellerman.[26] There are aspects of the story that bear no resemblance to Tanizaki's relationship to his sister-in-law, on which the novel is loosely based,[27] but it is clear that, just as Jōji was drawn to Naomi's un-Japanese features, Tanizaki was drawn to Hayama's resemblance to the Western screen beauties he admired: in a surviving still photograph from *Amateur Club,* Hayama poses in profile in her bathing attire, on tiptoe with her arms reaching upward, in an exact imitation of the Annette Kellerman pose described in *A Fool's Love.*[28]

Hayama Michiko in *Amachua
kurabu* (*Amateur Club*), directed
by Thomas Kurihara, 1920.
Courtesy of Fujita Mitsuo.

Tanizaki's wife (Chiyo) and
daughter (Ayu) make an
appearance as members of the
audience in *Amachua kurabu*
(*Amateur Club*). Courtesy of Fujita
Mitsuo.

Annette Kellerman. The caption reads "Human or mermaid?" *Katsudō kurabu*, October 1920. From Makino, ed., *Nihon eiga shoki shiryō shūsei* (*A Collection of Research Material from the Early Days of Japanese Film*).

Hayama Michiko in *Amachua kurabu* (*Amateur Club*). Imitating a famous pose by
Annette Kellerman. Courtesy of Fujita Mitsuo.

There were other factors that influenced Tanizaki's original story and
Kurihara's final draft of the *Amateur Club* script. Kaeriyama's *The Girl in
His Dreams* (released in June 1920), for example, his most successful film (it
is also credited as the first pure film comedy), is often mentioned as an
important inspiration. The story of an amorous woman and an unresponsive
man together on a desolate island, the film has been praised both for its
humor and the memorable performance of its seductive heroine, Azuma
Teru, who, according to the film's cameraman, appeared "nearly naked."[29]
Finally, as Tanizaki explained in "I Must be Grateful for that Happiness," he
and Kurihara were strongly motivated by the challenge of depicting the
everyday lives of contemporary Japanese on screen.[30] It is possible that

213

Miss Teru Azuma on location at Mt. Akagi.

Azuma Teru on location for Kaeriyama. A caption notes her bathing attire, horseback riding, and skill at walking barefooted ("like a Westerner"). *Kinema junpō,* 21 August 1920. From Makino, ed., *Fukkokuban Kinema junpō.*

Tanizaki was eager to work on the type of subject matter exemplified by *The Lust of the White Serpent,* material that gave him the opportunity to explore the nature of depicting the world of fantasy on screen. In "The Present and Future of the Moving Pictures," he had mused that it would not be possible to begin making "works of art" right away. Perhaps for this reason, he and Kurihara chose to begin with a comedy situated in a contemporary setting before attempting artistic adaptations of literature.

214

THE *AMATEUR CLUB* FILM SCRIPT

Kurihara wrote the final draft of the *Amateur Club* script, but according to Tanizaki, his own original scenario, which Kurihara used as a basis for his final draft, was "more than just a story." In "About Film," his recollections of his days at Taikatsu, he wrote: "My manner of writing was quite detailed, and I gave specific instructions for each scene. . . . I even divided the story into scenes, and made up titles. . . . Later, I gradually learned [how to write film scripts] myself, but at the time I knew nothing about film."[31] The original title of Tanizaki's scenario and the working title of the film was *Hishochi no sawagi* (*Commotion at a Summer Resort*); Tanizaki chose the title *Amateur Club* when the film was released.[32] Tanizaki's original work no longer exists, but in the script the action—the exploits of a group of young people, in particular, Miura Chizuko (Hayama Michiko) and Muraoka Shigeru—takes place during the course of one summer day, in the resort area along the Yuigahama shore near Kamakura, a city located between Tokyo and Yokohama. Chizuko, Shigeru, and Shigeru's friends are all children of well-to-do families vacationing at their villas in the area.

The first scene of the version of the script originally serialized in *Katsudō zasshi* in 1921 opens with a shot of the Yuigahama shore.[33] Instructions call for a "distinct shot of the landscape from one end to the other and overlap the following title midway through: 'Summer at Yuigahama Shore, Kamakura.'" This is followed by a "medium close-up" of a young man buried in the sand, which "gradually open[s] from the gently shifting sand into a full body shot" of the young man (2). A subsequent title and close-up (3) introduces Muraoka Shigeru, "a pompous young dandy at first glance, but in reality, a good-natured young man of good breeding." Shigeru is joined by three friends, who chide him for neglecting to rehearse for what we later learn is an amateur kabuki performance he and his friends (the Kamakura "Amateur Club" of the title) plan to stage at the Muraoka villa that evening (4–12). Just then one of the young men spots Chizuko swimming off in the distance (13–14). What follows establishes the thin plot of the story: the fumbling attempts of Shigeru and his friends to become acquainted with Chizuko. The young men are smitten by Chizuko's good looks and spirited vivaciousness. They applaud the cheekiness with which she reprimands the young maid sent to escort her home (22–32). An excellent swimmer, she scoffs at Shigeru's challenge to a race, much to the delight of his friends (44–51). And when she rejects Shigeru's gallant offer of his robe when her own is stolen, he only finds her all the more charming (56).

After this first sequence, the action divides into two parallel stories. At the Miura household, Chizuko's mother and the servants are in the process of

airing out the family heirlooms, while Chizuko queries her father on anecdotes of the Miura ancestry. In the meantime, at the Muraoka residence
Shigeru and his friends rehearse a double program of Western music and
kabuki, which they plan to present at the villa while Shigeru's disapproving
father is in Tokyo for business. The father leaves (121) after warning Shigeru
to behave himself while he is gone. Shigeru and his friends go ahead with
their performance (126). Everything proceeds according to plan until
Shigeru's father suddenly returns home on an early train and puts an abrupt
end to that evening's entertainment, sending both the guests and the performers—the latter in full kabuki regalia—scattering in all directions (160–178).
Meanwhile, Chizuko gives chase to the two robbers from the beach (who in
the meantime have taken an interest in the Miura heirlooms), but only after
she prudently avails herself of a full set of ancient armor (191–208). In the
second half of the script that follows, bemused police (they were changed
into detectives before the film's release for censorship purposes) join in a
wild chase for the lost daughter (dressed in armor), the disobedient son and
his entourage (in costume for scenes from the kabuki plays *Taikōki* and
Sendaihagi), and the very real robbers. After a race through Kamakura,
which includes a shot of Chizuko pursuing the hapless thieves past the Great
Buddha (224), the characters all come together at the Yuigahama shore. Mistaken identities are revealed (in a parallel to Chizuko's father mistaking
Shigeru for his daughter, Shigeru's father had mistaken Chizuko for his son),
and the film ends with the two fathers reunited with their respective children,
who end everything with a handshake. The final title expresses the snoring
noises of the rest of the exhausted members of the Amateur Club, fast asleep
(as we see in the subsequent and final scene) in a small boat rocked by waves
at the water's edge.

For current tastes, the somewhat cumbersome morality and awkward
plot of *The Glory of Life* give Kaeriyama's work, written only two years earlier, a peculiarly old-fashioned flavor in comparison, but there are interesting
similarities between the two scripts. Both stories, for example, are situated in
summer resorts: the opening scene of *The Glory of Life* calls for a shot of
Yanagisawa racing a yacht across the water.[34] In addition, the main characters of both stories belong to the privileged class. And even *Amateur Club* is
not without the strange, seemingly displaced fragments of Western culture
(Turgenev, Chaplin, children's church choirs) that are found in *The Glory of
Life*. The Amateur Club's selection of entertainment, for example—a pas-
tiche of Western music (soprano solo, violin duet, mandolin solo, etc.) followed by kabuki, and the jumble of old picture books, prints, and theatrical
magazines being used for reference alongside records and a gramophone
during the group's rehearsals—presents an unusual mix of East and West
(81–85). A notable difference is that in Kurihara's humorous script the for-

eign elements are more credible as a reflection of cultural contemporaneity rather than an indication of the director's need, as in Kaeriyama's case, to duplicate the mood of an American or European film in order to make an unprecedented break with tradition.

Although *Amateur Club* was more of a critical success than *The Glory of Life,* a majority of viewers in 1920 still judged the final film to be excessively imitative of foreign slapstick. Some went so far as to describe it as an amusing, yet still somewhat awkward translation of American visual gags and chase scenes to a Japanese setting.[35] Yet at least some moments in the script capture the flavor of ordinary, everyday life. This is particularly true in the scenes involving the Miura family. The description of a quiet summer evening spent together on the veranda is the most striking example:

> A mosquito smudge burns on edge of the veranda. Absorbed in idle conversation, Chizuko and her parents sit on the veranda enjoying the summer evening. Chizuko's mother is smiling and in a good mood, apparently having forgotten her harsh words earlier that day. With the assistance of spectacles, Chizuko's father scans the articles in the evening paper, talking with Chizuko and her mother as if he has read something of interest. Chizuko sits on the veranda; while gazing at the firefly cage and replenishing the smudge pot, she occasionally exchanges amused glances with her mother in response to her father's comments. A scene of a tranquil summer evening, overflowing with the sense of family harmony. (152)

This scene is followed by a brief sequence revealing the developments at the Muraoka residence, where the Amateur Club performers are engrossed in their rendition of a well-known scene from the kabuki play *Taikōki.* A note in the script indicates that the performance should be a humorous parody of "old-time" kabuki drama (appended to 158). After a few shots of the comically grandiose performance (153–158), we return to the Miura residence. The atmosphere here too has turned humorous, but quietly so:

> Chizuko's father lets the evening paper slip from his lap as he begins to doze; Chizuko and her mother look at him and laugh. The smoke from the mosquito smudge has grown quite thin. Then, shaking his head because a mosquito has landed on the tip of his nose, the father wakes with a start and glances up at the wall clock.
>
> Insert, the wall clock striking half past ten. Chizuko's father begins to mutter, as if to himself ("What, this late already! The night is brief . . ."). At this, Chizuko's mother turns to her and says:

> DIALOGUE TITLE: "CHIZUKO, DEAR, IT'S YOUR BEDTIME." (159)

217

The domestic scenes of the Miura family are both natural and believable in their simplicity. The family on the porch enjoying the evening breeze, the frustrations of Chizuko's mother when she is confronted with her daughter's unladylike behavior, and the fumbling attempts of Chizuko's father to mediate between Chizuko and her mother are all equally familiar situations. Nor do we need to be convinced of the sincerity of Shigeru's father when he scolds his son for wasting time on silly antics rather than doing his homework like a respectable boy. When the father returns home to discover that not only is the forbidden performance well under way, but the entire neighborhood seems to be present, his exasperation is entirely understandable.

The Glory of Life had consciously exploited the possibilities of location shooting in place of a studio set, but there is little mention of such locality in Kaeriyama's script. Kaeriyama's *The Tale of the White Chrysanthemum* (which opened in July 1920, a year after *The Glory of Life*) included many famous sights of Kyoto,[36] but what little explanation there is in *The Glory of Life* sounds more descriptive of a small resort village in Europe rather than Japan. In comparison, *Amateur Club* contains more specific indications for shots that make full use of the local landscape; films "using the natural beauty and picturesque landscape of our land as background" had been promised in the Taikatsu prospectus, and it is likely that Kurihara and Tanizaki chose the scenic Kamakura area as a setting for their film for this reason. The opening establishing shot of Yuigahama beach and the inclusion of such well-known sights as Kamakura's Great Buddha and Hase Temple (featured in the final chase scene, 210–212) are the most obvious examples of such landscape shots. The use of extras presumably added a sense of authenticity to the location shooting. Although *The Glory of Life* script calls for few extras, Tanizaki boasted of a cast for *Amateur Club* that included over one hundred people, some of whom no doubt played the part of the "students, children, young ladies, young couples, all apparently vacationers from the neighboring inns and villas" who are mentioned in the script as making up the audience for the Amateur Club's presentation (126).[37] When the film was shot the crowds on the beach indicated in the first scene were apparently authentic: at least one viewer later criticized the curious stares the bathers directed toward the camera, but at the same time praised the "unprecedented novelty" of featuring dogs and little children on screen.[38]

The predominant cutting back and forth between parallel action is the most noticeable difference in the structure of the *Amateur Club* script in comparison to *The Glory of Life*. In the first half of the film, this crosscutting is primarily between parallel developments at the Miura and Muraoka households, but there are also sequences, particularly in the beginning, where it involves alternate shots between Shigeru and his friends on the beach and Chizuko swimming, for example; or the two robbers making their way through belongings on the beach and the bathers, their unwitting victims; or the robbers hiding in the Miura garden and the members of the Miura family cleaning house. The rhythm of crosscutting gradually accelerates as the narrative becomes more complex. This begins with the sequence starting with the first shot of the Amateur Club's performance (126); during this sequence the established pattern of alternate shots is disrupted for the first time by the insertion between shots of the Miura family and the performance of a shot of the two robbers (138). After returning to the original pattern of alternate shots between the Muraoka and Miura residences, five shots suddenly follow in rapid succession, breaking up the action even further: the arrival of Shigeru's father at Kamakura station (160); Chizuko going to bed (161); the robbers approaching the Miura villa (162); and the audience and the Amateur Club performers at the Muraoka villa (163, 164).

The point at which Shigeru's father actually interrupts the performance occurs immediately after this brief sequence, almost precisely halfway through the story (168 out of a total of 265 shots). After this climactic sequence the action becomes increasingly fragmented as the viewpoint of the camera (as indicated in the script) moves from one character, or group of characters, to another, and each individual shot becomes shorter. The momentum builds as the two fathers, acting independently, call the police station for help in locating their wayward children (179–183, 229–230). These calls result in the two parallel chase sequences that become entangled in the end, with the characters converging on the now-deserted beach. Such a carefully constructed script suggests that Kurihara and Tanizaki hoped to achieve, through parallel editing, the kind of lively, "musical" rhythm Tanizaki admired in American comedies.

The *Amateur Club* script is considerably more detailed than *The Glory of Life,* which could be either a result of Kurihara's involvement or the larger overall scale of the Taikatsu project. As in Kaeriyama's script, the action is broken down into numbered shots, and the expository passages include lines of dialogue for the actors that helped them to stay in character during the shooting of the film. It is hard to be specific about the number of intertitles in *Amateur Club* because of overlapping changes in the serialized version, but they are divided into approximately forty-four *kotoba sōnyū* ("dialogue inserts") and twenty-five *taitoru* (expository "titles"). Beneath the directions for the location of each scene are indications for "interior" or "exterior" shots. Kurihara's expository passages are more descriptive, and contain detailed instructions for the actors, often including the direction from which they enter and exit a scene; in comparison, the action in *The Glory of Life* script is deduced from information contained in the dialogue. Kurihara and Tanizaki's choice of genre presumably influenced the more fluid colloquial style of the dialogue intertitles in *Amateur Club*.[39]

219

It may be unfair to compare two films of such different scale, but in general a wider range of shots are described in *Amateur Club* than in *The Glory of Life*. Although Kaeriyama included close-ups in his script, two-character shots predominated. Not only does Kurihara use close-ups more frequently, but he uses them in a more consistent manner: three of the main characters, for example, are introduced by an intertitle followed by a close-up shot of the character (unlike the characters in *The Glory of Life*, who are introduced through dialogue intertitles, each main character in *Amateur Club* is introduced with an individual intertitle).[40] In addition, shots often contain three or more characters; some shots of the Yuigahama shore and the audience at the Amateur Club presentation, for example, are composed for large crowds of people. Because Kurihara included instructions for positioning the camera (referred to as the "lens") in *Amateur Club,* he is also commonly credited with having been the first to introduce "camera angles" to the format of the Japanese film script; although he used precise technical terms (in both Japanese and English) for close-ups, long shots, fade transitions, iris shots, and overlap-dissolves, some directions for the positioning of the camera are less explicit. For example, one passage in the script reads simply, "shoot from a different angle" (*betsu no kakudo yori,* 37) instead of calling for a shot from a specific angle (eye level, low angle, reverse shot, etc.). On the other hand, there is a detailed description of an unusual panning point-of-view shot of Yuigahama beach, taken from "slightly above the surface of the water" in order to simulate Chizuko's viewpoint of the beach while she swims offshore (16).

Other than the establishing shot of Yuigahama shore and the point-of-view shot of Chizuko swimming, no other shots seem to suggest the use of a traveling camera. There are, however, three overlap-dissolve (referred to as "overlap") insert shots. One of these is a flashback—actually a repeat of an earlier shot—in the opening sequence. A man notices the commotion caused by a group of bathers, including Chizuko, when they discover they have been robbed while they were swimming (54). When he recalls having seen two suspicious characters a short while earlier, the shot in which he actually saw the two robbers (37) is repeated. The remaining two shots occur in the sequence in which Chizuko's father relates the background of a halberd and a suit of armor, part of the family treasure, which Chizuko has taken a particular interest in. In the first of these shots, Chizuko's father explains that the halberd belonged to his formidable grandmother, and as Chizuko picks up the weapon an overlap-dissolve transforms her into an image of herself dressed as her great-grandmother. After making "one or two thrusts" with the weapon, this image dissolves back into Chizuko (108). The final overlap-dissolve occurs when the father describes the former owner of the armor, the family's most valuable possession. As he is telling the story there is a brief dissolve of a young warrior dressed in the armor as he fights his first battle (111). These scenes also serve to introduce the armor, which Chizuko puts on when she later challenges the robbers who break into the family storehouse.

We can only imagine (with the help of production stills) the images that emerged from this script. The many ways in which such a script will inevitably differ from the completed film is a point elaborated upon in the editorial essay introducing *Amateur Club*'s publication in *Katsudō zasshi*.[41] In spite of any inconsistencies in the degree of detail in the *Amateur Club* script, the range of camera work indicated on the page alone confirms that the film's conception, at least, was considerably more ambitious than any previous pure film attempts. It is possible to hypothesize that *Amateur Club* still would have made an impression even without its explorations of camera technique. In contrast to the heavily painted, carefully concealed bodies of the female impersonator and the lugubrious plots of the *shinpa* melodrama, the novelty of Hayama's presence and comedy on both a visual and verbal (in the intertitles) plane alone might have been enough to draw an audience.

Much of the humor in *Amateur Club* depends on visual gags and is difficult to discuss based on how it is articulated in Kurihara's script. Certain sequences are entertaining to read, but a good deal is lost in the retelling. A few sequences are amusing enough to nevertheless warrant mention here. The chase sequences toward the end of the story are especially droll. In addition to mistaken identities and the hilarity generated by Chizuko, who by now is in a helmet, full armor, and carrying a long sword, the "Rat"—a member of the Amateur Club in costume for his part in the play *Sendaihagi*—becomes an increasingly important link between parallel sequences. He is in fact at the center of the most comical situations.[42]

The Rat's first misadventure occurs when, after being introduced by a title announcing him as "The Monster of Yuigahama" (212), he crosses paths with a gentlemen and his female companion enjoying a leisurely evening stroll along the moonlit beach (213–214). He manages to hide himself in the shadow of an abandoned boat, but they also decide to stop at the boat to rest and have a quiet chat (215–218). He jumps up in fright (219); as might be expected, the couple catch sight of him and faint straight away (220, 222). The poor Rat at this point has been chased all over town by the police and Shigeru's father, and is far more terrified than the dazed young man and his girlfriend. An even worse fate lies ahead, however, when the Rat is discovered by Chizuko. She immediately loses interest in the robbers and, ignoring the Rat's desperate squeals for mercy, readies herself for combat and starts swinging her impressive weapon in his direction (243). When he screams loudly for help the robbers are thrown off guard just long enough for the police to catch them, as the luckless Rat flees with the determined Chizuko close behind (250). She catches up with him at the Muraoka residence (254), but he gets a brief respite when Shigeru's father grabs Chizuko by her hel-met, thinking she is his wayward son. As Chizuko and Shigeru's father con-front each other in amazement, he seizes the opportunity to scurry out of the picture (256–259).

Several of the intertitles contribute to the humor of the script, such as those that playfully mock the Amateur Club's earnest efforts to stage a kabuki performance. Full of puns and high-spirited imitations of the lan-guage used in kabuki plays, however, the humor of these titles could be inter-preted as directed more toward kabuki itself than the histrionic attempts of Shigeru and his friends. The two figures of authority, the fathers of Chizuko and Shigeru, are also targets of jest, a comic device common in Keystone farce. Chizuko's ingenuous father, in particular, is often made to look the fool. He obviously dotes on his daughter and is completely oblivious to her mischief. When he rescues the tearful Chizuko from her mother's wrath, for example, Chizuko dashes outside and abruptly stops crying as soon as her parents are out of sight. The tears were only a ruse to fool her adoring father (74–75). One of the funniest moments in the entire script occurs when Chizuko's father calls the police station to inform them of his daughter's dis-appearance (as I explain below, this scene apparently contributed to censor-ship problems that influenced changes in the film's ending). Chizuko's father does not know that Shigeru's father has just reported the escape of a group of young men in medieval dress a few moments earlier. The police officer does his best to be polite: "I see. Your daughter has run away from home wearing scarlet-laced armor . . . very well, we shall search for her immediately." (230). A few scenes later, as Chizuko relentlessly pursues the doomed Rat, her distraught father chases after an embarrassed Shigeru (240). The father cries out "Chizuko! Chizuko!" Spotting Shigeru's warrior costume, he has mistaken the boy for his beloved daughter.

Not surprisingly, there reportedly were gags in the film that are not indi-cated in the script. The director Yoshimura Kōzaburō, who was ten years old when the film opened, over forty years later still remembered a shot of a young man buried up to his head in the sand. Tanizaki and Kurihara also had problems with the censors, which resulted in a last minute revision of the film's ending. The change is evident in the original published version of the script, which was serialized in *Katsudō zasshi* from June to October of 1921. Although the penultimate installment ends with scene 253, the subsequent and final installment begins with a rewrite starting with a title after the end of scene 251. A note at the top of the page explains that the ending had to be reformulated because the production crew was denied permission to shoot inside a police station.[43] In the final installment the Keystone Kop-inspired police officers (*junsa*) who had appeared earlier in the script are rewritten as detectives (*keiji*), and their role is less prominent. This could have diffused the humor of *Amateur Club,* and weakened any association to its commercially successful foreign models in the eyes of expectant viewers. As I discuss below, the disappointment in this respect does appear to have been great. Judging from film-related publications of the period, pure film rhetoric had escalated to the point that viewers anticipating a major change in the direction of the domestic industry had high expectations by 1920, and much attention was given to experiments with new screen comedy genres or forms.

The Audience Responds

The production of *Amateur Club* began in mid-August 1920, two months after Taikatsu published its prospectus in *Katsudō kurabu.* Tanizaki made it clear in his preface to the published script for *The Lust of the White Serpent*[44] that he had been active in its production, and despite his own decidedly "amateur" status at the time, he also appears to have participated throughout the production of *Amateur Club.* In a photograph taken of the staff and crew on Yuigahama beach, Tanizaki, looking dapper in a white suit and large straw hat, is seated in between Kurihara and Hayama. Kurihara, holding a pen, has what appears to be a shooting script balanced on his knee. (It is interesting to note that although the script was serialized in *Katsudō zasshi* under Tanizaki's name, the editorial essay introducing the script was accompanied by a large photograph of Kurihara sitting at a desk with a pen in his hand, accompanied by a caption that reads, "famous director Kurihara Tōmasu in the middle of the scriptwriting process." The opposite page features a smaller photograph of Tanizaki seated in a wicker chair, holding a cane and a cigar in his right hand.[45]) Benisawa Yōko later recalled that Tanizaki stood next to Kurihara on the set, giving instructions along with the director.[46] Tanizaki recalled being impressed with Kurihara's perfectionism during production. Describing the director's technique on location in "I Must Be Grateful for that Happiness," Tanizaki admitted that he was surprised to see Kurihara spend over an hour on a shot that was to be only one or two minutes long.[47] In all, it took a little over a month to shoot all five reels of *Amateur Club.* One portion had to be reshot, and it was finally released in November.[48]

The criticism of the pure film by opinion leaders of the "progressive audience," as it was styled in the Taikatsu prospectus, remained in 1920 overwhelmingly preoccupied with technical achievements. Pure film efforts continued to be evaluated in comparison with foreign films, and long passages were devoted to analyzing all Japanese films in terms of the number of "close-ups" or "cut-backs" that had been used;[49] such a preoccupation with imported technical terms, in fact, would prevail into the next decade and

The *Amateur Club* cast and crew on location on the beach at Yuigahama, Kamakura. In the front row, Benisawa Yōko (*second from left*), director Kurihara (*fourth from left*), Tanizaki, "famous Japanese Novelist" (*center, wearing white suit*), Hayama Michiko, and Takahashi Eichi (Okada Tokihito). *Kinema junpō,* 21 November 1921. From Makino, ed., *Fukkokuban Kinema junpō.*

reach a climax with the debate surrounding the introduction of sound technology. In short, while pure film enthusiasts in 1920 continued to welcome all attempts at pure film—any film, for example, that opened without the presence of a *benshi* narrator was still cause for celebration— they seem to have been less willing at this point to forgive the many other shortcomings such films might have.

The fate of Kaeriyama's Film Art Association illustrates this shift in the demands of pure film advocates. After the success of *The Girl in His Dreams* in June 1920, Kaeriyama's subsequent film, *The Tale of the White Chrysanthemum* (July 1920) received a relatively quiet reception. The production of the film had been hampered by differences of opinion among the members of the group (some members, including Murata Minoru, felt that Kaeriyama was not progressive enough). Displeasure on the part of the studio management and the fact that the film had been commissioned by a foreign concern may also account for the film's release in Kyoto and the decision never to show it in an Asakusa theater.[50] But it is also conceivable that part of the reason for the film's relative lack of success was Kaeriyama's choice of subject matter. There was something modern and sophisticated about *The Girl in His Dreams,* but *The Tale of the White Chrysanthemum,* a Muromachi-period (1338–1573) romance and sword fight film about a flower girl, suggests a return to the contrived stories of his earlier films. With the establishment of Taikatsu and Shōchiku, Kaeriyama's achievements were quickly obscured by the work of Hollywood-trained Kurihara and Kotani, and the Film Art Association was formally dissolved in July 1921.

Several factors influenced Tanizaki and Kurihara's choice of material for their first collaboration. It is evident that the demands of intellectual tastes and Tanizaki and Kurihara's desire to make a film with a popular appeal rather than an ambitious artistic endeavor were important considerations. Yet there are signs that suggest *Amateur Club* was motivated at least as much by Kurihara and Tanizaki's sheer enthusiasm and love of film—the film can even be understood as reflecting a certain amount of reflexivity in terms of being an "amateur" endeavor—and this proved to be one of the film's greatest attractions. Not only was *Amateur Club* unobstructed by Kaeriyama's quaint morality, but it had an uninhibited, playful quality that was appreciated by viewers no matter how critical they were of other aspects of the film. For example, although audiences were undoubtedly curious to see *Amateur Club* after all the publicity surrounding the establishment of Taikatsu and news of Tanizaki's collaboration, the first few minutes of the film were much more exciting than anything they had expected. There was nothing unusual about the title card, "Amateur Club," followed by a second title card with Tanizaki's name. But what came next was a bust shot of Tanizaki himself, in silhouette. After striking a match and lighting his cigarette, he exhaled, filling the screen with smoke. This was followed by a silhouette shot of Kurihara. Whether it was the presence of the popular Tanizaki on-screen, or merely the novelty of the technique, this was a memorable experience for the audience. Two months after the film opened, one viewer wrote: "For a moment we experienced that solemn feeling that comes from being faced with the extraordinary, and yet in our hearts we couldn't help being a little amused. It wasn't that we were laughing at Tanizaki Jun'ichirō or feeling embarrassed for him. It was because his mischievousness made us smile."[51]

In addition to having the advantage of lighter material, *Amateur Club* was critically judged technically superior to *The Glory of Life.* To begin with, very little fault was found with the acting and photography.[52] Kaeriyama had used amateurs in his films, but he usually cast trained actors with a background in the *shingeki* theater in the central roles. This was regarded as an improvement over the more standard use of kabuki and *shinpa* actors, but it was not as bold a commitment as Kurihara and Tanizaki's decision to use only amateurs.[53] Makeup and costumes in *Amateur Club* were also praised along with the energetic performances of the individual performers. Critics applauded the lighting, sets, and final tinting, and described the camera work as superior to that of the average film being made in Japan at the time.[54] The cameraman, Inami Yoshimi, had been trained in Hollywood like Shōchiku's Kotani; Shōchiku had approached Kotani first, and Inami had been the next choice.[55] Disregarding the numerous references to Tanizaki's contribution, however, the most enthusiastic praise was reserved for Kurihara, who was hailed as the first Japanese director to use the more American-style approach of investing the director with a more authoritative role in production.[56]

However much critics praised Kurihara's editing skills, and Kurihara and Tanizaki's attempt to create a comedy with a "musical" rhythm, some viewers found the tempo of *Amateur Club* too slow. One such viewer singled out the final chase sequences in particular as being too long, and complained of an overall unevenness, "as if the film had been shot in a hurry."[57] Iijima Tadashi concludes that the concept of two parallel stories actually spoiled the structure of the film because at some point they seemed to separate into two different stories.[58] It is also conceivable that contemporary audiences did not fully grasp Kurihara's attempts to achieve a style of continuity comparable to the relatively seamless narrative of a Hollywood film. At least one viewer has admitted that he was surprised to learn that a cutaway shot of the audience (a shot of a mother and child, played by Tanizaki's wife and young daughter, so described in the script) had not been improvised.[59]

Although the lighthearted spirit and technical achievements of *Amateur Club* were appreciated, it was commonly agreed at the time that no matter how cleverly Kurihara and Tanizaki managed to imitate Sennett's slapstick style, as a "Japanese" comedy the film was a failure. Envious of the popularity enjoyed by the steady stream of comedies being imported from abroad, and puzzled by a relative dearth of domestic comedy forms, supporters of the pure film had been discussing the problem of devising new forms of film comedy in Japan for some time before the release of *Amateur Club*. Not much was suggested in the way of a solution, however, and at least one writer concluded that the real problem was that the Japanese simply did not know how to appreciate comedy. "The Japanese have never known how to laugh," he wrote. "They love a good laugh, but they laugh with their mouths, not with their bellies. If you doubt me, just take a look around you." Examples of the typical situations regarded as humorous by the Japanese, he continued, were "such trivialities as a young girl dropping her chopsticks."[60] In hindsight some critics, like Iijima Tadashi, for example, are less inclined to criticize the narrative quality of *Amateur Club* because the very nature of slapstick requires an unbelievable, nonsensical plot. Nevertheless, even Iijima believes that modeling the film after American slapstick resulted in characters that, in the eyes of the average Japanese viewer, behaved in a manner that was essentially "un-Japanese."[61] Perhaps at that particular time the concept of ridiculing social conventions and the forces of law and order—unquestionably humorous in the context of a film of foreign origin—did not translate well, at least in terms of contemporary nationalistic sentiments, to a Japanese setting. It is equally conceivable that the censors who demanded last-minute revisions were at fault for whatever flatness audiences detected in the humor.

Kurihara and Tanizaki proposed to make a "popular" film showing the life of contemporary young Japanese, but *Amateur Club* (like *The Glory of Life*) was exclusively about members of the upper middle class. While such characters might have limited *Amateur Club*'s popular appeal, they also made it more accessible to the large intellectual contingency of pure film enthusiasts, the audience Kurihara and Tanizaki evidently had in mind from the start. The contemporary life film would not gain widespread generic diversity and appeal until much later in the decade, but for such supporters of pure film drama, *Amateur Club* represented an important step in that direction. It was still criticized as a "foreign imitation," but in spirit, at least, it was more in tune with contemporary taste than Kaeriyama's previous efforts. As one viewer recalled several years later:

> To tell the truth, when I saw *The Girl in the Mountain* by the Film Art Association I couldn't follow the story at all. The actors' gestures and expressions were childish in a manner that was inconceivable for Japanese, and I couldn't identify with them. There was also something unmistakably unnatural and foreign about *Amateur Club*, but I became absorbed in it right away. Perhaps it was because of the atmosphere of the Yūrakuza theater, where the film opened, or of Taikatsu, the production company, but the film had a lightheartedness that was within reach. [The credits] that, beginning with Jun'ichirō, introduced the faces of the cast and crew one by one, made me feel as if I knew them all, and I was glad that Tanizaki, a popular writer at the time, had written the scenario. The appearance in a bathing suit of his sister-in-law, Hayama Michiko, was unprecedented in a Japanese film, and I enjoyed her lively animation. I could feel a youthfulness that had been absent in Japanese films until then.[62]

Amateur Club represented a significant breakthrough for pure film enthusiasts for a number of reasons. To begin with, Kurihara's Hollywood background, Tanizaki's original story, a cast of amateurs, and the conscious exploitation of familiar locations made the film unquestionably the furthest removed from the theater of all pure film attempts until then.[63] In spite of an alleged sluggish pace, it also was considered technically superior to most, if not all other domestic productions: even though some viewers were more impressed by the sophisticated photography of Henry Kotani at Shōchiku, Inami's capable camera work was regarded as far better than average for the time. And although the film was not wholly successful in presenting characters that were credible as contemporary Japanese, Hayama and her colleagues were commended for their comparatively unassuming and natural performances. The unprecedented release at a prestigious first-run theater, the aura of exoticism surrounding the small Yokohama studio, and the fact that the picture was a domestic version of an American genre enjoying considerable popularity at the time (and a pioneer attempt at formulating a new brand of screen comedy in Japan) were all cited as additional factors enhancing the film's appeal. But most important, *Amateur Club* was the first contemporary drama film to be made by a director and a writer who had clearly defined responsibilities during the production of the film. In 1920 the solo *benshi* was extremely popular, and a glance at the continuity transcriptions of both foreign and Japanese pictures in the film literature of the late 1910s—with credits listing the title, studio, and cast, but neither the director nor the writer—gives some indication of the extent to which these two roles were ignored at the time.

It is true that a great deal of attention was given to the vivacious and modern Hayama: in her unusual costumes she romped about in an astonishing, uninhibited manner that would have been out of the question for a female impersonator. But the real stars of *Amateur Club* were the director and scriptwriter, who appeared—quite literally—in the opening credits of the film. Kurihara's talents as an actor had been appreciated in Japan even before he returned from Hollywood, and to an extent, the costumes, makeup, and spontaneity of the performers were attributed to his skill as an experienced actor. But Kurihara was also a director, and it was in this role, as a director who had had the opportunity to observe the work of such impressive Hollywood personalities as Ince and Griffith, that he was promoted by the Taikatsu management. This association would not have been lost on viewers aware of the increasingly visible presence of the director in Hollywood. Judging by the amount of positive critical response that focused on Tanizaki's involvement in the film, the significance of this important writer's participation was at least as great, if not greater, than that of Kurihara. The film underscored the necessity for original material written by accomplished writers; it was also regarded as further proof of Tanizaki's active support of pure film. As one pure film advocate observed, practical efforts like *Amateur Club,* however flawed, were still more efficient than empty theorizing. He pointed out that although *Amateur Club* "might seem trivial compared to the rest of Tanizaki's work," such a simple, lighthearted film was appropriate as a trial run for the Taikatsu studio. "However much they continue extolling idealistic theories," he argued, "the members of our film community should regard [this film] as a starting point from which they must continue to strive for works with some degree of harmony."[64]

It is obvious that viewers regarded Tanizaki's participation in the production of *Amateur Club* as significant, but how important Tanizaki himself considered the film is less clear. Iijima contends that Tanizaki was most interested in re-creating in a Japanese setting the "musical" rhythm that he admired in American comedies, while providing Kurihara with material that would complement the directing and production methods the director had learned in Hollywood.[65] It is also difficult to determine the extent of Tanizaki's contribution to the existing version of the film script, although it seems likely that Kurihara's revisions, rendering Tanizaki's original scenario into a version closer to a shooting script, were primarily technical: a more concise division of the action into individual scenes, and the addition of camera angles and technical terms that would have been less familiar to the inexperienced Tanizaki. Judging from the nature of Tanizaki's subsequent films at Taikatsu, and the fact that he never again attempted this type of comedy, it is conceivable that the experience of being present during the production of *Amateur Club,* his first experience of the kind, was more meaningful than the actual film itself. There is little doubt that his participation in the production of the film was an important influence in determining the future course of his involvement at Taikatsu. As he himself admitted in "I Must Be Grateful for that Happiness," seeing the manner in which Kurihara rewrote his original scenario made him all the more determined to master screenwriting technique. *Amateur Club* might not be the best example of Tanizaki's own expertise as a scriptwriter, but it is significant as an early example of a well-known writer providing the original story for a contemporary drama film.

THE TAIKATSU LEGACY

The importation of foreign films had been an important impetus in the founding of Taikatsu, but it was also a determining factor in bringing about its end. The appearance of an odd assortment of documentaries ("The Baseball Team of California University," "His Majesty the Crown Prince Observes a Boat Race," "Acrobats Tour America") in Kurihara's filmography under the year 1921 suggests that less than a year after the release of *Amateur Club* the small company was desperately in need of additional funds to pay import fees and the cost of distribution rights in addition to financing Kurihara's productions.[66] Although Taikatsu had started off with an unusually small amount of capital, employees had been confident at the time that the investment by a member of a powerful financial combine and the support of the intelligentsia would compensate for the relative scarcity of funds.[67] In spite of the limited finances, the Taikatsu management in the early days of the company appears to have been a "group of idealists" working "toward the realization of its ideals," just as it had described itself in the company prospectus. But the Japanese economy grew increasingly unstable after 1920. Asano was eventually forced to withdraw his investment after the production of *The Lust of the White Serpent,* signaling the end for the small studio.

According to some accounts, Asano withdrew from Taikatsu because he was disappointed with *The Lust of the White Serpent,* Kurihara and Tanizaki's last, most ambitious endeavor, which had been completed while Asano was temporarily in the United States.[68] The rumor was denied by the management,[69] but even without the difficulties caused by Asano's withdrawal, Taikatsu could not have continued to sponsor Kurihara and Tanizaki's pure films for much longer. Toward the end of 1921 the company's problems were compounded by a series of misfortunes: untimely purchases; censorship complications; and disputes with more powerful companies (Shōchiku, for example) over the enforcement of exclusive distribution rights for such potentially lucrative films as *Broken Blossoms, The Four Horsemen of the Apocalypse,* and *The Kid.* From the very start Taikatsu had prided itself on constructing luxurious theaters equipped with the most expensive projectors available from the United States and Germany;[70] perhaps for this reason it had only twenty or thirty theaters nationwide under its direct management, and it was impossible to circulate the steady stream of films being sent from the United States. To make matters worse, it was becoming increasingly clear that Kurihara and Tanizaki's production methods were too expensive, particularly in view of the limited number of viewers interested in pure films. During the production of the five-reel (about 5,000 feet) *Amateur Club,* for example, Kurihara had shot over 14,000 feet of negative.[71] According to Benisawa Yōko, the generous wages received by the studio staff were yet another factor contributing to the studio's rapid decline.[72]

It was obvious that Taikatsu would have to change its production policy if it intended to continue importing newly released foreign films. In October 1921, the company decided to begin sponsoring the production of *shinpa* films, which were guaranteed to bring in revenue from the provincial theaters where Kurihara's pure films had failed to create an audience. Taikatsu's import section also decided to concentrate on pictures that would appeal to the general public, and it invested in a large number of American serials. Unfortunately, the popularity of the serial in the United States had already started to decline, and Taikatsu found itself saddled with an enormous quantity of films of decidedly inferior quality.[73]

The end was surprisingly swift, beginning with complications during the production of *The Lust of the White Serpent* in 1921. Inami, the cameraman, had health problems that delayed the film's release until September. The decision to convert to the production of *shinpa* films was made in October. In spite of an announcement that month of a film (a comedy) to be directed by Tanizaki, as well as plans to produce his first script, *The Radiance of the Moon,* and another work titled *Irezumi no onna* (*The Tattooed Woman*),[74] Tanizaki left Taikatsu in November, apparently disgruntled over the change in policy. That same month the censors objected to a film starring Hayama Michiko, delaying its release.[75] Finally, in December, Taikatsu dissolved the contracts of the small band of actors that had been hand-picked by Kurihara and Tanizaki. At the time, Shimo Nariyasu, by then the managing director of the studio, explained that their dismissal was only temporary.[76] Other sources claimed the management took advantage of Kurihara's poor health, and released the actors under the pretense that Kurihara's doctor had ordered him to take an extended rest.[77]

By the end of the year there were rumors that Shōchiku had offered to hire Kurihara. According to the director's filmography, he had already made at least one *shinpa* film at Taikatsu before the new year, but only three documentaries are listed under 1922. Clearly, there was not much else Kurihara could do at the studio after losing the support of Tanizaki and the actors he had trained. In August 1922, Taikatsu reached an agreement with Shōchiku in which it essentially turned over all of its import concerns to the larger company. Taikatsu continued to produce *shinpa* films intermittently from April 1922 until October, at which point it was completely absorbed by Shōchiku.[78]

It is tempting to wonder what sort of pictures Tanizaki would have made had the Taikatsu management continued to promote the production of pure films; it is conceivable that he would not have left the company so abruptly if it had not changed its production policy. Taikatsu's announcement, in October 1921, of its decision to revert to *shinpa* films apparently took Tanizaki by surprise: he had just moved his family to Yokohama the previous month. If it is true that in October there were plans for Tanizaki to direct his own film, Taikatsu seems to have been equally startled by Tanizaki's sudden decision to leave. The company continued to issue statements hinting at a reconciliation.[79] Tanizaki's short entry in *Shinchō* in January 1922, in which he admitted that he would like to continue working in film, suggests that he may have considered such a reconciliation himself.[80]

In this short entry in *Shinchō,* Tanizaki suggested that he found it difficult to adjust to the "teamwork" the medium required. There are others who believe this was a major factor in the writer's decision to return to writing fiction full-time.[81] Iijima Tadashi attributes Tanizaki's apparent loss of interest in screenwriting to Kurihara's inability to match the writer's artistic sensibilities.[82] There may be some truth to this statement: Kurihara repeatedly postponed plans to film a number of works by Tanizaki, including *The Radiance of the Moon*, "The Growth with a Human Face," and *Jakyō* (*Heresy*).[83] But such changes in production plans could have been caused by a number of reasons (limited finances immediately comes to mind). Tanizaki cites Taikatsu's decline and Kurihara's worsening condition as the reasons behind his decision to leave the studio.[84] Regardless of what motivated him to end his association with Taikatsu, he retained a strong interest in film during his subsequent two years in Yokohama. He participated in the production of at least one film, *The Sparrow Who Lost His Tongue,* and his brother recalled animated discussions about film at frequent gatherings in Tanizaki's second Yokohama home.[85]

Kurihara never ceased his personal campaign to win more time and money for domestic productions, and he continued to stress the importance of making films that would appeal to foreign as well as domestic audiences. When asked why Japan could not produce such films, only a few months after Taikatsu began the exclusive production of *shinpa* films, Kurihara answered that, given enough time and money, everything was possible, implying that the entertainment management was to blame. As it was pointed out at the time, however, time and money are rarely given freely,[86] and Kurihara unfortunately lacked the physical stamina to continue. A year before his death from tuberculosis in 1926 at the age of forty-one, he made an appearance in Ogasawara Meihō's *Gokuraku shima no joō* (*The Queen of Paradise Island*). Although he had acted in his own films at Taikatsu, this was his first major role for another director since his Hollywood days. According to Ogasawara, Kurihara was planning a production of Tanizaki's *Heresy* after finishing *The Queen of Paradise Island,* and had arranged for Ogasawara to be his assistant director. But as *The Queen of Paradise Island* neared completion, Kurihara could barely stand without his wife's support, and it was to be his last production.[87] In a eulogy written two months after Kurihara's death, Tanizaki called the director's short life, which ended in excruciating pain and poverty, a tragedy. He closed, however, with the comment that although his former colleague became increasingly irritable toward the end of his long illness, the Thomas Kurihara that he remembered from his days at Taikatsu had been a "rare and heroic" person.[88]

CONCLUSION: BEYOND PURE FILM

WHEN THOMAS KURIHARA died in September 1926, Tanizaki had already moved to Kansai; that year he made his second trip to Shanghai, and gave up the Western-style life he had pursued in Tokyo and Yokohama. Tanizaki did not write for the screen again after he left Yokohama, but even excluding his own original film scripts, his work has provided material for over fifty films. The small Taikatsu studio in Yokohama never grew to the scale of a Hollywood studio as Kurihara and Tanizaki had envisioned—in the end it was surpassed in this respect by Shōchiku—but the actors that Kurihara and Tanizaki had assembled there brought their experience and training with them when they left the studio. In 1922, for example, a group including Uchida Tomu and Benisawa Yōko went to work at Makino Shōzō's studio in Kyoto, where they appeared in one of his many versions of *Chūshingura* (*The Loyal Forty-Seven Ronin*), and Hayama Michiko and Okada Tokihiko acted for other directors, including Kaeriyama Norimasa. Other Taikatsu protégés who went on to important careers were the directors Futagawa Buntarō and Inoue Kintarō and the actors Egawa Ureo and Watanabe Atsushi.

In 1926 Kaeriyama Norimasa had already retired from film production, but many of his former colleagues were among the most active figures working in the contemporary drama film. Notably, Murata Minoru, already known for his contemporary drama films *Omitsu to Seizaburō* (*Omitsu and Seizaburō*, 1923) and *Seisaku no tsuma* (*Seisaku's Wife*, 1924), had just returned from a trip to Europe, where he and Mori Iwao, his screenwriter, held screenings of *Machi no tejinashi* (*The Street Juggler*, 1925) for audiences in London, Berlin, and Paris. In Japan the script for this film was praised as an original work at a time when adaptations (translations would be a more

233

Okada Tokihiko, who appeared in several Kurihara-Tanizaki features. Courtesy Kawakita Memorial Film Institute.

suitable word) of foreign literature were most popular. European audiences, however, were not impressed—they criticized the film for being too slow, too gloomy, and most of all for being too imitative of Western melodrama—and Murata, a passionate admirer of European culture, returned home broken-hearted, sending Mori on to Hollywood alone. The rumor that the director Ernst Lubitsch liked *The Street Juggler* provided some consolation for Murata, but the film failed to appeal to the American audience as well.

Foreign reaction to Murata's work had little effect on his reputation in Japan, and when he returned he became head of the contemporary drama division of the Nikkatsu Taishōgun studio in Kyoto. That year he and Mori Iwao organized a separate department at the Nikkatsu studio, the Kinyōkai, to foster the improvement of contemporary drama film scripts. Active in both the *shingeki* and pure film movements, Murata's loyalties lay with the intel-

234

Seisaku no tsuma (*Seisaku's Wife*), directed by Murata Minoru. Urabe Kumeko. Courtesy Kawakita Memorial Film Institute.

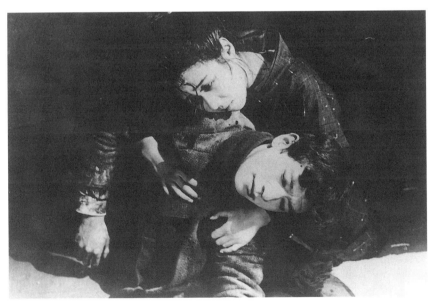

Machi no tejinashi (*The Street Juggler*), directed by Murata Minoru from a script by Mori Iwao, 1925. Okada Yoshiko (*top*) and Kondō Iyokichi. Courtesy Kawakita Memorial Film Institute.

lectuals who believed that a thorough understanding of Western drama was essential to the realization of the modern Japanese film, rationalizing that only this type of knowledge would erase any lingering influence of the traditional theater. As a champion of realism, he was gradually superseded in the 1930s by Mizoguchi Kenji, a protégé of Tanaka Eizō. Tanaka, unlike Kaeriyama and Murata, made notable innovations in the contemporary genre while working within the framework of the commercial *shinpa* film at the Nikkatsu Mukōjima studio. Tanizaki's film scripts at Taikatsu had been inspired by his familiarity with European and American films and Kurihara's knowledge of Hollywood technique; Kaeriyama and Murata's contemporary drama films were influenced by their admiration of European and American films and, particularly in Murata's case, the *shingeki* movement to modernize the Japanese theater. In this sense, Tanizaki, Kaeriyama, and Murata shared common ground in their close affinities with an intellectual audience. Tanaka Eizō, whose association with Osanai Kaoru and the *shingeki* movement signals an active interest in non-Japanese forms of dramatic narrative and narrative technique, shared this commonality as well.

The view popularized by Anderson and Richie's scholarship in the 1950s, encouraged by the work of traditional historians like Tanaka Jun'ichirō, is that the pure film movement is important as marking the point at which Japanese cinema becomes interesting precisely because it becomes "Westernized." As further research in this key transitional period continues to add depth to our perceptions of it, unfamiliar or even forgotten names, titles, and traces of information will no doubt be brought into sharper focus. It is clear nevertheless that at the very least, the movement brought together many of the important creative figures in Japanese cinema of the 1910s and 1920s in an unprecedented way, and with long-lasting consequences. That these individuals came from a variety of backgrounds and, subsequently, promoted a wide range of creative and critical attitudes toward film is a crucial aspect of the period that is all too easily overlooked in the scramble to separate and differentiate East from West.

In the 1910s, the contemporary drama genre took shape at a time when the *shingeki* spirit of reform collided with *shinpa* practice and tradition in an increasingly cosmopolitan domestic marketplace. Japan may not have been a key exporter of films, but as a seasoned consumer of the European and American product it did not exist in a vacuum, cut off from changing trends in the international film market: the popularization of continuity devices; shifts in audience expectations and the conception of new genres; the formulation of mass-market perceptions of authorship and related issues of cultural quality and creative control; the idea of cinema as a product with a national identity; and the view of cinema as art, to name just a few. The new diversity of approach in terms of production and exhibition encouraged a new interdependence between filmmakers (directors and writers), film actors, and the written word (both in the form of the screenplay and intertitles). At the same time, it inspired debate that forged a seminal relationship between production (the author) and consumption (the spectator) through the emergent venue of popular journalism.

In its wake, the movement left ripples of change that determined the direction of the newer studios established in the early 1920s as well as the direction of the industry as a whole after the devastation and reconstruction precipitated by the 1923 Kanto Earthquake. The *benshi* remained an important element of the industry until the standardization of sound technology in the 1930s, but so did the use of titles. Female impersonators were already deemed an anachronism before the earthquake, and the female star became the new personality on the block at Shōchiku as well as Nikkatsu, the former core of *shinpa* production. The screenplay remained a central creative element and the screenwriting department an essential aspect of film production. The participation of prominent writers like Tanizaki Jun'ichirō in script development had an important effect not only on the industry, but in many cases, on their own fiction as well. It seems moot to argue that many of these changes might have happened anyway. Although difficult to define given the complexity of the period, the gaps that remain in our history, and the dangers involved in applying present-day criteria, the pure film movement irrefutably provided a milieu that favored the developments I have described.

Where can we go from here? The prominent position the screenplay continues to enjoy in Japanese film culture remains a topic rich with possibility. The pure film movement only partially explains this enduring phenomenon, but further studies of many of the important screenwriters of the late silent and early sound period will undoubtedly reveal formative links to individuals central to this period. Yoda Yoshikata, who later became the principal writer for the director Mizoguchi Kenji, is a good example. Yoda entered Nikkatsu and began to work with Murata Minoru in 1930 before moving on to Mizoguchi's entourage (Mizoguchi himself was a protégé of both Murata and Tanaka). A closer analysis of Yoda's career, like that of many members of his generation of contemporary drama screenwriters working in the Kyoto Nikkatsu studio (where the contemporary drama division moved after the Kanto Earthquake), might be the key to unraveling the intriguing interplay between a healthy respect for foreign influence, like that fostered by Murata, Mizoguchi, and even Tanaka Eizō, and the elements of *shinpa* dramaturgy that also appear to have figured so prominently in their work.

On a more general note, this study of the pure film movement inevitably encourages further research in the lost genres that existed in the forms of the *shinpa* film and chain drama, a direction outlined in chapter 1. The period film, the female impersonator, and the *benshi* all deserve more space than I have been able to allow them here. The *benshi* in particular has been a special focus of researchers working in both Europe and the United States. Recent scholarship in Japan has made much of the journalism of the period available to researchers worldwide in the form of reprints of important magazines like *Katsudō shashinkai* and *Kinema Record.* The recuperation of and accessibility to whatever survives in the form of scripts, scenarios, screenplays, and *benshi* scripts are sure to raise new opportunities for understanding the lively competing forces of this period that, to our current knowledge, has left us so little in the form of surviving prints. At the very least, we can attempt to approach these lost visions on the flickering screen of our imagination.

APPENDIX

Translator's Note

SCREENWRITING STYLE HAS always been open to variables, but there are a few aspects of the following translations that warrant mention apart from stylistic considerations. In general, the translations reflect the format of the original text as closely as possible, but I have also tried to keep notes to a minimum.

English approximations are used when they do not unduly detract from the effect of the original (for example, "veranda" for *engawa* in *Amateur Club,* although these two words are not entirely interchangeable).

The original Japanese is retained when the closest English approximation seems inappropriate, misleading, or, at best, vague.

Whenever possible, "incorporated footnotes" are restricted to first appearance of the original Japanese, which follows in brackets. The original Japanese is used thereafter.

Any terminology that appears in capitals in the original (i.e., CU for close-up) is retained in the translation.

Punctuation has been retained whenever possible; it is worth noting that a casual, or at least unconventional, attitude toward punctuation is one of the characteristics of *Amateur Club* (for example, double exclamation points, no quotation marks, phrases in place of conventional sentence structure).

In the following translations, it is not my intention to provide a detailed analysis of the terminology of the period, but because the use of "technical terms" and degree of detailed description is an informative aspect of these scripts, I include references to the original as much as possible. In general, there is a pronounced lack of consistency in the use of basic terminology in these scripts. There are often basic variations even within a single script. *The Glory of Life* uses such terms as "fade in," "fade out," "Vision," and "close-up" most consistently. The *Amateur Club* and *The Lust of the White Serpent* scripts were both published along with a terminology key, but the terms provided are not used consistently. In *Amateur Club,* for example, *ōutsushi, sessha,* and CU are all apparently used interchangeably to indicate a "close-up" or "close shot" (there is no way to systematically distinguish between the two); *ōutsushi* is a common term for "close-up," but *sessha* is the term provided in the explanatory key. LS and *tōutsushi* are both used to indicate a "long shot." In such cases, it is not clear whether the different terms imply variation in the relative proximity of the camera to its object. Although my intention was to retain the original usage as much as possible, in one instance I deliberately chose an alternative interpretation. In both *Amateur Club* and *The Lust of the White Serpent,* *yōmei* and *yōan* are described as "dissolve in and out." No mention is made in either script of the more likely terms, "fade in" and "fade out." (In *The Glory of Life* as well as *The Production and Photography of Moving Picture Drama,* Kaeriyama Norimasa uses the terms *shiboriaku* ["fade in"] and *shiboru* ["fade out"].) The absence of any mention of fades suggests possible confusion between fades and dissolves on Tanizaki's part, and I have translated *yōmei* and *yōan* as "fade in" and "fade out."

Any alterations in the formatting that I have made in the following translations is for the purpose of coherence and accessibility. In this regard too I have tried to remain as faithful to my sources as possible, but it should be noted that all translations here are from published versions of the scripts. It is entirely possible that to some extent the scripts already underwent some kind of editorial process during their initial publication and that the form in which they eventually appeared as published may not exactly correspond to how the screenwriter conceived of putting the text on the page.

Mizusawa Takehiko [Kaeriyama Norimasa]: *The Glory of Life* (*Sei no kagayaki*, 1918–1919)

The Glory of Life

CREDITS:

Original story Mizusawa Takehiko [Kaeriyama Norimasa]

Director	Kaeriyama Norimasa
Photography	Ōmori Masaru
Titles	Nogawa Tatsu

CAST:

Yanagisawa Yasuhiko	Murata Minoru
Yamashita Juntarō	Kondō Iyokichi
Shimazaki Teruko	Hanayagi Harumi
Yō-chan	Ishida Yōichi
Teruko's father	Aoyama Sugisaku

Hanayagi Harumi as Teruko and Murata Minoru as a repentant Yanagisawa, scene 89 of *Sei no kagayaki* (*The Glory of Life*), directed by Kaeriyama Norimasa, 1918–1919. Courtesy Kawakita Memorial Film Institute.

241

1. On the lake

TITLE: "SUMMER HAS ARRIVED. HE HAS COME TO THE RESORT, AS HE DOES EVERY YEAR.

The Viscount's son, YANAGISAWA YASUHIKO . . . MURATA MINORU"
Yasuhiko is sailing his yacht on the lake.
(2–3 shots, add a close-up [*ōutsushi*])

2. Near the lake #1

TITLE: "YAMASHITA AND TERUKO HAVE BEEN FRIENDS SINCE CHILDHOOD.
The young chemist, YAMASHITA JUNTARŌ . . . KONDŌ IYOKICHI
THE WELL-TO-DO YOUNG WOMAN, SHIMAZAKI TERUKO . . . HANAYAGI HARUMI"
Yamashita and Teruko are about to put their boat in the water.

3. Near the lake #2

TITLE: "YŌ-CHAN, TERUKO'S YOUNGER BROTHER . . . ISHIDA YŌICHI"
Yō-chan comes running toward the lake from afar. As he runs forward, he looks ahead and laughs.
Yō-chan: "Sister!"
(Close-up) Yō-chan's face. He breaks into a run.

4. Near the lake #1

Yamashita and Teruko push their boat into the water. Yō-chan comes running toward them.
Yō-chan: "Please take me too."
Yamashita: "Oh, it's you—get in."
Teruko: "Yō-chan, don't rock the boat, it's dangerous."
Yō-chan: "Don't worry, I won't."[1]
Yamashita and Yō-chan launch the boat. Teruko gets on board. The other two also get in and they take off.

5. On the lake

Yanagisawa's yacht sailing on the lake. The yacht carrying Yamashita and the others sails behind it. The two boats gradually draw nearer to each other until Yamashita and Yanagisawa are sailing neck and neck. They race their yachts.

6. The shore of the lake

The two boats reach the shore. The four passengers disembark and walk ashore. Yamashita introduces Teruko to Yanagisawa.
Yamashita: "Allow me to introduce you. This is Miss Shimazaki."

Yanagisawa: "How do you do. My name is Yanagisawa. My summer house is in the neighborhood, so please come visit."

Teruko: "Why, thank you, I will."

Yanagisawa is moved by Teruko's beauty.

Yanagisawa: "Well, let's meet again."

Yamashita: "Goodbye, we'll stop by to visit you sometime."

Yanagisawa says goodbye and leaves. The remaining three watch him depart. Teruko looks thoughtful as she gazes after him.

(Insert setting sun.) Fade out [*shiboru*]

7. The garden of Yanagisawa's summer house

TITLE: "THE AWAKENING OF LOVE"

In the garden, Yangisawa is gazing at the lake. (It is toward evening, at dusk.) The evening moon illuminates the ground. Yanagisawa recalls the events of the day, and Teruko's face.

(Insert: the two yachts, and Teruko's face)

8. At a window, Teruko's house

Outside it is dark, and a chill wind blows in through the window. Teruko sits in a chair by the window, with a lamp beside her. She is slightly slouched in the chair, reading a novel.

(Close-up) Teruko and her book. The title is visible:

"*A Nest of Gentlefolk* by Turgenev."

(Back to) Teruko, her book slips from her hands. Teruko's face is clearly visible—she is lost in thought.

(Close-up) Teruko's face. She looks hesitant.

(Back to) Teruko, reflecting on what happened earlier in the day.

TITLE: "IF ONLY IT WOULD COME TRUE. . . ."

(Vision [*gensō*]) Teruko and Yanigisawa riding in an automobile.

(Close)[2]

9. Yamashita's laboratory

Yamashita works alone on his research.

10. In the woods #1

TITLE: TWO FLUTTERING BUTTERFLIES (INSERT)

Yanagisawa awaits Teruko by some tall trees in the woods.

11. In the woods #2

Teruko, walking on her way to see Yanagisawa.

12. In the woods #3

Yanagisawa seen from a distance. Teruko approaches him, recognizes him, and runs toward him.

13. Back to In the woods #1

Yanagisawa and Teruko holding hands as they take a walk together.
Teruko: "Could you please slow down?"
Yanagisawa: "No, I had to wait for you quite a long time. I was just beginning to think that you might not come."
Teruko: "Really? . . . let's take a walk over there."
The two of them walk off.

14. On the mountain

Yanagisawa and Teruko walking and chatting. Yanagisawa asks,
TITLE: "WHAT IS YOUR PHILOSOPHY OF LIFE?"
Fingering some flowers, Teruko answers cheerfully,
TITLE: "LIFE? WELL, ONE SHOULD BE HAPPY AND LIVE A FULL LIFE, OF COURSE . . . I HATE A GLOOMY OUTLOOK, YOU KNOW."
As soon as Yanagisawa hears this, he says,
TITLE: "YES. WE SHOULD EAT WHATEVER WE WANT AND DO WHATEVER WE LIKE. ONE MUST LIVE LIFE TO THE FULLEST."

15. On the mountain

16. On the mountain

(same. LS, fade out)

17. Teruko's father's room

TITLE: "TERUKO'S FATHER IS AN ARDENT OLD BOTANIST—OBLIVIOUS TO EVERYTHING BUT HIS WORK.
TERUKO'S FATHER . . . AOYAMA SUGISAKU."
Surrounded by numerous old books and plant specimens, Teruko's father is engrossed in studying something under his microscope. Beside him Yō-chan is looking through his father's magnifying glass at insects in a box.
(Close-up) Yō-chan looks at the insects. A shot of the insects fighting.
Yō-chan: "Come on, come on—no, no good, you lost."
His father notices his loud voice, looks up from his microscope and scolds Yō-chan,
Father: "What are you saying? Go away, you're too noisy."
As if making fun of his father, Yō-chan squints with one eye, makes a face,

and leaves. His father is in a huff, but quickly turns his attention back to his work.

18. The garden, #1:1 (fade in)

TITLE: "ONE MORNING"
Yamashita, Yangisawa, and Teruko are playing tennis.

19. The garden #2:1

Yō-chan and a group of other children are imitating their favorite movie actors.

20. The garden #1:2

Tennis

21. The garden, and Teruko's father's room #2

The father, engrossed in his research.

22. The garden #2:2

Yō-chan imitates Charlie Chaplin.

23. The garden #1:3

A tennis ball flies through the air. Teruko makes a face as she misses it.

24. Again, Teruko's father's room #2

The ball hits Teruko's father in the face. He is startled and angry.

25. The garden #1:4

Teruko: "Let's quit, my father's annoyed."
Yanagisawa: "Well then, shall we go?"
Yamashita: "I'll catch up with you. I'm going to straighten up a bit here before I go."
Teruko: "Thank you, I'm sorry to leave this to you."
They leave, and Yamashita gathers up the rackets, balls, and other equipment.

26. In the shade of some trees #1

Teruko arrives first and sits on the grass.
Teruko: "Why don't you come over here where it's cool?"
Yanagisawa: "Me? I'm covered with sweat. It certainly is hot."

Yanagisawa sits down. Teruko discovers a caterpillar on his sleeve.
Teruko: "Wait, just a minute—"
Yanagisawa: "What? There's nothing there. What a nuisance you are!"
Teruko: "No, see—a caterpillar!"
(Close-up, Teruko grabs the caterpillar).
Yanagisawa: "What a horrible feeling. I wonder where it came from?"
Teruko flicks the caterpillar away. Yanagisawa wipes his hands on his clothes.

27. A road at night

Yamashita approaches.

28. In the shade of some trees #2

Yanagisawa gives Teruko a gift. As they happily embrace, Yamashita comes from behind and approaches them warily. Teruko sees him and stands up.
Yamashita: "Teruko! Why, I didn't realize . . . is it all right for me to have come?"
Teruko: "Of course. There's something I forgot to do. I'll be back."
Yanagisawa: "Teruko, can't it wait?"
Teruko: "But I'll be back."
Yanagisawa: "Then, I'll be seeing you . . ."
Yamashita gazes after Teruko as she leaves.

29. The garden 2:3

(Insert, fade in and out)[3] The children playing in the garden.

30. In the shade of some trees #2

Yamashita speaks to Yanagisawa.
TITLE: "DO YOU LOVE HER?"
Yanagisawa: "Well, I don't know. I'm not really sure."
Yamashita: "I see."
He looks uneasy. He tries to hide his growing anger as he continues,
Yamashita: "But think about what you're doing."
Yanagisawa: "—what does it matter?"
Yamashita: "What do you mean, 'what does it matter'—?"
TITLE: "THERE IS NO NEED FOR ME TO THINK ABOUT TOMORROW, OR ANYTHING OTHER THAN MY PRESENT HAPPINESS."
Yamashita: "I see—then goodbye."
He leaves, and Yanagisawa looks annoyed at having been caught in the act by Yamashita, of all people.

31. In the shade of some trees in the garden

Teruko looks out from between some trees. Yamashita approaches. Teruko hides. Looking sad, Yamashita walks right by her hiding place. Teruko sticks her head out once again.

(Close-up) A close-up of Teruko, her eyes filled with tears. She leaves her hiding place.

32. Under the shade of some trees #3

Teruko approaches Yanagisawa. Yanagisawa placates her.

Yanagisawa: "You mustn't worry. What is there to worry about?"

Teruko hides her tear-streaked face. Then the two of them exchange a meaningful look, and passionately embrace one another.

(Close-up) The expression on Teruko's face as it wavers between apprehension and joy.

(Close-up) Yanagisawa's face: there are traces of uneasiness, but his expression also seems to be reassuring Teruko. (Slow fade out)

33. A table by the lakeside

Yanagisawa Yasuhiko, Teruko, and her younger brother are seated around the table, eating a meal. A manservant approaches the garden with a telegram.

(Insert close-up) The telegram,

"FATHER CRITICAL RETURN IMMEDIATELY

YANAGISAWA"

Yanagisawa is alarmed. Because he is facing Teruko, he composes himself and tries to hide the telegram. Teruko notices, and looks at him.

Teruko: "What is it?"

Yanagisawa: "It's nothing. . . ."

Teruko (reaching for the telegram): "Something must have happened. Please let me have a look."

Yanagisawa makes a move to intercept her, but she forcibly snatches it out of his hand and reads it. She stares at him in surprise and concern.

Yanagisawa: "I must go home."

Teruko: "Are you leaving, then? I suppose it can't be helped."

With a look of resignation, Yanagisawa abruptly rises from his chair. Teruko sighs, shaken by this turn of events.

34. A room

Yanagisawa prepares for his trip. His maid and a steward look concerned as they assist him.

(Appropriate conversation)

35. In front of Yanagisawa's summer house

An automobile is waiting. Yanagisawa and Teruko come out of the house. They stand in front of the automobile. (With servants, attendants)

Yanagisawa: "I plan to return right away. There's no need for you to be concerned, I'll be sending you a letter directly."

Teruko: "Yes, please let me know how things are as soon as you can. I'd like to go with you as far as the railway station. . . ."

TITLE: "I'LL BE BACK SOON, AND WHEN I DO RETURN WE'LL HAVE MUCH TO TALK ABOUT—GOODBYE."

Teruko: "Goodbye, please write. . . ."

They exchange glances, and Yanagisawa gets into the automobile. It drives off. Teruko stares after it.

36. A road

An automobile travels rapidly along the road. (Fade out)

37. Teruko's father's room #2

Teruko's father and Yamashita are discussing some scientific matter.

Father: "Yamashita, yesterday I went into the mountains. I made an interesting discovery."

Yamashita: "Really? What is it?"

Father: "Well, take a look in the microscope. I have never seen anything so magnificent."

Yamashita takes a look.

(Close-up) Microbes seen through the microscope.

Yamashita: "Indeed! Where did you discover this?"

Father: "Isn't it something? On the far mountain, to the back of the range. . . ."

Teruko enters looking sad. She looks the other way. Her father notices.

Father: "Teruko, what is the matter? You don't look well at all."

Teruko: "It's nothing. . . ."

Understanding something of the situation, Yamashita sighs. Teruko's father acts as though nothing of concern is going on.

Father: "I'm going back to the same place again. I'd like to collect some better samples."

The two men continue their conversation. Teruko walks across the room. (She looks very sad.)

38. Teruko's bedroom (night)

TITLE: "DAY AFTER DAY, MONTH AFTER MONTH, THE TIME PASSES, BUT NO NEWS ARRIVES FROM YANAGISAWA."

In her white nightgown, Teruko sits at her desk. She is overcome with sadness as she gazes at a photograph of Yanagisawa.
(Close-up) Yanagisawa's photograph.
She extinguishes the lamp and gets into bed. But she has trouble sleeping, and stares at the ceiling with her eyes wide open. Growing increasingly despondent, she bursts into tears.

39. Tokyo

TITLE: "YANAGISAWA IS HELD CAPTIVE BY THE SEDUCTIVE DREAM OF CITY LIFE."
Yanagisawa and an actress leave the Teikoku Theater by car. They drive through the streets of Ginza, arriving at the Mitsukoshi Department Store.

40. The laboratory

(Quick fade in and out)[4] Yamashita's room. He is conducting an experiment.

41. Behind Teruko's house (night)

Teruko quietly opens the back gate and leaves, inching along the wall.

42. In front of the railway station

Teruko enters the railway station.

43. A platform

Teruko boards a train.

44. Inside the train

TITLE: "VISITING YANAGISAWA IN TOKYO"

45. Railroad tracks

The train moves off into the distance. (Fade out)

46. In front of Tokyo station

Teruko exits the station.

47. On the road

Walking along the road, Teruko stops to ask a passerby for directions to the house of Viscount Yanagisawa. The person points out the house.

48. The wall of Viscount Yanagisawa's residence

Nodding in recognition, Teruko walks toward the gate.

49. In front of the gate

Teruko hesitates before entering the wide gate.
(Close-up) The hesitant expression on Teruko's face.
After a moment, the sound of a carriage (automobile) is heard.

50. An automobile traveling along the road

The automobile approaches. Yanagisawa and the actress are inside.

51. Back to the gate

Teruko attempts to hide as the automobile enters the gate. Teruko recognizes it. She steps out to look through the gate at what is inside.

52. Beside a telephone pole

Teruko looks around, then leans against a telephone pole. Stunned and weak, she bursts into tears. She then leaves. (Fade out)

53. Inside the train

Teruko sadly looks out the train window. (Fade out)
TITLE: "RETURNING HOME AGAIN"

54. A road in Teruko's hometown (night)

Teruko walks home alone through the picturesque natural landscape of mountains and trees.

55. In front of the house

She approaches her house. Pausing for a moment, she enters.

56. Teruko's father's bedroom

Teruko's father is asleep. Teruko quietly opens the door, looks in on him, and then closes the door again.

57. Teruko's bedroom

Teruko listlessly enters her bedroom. After a pause, she collapses onto the bedding and cries. Finally, she undresses.

58. The laboratory (night)

Yamashita reads a book as his assistant yawns beside him. Soon Yamashita also grows tired. He taps his assistant on the shoulder to say that he is going out for a walk and will return.

59. Teruko's bedroom

Teruko lies in bed, but her mind is in a turmoil and she is unable to sleep. (Vision) The mocking faces of frightful demons, Yanagisawa's face and then Yamashita's stern face come to mind. In a half-mad state, she leaves the room (her face strangely composed).

60. Alongside the house (night)

Teruko leaves the house in her bare feet.

61. Lakeside #1 (night)

Teruko runs toward the riverbank. She gets into a boat that is tied up there and pushes off.

62. On the lake (night)

She throws the boat's oars into the water and, sadly, stands up in the boat. Her decision is made.

63. Lakeside #2 (night)

Yamashita is taking a walk when he sees a boat out on the lake. Noticing someone dressed in white, he breaks into a run.

64. Lakeside #3 (night)

Yamashita pushes off in a boat and begins to row.

65. On the lake

Yamashita rows the boat. An empty boat drifts toward him. Looking ahead he sees a woman's body floating in the water and hastens toward it.

66. On the lake

Yamashita lifts the woman out of the water.

67. Aboard the boat

Yamashita, having saved Teruko, rows the boat.

68. The shore of the lake

The boat reaches the shore. Yamashita walks ashore with Teruko in his arms.

69. Within the gate of Teruko's house

Yamashita holds Teruko in his arms. A maid comes out of the house and together she and Yamashita help Teruko inside.

70. Teruko's bedroom

Yamashita brings Teruko into the bedroom. Her father enters in his night-clothes. The maid is busily attending to things. Teruko's father tells Yamashita to give Teruko some smelling salts, and the maid helps her out of her wet clothes. Yamashita leaves to go for the doctor.

71. In front of the gate and within the gate

Yamashita hurries to the doctor's by car.

72. An automobile traveling along the road

73. In front of the doctor's house

Yamashita gets out of the car, bangs on the door, and calls out. The doctor comes out.

74. Teruko's bedroom

Teruko has changed her clothes and is asleep in bed. Yamashita and the doctor hurry to her side. The doctor promptly looks at her and says, "She's all right. There is no need to be concerned." Everyone is relieved. Teruko moves slightly.

75. Teruko's bedroom (morning)

TITLE: "THE MORNING LIGHT"
The window is open, and the morning sun streams into the room. Teruko remembers nothing from the day before and attempts to get out of bed. Her head feels slightly heavy. She forces herself to get up, and she goes to the window to look outside.

76. A part of Teruko's house

Yamashita pays a visit. He meets Teruko's father in the garden, briefly greets him, and hastens to Teruko's room.

77. Teruko's bedroom

Yamashita's entrance takes Teruko completely by surprise. She hurriedly throws some clothes on over her nightdress and awkwardly sits on the bed. Yamashita sits down in a chair in front of her.
Yamashita: "How are you doing? Do you feel better?"
Teruko: "Yes."
She answers him, then sadly turns away, her head bowed. Sympathetic as well as reassuring, Yamashita says,
Yamashita: "This won't do, what is it that is making you sad?"
TITLE: "LAST NIGHT YOU TRIED TO DIE. . . ."

78. Talking about the night before (insert)

TITLE: "THIS IS THE ULTIMATE DILEMMA. WE MUST WORK FOR LIFE WITH AN EFFORT GREATER THAN DEATH. WE STRIVE. WE WORK. IT IS THE COWARD WHO BECOMES FRUSTRATED IN THE ENDEAVOR TO LIVE AND HASTENS DEATH. . . ."
Teruko gradually takes heart.

79. The interior of the church

The children at Sunday service are singing a hymn in chorus.

80. Teruko's bedroom

Teruko listens. The song gradually fades, transforming into a title.
TITLE: "REJOICE YE MYRIADS! WHEN THE LORD JESUS DEFEATS THE KINGDOM OF THE DEAD, THE POWER OF DEATH WILL HAVE VANISHED, AND OUR LIVES WILL BE EVERLASTING."
Teruko is deeply moved, and says to Yamashita,
Teruko: "You know, for some reason I'm feeling better."
Teruko appears happy, yet her face is still tinged with sorrow. Yamashita leads her to the window.
Yamashita: "Just look at that blue sky, those green trees!"
TITLE: "EVERYWHERE THE WORLD IS CHARGED WITH THE VITALITY OF LIFE."

81. (Insert) A blue sky

Two dogs come out of the forest and romp in the sunshine.

82. Back to Teruko's bedroom

Teruko feels increasingly happier. In due course, Yamashita says:
"I'll come again. Take good care of yourself."

He leaves.

Teruko thanks him as she sees him off, and once again admires the view out the window.

(Close-up) Her face, lost in thought.

Yamashita's face comes to mind, but then again so does Yanagisawa's. Teruko resolves to do her best not to think of Yanagisawa.

83. Yanagisawa's room (night)

Yanagisawa returns home drunk, but he is definitely not happy in his drunken oblivion. He picks up the photo of an actress on his desk.

(Close-up of the actress's photograph)

He then tears it up. In anguish, he takes a photo of Teruko from his desk drawer and stares at it. As he does so, Teruko appears before him and speaks to him. (Vision)

In frustration Yanagisawa buries his head in his hands. He then drinks some water from a pitcher beside him.

84. Yanagisawa's room (before noon)

Yanagisawa is now awake, brushing his teeth and washing his face. An elderly steward enters and sadly shows him an announcement in the newspaper.

(Newspaper announcement)

AUCTION OF YANAGISAWA COLLECTION IN HAMACHŌ, NIHONBASHI WARD. BIDDING ON JULY 15TH AND 16TH. PREVIEWS IN THE MORNING, JULY 4TH AND 5TH.

Steward: "Sir, what is this announcement all about?"

Yanagisawa hesitates.

Yanagisawa: "Oh, it's nothing, I'm just selling off some old things."

Steward: "But these are family heirlooms, left to you by your ancestors. Why are you doing this. . . ?"

Yanagisawa: "But I need the money. Why fuss over a few heirlooms?"

Steward: "Sir, what a monstrous thought . . . but I suppose it can't be helped."

The steward bows his head, balking at the very idea. Yanagisawa looks discomfited as he dries his face with a towel.

85. The garden of Teruko's house

Teruko's father is tending his flower garden. Teruko is playing quoits with her brother, Yō-chan; she sits down on a nearby fence and thinks for a moment.

(She recalls sailing with Yanagisawa) (Insert)

But she shrugs it off as something that happened long ago. She then thinks of Yamashita.
(With Yamashita, conducting an experiment) (Insert)
"Yamashita is the more manly of the two," she thinks.
Yō-chan: 'Sister, what are you thinking about? It's your turn.'
Teruko: "Oh, so it is. I had completely forgotten."
She tosses another ring. Her father makes a strange face and laughs.
(Close-up) Teruko's father's face.

86. The laboratory

Yamashita is working in the laboratory with his assistant. Teruko suddenly visits the garden.
Teruko: "May I come in?"
Yamashita: "Teruko? Yes, please do. But it's very dirty in here."
Teruko: "What are you doing?"
Yamashita: "This is radio-carbonium, a component for a wireless electric light. I'm nearly finished with my experiment, and if I'm successful . . ."
Teruko: "Oh, my—!"
Yamashita: "Don't touch that, it's dangerous! It has an electric current running through it."
Teruko: "Don't frighten me so! Can I see it?"
She draws closer to look. The electric light has a phosphorescent glow. They both watch it.

87. Teruko's room (night)

TITLE: "A STORMY NIGHT"
It is a stormy night. Teruko is in bed. There are lightning flashes and the sound of heavy rain.

88. Storm

Outdoors, cracks of lightning in the violent rainstorm. (Do something appropriate with this scene)

89. Teruko's room

A short while later, an anonymous figure shrouded in a black cloak enters the room. He walks across Teruko's room and approaches her bed.
(Close-up) Teruko is sleeping.
The man looks into Teruko's face, and at that very moment upsets a small figurine beside her. Surprised, the man tries to hide himself. Teruko wakes and switches on the lamp.

(Back)

She sees the person in black furtively standing in front of her bed and is about to scream. The man draws close to Teruko and places his hand over her mouth.

Yanagisawa: "Please, wait—I'm not a thief!"

Then he pulls back the cloak's hood. Teruko, surprised, recognizes Yanagisawa.

Teruko: "Why have you come here? Please go away!"

Yanagisawa: "No, I've come to offer you an apology."

Yanagisawa speaks gently to Teruko. He sits in a chair by her side, and they are both silent for a moment.

TITLE: "MISS SHIMAZAKI, I'VE COME TO APOLOGIZE TO YOU. I INTENDED ONLY TO LEAVE YOU THIS LETTER, I DID NOT MEAN TO WAKE YOU."

He gives her the letter and buries his face in his hands. Teruko takes the letter over to the light and reads it.

(The contents of the letter) Insert . . .

Teruko: "I understand. . . ."

She runs her hand over Yanagisawa's head.

TITLE: "UNTIL NOW I HAVE BEEN DELUDED. I AM LEAVING TO GO ABROAD. . . ."

Teruko: "I understand, please take good care of yourself."

Her eyes glisten with tears.

Yanagisawa: "From now on I intend to live an honest life."

The two clasp hands, and then part.

TITLE: "GOODBYE. . . ."

Teruko weakly sits down on the bed as she watches Yanagisawa leave.

90. Storm

Violent wind and rain, cracks of lightning. Wrapped in his cloak, Yanagisawa vanishes into the darkness and the steadily falling rain.

91. On the mountain

Teruko and Yamashita are sitting on the mountainside.

TITLE: "THE STORM HAS CLEARED"

Teruko: "Did you know that Viscount Yanagisawa's son has gone abroad?"

She shows Yanagisawa's letter to Yamashita.

Yamashita: "I received a letter as well."

He takes a letter from Yanagisawa out of his pocket.

Yamashita: "For the first time, he will live an honest life. I'm happy for him."

Yamashita points in the distance.

(Insert) Smoke rises from the black chimney of a factory nestled in the hills.

They watch the rising smoke.

TITLE: "THAT BLACK SMOKE REPRESENTS THE LIFE EACH ONE OF US HAS. IT IS ENERGY. LET US WORK, LET US FACE THE GLORY. . . ."

92. The harbor

A steamship quietly leaves the harbor.

93. Aboard ship

Standing at the railing, Yanagisawa reluctantly watches the blue sky of his homeland recede in the distance. He takes off his hat and bows his head, his expression one of determination.

94. The sky at sunrise

The words "Life is effort" appear in the sky at dawn. (Fade out).

Masumoto Kiyoshi: *A Father's Tears*
(excerpt, *Chichi no namida,* 1918)

As a moving picture scenario [*katsudō shashingeki no daihon*], this script [*kyakuhon*] is stylistically very different from Ide Shōichi's ideal.[1] Instead it may seem old-fashioned for a moving picture scenario. It is more or less standard, however, for a scenario that accommodates industry executives who endorse the *kowairo* style of *benshi* delivery, and expect a great deal from the effect of spoken lines as well as from the picture [*shashin*]. Also, this work artistically leaves much to be desired, but it is far more difficult to disassociate businessmen from the moving pictures in comparison to stage drama. For this reason, one must tolerate annoyances such as compromises, concessions, and half-measures. In order [for a film] to be commercially viable, the cost and schedule of shooting are prescribed by more or less uniform restrictions. As a result, one must limit the number of scenes and, to an extent, infringe on the domain of stage drama. I am in full agreement with Mr. Ide's opinions concerning moving picture drama, and I too believe that the future of the moving pictures lies in that direction. Nonetheless, I should like to explain that my bold choice of such a compromised style was solely for commercial purposes.

—Masumoto Kiyoshi

CAST OF CHARACTERS:

Hata Shingo	A blind vagrant, Yuriko's biological father
Sakatani Tetsuzō	A vagrant posing as Yuriko's biological father
Nitta no Okuma	Beggar, Tetsuzō's former lover
Hamaguchi Tomoe	Bank president, Yuriko's adoptive father
Hamaguchi Saiko	Tomoe's second wife
Hamaguchi Masaya	Tomoe's first wife's child
Hamaguchi Yuriko	Tomoe's adopted daughter, Masaya's fiancée
Utagawa Tamaji	Saiko's child, an actress
Adachi Taiji	Tamaji's lover
Tomita Eizō	Shipowner
Otake	Maid employed at the Hamaguchi residence
Others:	jinrikisha man, maid, owner of a cheap lodging house, drivers, actresses, peddlers, traveling performers, and various others

Scene #1

A Wanderer[2]

Fade out on the previous title; fade in, full frame of a sign with the following inscription:[3]

Missing Person

Daughter, born 1900. Real name, Hata Hana. Missing since being given as a foster child to Yasuura Kuma in the Ōmiya domain in the middle of 1908. I should be grateful if anyone who knows of Hana's whereabouts would kindly let me know.

This sign hangs on the back of Hata Shingo. As the lens slowly pulls back he turns around and we see a three-quarter shot of him with this sign on his back, playing a *shakuhachi*.[4] Before long, Shingo deliberately turns back around while playing the *shakuhachi,* and after a moment, he quietly walks off. Two or three delivery men appear (they should stand still when three-quarters of their figures are visible as well). They point to the wooden sign on Shingo's back and whisper to one another, appearing sympathetic.

Scene #2

Related, Unrelated

The foot of a bridge, a moonlit night.[5] Shingo stands at the foot of the bridge and begs for alms from the people passing by as he plays his *shakuhachi*. Gentlemen and geisha come and go before him, but not one of them shows him any charity. Finally, even the intermittent, plaintive notes grow faint from his sadness. Shingo is startled as a motorcar comes dashing toward him. He attempts to move out of the way, stumbles, and falls, unable to get up. The car comes to a stop nearly twelve meters beyond him and the driver opens the car door and jumps out. Hamaguchi Yuriko, elegantly dressed, steps out of the car and follows the driver. The driver helps the fallen Shingo to his feet.

Driver: Are you alright? Are you hurt?

Shingo: It's not serious, thank you.

Driver (brushing the mud from him): I'm terribly sorry.

Shingo (as if looking for his *shakuhachi,* which flew out of his hands): My *shakuhachi,* it must have fallen somewhere.

Yuriko (she picks up the *shakuhachi;* wiping the mud from it with her sleeve, she takes Shingo's hand and gives it to him): Here it is—why, you're blind, aren't you?

Shingo (he raises the *shakuhachi* slightly in thanks): Yes, I'm afraid so.

Yuriko: I am so sorry, please wait one moment.

(She deftly takes a five-yen bill from her purse.)[6]

> This is just a small sum, a five-yen bill. Please take it and quickly go home and rest for today.

> Shingo: No, no. I'm not injured, so there is no reason to accept such a large sum of money.

> Yuriko: It's alright. I would like you to accept it for my sake.

(She takes Shingo's hand and forces him to take the money.)

> Shingo: Well then, thank you very much.

(*He accepts the money. As if not wanting to reveal his obvious destitution, he turns aside, takes out his purse, and puts the bill away.*)

Yuriko suddenly notices the wooden sign on his back.

> Yuriko: What's this? Please let me read your sign. Hoshino, strike a match.

The following appears in close-up.[7] The driver strikes a match and hands it to her. As Yuriko reads her eyes gradually fill with tears. The driver lights another match. Yuriko finishes reading.

> How sad. Then who do you live with now, old man?

> Shingo: I have no one to talk to. Longing for my daughter, I wander about aimlessly searching this gate here and that crossing there, entrusting this worthless life to a single *shakuhachi*.

> Yuriko: Then how your daughter must also be searching for you! Hearing your story makes me somehow feel as if it is my own, and I am moved to tears.

> Shingo: What a shame! Why liken a person in your circumstances to the daughter of someone like me?

> Yuriko: But I am sure you would cry if I were to tell you about my situation. I will tell you someday. I am the daughter of the Hamaguchi family—their main residence is in Shinkoume—but I am actually their adopted child. The father I have now is truly a good person, but my real father only abuses me. I wouldn't even mind being adopted by you, so it would be wonderful if a kind man like you were my real father!

Shingo listens to her attentively.

> Why don't you come around to our house? When you come to Shinkoume, mention the name Hamaguchi and you'll find it right away. As long as I'm at home, I'm certain you'll be given enough money to buy rice again. Please come, won't you? I'll be waiting. Well then, until we meet again. Today you'd better return home.

Shingo quietly bows his head and, without saying goodnight, only faintly answers yes, yes, under his breath. Yuriko reluctantly gets into the car, watching him from the window as it drives off. After a moment Shingo walks away, retracing his steps as he quietly plays the *shakuhachi*.

Scene #3

A New Actress

Tomita Eizō's private theater. On stage the curtain is still closed. It is time to begin, and elegantly dressed guests leisurely enter and take their seats. The last to enter is Hamaguchi Masaya, preceded by Hamaguchi Saiko, who sit down side by side. When the bell rings Eizō appears, parting the curtain. The guests all applaud.

>Eizō: Before the performance begins, I would like to thank you all for expressly taking the trouble to honor us with your presence, and take this opportunity to say a word about the incentive behind my establishing this entertainment hall (the audience applauds). Being by nature a complete layman concerning the arts, I could say something about my profession, shipbuilding, and then withdraw. I would only like to say, however, that I did not meaninglessly spend money toward the cost of establishing this entertainment hall. Ever since the Great War in Europe, the Japanese have day by day taken up an interest in depravity, in an inverse proportion to the expansion of our country's wealth. It is indeed regrettable that this is an especially pronounced reality among those of us in industry; perhaps this why our kind, designated as the "nouveau riche," are looked down upon in public and summarily condemned. It is indeed truly such misguided avocations as wasting money in the companionship of prostitutes and spending lavishly on mansions and clothes that have given people this idea. (The audience applauds.) In order to redress these vices, however slightly, one can only strive for an improvement of such avocations. I thought it would be most expedient at this moment to present refined entertainment, and I invested my own modest fortune in the construction of this entertainment hall. I humbly asked you all here today for the opening of this theater, and to introduce to you the premiere actress of our theater world, Miss Utagawa Tamaji (newly returned from abroad) in her most renowned role in a typhoon drama.[8] As there is no need for me to indulge any further in idle talk about Miss Tamaji and this drama, we will immediately proceed to begin the performance. Please relax and enjoy the show.

The audience applauds enthusiastically. Eizō bows and leaves. Saiko appears to be telling Masaya all about Tamaji when the bell rings. The audience applauds as the curtain opens.

Scene #4

The play within the play. Tamaji acts the part of the heroine in the typhoon drama. (Omitted from the script.)

Scene #5

Close-up centered on Saiko and Masaya's seats.

    Saiko: Well, well, this Tamaji really is the talk of the town.

    Masaya: Yes, she's quite beautiful, isn't she?

    Saiko: Her acting is extraordinary as well.

    Masaya: Mother, you certainly favor Tamaji, don't you!

    Saiko: First of all, she is a world apart from the others. Why don't you take this opportunity to meet her? Actually, I'd like to meet her too.

(She stands up.)

    Why don't we go backstage? Let's go together.

The two exit together.[9]

262

Tanizaki Jun'ichirō/Thomas Kurihara: *Amateur Club* (*Amachua kurabu*, 1920)

Amateur Club

CREDITS:

Original story and scenario	Tanizaki Jun'ichirō
Director	Thomas Kurihara
Photography	Inami Yoshimi
Stage manager[1]	Ozaki Shōtarō
Titles	Ueno Hisao

CAST:

Miura Chizuko	Hayama Michiko
Muraoka Shigeru	Ueno Hisao
Muraoka Natsuko	Kamiyama Sango
Miura Chizuko's Father	Naitō Shiren
(Chizuko's Mother)[2]	

Kurihara and Tanizaki's *Amachua kurabu* (*Amateur Club*), 1920. Hayama Michiko (*third from right*). Courtesy Kawakita Memorial Film Institute.

Muraoka Shigeru's Father	Shiraishi Shikō
Katō Kenzō (Takechi Mitsuhide)	Sugiura Ichirō
Hattori Ichirō (Misao)	Takemura Nobuo
Thief (Thief)	Hanabusa Takeshi
Ōno Kamekichi (Mitsuhide's mother, Satsuki)	Murakami Tetsuji
Inoue Hideo (Hatsugiku)	Takahashi Eichi
Suzuki Risaburō (Hashiba Hisayoshi)[3]	Ōhashi Sōgo
Nakamura Hiroshi (Nikki Danjō)	Horikiri Morinosuke
Koizumi Nobuichi (Otokonosuke)	Murata Takeo
Watanabe Yoshitaro (Rat)	Sakano Hirokichi
Passerby (Scene #37, passes by thieves)	Ozaki Shōtarō
Gentleman (Scene #214)	Matsumura Kameichi
Geisha (same)	an anonymous geisha
Chizuko's Maid (Scene #19)	Benisawa Yōko
Mother in the audience (Scene #166)	Mrs. Tanizaki
Child (same)	Miss Tanizaki

(Names in parentheses are the names of the characters in the kabuki performance)

Scene #1. Exterior. Beach

Fade in and out. An actual view of the Yuigahama seaside resort. Take a distinct shot of the landscape from one end to the other and overlap the following title midway through:

TITLE #1: SUMMER AT YUIGAHAMA SHORE, KAMAKURA

Scene #2. Exterior. Beach

Iris in [*kōmei*]. Medium close up [*chūsessha*] of Muraoka Shigeru buried in the sand. Gradually open from the gently shifting sand into a full body iris shot of Muraoka, and cut.

TITLE: MURAOKA SHIGERU. A POMPOUS YOUNG DANDY AT FIRST GLANCE, BUT IN REALITY, A GOOD-NATURED YOUNG MAN OF GOOD BREEDING.

Scene #3. Exterior. Beach

CU Muraoka's face. The intelligent, attractive, and pleasant expression and gestures of a lively young man. Hearing someone call he turns his head to the right. Acting as if he does not want to be recognized by whoever is calling him, he returns to his former position, and closes his eyes as if he is asleep and oblivious to everything.

TITLE: MURAOKA'S FRIENDS. INOUE, HATTORI, KATŌ.

Scene #4. Exterior. Beach

Three lively young men enter from BG, call Muraoka and, looking around and thinking it strange that they can't find him, they exit stage left.

Scene #5. Exterior. Beach

The above three youths enter from the right. When they come to the place where Muraoka is buried they call Muraoka again. Muraoka suddenly gets up and yells, "Over here!" The three are taken by surprise, and slap each other on the shoulder and break up in laughter as they sit down on the sand.

Scene #6. Exterior. Beach

Close-up [*sessha*] of the four. Inoue turns toward Muraoka:
TITLE #4: "COME ON, LET'S HURRY HOME AND REHEARSE A BIT MORE."

Scene #7. Exterior. Beach

A continuation of the previous scene. Inoue pronounces the previous title and, making a strange gesture, pleads, "Lord Mitsuhide, you're not listening at all." Muraoka feigns slight disappointment.

DIALOGUE INSERT #5: I WOULDN'T MIND, IF ONLY HATSUGIKU WEREN'T SUCH A LOUSY ACTOR—

Saying this, he continues what he was doing previously. Inoue, unsettled, pouts and mutters something like, "if only Jūjirō were more reliable." . . . Muraoka peers a little off to the side, as if having spotted someone.

Scene #8. Exterior. Beach

A group of men and women in bathing attire . . . Long shot [*tōutsushi*] of a fat woman flirting with the man beside her.

Scene #9. Exterior. Beach

Close-up. The woman in the previous scene coquettishly clings to the man.

Scene #10. Exterior. Beach

Close-up of the four: Muraoka, Inoue, Hattori, and Katō. Pick up on Muraoka's gaze at the end of #7. Trying to keep a straight face, he attracts Inoue's attention.

Scene #11. Exterior. Beach

Continue the close-up in #9 for approximately three feet.

Scene #12. Exterior. Beach

A continuation of #10 . . . Muraoka speaks:
DIALOGUE INSERT TITLE: "LOOK, THAT'S IT! THAT'S THE SPIRIT!"
Inoue grows increasingly sullen. . . . Paying no attention and silently staring off into the distance, Hattori acts as though he has suddenly discovered something interesting. "Look at that," he says, pointing out to sea. The others nod in acknowledgment. Katō says:
DIALOGUE INSERT: "HEY, THAT GIRL'S SWIMMING AGAIN."

Scene #13. Exterior. In the water

Long shot of Chizuko swimming in the water.

Scene #14. Exterior. Beach

A continuation of #12—all four youths gazing out to sea. Now Katō says:
DIALOGUE INSERT: "THAT GIRL SWIMS AWFULLY WELL. SHE WOULDN'T BE A FISHERMAN'S DAUGHTER, WOULD SHE?"
Muraoka responds: "Don't be silly, would a girl that pretty be a fisherman's daughter?"
DIALOGUE INSERT: "SHE'S THE DAUGHTER OF AN OLD FAMILY LIVING IN ŌGIGAYATSU IN KAMAKURA, THE MIURA FAMILY."
Muraoka says this with an air of importance,and the other three laugh lightly. Then they again stare out to sea.

Scene #15. Exterior. In the water

Medium close-up, Chizuko, all alone, unconsciously and effortlessly swimming various strokes.

Scene #16. Exterior. Beach

Positioning the lens at the same height as the young woman's eyes at the surface of the water, a shot of Yuigahama in the distance as it would appear to someone swimming parallel to the shore.

Scene #17. Exterior. In the water

A continuation of #15. Chizuko swims.
TITLE: CHIZUKO, THE MIURA FAMILY'S TOMBOY

Scene #18. Exterior. In the water

Close-up of Chizuko swimming. This scene calls for some graceful action.

Scene #19. Exterior. Beach

The Miura family maid (eighteen or nineteen years old?) enters from the right, stands in front facing the camera and looks around as if searching for someone she can't find. Muttering, she exits to the left.

Scene #20. Exterior. Beach

The place where Miura and the other three youths are. All four of them are still intently staring off to sea and talking among themselves.

Scene #21. Exterior. In the water

Chizuko still continues to swim.

Scene #22. Exterior. Beach

Miura and the other three youths just as before . . . the maid enters from the right and stands in front, still looking around as she mutters to herself. Suddenly she spots Chizuko out to sea and calls out in a loud voice:
DIALOGUE INSERT: "MISS!!!"
The maid continues to scold her even more.

Scene #23. Exterior. In the water

Chizuko continues swimming as if she still hasn't heard the maid calling her.

Scene #24. Exterior. Beach

The maid calls out, "Miss, Miss Chizuko," as loudly as she can.

Scene #25. Exterior. In the water

Chizuko looks toward the beach, laughs gleefully, and draws nearer to the shore. Then, making faces and playfully cheering with her hands in the air, she escapes further out into the water.

Scene #26. Exterior. Beach

A shot of the maid with Muraoka and the other three behind her . . . the maid is in a huff. The four youths laugh. The maid continues her scolding: "Miss! What kind of a person are you? Didn't you just pay your respects at the temple today in your mother's place? I'm amazed that in spite of that here you are swimming in such a place!"
DIALOGUE INSERT: "COME NOW, LET'S HURRY HOME OR YOU'LL GET A SCOLDING FROM YOUR MOTHER."

Scene #27. Exterior. In the water

Chizuko stands up in the water and calls out, beckoning the maid:
DIALOGUE INSERT: "WELL THEN, COME HERE AND CATCH ME. COME ON!"

Scene #28. Exterior. Beach

Close-up of the four youths convulsed with laughter.

Scene #29. Exterior. Beach.

Close-up from behind the maid. She abruptly turns around and takes her anger out on the young men, shouting crossly:
DIALOGUE INSERT: WHAT DO YOU THINK IS SO FUNNY?

Scene #30. Exterior. Beach

Close-up. The four young men stop laughing at once and look embarrassed.

Scene #31. Exterior. Beach

The maid leaves, still fuming at them. (Exit to the right.)

Scene #32. Exterior. Beach

The young men watch her go and together burst into laughter.

Scene #33. Exterior. In the water

Close-up. Chizuko was also watching the maid leave, but hearing the boys' laughter she suddenly looks in their direction.

Scene #34. Exterior. Beach

Close-up. The four young men were pointing in the direction of the departing maid and roaring with laughter, but, suddenly realizing that Chizuko is standing and staring at them, they all muffle their laughter.

Scene #35. Exterior. In the water

A continuation of #33. In the end Chizuko also laughs cheerfully at them. Fade out.

Scene #36. Exterior. Beach house

(Fade in) A shot of two thieves now walking around stealing wallets, watches, and other articles of value from among the clothes that the bathers have shed here and there. They come upon a young woman's dressy outfit that has been nonchalantly cast aside, and exchanging meaningful glances one of them tucks the sash and handbag under his arm, and the other rolls the garment tightly into a ball and stuffs it inside a towel. After artfully pilfering the loot they sneak away, glancing around in all directions.

Scene #37. Exterior. Beach house

Shoot from a different angle.
When the two thieves attempt to slip around the side of the beach house, they run into a man holding a bundle of bathing clothes. Although the two are taken by surprise, they immediately feign innocence and pass him by. With a suspicious air, the man watches them go. —Cut—

Scene #38. Exterior. Beach

Chizuko gets out of the water and, a short distance from the group of young men, lies down and stretches out her legs. (Shoot with the men visible behind her.)

Scene #39. Exterior. Beach

Now and then stealing a playful glance at the young woman, the four young men chat among themselves.

Scene #40. Exterior. Beach

Close-up. Chizuko squares her shoulders and glares at them.

Scene #41. Exterior. Beach

Continuation of #39. . . . One of the four, Hattori, raises his hand in greeting.

Scene #42. Exterior. Beach

Chizuko impulsively beams back.

Scene #43. Exterior. Beach

The four take this as an opportunity to stand up and move next to her.

Scene #44. Exterior. Beach

Long shot. With Chizuko in FG . . . the four approach from BG and sit down around Chizuko.

Scene #45. Exterior. Beach

Close-up. Muraoka addresses her:
DIALOGUE INSERT: YOU'RE QUITE A GOOD SWIMMER. HOW ABOUT RACING WITH ME?

Scene #46. Exterior. Beach

Chizuko:
DIALOGUE INSERT: GLADLY, I'M NOT ABOUT TO LOSE TO A MAN!

Scene #47. Exterior. Beach

Muraoka says evenly:
DIALOGUE INSERT: BUT I'M BETTER THAN YOU ARE, CHIZU.

Scene #48. Exterior. Beach

Chizuko opens her eyes wide in surprise:
DIALOGUE INSERT: HOW DO YOU KNOW MY NAME?

Scene #49. Exterior. Beach

Long shot. Muraoka continues speaking:
DIALOGUE INSERT: OF COURSE I KNOW IT, I'VE CHECKED UP ON YOU.

Scene #50. Exterior. Beach

CU Chizuko:
DIALOGUE INSERT: AH, SO YOU'RE A DETECTIVE!

Scene #51. Exterior. Beach

Muraoka and the others. Muraoka speaks:
DIALOGUE INSERT: OF COURSE I'M NOT A DETECTIVE, BUT HOW COULD I
RESIST FINDING OUT ALL ABOUT SOMEONE AS PRETTY AS YOU?
When Muraoka says this and laughs suggestively, Chizuko frowns:
DIALOGUE INSERT: WHAT A LOATHSOME FELLOW!
With this parting remark she strides off toward the beach house. Muraoka is
struck speechless and blankly watches her go. The other three clap their
hands and poke fun at Muraoka. Fade out.

Scene #52. Exterior. Pine grove

Fade in. The two robbers from before are spreading out the items they have
stolen one by one and happily examining them. Then they bury them in the
sand at the foot of a pine tree and again go off to work.

Scene #53. Exterior. Beach house

Having reached the beach house, Chizuko has looked everywhere for her
clothes in order to change, but she can't seem to find them at all. Shortly a
crowd of people come forward saying their wallets have been stolen and their
watches have disappeared. The man from #37 is also in the background listening.

Scene #54. Exterior. Beach house

Close-up, the man from #37 has been listening to what everyone is saying,
and makes a face as if he has suddenly recalled something. Overlap with
shot #37 of the robbers passing the man by. Everyone turns upon the man,
but Chizuko reasons with them and points out that he didn't commit the
crime.

Scene #55. Exterior. In front of the beach house

Muraoka and his friends are standing listening to the conversation between
Chizuko and the others. Then they each try to lend her his clothes. In the end
they toss for it and Muraoka wins. Muraoka, triumphant, exits the scene and
heads toward the beach house.

Scene #56. Exterior. Beach house

Chizuko and two or three others. Although Chizuko has placated the crowd, she is now upset that she herself won't be able to return home; Muraoka enters at this point.

DIALOGUE INSERT: CHIZUKO, EXCUSE ME FOR BEING FORWARD, BUT I'LL LEND YOU MY CLOTHES.

He addresses her in a friendly manner, but Chizuko is irritated to see him again and gruffly responds:

DIALOGUE INSERT: I DON'T NEED TO BORROW YOUR CLOTHES!

So saying, she hastily leaves in her bathing attire. Muraoka is disappointed once again, but he can't help smiling because Chizuko's ingenuous manner is charming nevertheless.

#56A. Seeing Muraoka fail a second time, his three friends laugh at him.

TITLE: THE SUMMER AIRING OF ARTICLES AT THE MIURA RESIDENCE IN ŌGIGAYATSU[4]

Scene #57. Interior. Sitting room [*zashiki*] in the Miura residence seen from the veranda [*engawa*]

A general view of the front of the Miura residence. Because they are an old family dating back to the time of the Yoritomo, there are a very large number of heirlooms that have been passed down by the preceding generations. Today these are laid out for summer airing throughout the room and on the veranda. Chizuko's mother is preparing everything to be aired.

TITLE: CHIZUKO'S MOTHER

Scene #58. Interior. Miura residence

CU Chizuko's mother.

Scene #59. Exterior. Veranda

Chizuko's mother has come from the room out to the veranda and is dusting off the treasures that have been laid out everywhere when the maid returns from the beach. Vexed, she tells the mother about Chizuko. The mother listens with a worried expression.

Scene #60. Exterior. Garden of the Miura residence

Choose a spot with a hedge or a shaded area. The two thieves seen earlier appear in the shadows, quietly whispering to each other as they furtively peer into the room.

Scene #61. Exterior. Miura residence

A flash shot of the veranda; the maid exits.

272

Scene #62. Exterior. Garden of the Miura residence

A continuation of #60 . . . the two appear to have heard a noise.

Scene #63. Exterior. Part of the Miura garden. Footsteps, 3 feet of film

Scene #64. Exterior. Garden of the Miura residence

A continuation of #62. . . . The two hide their faces. Chizuko enters in her bathing attire, stands still in FG and looks in the direction of the veranda.

Scene #65. Exterior. Veranda of the Miura residence

Chizuko's mother is busy laying things out to air.

Scene #66. Exterior. Garden of the Miura residence

A continuation of #64. . . . Chizuko sees that her mother is on the veranda and then looks down at what she has on. Too late, she realizes her predicamen . . . determined at last, she walks toward the veranda.

Scene #67. Exterior. Veranda of the Miura residence

Chizuko's mother continues as in #65. . . . Chizuko enters—she puts on a tearful face as she greets her mother and lingers despondently at the edge of the veranda.

Scene #68. Exterior. Veranda of the Miura residence

Close-up. Chizuko's mother momentarily glances up and down at her daughter's appearance incredulously.

Scene #69. Exterior. Edge of the veranda of the Miura residence

A full-body close-up [*ōutsushi*] of Chizuko—she is flustered, as if unable to endure her mother's steady gaze.

Scene #70. Exterior. Veranda of the Miura residence

CU mother. When she learns of the robbery, she is extremely displeased. Blinking back tears, she scolds Chizuko.

Scene #71. Exterior. Edge of the veranda of the Miura residence

Chizuko, severely reprimanded by her mother, collapses in tears on the veranda.

Scene #72. Exterior. Veranda of the Miura residence

LS, a continuation of previous scene. Chizuko's father emerges from within the house, stops in the middle of the room, and looks at the veranda.
TITLE: CHIZUKO'S FATHER

Scene #73. Exterior. Sitting room of the Miura residence

Close-up, Miura. He has been watching Chizuko and her mother on the veranda and, smiling, lightly shakes his head as he exits in the foreground.

Scene #74. Exterior. Veranda

His daughter cries, cowering on the veranda, and her mother scolds her. The father advances from the background, placates the mother, and turns toward Chizuko.
DIALOGUE INSERT: CHIZU! IT LOOKS LIKE YOU'VE PULLED SOME PRANK AGAIN. I'LL APOLOGIZE TO YOUR MOTHER, SO STOP CRYING AND GO INSIDE AND CHANGE YOUR CLOTHES.
Chizuko exits, behaving like a spoiled six- or seven-year-old.

Scene #75. Exterior. At the well in the backyard

Chizuko enters pretending to cry. When she reaches the well she abruptly stops pretending, sticks out her tongue, and laughs. Fade out as she prepares to dash water on herself.
TITLE: IN THE SITTING ROOM, CHIZUKO'S MOTHER AND FATHER ARE DISCUSSING HOW TO DISCIPLINE THEIR DAUGHTER.

Scene #76. Exterior. Veranda

The mother complains: "Really! She's such a tomboy."
"Nah, when they're young, whether they're a boy or a girl, they need to be lively. You shouldn't scold her like that." The father pays no attention to the mother's grumbling and just laughs indulgently.
"Your acting like that is the problem. Because you're too lenient with her, that girl will always act like a child."
"Act like a child! That's a good thing—people should always be a child at heart."
The father turns a deaf ear, and the mother, looking increasingly displeased, leaves teary-eyed.

Scene #77. Exterior. The garden

Fade in and out. The two thieves are looking toward the veranda.

274

Scene #78. Exterior. Miura residence. Veranda

The father, as in #76. . . . Having changed into a cool summer kimono [*yukata*] (any color but white), Chizuko enters looking like a well-mannered young lady. She looks at her father and, smiling, heads back to the garden. Her father stops her and tells her not to go anywhere else today because he has something interesting to tell her. Chizuko reluctantly goes over to her father's side and stands. He has her sit down.

DIALOGUE INSERT: ALL THE THINGS HERE ARE OUR FAMILY TREASURES. THEY ARE THE LEGACY OF OUR ANCESTORS FROM LONG AGO.

The father picks up the apparel, paintings and calligraphy, and utensils, and one by one tells Chizuko about their origins. As she listens to her father, Chizuko puts her hand through the sleeve of a robe [*hitatare*], tries on a black lacquered hat [*eboshi*], and attempts drawing a bow. Meanwhile, the two advance to the next room.

Scene #79. Exterior. Garden of the Miura residence

As soon as they see the father move on to the next room, the two thieves glance all around and stealthily go to the shadow of the stone lantern next to the veranda. Again keeping a sharp eye on the lookout, they stare in the direction of the room where things have been laid out to air. Fade out.

TITLE: THE MURAOKA VILLA

Scene #80. Exterior. Muraoka villa

Iris in and out. A full shot of the villa.

Scene #81. Interior. Shigeru's room

Fade in. LS, Muraoka, Inoue, Hattori, Katō, Natsuko, and three or four others are present in the scene. Natsuko and Hattori make a mimeograph and Shigeru stands beside them trying to see the result. Inoue is by the gramophone looking for a record. Katō Kenzō is absorbed in practicing the violin. Koizumi, who will play the character Otokonosuke, studies kabuki makeup techniques [*kumadori*] before a mirror while consulting photographic illustrations in [the entertainment review] *Engei gahō*. . . . Nakamura, who plays the role of Nikki Danjō, is making strange facial expressions, raising his eyes, pursing his lips, and so on.

Scene #82. Interior. Shigeru's room

Shigeru picks up the program that Natsuko and Hattori have finally finished printing and solemnly examines it.

Insert of the printed program:

THE KAMAKURA AMATEUR CLUB
THIRD PERFORMANCE
Seven o'clock this evening at the Muraoka villa on Hase Shore
PROGRAM

Opening Address	Muraoka Shigeru
PART ONE	Western Music
Soprano solo	Miss Muraoka Natsuko
Violin accompaniment	Katō Kenichi[5]
Violin solo	Inoue Hideo
Mandolin solo	Muraoka Shigeru
Duet	Muraoka Natsuko
	Hattori Ichirō

15 minute intermission

PART TWO	HISTORICAL DRAMA
THE TAIKŌKI	ACT X
Takechi Mitsuhide	Katō Kenzō
Takechi Jūjirō	Muraoka Shigeru
Hatsugiku	Inoue Hideo
Mitsuhide's mother, Satsuki	Ōno Kamekichi
Mitsuhide's wife, Misao	Hattori Ichirō
Hashiba Hisayoshi	Suzuki Risaburō
THE DISPUTED SUCCESSION	"UNDER THE FLOOR"
Nikki Danjō	Nakamura Hiroshi
Arajishi Otokonosuke	Koizumi Nobuichi
The Rat	Watanabe Yoshitarō

Performance ends at 11 o'clock in the evening

Muraoka gives his approval and asks them to run off several copies.

Scene #83. Interior. Shigeru's room

Inoue finally locates the record he has been looking for.
Insert, close-up of the record: THE TAIKŌKI, ACT X, "AT AMAGASAKI"
Inoue rejoices and places it on the gramophone, turns to one side, and calls Shigeru.

Scene #84. Interior. Shigeru's room

Natsuko and Hattori are following Shigeru's instructions. Shigeru turns in the direction of Inoue's call and asks what he wants.

Scene #85. Interior. Shigeru's room

Inoue points to the record and tells him to come quickly to rehearse . . . at the same time, the record begins turning.

Scene #86. Interior. Shigeru's room

Shigeru takes leave of Natsuko and Hattori and exits the scene.

Scene #87. Interior. Shigeru's room

Shigeru goes over to where Inoue is and starts rehearsing.
TITLE: CLINGING, APPEALING TO HIM TO THINK BETTER OF IT
Inoue and Shigeru make the appropriate gestures for this scene.

Scene #88. Interior. Shigeru's room

Katō practices the violin.

Scene #89. Interior. Shigeru's room

Koizumi, hard at work studying makeup. Insert photo from *Engeki gahō*.

Scene #90. Interior. Shigeru's room

Nakamura, who will play Nikki Danjō, is engrossed in his study of facial expressions.

Scene #91. Interior. Detached tearoom

LS. Shigeru's father Tamotsu is lying down and indulging in a short nap, the Chinese book he was reading spread open by his pillow (his face covered with a fan).
TITLE: SHIGERU'S FATHER

Scene #92. Interior. Detached tearoom

Close-up. Although still half asleep, he stretches out his left hand holding the fan onto the tatami matting, quietly shows his sleepy face for a moment, and suddenly opens his eyes as if he has been awakened by a sound. He appears to be contemplating an annoying noise. Include in the close-up the unfinished collection of Tang and Sung dynasty poems . . . a page with small red dots for emphasis here and there . . . (he is an elderly man, the politician type). The old man seems to understand where the sound is coming from . . . he sits up.

Scene #93. Interior. Shigeru's room

Full shot. All present are feverishly absorbed in their rehearsing.

Scene #94. Interior. Detached tearoom

Shigeru's father deliberately stands and leaves the scene.

Scene #95. Interior. Shigeru's room

As the rehearsing grows increasingly intense, Shigeru's father Tamotsu unceremoniously enters the room looking very displeased. At once, everyone goes silent and cowers. "What is going on? Just what do you think you're doing?" he says, eyeing them one by one, his eyes riveting on Koizumi, who is made up to play the role of Otokonosuke.

Scene #96. Interior. Shigeru's room

Close-up of Koizumi, looking as if he is at a disadvantage.

Scene #97. Interior. Shigeru's room

Tamotsu walks over to Koizumi and rubs at his face, glaring hard enough to bore a hole through him.

Scene #98. Interior. Shigeru's room

CU gramophone, the record spinning serenely.

Scene #99. Interior. Shigeru's room

CU of Shigeru. He looks at the gramophone and hurries over to it.

Scene #100. Interior. Shigeru's room.

Position the lens so that from the gramophone to where Koizumi and Tamotsu are standing is visible. Shigeru reaches the gramophone. Tamotsu sees this and approaches Shigeru.

Scene #101. Interior. Shigeru's room

CU, Shigeru's hand stopping the rotation of the gramophone.

Scene #102. Interior. Shigeru's room

Natsuko and Hattori from the point at which Shigeru is standing. Natsuko and Hattori are desperately clearing away the handbills. Tamotsu is giving Shigeru a good scolding.[6] Tamotsu spies the handbills, approaches Natsuko, and takes one.

(Insert, handbill)

Scene #103. Interior. Shigeru's room

CU, Tamotsu's expression turns even uglier after reading the handbill.

Scene #104. Interior. Shigeru's room

LS, the father thrusts the hand bill under Shigeru's nose.

DIALOGUE INSERT: WHO GAVE YOU PERMISSION TO DO SUCH A THING? THIS HOUSE IS NOT A PLAYHOUSE!![7] IT IS NOT A PLAYGROUND FOR JUVENILE DELINQUENTS!!

He grows sharper with each word, and Shigeru pleads his case.

DIALOGUE INSERT: BUT FATHER, WE'RE HARDLY JUVENILE DELINQUENTS, WE HAVE A SERIOUS MOTIVATION FOR STUDYING DRAMA.

With this, the father grows even more furious: "'Studying drama.' Don't make me laugh, if you have that kind of time on your hands, study your lessons. Students have no business studying drama!!" When Shigeru persists in saying another word or two on his own behalf, his father becomes even more imperious:

DIALOGUE INSERT: I'VE HAD ENOUGH! NO MATTER WHAT YOU SAY I POSITIVELY WILL NOT PERMIT IT.

Giving them all a withering look, his father leaves in a rage. They all watch him go with bated breath. Shigeru calls them all to gather around him.

Scene #105. Interior. Shigeru's room

Close-up of the group. Shigeru says in a low voice:

DIALOGUE INSERT: FATHER IS LEAVING FOR TOKYO ON THE FOUR O'CLOCK TRAIN AND HE'S NOT COMING BACK TONIGHT SO DON'T WORRY.

Fade out on the group in a huddle.

Scene #106. Exterior. Garden of the Miura residence

Fade in. The two robbers are still indefatigably looking in the direction of the sitting room.

Scene #107. Exterior. Veranda of the Miura residence

The room is actually two rooms adjacent to each other; Chizuko and her father have already arrived in one of these adjoining rooms and are admiring an endless array of valuables. Chizuko immediately grabs a halberd [*naginata*] laying there and begins questioning her father. Her father responds:

DIALOGUE INSERT: THAT WAS USED BY MY GRANDMOTHER. SHE WAS AS ROBUST AS A MAN!!

Scene #108. Exterior. Veranda of the Miura residence

Chizuko, listening, is unable to contain her delight and impulsively flourishes the halberd. Overlap at this point: Chizuko dressed as a woman of long ago, brandishing the halberd once or twice and then changing back to the former Chizuko.

Scene #109. Exterior. Veranda of the Miura residence

Father and daughter. He stops her, pointing out that what she is doing is dangerous. Chizuko suddenly spies a suit of armor laid out.

Scene #110. Exterior. Veranda of the Miura residence

CU of armor.

Scene #111. Exterior. Veranda of the Miura residence

Chizuko asks her father to tell her about this armor. With evident pride, her father says:

DIALOGUE INSERT: THIS? THIS IS THE MOST VALUABLE ITEM IN OUR FAMILY, SO YOU SHOULD LISTEN CAREFULLY AND REMEMBER WHAT I TELL YOU. LONG AGO AMONG OUR ANCESTORS THERE WAS A GREAT SAMURAI. AT THE AGE OF FIFTEEN HE DISTINGUISHED HIMSELF IN HIS FIRST BATTLE.

Overlap the father's monologue with a young warrior wearing this armor felling the enemy leader, or something of the sort, and close with Chizuko's father. Chizuko is touching the armor with evident delight, saying "So this was worn by a child! My, what a fetching set of armor!" or something of the sort.

Scene #112. Exterior. Garden of the Miura residence

Sensing opportunity, the two thieves tiptoe toward the sitting room and hide under the veranda.

Scene #113. Exterior. Veranda of the Miura residence

Trying on a dragon-crested helmet and waving a long sword, Chizuko is thoroughly delighted and makes no effort to leave their side.

Scene #114. Exterior. Under the veranda of the Miura residence

Keeping an eye on the adjacent room, one of the thieves furtively reaches out and grabs an article on the veranda . . . then the two whisper to each other under their breath.

Scene #115. Exterior. Veranda of the Miura residence

Engrossed with the armor, Chizuko casually looks in the direction of the veranda and is surprised.

Scene #116. Exterior. Veranda of the Miura residence

CU, a hand quietly reaches out from under the veranda.

Scene #117. Exterior. Veranda of the Miura residence

Chizuko whispers something in her father's ear. Her father picks up an iron-ribbed fan beside him and tiptoes out of the scene.[8] As if suddenly struck with an idea, Chizuko tucks the halberd under her arm and jumps down into the garden.

Scene #118. Exterior. Veranda of the Miura residence

The hand that reached out from under the floorboards takes hold of one of the heirlooms there, and is about to disappear again under the floorboards when Chizuko's father approaches, it is whacked with the iron-ribbed fan, and it drops the item. At the same moment the two thieves jump out from under the veranda and beat a hasty retreat.

Scene #119. Exterior. Part of the garden of the Miura residence

The two thieves run in and out [of the frame]. Chizuko chases after them waving the halberd. Right behind her run five or six menservants and maids, each of them crying, "Miss! It's dangerous!"

Scene #120. Exterior. Garden of the Miura residence

The two thieves enter and, dodging their pursuer, disappear. . . . Chizuko enters and is determined to chase them down, but the menservants and maids restrain her and take her away.

Scene #121. Exterior. Garden of the Miura residence

Chizuko enters while angrily berating the servants: "What a shame! . . . they've managed to get away!! It's all your fault for dawdling around!" Chizuko's father enters from FG and comforts his daughter:
DIALOGUE INSERT: IF THEY'VE ESCAPED, IT'S BETTER TO LET THEM GO— THEY DIDN'T MAKE OFF WITH ANYTHING.
Chizuko, seemingly even more vexed, says:
DIALOGUE INSERT: THE NEXT TIME THEY COME HERE, I'LL MAKE THEM PAY!

Her father, in his usual good humor, jokes, "I hope they don't come too often."

Scene #122. Exterior. Entrance to the Muraoka residence

A jinrikisha waits off to one side.[9] Muraoka Tamotsu comes out from the entrance ready to go out; Shigeru also comes to the entrance in order to see him off. Tamotsu sternly passes sentence upon Shigeru once again:
DIALOGUE INSERT: WELL THEN, I'LL BE ON MY WAY, AND WHILE I'M GONE THERE IS TO BE NO FOOLISHNESS. I ABSOLUTELY WILL NOT HAVE IT.
Shigeru merely nods in consent, secretly thinking success is in sight. His father gets in the jinrikisha and leaves.

Scene #123. Exterior. Entrance to the Muraoka residence

Close-up. As soon as his father's figure disappears, Shigeru dances a little jig and enters the house.

Scene #124. Interior. Shigeru's room

The group is out of spirits when Shigeru enters and in a loud voice says, "Hey, my father just left. We're safe, come on, let's hurry it up." Hearing this the group takes heart and leaves the room.

Scene #125. Interior. *Hiroma*[10]

The group enters carrying in their hands various scenery and stage props. Shigeru supervises the group. Fade out on the group, their spirits revived, as they go about setting everything up.
TITLE: SEVEN O'CLOCK THAT EVENING

Scene #126. Interior. *Hiroma* (night)

Fade in. Preparations are complete, and the invited lot are pouring into the room in droves. Students, children, young ladies, young couples, all apparently vacationers from the neighboring inns and villas. . . . Out . . . .[11]

Scene #127. A room in the Miura residence

Following Chizuko's father's orders, Chizuko's mother and three maids work in groups: they are folding garments, rolling up hanging scrolls, wrapping utensils in cotton padding, tying boxes with cords, and cleaning with feather dusters.

Scene #128. Interior. *Hiroma* (night)

Shoot from the stage, facing the crowd. All together the spectators clap their hands.

Scene #129. Interior. *Hiroma* (night)

Set the camera up behind the crowd and shoot facing the stage. Summoned by the applause, Muraoka Shigeru appears onstage and bows to the audience.

Scene #130. Interior. *Hiroma* (night)

Close-up of Muraoka Shigeru. He begins his opening address. (Affectedly)
DIALOGUE INSERT: LADIES AND GENTLEMEN!! WE HEREBY PRESENT THE RESULTS OF OUR STUDIES OF WESTERN MUSIC AND KABUKI DRAMA. WE WISH TO PASS AN EVENING OF PLEASURE IN YOUR COMPANY, AND HUMBLY REQUEST YOUR COMMENTS AS WELL.
Shigeru concludes the above title.

Scene #131. Interior. *Hiroma* (night)

CU, choose a group of lively youths in the audience. Some shout "hear, hear!" while others, laughing, applaud.

Scene #132. Interior. *Hiroma* (night)

LS, position the camera behind the crowd; Shigeru adds a word or two in closing and withdraws. Everyone applauds. (Highlight the action in FG.) Fade out.

Scene #133. Interior. A room in the Miura residence

One by one, the articles packed in boxes are carried out toward the storehouse at the back of the residence. The menservants and maids work diligently, following the instructions of Chizuko's father.

Scene #134. Interior. Entrance to the storehouse

The servants carry in the boxes.

Scene #135. Interior. *Hiroma*

Shoot from behind the crowd. Onstage Natsuko is singing a soprano solo to Katō Kenzō's violin accompaniment.

Scene #136. Interior. *Hiroma*

CU, Natsuko's solo.

Scene #137. Interior. *Hiroma*

The camera is in the same position as in #135. The soloist finishes singing amid thunderous applause, bows politely, and steps down from the stage, beaming at the audience. Their programs in hand, the audience awaits the next number.

Scene #138. Exterior. A pine grove at the shore (iris in)

The two thieves have returned to shadows of the pine grove, and are again discussing something.

DIALOGUE INSERT: LET'S GO BACK ONCE MORE TONIGHT BETWEEN ELEVEN O'CLOCK AND MIDNIGHT.

When one of them says this, the other nods in agreement. (Iris out)

Scene #139. Interior. Sitting room in the Miura residence

For the most part the items belonging to the Miuras that had been laid out to air have already been put away, and all that is left is the scarlet-laced suit of armor.[12] Chizuko, whose eyes had been riveted on the armor, turns to her father with evident reluctance and asks:

DIALOGUE INSERT: FATHER, WILL THIS ARMOR BE PUT AWAY TOO?

Her father looks doubtful.

DIALOGUE INSERT: BUT I'D REALLY LIKE TO TRY IT ON.

Her father humors her.

DIALOGUE INSERT: NOW THAT'S PRECISELY WHY YOUR MOTHER SCOLDS YOU! IF YOU WANT THE SUIT OF ARMOR, IN TIME I'LL GIVE IT TO YOU— EVERYTHING IN THIS HOUSE WILL BE YOURS.

As he is speaking, his wife and a maid enter, put the armor in its chest, and carry it away.

Scene #140. Interior. Sitting room in the Miura residence

Close-up of Chizuko, gazing after it wistfully. (Iris out)

TITLE: THE AMATEUR CLUB'S PROGRAM PROCEEDS PIECE BY PIECE. THE WESTERN MUSIC PORTION HAS JUST ENDED.

Scene #141. Interior. *Hiroma*

From the notice "15 minute intermission" onstage to the seats in the audience. The seats are tightly packed together, giving the appearance of a great success. The members of the audience are fanning themselves, drinking tea, and chatting noisily.

Scene #142. Interior. Shigeru's room (backstage)

LS the group is making quite a racket preparing for the period drama.

Scene #143. Interior. Backstage

Close-up, Shigeru as Jūjirō faces Hattori as Misao and appears to be doing his makeup.

TITLE: *GIDAYŪ* PERFORMANCE TAKEMOTO UDAYŪ

SHAMISEN TSURUSAWA MANSUKE

Scene #144. Interior. Backstage

CU The two professional artists dressed in *kataginu* and *hakama* politely wait in one corner.[13] Just as one of them flicks the ash from his cigarette he suddenly looks up and gets the attention of the other.

Scene #145. Interior. Backstage

Close-up, Inoue as Hatsugiku has completed his makeup. He is now having a maid stick an ornament in his hair, but she has just greatly mistaken where to poke it.

Scene #146. Interior. Backstage

Close-up, the *gidayū* chanter and the *shamisen* player. They should show as little expression as possible. They look like they are trying hard not to smirk.

Scene #147. Interior. Backstage

Katō as Mitsuhide and Ōno as Satsuki are both having maids help them into their costumes.

Scene #148. Interior. Backstage

The two professionals look away. One of them yawns, the other sighs. They calmly dismiss everything in a quiet and patronizing manner (as if emphasizing that they themselves are not amateurs). Fade out.

Scene #149. Interior. *Hiroma*

Fade in. The intermission sign is removed, and the curtain finally opens on act 10 of *Taikōki*. The crowd applauds. The chanter begins his performance.

Scene #150. Interior. *Hiroma*

CU, chanting.

Scene #151. Interior. *Hiroma*

The audience grows quiet and appears to be listening attentively.

Scene #152. Exterior. Veranda of the Miura residence (night)

A mosquito smudge burns on the edge of the veranda. Absorbed in idle conversation, Chizuko and her parents sit on the veranda enjoying the summer evening. Chizuko's mother is smiling and in a good mood, apparently having forgotten her harsh words earlier that day. With the assistance of spectacles, Chizuko's father scans the articles in the evening paper, talking with Chizuko and her mother as if he has read something of interest. Chizuko sits on the veranda; while gazing at the firefly cage and replenishing the smudge pot, she occasionally exchanges amused glances with her mother in response to her father's comments. A scene of a tranquil summer evening, overflowing with the sense of family harmony.

Scene #153. Interior. *Hiroma*

Full view of the stage, Satsuki's monologue: the bridal toast, a celebratory cup of sake to both marriage and departing for battle.[14]
TITLE: JOY, YET THE INCREASING SADNESS OF FAREWELL

Scene #154. Interior. *Hiroma*

Close-up, chanter and *shamisen* player. The chanter is reciting at full force, steam rising from his head, and the *shamisen* player is no less enthusiastic.

Scene #155. Interior. *Hiroma*

CU Hatsugiku, her smiling face concealing her sorrow at the thought that even though she has such a fine husband, this could be a toast to farewell (appropriate gestures).

Scene #156. Interior. *Hiroma*

The general audience, some clapping, some shouting.

Scene #157. Interior. *Hiroma*

Close-up of five or six people, shouting repeatedly
DIALOGUE INSERT: NARIKOMAYA! SUKETAKAYA![15]

Scene #158. Interior. *Hiroma*

A full view of the stage. What follows is the scene where Hatsugiku says, "achieve distinction and do meritorious deeds, let us drink to victory at least for tonight, then afterwards, unspeakable anguish," and so on and so forth. (The main purpose of the amateur theatrical performance is a burlesque of old-time kabuki drama and *gidayū;* it should be comical.)

286

Scene #159. Exterior. Veranda of the Miura residence

Chizuko's father lets the evening paper slip from his lap as he begins to doze; Chizuko and her mother look at him and laugh. The smoke from the mosquito smudge has grown quite thin. Then, shaking his head because a mosquito has landed on the tip of his nose, the father wakes with a start and glances up at the wall clock.

Insert, the wall clock striking half past ten. Chizuko's father begins to mutter, as if to himself ("What, this late already! The night is brief. . . ."). At this, Chizuko's mother turns to her and says:

DIALOGUE TITLE: "CHIZUKO DEAR, IT'S YOUR BEDTIME."

Chizuko's mother summons the maid and issues her orders, and they go inside. Fade out on the woman as she closes the shutters.

TITLE: SHIGERU'S FATHER, WHO WAS NOT EXPECTED TO RETURN, HAS ARRIVED AT THE KAMAKURA STATION ON THE 10:50 TRAIN.

Scene #160. Exterior. In front of the Kamakura train station

Fade in and out, At the train station, Shigeru's father Tamotsu calls for a jinrikisha, gets in, and rides away.

Scene #161. Interior. Chizuko's room

Chizuko looks content, sound asleep within a mosquito tent.

Scene #162. Exterior. Garden of the Miura residence

The two thieves walk from FG to BG.

Scene #163. Interior. *Hiroma*

Shoot from behind the audience, everyone is silent.

TITLE: APPEARING FROM THIS SIDE OF THE GOURD TRELLIS . . .

Scene #164. Interior. *Hiroma*

Close-up of the chanter, he is sitting erect (about three feet [of film]).

TITLE: TAKECHI MITSUHIDE!!

Overlap this title with the next scene.

Scene #165. Interior. *Hiroma*

Mitsuhide emerges from the bamboo grass at the rear of the stage, approaches the camera, gestures with the sedge hat that he is carrying, glares, and strikes a pose.[16]

Scene #166. Interior. *Hiroma*

CU, a mother and child in the audience only. The five- or six-year-old child is frightened by Mitsuhide's face and suddenly bursts into tears, clinging to her mother.

Scene #167. Interior. *Hiroma*

Another portion of the audience, the four or five people from a previous scene will do. They shout enthusiastically:
DIALOGUE INSERT: NARITAYA!! BRAVO!!

Scene #168. Exterior. In front of the entrance hall of the Muraoka residence

Fade in. Tamotsu, who has just now stepped down from the jinrikisha, hears the commotion, dismisses the ricksha driver, and gruffly goes inside.

Scene #169. Interior. *Hiroma*

From behind the audience. Natsuko is in FG. Natsuko had been fixated on the stage, but thinking she might have heard something, she suddenly turns around.

Scene #170. Interior. Entrance

From the entrance with the door in the background.
The father enters through the door and gruffly advances forward.

Scene #171. Interior. *Hiroma*

Stunned, Natsuko stumbles inside.

Scene #172. Interior. Shigeru's room (backstage)

Appearing in the next number, *The Disputed Succession,* Nikki Danjō, Otokonosuke, and the Rat wait in full costume backstage. Natsuko comes bounding in. Shouting "Oh no!! Oh no!!," she announces that her father has returned. The group panics, not knowing what to do.

Scene #173. Interior. *Hiroma*

From behind the audience. The father flies into a rage, and with a menacing look leaps over the spectators' seats, dashes up onto the stage, and wallops the actors one after another. Hatsugiku's wig is knocked off and she keels over, her hairy legs in the air.

Scene #174. Interior. *Hiroma*

CU chanter and *shamisen* player, dumbfounded, their eyes opened wide in astonishment.

Scene #175. Interior. *Hiroma*

After toppling Hatsugiku, the father eyes the two entertainers and heads in their direction.

Scene #176. Interior. *Hiroma*

Just as the two entertainers are trying to gather up their *shamisen* and the like, the father approaches and starts to wallop them too.

Scene #177. Interior. *Hiroma*

From behind the audience. All flee in terror. Onstage, the actors are overwhelmed and flee backstage. The father chases after them.

Scene #178. Interior. Shigeru's room

The group noisily enters the room. The father is chasing after them, so with Shigeru's Jūjirō in the lead, Mitsuhide, Hisayoshi, Misao, Hatsugiku, Satsuki, Nikki Danjō, Arajishi Otokonosuke, and finally the Rat too dash back and forth in full costume, dispersing in all directions and saying "Run away, run away!" Grumbling, the father returns to the *hiroma*.

Scene #179. Interior. One section of the *hiroma*

The father enters from Shigeru's room, approaches a telephone, and picks up the receiver.

Scene #180. Interior. One section of the *hiroma*

Close-up, the father, Tamotsu, is feverishly making a phone call.

Scene #181. Interior. Superintendent's office

The superintendent who is in charge hears the phone ring, picks up the receiver, and responds with "hello."

Scene #182. Interior. One section of the *hiroma*

Tamotsu begs the superintendent to apprehend the youths.

Scene #183. Interior. Superintendent's office

Stifling his laughter because the situation is so comical, the superintendent dispatches five or six policemen to make the arrest.

Scene #184. Interior. Chizuko's room

Chizuko continues sleeping peacefully.

Scene #185. Interior. *Hiroma*

Natsuko, the only one caught by her father, has been scolded and is sobbing.

Scene #186. Exterior. Hase Road (night)

The wigless Hatsugiku, Mitsuhide, and Otokonosuke run head over heels down the main road of Hase. Behind them the old woman character Satsuki runs with her kimono skirts tucked up, and behind her runs the Rat. The group runs from FG to BG in this shot [*gamen*].

Scene #187. Exterior. Another street

Now they run up in the previous order from BG to FG, stop in FG and, as if suddenly seeing something, abruptly turn around and hide left and right. The group of policemen enter from alongside the camera and chase after them.

Scene #188. Exterior. Yet another road

Dressed in his scarlet-laced armor, Muraoka Shigeru is cornered by a policeman, and takes refuge in some grass.

Scene #189. Exterior. Entrance to the storehouse, the garden of the Miura residence

The two thieves are climbing over a wall (reverse the order of #188 and #189).

Scene #190. Exterior. Entrance to the storehouse

The thieves have arrived at the entrance to the storehouse, and are trying to break the lock.

Scene #191. Interior. Chizuko's room

The sleeping Chizuko is awakened by a strange sound and listens intently.

Scene #192. Exterior. Entrance to the storehouse

The thieves finally break the lock and enter the storehouse.

Scene #193. Interior. Chizuko's room

Listening intently, Chizuko gets up and leaves the room (carrying a candle-stick and matches in her hands).

Scene #194. Interior. Inside the storehouse, ground floor

The entire place is filled with heaps of large boxes of valuables; the armor case is in the most conspicuous spot. The two thieves poke around with their flashlights, but seeing only boxes that are too large, they soon proceed to the second floor.

Scene #195. Exterior. Entrance to the storehouse

When Chizuko enters from the hallway and arrives at the entrance to the storehouse, the door is open and she suspects thieves. Soon hearing footsteps going up to the second floor, Chizuko lights her candle and stealthily enters the storeroom, shading the light with a sleeve.

Scene #196. Interior. Inside the storehouse (ground floor)

Chizuko tiptoes in, makes her way to the bottom of the stairs and looks up at the second floor.

Scene #197. Interior. Inside the storehouse, second floor

The two thieves unfold large squares of cloth [*furoshiki*]; on them they pile up moderately sized articles.

Scene #198. Interior. Inside the storehouse (ground floor)

Chizuko is looking up at the second floor, but hearing nothing more, she is relieved. She happens to look in front of her and sees the armor case. Chizuko instantly has an idea and, nodding to herself, quietly removes the armor and starts putting it on

Scene #199. Interior. Inside the storehouse (second floor)

The two thieves prepare to wrap up the last of the loot in their *furoshiki*.

Scene #200. Interior. Inside the storehouse (ground floor)

Chizuko hastily puts on the armor, now and then attentively glancing up at the second floor.

Scene #201. Interior. Inside the storehouse (second floor)

Carrying the various articles over the shoulders, the two thieves approach the stairs.

Scene #202. Interior. Inside the storehouse (ground floor)

Hearing the footsteps above, Chizuko clicks her tongue disapprovingly and briefly hides beneath the stairs. Still unaware that someone is there, the thieves hurry by. Chizuko comes out and hastily puts on the rest of the armor.

Scene #203. Exterior. Entrance to the storehouse

The two thieves exit and head toward the corridor.

Scene #204. Interior. Inside the storehouse (ground floor)

Chizuko finishes putting everything on. Thoroughly preparing herself, she takes the dragon-crested helmet and carries a gold-mounted sword and sheath at her side.
TITLE: CHIZUKO'S FIRST BATTLE
Chizuko hastens after the thieves.

Scene #205. Exterior. Garden of the Miura residence

The two thieves are frantically clambering up the wall; they suddenly look in the direction of the garden.

Scene #206. Exterior. Garden of the Miura residence

With the camera at the same height as the wall, shoot someone wearing armor wielding a drawn sword coming after the thieves from the far distance.

Scene #207. Exterior. Garden of the Miura residence

Close-up. The two thieves atop the wall, startled, scurry down the other side of the wall.

Scene #208. Exterior.

The two thieves jump down from the wall and continue to flee; Chizuko comes after them, jumps over the wall, and follows relentlessly.

Scene #209. Exterior. Pine grove

The policemen follow after Hatsugiku, Mitsuhide, and Nikki Danjō fleeing willy-nilly through the dunes and pine groves.

Scene #210. Exterior. Stone stairs to the Temple of Kannon at Hase

Misao, Satsuki, and Otokonosuke desperately run up the stone steps.

292

Scene #211. Exterior. Temple grounds, Temple of Kannon at Hase

Just as the three from the previous scene run up and crawl under the veranda of the temple, the policemen approach from the opposite direction, so the three double back.

Scene #212. Exterior. Stone stairs to the Temple of Kannon at Hase

The three scramble down the stone steps. The policemen chase after them.
TITLE: THE MONSTER OF YUIGAHAMA

Scene #213. Exterior. Beach

The Rat of *The Disputed Succession* is left all alone, and runs for dear life along the shore of Yuigahama.

Scene #214. Exterior. Beach

A gentleman and a geisha dressed in *yukata* are strolling hand in hand, enjoying the view of the moonlit shore.

Scene #215. Exterior. Beach (fishing boat)

Off to the side in FG is a fishing boat. The Rat comes running from BG, pauses for a moment, and looks ahead.

Scene #216. Exterior. Beach (fishing boat)

The gentleman and geisha come walking.

Scene #217. Exterior. Beach (fishing boat)

Continuation of #215, instantly, the Rat hides in the boat's shadow. The gentleman and geisha enter and lean against the boat with an appearance of extreme intimacy.

Scene #218. Exterior. Beach (fishing boat)

Close-up. The gentleman and the geisha seen from behind; the two chat quietly, billing and cooing.

Scene #219. Exterior. Beach (fishing boat)

CU Rat. Listening to the two, he suddenly has an idea and stands up, emitting a bizarre cry.

Scene #220. Exterior. Beach (fishing boat)

Close-up. The gentleman and the geisha from behind. Startled by the bizarre cry, they turn around, opening their eyes wide.

Scene #221. Exterior. Beach (fishing boat)

The Rat is motionless.

Scene #222. Exterior. Beach (fishing boat)

Close-up, the gentleman and the geisha, eyes open wide, collapse in a faint. Paying little heed, the Rat hides inside the boat.

Scene #223. Exterior. The other road (some grass)

Shigeru, perfectly still, conceals himself.

Scene #224. Grounds of the Temple of the Great Buddha

Chizuko, brandishing the sword, pursues the two thieves. Entering the grounds of the Temple of the Great Buddha, the three momentarily chase each other around the Great Buddha statue and then run off in a different direction.

Scene #225. Interior. The shutters along the corridor

Chizuko's father enters and, thinking it strange that the shutters have been left open, exits in the direction of the storehouse.

Scene #226. Exterior. Entrance to the storehouse

The father enters and goes inside.

Scene #227. Interior. Inside the storehouse (ground floor)

The father enters and, discovering Chizuko's nightclothes flung off in front of the armor case and the armor missing, hurriedly turns back.

Scene #228. Interior. Chizuko's room

The father enters, looks inside the mosquito tent and, surprised to find the bed empty, awakens the whole house. With the mother leading the way, the maids and manservants enter, some with their eyes wide in astonishment, others still half asleep. They all raise an uproar. The father quickly exits.

Scene #229. Interior. Telephone room, the Miura residence

The father quickly enters and makes a call.

Scene #230. Superintendent's office

The superintendent is listening on the phone—
DIALOGUE INSERT: I SEE. YOUR DAUGHTER HAS RUN AWAY FROM HOME
WEARING SCARLET-LACED ARMOR . . . VERY WELL, WE SHALL SEARCH FOR
HER IMMEDIATELY
The superintendent hangs up the phone and summons a subordinate. The
subordinate enters, salutes, and says:
DIALOGUE INSERT: "ARMOR AGAIN?"
Laughing, the superintendent replies:
DIALOGUE INSERT: "THAT'S RIGHT. THIS TIME IT'S A GIRL."
The policeman energetically dashes outside.

Scene #231. Exterior. Beach

The gentleman and the geisha lie senseless. The policemen enter and help the
two up and on their way. The Rat, hiding inside the boat, unexpectedly
appears and takes off in the direction of the sand dunes. The policemen chase
after him.

Scene #232. Exterior. Pine grove (square)

The two thieves enter, turn back around in FG, point off to the side, and break
into a run. A moment later, Chizuko enters and, as if having lost sight of the
thieves, suddenly looks ahead.

Scene #233. Exterior. Pine grove

LS, the Rat runs down a sand dune and flees [in the direction of Chizuko].

Scene #234. Exterior. Pine grove (a bend)

Chizuko hides in the shade under some pine trees.

Scene #235. Exterior. Pine grove

The Rat flees, approaching ever closer.
TITLE: BEHOLD THE MONSTER

Scene #236. Exterior. Pine grove (a bend)

From behind Chizuko, who is hiding in the shade of some trees, shoot the
Rat's approach. Chizuko takes the defensive, instantly blocking the Rat's
path.

Scene #237. Exterior. Beach (fishing boat)

Mitsuhide, Hatsugiku, and Nikki Danjō finally reach the shore and hide in the boat where the Rat had taken cover a few moments ago.

Scene #238. Exterior. Street

Mr. Miura enters accompanied by a manservant, searching here and there. They approach FG and look ahead.

Scene #239. Exterior. The other road (some grass)

Long shot of Shigeru crouching in the grass.

Scene #240. Exterior. Road

A manservant tells Chizuko's father that the figure crouching in the grass in the distance is Chizuko. The father is overjoyed, and leaves the scene, shouting "Chizuko! Chizuko!"

Scene #241. Exterior. The other road (some grass)

Thinking it strange that they seem to be chasing him, Shigeru makes a break for it. The father and the manservant follow.

Scene #242. Exterior. Beach (fishing boat)

Misao, Satsuki, and Otokonosuke run up from BG. Mitsuhide, Hatsugiku, and Nikki Danjō stick their heads out from the fishing boat in FG and wave to them. The other three quickly crawl in.
TITLE: CHIZUKO'S CONQUEST OF THE RAT

Scene #243. Exterior. Pine grove (a bend)

The endangered Rat backs off because Chizuko brandishes the sword, but seizing an opportunity, he knocks down Chizuko's sword and starts wrestling with her. As a result of the rough scuffle, Chizuko has lost her helmet, but shortly after she picks up her sword and starts swinging. The Rat bows repeatedly and surrenders, begging for mercy with clasped hands. Chizuko won't hear of it and continues swinging the sword. The Rat cries:
DIALOGUE INSERT: "HE-ELP! MURDER!"

Scene #244. Exterior. Pine grove

A policeman enters looking all about, but he apparently hears something and leaves in a hurry.

Scene #245. Exterior. Pine grove (a bend)

The Rat flees for dear life. Chizuko follows in pursuit.

Scene #246. Exterior. Pine grove

Flash scene, The Rat and Chizuko.

Scene #247. Exterior. Pine grove (a bend)

The policeman enters, picks up the fallen dragon-crested helmet, and examines it.

Scene #248. Exterior. Pine grove (the thieves encounter the Rat)

The two thieves enter with their bundles slung over their shoulders and dig up the watches, wallets, Chizuko's clothes, and such that they had buried that afternoon.
TITLE: "MURDER!"
The Rat runs by them screaming. The two thieves are startled and faint.

Scene #249. Exterior. Pine grove (a bend)

The policeman hears the scream and, carrying the helmet, exits the scene.

Scene #250. Exterior. Pine grove (the thieves' hideout)

Chizuko chases after the Rat without so much as a glance at the thieves. The policeman enters, ties a rope around the two thieves in a huddle, and leads them away.
TITLE: THE END OF JŪJIRŌ

Scene #251. Exterior. Street

Shigeru comes running from BG. Mr. Miura and the manservant follow in pursuit, still repeatedly calling out, "Chizuko! Chizuko!"[17]
TITLE: THE RAT RUNS INTO THE MURAOKA RESIDENCE IN A DAZE

Scene #252. Exterior. Gate in front of the Muraoka villa

The Rat enters and Chizuko follows. Both of them enter the house from the front entrance.

Scene #253. Interior. *Hiroma*

Tired of waiting, Shigeru's father paces around the room.
TITLE: "MURDER!"

Scene #254. Continuation of the previous scene

Unaware that Shigeru's father is in the room, the Rat runs in shouting "Murder!," stumbles, and falls. Chizuko also falls down on top of him and begins to wrestle with him.

Scene #255. Interior. *Hiroma*

Close-up of Shigeru's father. Thinking Chizuko to be his son, he energetically steps forward and grabs at the two.

Scene #256. Interior. *Hiroma*

Long shot. Shigeru's father separates Chizuko, who is on top in the struggle, and swats her hard. Chizuko shrieks and tumbles over.

Scene #257. Interior. *Hiroma*

Close-up, the Rat looks at Shigeru's father's face and opens his eyes wide in amazement.

Scene #258. Interior. *Hiroma*

Close-up of Chizuko and Shigeru's father. The father grabs her collar and pulls her to her feet; on closer look he realizes she is not his son and is dumbfounded. Chizuko, flustered, apologizes.

Scene #259. Interior. *Hiroma*

Shigeru's father also apologizes to Chizuko for having spanked her. Chizuko cries; in the meantime, the Rat sneaks away. Chizuko leaves the scene accompanied by Shigeru's father. Fade out.

Scene #260. Exterior. The final street

Jūjirō comes running from BG. Chizuko's father and the manservant chase after him. The manservant finally catches Shigeru in FG. The father runs up and soothingly says, "Chizuko, why run away like that when I call to you so?" Shigeru looks down, trying to hide his face. Gently lifting Shigeru's face in order to remove the helmet, the father is taken aback.

Scene #261. Close-up of the previous scene

Scene #262. Continuation of the previous scene

Shigeru explains the night's events to Chizuko's father. Although the father listens, laughing, he is all the more worried about what has become of

Chizuko. The manservant turns around and sees Chizuko approach, accompanied by a gentleman, and tells her father. The father rejoices and looks behind him as Chizuko, weeping, enters accompanied by a gentleman. Shigeru's father introduces himself and hands over Chizuko. Chizuko's father hands over Shigeru as well.

At this point, the detective (Yamazaki) happens to enter, leading the two thieves. He salutes Chizuko's father and points to the stolen goods. He says they will be returned at the station and leaves the scene.

Chizuko's father and Shigeru's father talk to each other as they watch them go. Behind their fathers, Shigeru and Chizuko shake hands.

Scene #263. Same as the previous scene

Close-up of the manservant's expression as he looks at Shigeru and Chizuko getting along with one another.

Scene #264. Same as the previous scene

Close-up of Chizuko and Shigeru, talking in a friendly manner. Fade out.
TITLE: ZZZZZZ, ZZZZZZ

Scene #265. The shore. Fishing boat

With the fishing boat in FG, the waves picturesquely lapping the seashore. Emphasize the moonlit scenery.

Tanizaki Jun'ichirō: *The Lust of the White Serpent* (excerpt, *Jasei no in*, 1921)

Period: not necessarily specific, but the costumes and manners should be appropriate to the early 1300s.[1]

Setting: should resemble the area along the road to Yamato in the province of Kii.[2]

(TITLE) Fade in and out[3]

LONG AGO, ON CAPE MIWA IN THE PROVINCE OF KII, THERE WAS A FISHERMAN NAMED ŌYAKE NO TAKESUKE. SEVERAL FISHERMEN WORKED UNDER HIM, AND HIS HOUSEHOLD WAS PROSPEROUS.[4]

Scene #1. Exterior. Seashore

Fade in. The shore of Cape Miwa, Kii province. Five or six fishing boats have just pulled ashore. Many fisherman (if possible, use real fishermen, altogether about twelve or thirteen men and women) are climbing out of the

Kurihara and Tanizaki's *Jasei no in* (*The Lust of the White Serpent*), 1921. Okada Tokihiko (*left*) and Benisawa Yōko (*right*). Courtesy Kawakita Memorial Film Institute.

boats. They gather on the beach, carrying fishing nets and baskets of various kinds of fish. Standing on the righthand side of the shore, awaiting their arrival, is Ōyake no Takesuke, who approaches and inspects their catch. Takesuke's oldest son, Tarō, is among the fishermen, directing the men and women on stage right. The fishermen empty out the baskets of fish onto the sand.

Scene #2. Exterior. Beach

CU of part of the group, including Takesuke and his son, with the accumulation of fish in the center of the frame. Tarō counts the fish, sorting them one by one according to their size. Smiling, Takesuke watches him. The father and son exchange glances and appear to be pleased with the large catch.

Scene #3. Exterior. Beach

CU of Takesuke and his son. "What do you say, Father? Look at the splendid sea bream we caught," Tarō says, displaying a fish before his father. They look at each other and laugh.
(Insert Title)
HIS SON TARŌ, FOLLOWING HIS FATHER'S VOCATION, WORKED HARD EVERY DAY.
Takesuke is forty-five or -six years old, an aged man with a kind face. He is wearing a black lacquered hat [*eboshi*], a proper robe with long, voluminous square sleeves [*hitatare*], and straw sandals on his bare feet. Tarō is a young man twenty-four or twenty-five, wearing pleated trousers [*hakama]* over a slightly soiled padded jacket [*kosode*]. Iris out at the end of this scene.

Scene #4. Interior. Yumimaro's room

Fade in. The room of Abe no Yumimaro, a Shinto priest at the Shingū Shrine.[5] In BG, two thick columns stand a short distance apart. Latticework has been inserted between the top and bottom of the columns. The top lattice is propped open, and light shines into the room. The floor is made of well-polished wooden boards. A desk stands in the center of the room. Facing it on the left is Abe no Yumimaro, seated on a tatami mat, and on the right, Toyoo, seated on a straw mat. A Chinese book is open on the desk, and Yumimaro is reciting the Chinese text aloud for Toyoo's benefit.
(Insert Title)
TAKESUKE HAD A YOUNGER SON, TOYOO. ALTHOUGH BORN TO A FISHERMAN, HE WAS COMPLETELY DIFFERENT FROM HIS OLDER BROTHER, TARŌ. TOYOO YEARNED FOR THE ELEGANCE OF THE CAPITAL CITY OF KYOTO, AND SO HE REGULARLY VISITED THE SHRINE'S HEAD PRIEST, WHO WAS EDUCATING HIM.
Toyoo raises his head and, pointing to a passage in the text, asks Yumimaro a

question. (Toyoo is about eighteen or nineteen years old. He is wearing a silk hunting robe [*kariginu*], an *eboshi*, and loose, full silk trousers [*sashinuki*]. Yumimaro is around forty, and wears a priest's garments.)

Scene #5. Interior. Yumimaro's room

CU of Toyoo, asking a question. He is a handsome youth with a pleasant expression.

Scene #6. Interior. Yumimaro's room

CU of Yumimaro, reading aloud in answer to Toyoo's question.

Scene #7. Interior. Yumimaro's room

Full shot of both figures. Yumimaro continues to read, Toyoo listens. Fade out.
(Title) Fade in and out
IT WAS CLOSE TO THE END OF THE NINTH MONTH. BUT THAT DAY THE SEA HAD TURNED EXCEPTIONALLY CLEAR, AND THE SUDDEN RAIN RELEASED BY THE SOUTHEAST CLOUDS SOFTLY DRIZZLED.

Scene #8. Exterior. Seashore

Fade in. A shot of the clouds in the sky. A suspicious rain cloud wells up in one corner of the heavens. Blown by the wind, it spreads darkly, widely, from the bottom to the top of the frame.

Scene #9. Exterior. Seashore

Same location as #1. Because of the sudden change in the weather, Takesuke, his son, and the fishermen quickly gather their things and pull the boats onto the beach.

Scene #10. Interior. Yumimaro's room

Having finished his daily lesson, Toyoo is about to take leave of his teacher and return home. Yumimaro takes a look outside and, knitting his brow, says, "Oh dear! What terrible weather. You should wait for the rain to stop." "No, it is nothing," Toyoo answers. He stands and exits to the left. Yumimaro, still anxious about the weather, sees Toyoo off.

Scene #11. Exterior. Outside Yumimaro's room

The veranda outside the room, shot from the garden. The rain is falling more heavily, and Yumimaro stops Toyoo. "You will have trouble in this down-pour. You should take an umbrella," Yumimaro says, as he prevents Toyoo from leaving and goes for the umbrella. Toyoo sits down on the steps and stares absentmindedly at the rain in the garden.

Scene #12. Exterior. Seashore

Continuation of #9. The fishermen have finished pulling the boats up onto the beach, and they run off to the right through the driving rain.

Scene #13. Exterior. Outside Yumimaro's room

A shot of Toyoo sitting on the steps. Yumimaro comes out and gives him the umbrella. Toyoo thanks him courteously and exits to the right, holding the umbrella over himself. Yumimaro looks after him. Fade out.
(Art Title) Fade in and out
WHAT HARDSHIP, THIS RAIN THAT FALLS ON CAPE MIWA!
AND YET AT SANO CROSSING NO HOUSE IS IN SIGHT[6]

Scene #14. Exterior. Seashore

Fade in. A view of the long coastline and Cape Miwa in the rain. The sky increasingly shows signs of an impending storm, and there is no trace of any-one on either the sea or land. Soon the solitary figure of Toyoo approaches BG to FG, holding the umbrella against the wind. MCU Toyoo, as he stops and tilts the umbrella as if looking for shelter from the rain. After glancing around, he takes a few more steps and looks straight ahead.

Scene #15. Exterior. Rush hut of a fisherman

LS. A single rush-thatched hut by the sea.

Scene #16. Exterior. Seashore

A continuation of #15. Toyoo spies the hut in the distance and exits to the left, passing the camera.

Scene #17. Exterior. Hut

In front of the hut. Entering from the right, Toyoo approaches the shadow of the hut. As Toyoo shuts the umbrella and opens the cedar door, an old fisher-man about fifty years of age appears from within. Seeing Toyoo, he politely bows his head. "Please come in," he says as he leads him inside. Toyoo enters the hut.

Scene #18. Interior. Inside the hut

The interior is a dim space enclosed by wooden boards and a low ceiling. Sunlight shines faintly through the thatched eaves in front of the hut. No planks cover the dirt floor, which had been spread with straw mats. The old man guides Toyoo from the wooden door facing the camera and quickly closes it. He lays a round straw mat on the dirt floor and invites Toyoo to sit, saying, "this is a poor dwelling, but please rest here a moment." (The old man is wearing an *eboshi*, a *kosode*, and *hakama*.) Toyoo is being treated so politely that he says, as if he is inconveniencing the old man, "Please don't go to such trouble for my sake." From time to time, rain leaking through the rushes blows violently into the room.

Scene #19. Interior. Inside the hut

Cowering from the rain, Toyoo and the old man banter on about the terrible weather (full shot of them both). The sound of the rain and the echo of the wind seem to be growing ever more violent. Then, as if he hears someone's voice, the old man goes to the cedar door on the right.

Scene #20. Interior. Inside the hut

From within, the old man puts his left ear to the door and asks, "Who is it, who's there?" Outside, someone taps on the door.

NOTES

INTRODUCTION

Except for names that commonly appear in the Western order, such as Sessue Hayakawa, all Japanese names appear in the Japanese order of family name first.

1. *Sei no kagayaki* has previously been translated as *The Glow of Life*: *kagayaki* can be translated as both "glow" and "glory." An article in the contemporary film publication *Kinema junpō* refers to the film in English as *The Glory of Life*. See Anon., "New Epoch Will Be Made" (in English), *Kinema junpō* (November 1920): p. 4.

2. Komatsu Hiroshi, "Yume no tekusuto—shoki no eizō to gensetsu no aida," in Makino, ed., *Fukkokuban Katsudō shashinkai,* part 1: 15–22; "Kioku no mokuroku," in Makino et al., eds., *Fukkokuban Kinema rekōdo,* 1: 15–28.

3. See Penelope Houston, *Keepers of the Frame: The Film Archives* (London: BFI Publishing, 1994), p. 69.

4. Susan Sontag, *On Photography* (New York: Anchor, 1990), p. 71.

5. See in particular Paolo Cherchi Usai's consideration of the variables at work in silent cinema research, "The Ethics of Research," in Cherchi Usai, *Burning Passions,* pp. 86–90. As Cherchi Usai points out, this does not imply that the traditional histories at our disposal are entirely invalid sources of information.

6. Patrick Loughney uses this term to encompass some of the various "permutations" in, for example, the American industry. See Loughney, "*Rip Van Winkle* to *Jesus of Nazareth,*" pp. 277–289. I address this problem of terminology in the Japanese context in more detail in chapter 1.

7. Isabelle Reynauld makes this argument in favor of studying screenwriting practice most eloquently in "Written Scenarios of Early French Cinema." Although dealing with American cinema and concerned with an earlier period than my study, two other articles in the same issue of *Film History* (on screenwriters and screenwriting) provide helpful examples of the potential for such studies. See Loughney, "*Rip Van Winkle* to *Jesus of Nazareth*" and Azlant, "Screenwriting for the Early Silent Film."

8. Although his scope is different from my own, I find the rationale Alan Williams applies

to his history of French cinema applicable to my own approach. Like Williams, I am aware that although "the notion . . . of an established *canon* of significant films" is problematic for many modern critics, it provides—with "a modest amount of tinkering (almost always in order to expand, rather than contract, the canon)"—a framework useful to my study. Like Williams, I remain open to possibilities for "tinkering" with the accepted boundaries of the pure film "canon." See Williams, *Republic of Images: A History of French Filmmaking* (Cambridge: Harvard University Press, 1992), particularly pp. 2–4.

CHAPTER 1

1. Satō Tadao, "Nihon eiga no seiritsu-shita dodai," in Imamura Shōhei et al., eds., *Nihon eiga no tanjō,* p.40; Tanaka Jun'ichirō, *Nihon eiga hattatsu shi,* 1: 312–315; Anderson and Richie, *Japanese Film,* p. 42. A photograph of Taguchi Ōson and two colleagues posing with Roscoe ("Fatty") Arbuckle at "the Lasky studio" appears in *Katsudō kurabu* 3 (October 1920).

2. Yoda, *Mizoguchi Kenji,* pp. 36, 38.

3. See for example the "Questions and Answers" column of *Kinema junpō* (11 August 1920): p. 4. In response to a reader who apparently inquired about why the term "pure film drama" [*jun-eiga-geki*] had been applied in a particular case, the writer offers his interpretation of the term as "that which possesses all the elements of a film drama [*eiga-geki*] and goes beyond being a film adaptation [*eiga-ka*] of a stage play [*butai-geki*]," then suggests that the term was used to market Kaeriyama's *Gen'ei no onna* (*The Girl in His Dreams,* 1920) and Edamasa Yoshirō's *Aware no kyoku* (*Song of Sadness,* 1919) because these films were "more advanced than other Japanese films until now and closer to Western films." The writer suggests that the use of the term to advertise the particular film in question was just good marketing.

4. In his study focusing on censorship legislation and discourse on and about film during the silent period, Aaron Gerow views pure film and, consequently, the relationship between the pure film movement and contemporary screenwriting practice, from a different perspective. For Gerow, the pure film movement was one in which "words were to be exiled from the domain of the filmic text." In his analysis, the "pure" of pure film implies the conviction that film is an "inherently silent visual medium" uncontaminated by the taint of the word (a definition in which "word" seems to play multiple roles as the "word" of the preproduction script and the intertitle as well as the "word" of film criticism, nationalistic rhetoric, and film censorship legislation). This perspective is complicated by the fact that while it is contingent upon or at least presumes a precise definition (and our complicit understanding) of the nature and function of "image," "word," and "silence" in silent cinema, it simultaneously creates considerable slippage between these terms. See Gerow, "Writing a Pure Cinema," pp. 275, 278, 338.

5. Kaeriyama, *Katsudō shashingeki no sōsaku to satsuei hō,* p. 41.

6. See, for example, Satō, "Nihon eiga no seiritsu-shita dodai," p. 35.

7. The scripts of several pure films do survive, although *Souls on the Road* and Tanaka Eizō's *Kyōya eriten* (*The Kyōya Collar Shop,* 1922) have been reconstructed. *Souls on the Road* was rewritten from memory by the author, Ushihara Kiyohiko, with additional help from a surviving *benshi* script, the two novels that provided the source material for the film, and a handwritten transcription of the film itself. *The Kyōya Collar Shop* "screenplay" is actually a condensed version, written by Kobayashi Masaru, of a story Tanaka Eizō wrote based on his original film script a year after the film was made. Both reconstructions can be found in Nihon shinario sakka kyōkai, eds., *Nihon shinario taikei.*

8. Satō, "Nihon eiga no seiritsu-shita dodai," p. 52.

9. Yoda, "Kantoku Murata Minoru," in *Musei eiga no kansei,* vol. 2 of *Kōza nihon eiga* (Tokyo: Iwanami, 1986), p. 214.

10. Anderson and Richie, *Japanese Film,* p. 31.

11. I thank Tom Gunning for pointing out that given Griffith's pace, Makino's rate of production, usually referred to as "phenomenal," was not that excessive for the time.

12. Shindō Kaneto, "Shinario tanjō zengo," in Imamura Shōhei et al., eds., *Nihon eiga no tanjō,* p. 176.

13. Personal interview with Yoda Yoshikata, 21 June 1988.

14. Chiba et al., *Nihon eiga shi,* p. 14.

15. Shindō Kaneto, "Ichi suji, ni nuke, san yakusha," in *Musei eiga no kansei,* p. 154.

16. There are different versions of Makino's words: according to some sources, "the negative" precedes "the script." "First, the story . . . ," however, is the version generally acknowledged to be correct, and Takizawa Osamu, who knew Makino personally, supports this version. See Takizawa Osamu, "Makino Shōzō hyōden," in Misono, ed., *Kaisō Makino eiga,* p. 54.

17. See, for example, Stempel, *Framework,* pp. 35–38. As Stempel points out, the early use of intertitles was inconsistent, and dialogue titles were particularly scarce until the midteens.

18. Kristin Thompson, "The Formulation of the Classical Style, 1909–1928," in Bordwell, Staiger, and Thompson, *Classical Hollywood Cinema,* p. 186. Thompson notes that during this period, "scriptwriters seemed to assume that every title in a film betrayed a weak point where its author had failed to convey the situation properly through images."

19. Ibid., p. 27. It is interesting to note that after 1917, expository titles commonly appeared as (often highly stylized) art titles, which were increasingly distinguishable from dialogue intertitles in their lettering style (font) or degree of background detail.

20. Eisner, *Haunted Screen,* pp. 179, 206. The term *titelloser film* ("titleless film") is used to refer to such productions.

21. Manvell, "Screenwriting," p. 450.

22. Hannon, *The Photodrama,* p. 38. Hannon is paraphrasing E. W. Sargent, author of the early screenwriting handbook, *Technique of the Photoplay* (1912).

23. Weston, *Art of Photo-Play Writing,* p. 39.

24. Edward Azlant highlights this particular role of silent scenarists, and offers Loos, Marion, and Sullivan as examples. Loos wrote for Douglas Fairbanks, Marion for Mary Pickford, and Sullivan for William S. Hart. See Azlant, "Screenwriting for the Early Silent Film," p. 245.

25. Weston, *Art of Photo-Play Writing,* p. 39.

26. Donald Kirihara puts the *benshi*-bunraku comparison in perspective in "Institution of the Benshi." For an example of an early assertion that the *benshi* must watch the film carefully, and understand why any given picture was made before attempting to "explain" it, see the article by the resident *benshi* of the Ōsaka Naniwaza, "Katsudō shashin no setsumeisha," in *Katsudō shashinkai,* no. 2 (October 1909): pp. 7–9.

27. Personal interview with Yoda Yoshikata, 21 June 1988; Anderson and Richie, *Japanese Film,* pp. 24–25. Tanaka Jun'ichirō transcribes an excerpt from a *benshi* script in "Onoe Matsunosuke-geki *Bingo Saburō,*" pp. 27–29. In this article, Tanaka provides commentary on four early examples of "scripts" (or proto-scripts), including the prologue to a thirty-eight-scene *benshi* script by Masumoto Kiyoshi, *Chichi no namida* (*A Father's Tears,* 1918), a *shinpa* film produced by Nikkatsu. A portion of this script, translated from the original published version in *Katsudō no sekai* 3 (June 1918), is provided in the appendix. To my knowledge, accessible handwritten *benshi* scripts in the collection of the National Film Center at the Museum of Modern Art in Tokyo date back only as far as the early 1920s.

28. Kirihara, "Institution of the Benshi," p. 47. Kirihara emphasizes that the attraction of the *benshi* lay in the "interplay" between his delivery and the projected images; in other words, it was not necessarily "a battle for dominance between the benshi's interpretation and the events depicted in the images and the intertitles."

29. Joseph L. Anderson, "Second and Third Thoughts about the Japanese Film," in Anderson and Richie, *Japanese Film*, p. 439.

30. Hazumi, *Eiga gojūnen shi*, p. 124. The Japanese screenplay has been referred to as *kyakuhon* ("script") and *shinario* ("scenario," a loan word from the West and a later addition) since the silent period. After the mid-1910s, *katsudōgeki kyakuhon* ("moving picture script") and *eigageki kyakuhon* ("film script") were used interchangeably, together with *shinario*. The *benshi* narration script was commonly referred to as the *benshi daihon*.

31. Burch, *To the Distant Observer*, p. 79.

32. See Tsivian, "Spoken Titles in Russian Films," for an interesting analysis of the course taken by spoken titles during the "oral craze" in Russia. Tsivian uses Barry Salt's estimation of 1908 as marking the beginning of an increase in the use of dialogue titles. See Salt, *Film Style and Technology: History and Analysis* (London: Starword, 1983), pp. 107–108. I date the rise in interest in intertitle experimentation in Japan from the gradual popularization of the concept of pure film beginning in the early 1910s.

33. Examples can be seen in the surviving print of the 1922 *shinpa* film *Futari Shizuka*. See also Hazumi, *Eiga gojūnen shi*, p. 64 for samples of title cards from *shinpa* and *kyūha* films.

34. Personal interview with Yoda Yoshikata, 21 June 1988. It should be noted that this was also true of directors elsewhere. Tom Gunning points out that Marcel L'Herbier, for example, found titles to be an important aspect of his early films in the late 1910s and early 1920s.

35. Anderson, "Second and Third Thoughts," p. 441.

36. Tanaka, *Eiga nandemo kojiten* (Tokyo: Shakai shisōsha, 1980), p. 323.

37. Kinugasa, *Waga eiga no seishun*, pp. 21–22.

38. Anderson, "Second and Third Thoughts," p. 442.

39. Maruyama Masao and Haniya Yutaka, "Bungaku no sekai to gakumon no sekai," *Yūrika* 10 (March 1978): pp. 87–88. Tokugawa Musei is also remembered for his narration of *Souls on the Road*.

40. The *benshi* never disappeared completely. Even today it is possible to enjoy *benshi* performances in Japan, primarily at special screenings, libraries, and civic centers. Sawato Midori, a disciple of the late Matsuda Shunsui, the most active *benshi* in recent years, has performed at foreign film festivals in addition to making regular public appearances throughout Japan. She has also provided *benshi* commentary for televised broadcasts of both Japanese and foreign silent films: a 1991 television broadcast of D. W. Griffith's *The Birth of a Nation*, for example, featured her own original commentary. Videotapes of silent Japanese classics narrated by Matsuda himself are also available. A different view of the significance of this practice is offered by Iijima Tadashi, who was of the opinion when he was still a teenager that the *benshi* should be abolished. He admits that while he is not in favor of such videotapes, he can understand their attraction for modern audiences; however, he still asserts that watching videotapes featuring *benshi* commentary and narration constitutes a form of entertainment that should be distinguished from watching a silent film without narration. See Iijima, *Jidenteki essei*, p. 39. Joseph L. Anderson, coauthor, with Donald Richie, of *The Japanese Film: Art and Industry* (the definitive history of Japanese cinema in the English language since it was first published in 1959) is said to be an accomplished *benshi* and has given performances in the United States.

41. David Bordwell's analysis of the 1922 *shinpa* film *Futari Shizuka* provides a clear picture of the visual style of this ostensibly "impure" genre only four years after the production of *The Glory of Life*. See Bordwell, "Visual Style in Japanese Cinema." For an example of a 1910s kabuki (*kyūha* or *kyūgeki*) film, *Masamune Gorō* (1915), see also Komatsu's article in the same issue of *Film History*, "The Meaning of Tenkatsu Company," pp. 81–86.

42. I am grateful to Ōta Yoneo for bringing my attention to the degree, for example, to which the concept and function of (and terminology for) "set" and "set design" in Kyoto was

affected by the extent to which the "set" for a period film, a major part of Kyoto production, was a location that companies there could customarily take for granted.

43. Abel, "The 'Blank Screen of Reception.'"

44. See *Nihon eiga sakuhin jiten senzenhen.* The foreword to this reference book, which has the English title *Complete Dictionary of Japanese Movies from 1896 to August 1945,* acknowledges that it is not likely to be an exact record of all films produced and screened in Japan before 15 August 1945. It was compiled from three main sources: *Firumu ken'etsu jihō* (published by the Naimushō keihōkyoku); *Kurashikku eiga nyūzu (Classic Film News),* numbers 1–400, the monthly publication of the Musei eiga kanshōkai (Silent Film Association), sponsored by Matsuda Film Productions; and *Nihon eiga sakuhin taikan* 1–7, supplementary volumes of *Kinema junpō* (Kinema junpōsha). The *Firumu ken'etsu jihō* are censorship records compiled by the surveillance division (Police Bureau) of the Home Ministry (Ministry of Domestic Affairs), abolished after World War II.

45. Speaking within the general context of Japan's theatrical tradition, Thomas Rimer made this point most convincingly in his contribution to "The Formation of Artistic and Literary Canons," the sixth plenary session of the *Meiji Studies Conference,* sponsored by the Edwin O. Reischauer Institute, Harvard University (6–8 May 1994).

46. Bordwell, "Visual Style in Japanese Cinema."

47. For a comprehensive study of this topic in the context of Europe and the United States, see Kern, *Culture of Time and Space.*

48. Satō Kōroku, "Katsudō shashin no kyakuhon," *Katsudō shashinkai,* no. 8 (April 1910): p. 4. Beginning with the inaugural issue, the cover of *Katsudō shashinkai* also consistently featured the English-language title *The Cinematograph.* Issues 1–21 and 26 are also available in facsimile copies, which preserve the magnificent color of all the extant illustrated covers (the cover of the first issue survives only in copy form). See Makino, ed. *Fukkokuban Katsudō shashinkai.*

49. Pollack, *Reading against Culture,* p. 39.

50. In their introductions to the 1999 reprint edition of *Katsudō shashinkai,* Komatsu Hiroshi and Makino Mamoru emphasize the fan-oriented nature of this publication. According to Komatsu, it was sold (rolled up) during intermission at all Yoshizawa theaters. Komatsu also notes that although the publication was sponsored by the Yoshizawa Company, it was issued by a publishing entity called the *Nihon katsudōsha.* See Komatsu, "Yume no tekusuto—shoki no eizō to gensetsu no aida," pp. 16–17. Makino points out that to whatever extent *Katsudō shashinkai* was sponsored by the Yoshizawa Company, the publication doesn't necessarily give the impression of being a publicity magazine. See Makino, "Meijiki no bunmeikaika to zasshi *Katsudō shashinkai,*" in Makino, ed., *Fukkokuban Katsudō shashinkai,* p. 24. This view is supported by an article appearing in the May–June 1911 issue, no. 21, p. 23 ("Katsudō shashin zasshi"), which points out that although the publication resembles the house organ of the Yoshizawa Company, it remained fairly unreserved in criticizing Yoshizawa productions, and was not at all reluctant to point out the positive qualities of films made by rival production companies.

51. "Hakkan no shūi," *Katsudō shashinkai,* no. 1 (June 1909): p. 4.

52. Uchida Shigenori, "Honpō ni okeru fūzoku firumu," *Katsudō shashinkai,* no. 17 (January–February 1911): p. 2. There are a number of possible readings of the author's first name.

53. *Katsudō shashinkai,* no. 12 (August 1910): n.p.

54. See for example "The Kinema-Record Film Index" (the title is in English), in *Kinema Record* 42 (December 1916): pp. 546–551. This is an index of releases reviewed in the previous issues 37–41. The actual index is preceded by a small guide (or key) to the system of classification that is used. According to this guide, Japanese films are classified as *shinpa, kyūha,* comedy

(*kigeki*), news, (*jiji*), and "other;" foreign films are divided into drama (*geki*), comedy, education (*kyōiku*), news, and "other." The index itself is divided into four sections. The first is for "Japanese Made Films," and features only the classifications *shinpa* and *kyūha*. "Foreign Made Films" take up the remaining three sections: "Drama (Social, Tragic, Artistic, Sensational, Historical etc.)"; "Comic (Farce, Comedy, Trick, Etc.)"; and "Education (Scientific, Topical, Travel, Scenic Etc.)." Japanese films are individually classified, but foreign films are not. Rather, the above classifications are given in both Japanese and English (the terms in the two languages do not always directly correspond) as a general heading at the top of each of the three sections.

55. It is also possible that this shift was influenced by fluctuations in classification terminology abroad, which then affected Japanese trends at the point of appropriation. In this respect, a closer comparative reading of contemporary periodicals in Europe, the United States, and Japan would be useful.

56. *Katsudō kurabu* 6 (February 1923): pp. 52–57.

57. Although immensely popular during its peak from 1914 to 1917, and important as a venue for women actors, the chain drama was banned in the late 1910s because of censorship considerations. Iwamoto Kenji points out the irony that the establishment of *Kinema Record* neatly coincided with the ascendancy of the chain drama. See Iwamoto's introduction to the 1999 reprint edition of *Kinema Record*, "Ōbei eiga o kagami toshite," in Makino, ed., *Fukkokuban Kinema rekōdo*, part 1: 6–7.

58. Pollack, *Reading against Culture,* p. 39. Pollack points out that this is what the Meiji political thinker Fukuzawa Yukichi meant by "national independence through personal independence."

59. Gioia Ottaviani describes the essential problem of the *shingeki* theater as an effort "not only to create a modern theatre, but to confront the modern world with the theatre, in particular, modern Japan." See Ottaviani, "Shingeki Movement," p. 178.

60. For a vivid account of viewing a chain drama, see Tanaka Jun'ichirō, "Onoe Matsunosuke-geki *Bingo Saburō,*" p. 29. Tanaka describes an experience he had in an Asakusa theater sometime early in 1917:

> As four or five actors were performing onstage, a woman shrieked and fled through the curtain. Two or three men and women chased her through the curtain. In an instant, the stage became dark, a white curtain slid down in front of the stage, and on it was [projected] a shot of a park. The woman came running into this park, and there was a struggle between her and the people who were chasing her. A car passed by, picked up the woman pleading for help, and drove off. The men followed after her.
>
> The car arrived at what appeared to be the mansion of a wealthy person. The woman, accompanied by the evil-looking man who was driving the car, entered the mansion and was ushered into the drawing room. At this point the film suddenly disappeared. When the white curtain was raised the stage was arranged just like the film scene of the drawing room, and the same woman and man that had been in the film continued performing just as they were. At the time, I found the changes interesting.

61. Tanaka Jun'ichirō's *Nihon eiga hattatsu shi,* vol. 1, emphasizes those *shinpa* melodramas that had what he considered to be outstanding technical merit (Tanaka was a former pure film advocate). Leftist critic Iwasaki Akira laments the *shinpa* film's inherent feudalistic ideology in "Nihon eiga shi I," in Yamada Kazuo, ed., *Eiga no rekishi,* vol. 2 of *Eigaron kōza* (Tokyo: Godō shuppan, 1977), pp. 12–14. See also Hazumi Tsuneo, *Eiga gojūnen shi.* Hazumi especially criticized the *shinpa* melodrama for gratuitous misogynism (pp. 50–52). Additionally, such criticism can cloud our understanding of both the *shinpa* and pure film by tailoring them to fit within a strict oppositional East vs. West (as in "old vs. new") paradigm. Komatsu has also characterized Japanese film before the 1920s as being "the opposition of two antithetical modes" (a conflict between "Japanese cinema" and "non-Japanese cinema practice"). His work suggests an admiration for

the ability of such Japanese forms as the *shinpa* melodrama to resist "occidental" film style. See for example his "The Fundamental Change" and "Before the Great Kanto Earthquake."

62. Meadow, "Japanese Character Structure."

63. See McDonald, *From Book to Screen,* pp. 3–16 for background (including original serialization dates and stage adaptations) and descriptive synopses of literary and/or film versions of *The Cuckoo, One's Own Sin* (also called *My Sin*), and *Foster Sisters,* as well as several other popular pieces from the *shinpa* repertory. According to McDonald, *Foster Sisters* was inspired by an English novel, *Dora Thorn,* and uses "a kind of Cinderella story to argue for the superiority of Christian morality over Confucianism as it applied to family matters in Meiji Japan."

64. Kishi Matsuo, "*Kyōya eriten,*" in Shinario sakka kyōkai, ed., *Nihon eiga shinario taikei* (Tokyo: Chūō kōronsha, 1978), 1: 797.

65. Hazumi, *Eiga gojūnen shi,* p. 50

66. I first presented some of the following ideas on women actors during the 1910s in an unpublished paper, "Women on the Silent Screen: The Actress Debate, 1913–1923," at the conference "Women in Japanese Culture," University of Texas at Austin, 24–25 February 1995.

67. About fifteen minutes of Nakamura Kasen's work survives in footage of the 1908 M. Pathe film *Taikōki judanme* and the 1916 *Kyara Sendaihagi,* housed at the Kawakita Memorial Film Institute in Tokyo.

68. "Gureesu Kanaado no kenkyū," *Katsudō no sekai* 1 (September 1916): pp. 147–164.

69. Ichikawa Shizue, "Joyū shibō no katagata e," *Katsudō gahō* 1 (May 1917): p. 46. The experience was no easier for men. One year earlier, Inoue Masao, whose career later included, notably, the central role in Kinugasa Teinosuke's *Kurutta ippeiji (A Page out of Order/A Page of Madness,* 1926), noted in "Chikaku tōbei shitai," *Katsudō no sekai* 1, no. 3, p. 38: "[Making] a chain drama is hard work. I wake up at six in the morning. Without even washing my face, I leave for the Nippori studio. When I'm done, I eat lunch and then immediately go onstage. It is not that hard work bothers me, but living like this, without an hour to spare, I get depressed wondering when I can work on improving my performance."

70. "Yaoko kara mōshiage sōrō," *Katsudō gahō* 1 (March 1917): pp. 111–112.

71. "Rakuba no hanashi," *Katsudō gahō* 1 (April 1917): pp. 68–69.

72. Murata Minoru, "Nihon eiga no shin keikō," *Kinema junpō,* no. 181 (January 1925): p. 53.

CHAPTER 2

1. See "Shinario nenpyō," *Shinario taikei,* 1: 814. The crown prince was ahead of him: on November 20, 1896, he saw Edison's Kinetoscope, an experience that made him one of the first to see moving pictures in Japan.

2. Ibid., p. 814.

3. Satō Kōroku, "Kōan-bu no hōshin," *Katsudō shashinkai,* no. 9 (May 1910): p. 3.

4. "Katsudō shashin zasshi," p. 23.

5. See *Katsudō shashinkai,* no. 18 (February–March 1911): pp. 26–27 for a description and critique of *Matsu no midori.* For secondary source references to the film, see Kishi Matsuo, "Masumoto Kiyoshi," in *Nihon eiga Kantoku zenshū* (Tokyo: Kinema junpōsha, 1976), pp. 370–371, and Tanaka, *Nihon eiga hattatsu shi,* pp. 141–142.

6. Kishi, "Shinario tanjō izen," p. 794.

7. Ibid.

8. Lindsay, *Art of the Moving Picture,* p. 17. See Azlant, "Screenwriting for the Early Silent Film" for more on the background of early writers in the U.S. circa 1897–1911.

9. Staiger, "The Hollywood Mode of Production to 1930," in Bordwell, Staiger, and Thompson, *Classical Hollywood Cinema,* pp. 126, 137–139; Thompson, "The Formulation of the Classical Style," p. 165.

10. For a comparison between American screenwriting practice during the 1910s and 1920s and those of France, Germany, and the Soviet Union, see Kristin Thompson, "Early Alternatives to the Hollywood Mode of Production: Implications for Europe's Avant-gardes," *Film History* 5, no. 4 (1993): pp. 386–404.

11. Azlant, "Theory, History, and Practice of Screenwriting," pp. 128–132.

12. "Katsudō shashin no benshi," *Katsudō shashinkai,* no. 19 (March 1911): p. 1.

13. Weston, *Art of Photo-play Writing,* p. 28.

14. Satō Kōroku, "Katsudō shashin no kyakuhon," *Katsudō shashinkai,* no. 8 (April 1910): p. 4. A month earlier, in the May 1910 issue of *Katsudō shashinkai,* Satō was slightly more equivocal about the quality of Yoshizawa films in comparison with those of Europe and the United States (despite claiming relative ignorance about European and American films he knew enough to point out that mediocre films were produced by these industries too). See Satō, "Kōan-bu no hōshin," p. 3.

15. See "Shinario nenpyō," p. 814.

16. For more detail on the individuals involved in *Katsudō no tomo,* see Makino Mamoru, "Meijiki no bunmeikaika to zasshi *Katsudō shashinkai,* pp. 23–33 and Makino, "Eiga jyanarizumu no genryū, *Firumu rekōdo* to *Kinema rekōdo* no wakaki gunzō," in Makino, ed., *Fukkokuban Kinema rekōdo,* 1: 29–39.

17. In his introduction to the reprint edition of *Kinema Record,* Iwamoto Kenji points out that *Kinema Record*'s generally negative view of Japanese films distinguishes it significantly from the more magnanimous and positive outlook reflected in *Katsudō shashinkai,* perhaps because the latter was to some extent sponsored by Yoshizawa, a conspicuous component of the domestic trade industry. See "Ōbei eiga o kagami toshite," in Makino, ed., *Fukkokuban Kinema rekōdo,* p. 13.

18. Tanaka Jun'ichirō, "Kaeriyama Norimasa," in *Nihon eiga kantoku zenshū,* p. 110.

19. Welsh, *A.B.C. of Motion Pictures,* p. 90.

20. Kaeriyama is often referred to in secondary sources as the originator of the term *eiga* (film), but the word was among many in common usage by the midteens (*eiga* had originally been used to refer to the magic lantern). Komatsu points out that in the early 1910s there was no standard word for film in Japan or elsewhere. See Komatsu, "Kioku no mokuroku," in Makino, ed., *Fukkokuban Kinema rekōdo,* 1: 17–18. The articles in *Katsudō shashinkai,* including those by Kaeriyama, are a good reflection of this phenomenon. *Katsudō shashin (geki), eiga (geki), firumu* or *fuerumu* (these latter sometimes appearing as alternative phonetic readings, or *rubi,* alongside the Chinese characters for *katsudō shashin* or *eiga*) appear throughout the magazine's run, often being used interchangeably within a single article.

21. Kishi, "Shinario tanjō izen," p. 795.

22. Yoshida Chieo gives this approximate price in Yoshida, "Kaeriyama Norimasa to *Sei no kagayaki no shuppatsu made,*" in Imamura et al, eds., *Nihon eiga no tanjō,* p. 242. It is difficult to assess the film's eventual impact on a professional level. Anecdotal evidence suggests at least one important scriptwriter of the period, Susukita Rokuhei (1899–1960), was inspired by the book (an avid movie fan, he is said to have came across a copy one day in the neighborhood library, and was impressed by Kaeriyama's advice). Working in the *jidaigeki* genre, he adapted his own popular novels into original film scripts with psychological depth, and is considered one of the first scriptwriters to express a personal individuality. See Kishi, "Shinario tanjō izen," p. 798, and Satō, "Nihon eiga no seiritsu- shita dodai," p. 49.

23. Kaeriyama, preface, *Katsudō shashingeki no sōsaku to satsuei hō,* p. 1.

24. Kaeriyama, *Katsudō shashingeki no sōsaku to satsuei hō,* pp. 1–2. Under the heading

"Honsho chosaku ni kansuru sankōsho" ("books used as reference for this publication"), Kaeriyama cited references from France, Italy, and Germany in addition to English-language sources.

25. Ibid., pp. 42, 45.

26. Ibid., p. 41.

27. Iijima Tadashi, "Nihon eiga no reimei: jun'eigageki no shūhen," in Imamura et al., eds., *Nihon eiga no tanjō,* p. 105. Iijima remembers the audience calling out, "mattemashita!" (literally, "this is what I've been waiting for!") when the *benshi* came on stage.

28. "Geijutsu toshite no katsudō shashin," *Katsudō shashinkai,* no. 19 (March –April 1911): pp. 15–16 and "Katsudō shashin geijutsuron," *Katsudō shashinkai,* no. 26 (November 1911): p. 4.

29. Komatsu, "Yume no tekusuto—shoki no eizō to gensetsu no aida," in Makino, ed., *Fukkokuban Katsudō shashinkai,* part 1: 20.

30. "Geijutsu toshite no katsudō shashin," p. 16.

31. Komatsu, "Yume no tekusuto," p. 20.

32. Tanaka, *Nihon eiga hattatsu shi,* p. 282.

33. Mizusawa Takehiko [Norimasa Kaeriyama], *Sei no kagayaki,* in Shinario sakka kyokai, ed., *Nihon shinario taikei* (Tokyo: Eijinsha, 1973), 1: 7–17. My translation in the appendix was made from this most recent publication of the scenario. The first imprint of *The Glory of Life* in 1959 was based on a carbon copy of the scenario that Kaeriyama had kept in his home. He had written it himself on Minō paper, a particularly sturdy type of Japanese paper from Gifu prefecture. See "Henshū o owatte," in *Nihon eiga daihyō shinario zenshū* (Tokyo: Kinema junpō, 1959), vol. 6: 180. The script appears on pages 157–161. The script has also been published in *Nihon eiga shinario koten zenshū* (Tokyo: Kinema junpō, 1965), 1: 14–21. Except for the addition of a number "2" after the heading for scene no. 21 in this version, all three versions are identical.

34. *Nihon eiga daihyō shinario zenshū,* vol. 6: 156.

35. See, for example, the following reviews of and references to *The Glory of Life, The Girl in the Mountain* and *The Girl in His Dreams: Kinema junpō* (1 October 1919): pp. 2, 4; (11 October 1919): pp. 7–8; (1 June 1920): pp. 4, 10; (11 June 1920): p. 4; *Katsudō no sekai* (October 1919); *Katsudō kurabu* (November 1919): pp. 44–45. Selected reviews are also included in Okabe, ed., *Kaeriyama Norimasa to Tōmasu Kurihara,* pp. 21–28. *The Glory of Life* and *The Girl in the Mountain* were completed in 1918. Their release was delayed until 13 September 1919, when they opened simultaneously at two different theaters.

36. Yamamoto, *Katsudōya suiro,* pp. 31–33. Kishi Matsuo believed that Yamamoto confused his recollections of Kaeriyama's first films, and in this passage he is actually referring to the second film, *The Girl in the Mountain* (the theater Yamamoto refers to is the one in which this film, not *The Glory of Life,* opened). See Kishi, *Jinbutsu nihon eiga shi,* pp. 265–266. "Film Art Association" is my translation of Eiga geijutsu kyōkai, the name chosen by Kaeriyama's production group at Tenkatsu. This group is referred to as "L'Association des Artistes Cinématographiques" in Anon., "New Epoch Will Be Made," p. 4.

37. See Rimer, *Toward a Modern Japanese Theatre,* pp. 15–16.

38. Ibid., p. 19. Bordwell discusses in detail some of the dynamics and implications of this "cultural exchange" in "Visual Style in Japanese Cinema," pp. 14–18.

39. Seidensticker, *High City Low City,* p. 274. Seidensticker emphasizes the role film played in putting international celebrities "in front of everyone."

40. *Japan Times Weekly and Mail,* July–September 1919.

41. Nakura Bun'ichi, "Katsudōgeki no kyakuhon no kakikata," *Katsudō no sekai* (February 1916): pp. 70–77, in Makino, ed., *Nihon eiga shoki shiryō shūsei,* hereafter cited as *NES.*

42. One example is Ushihara Kiyohiko, who has written that his scenario for *Souls on the*

Road was influenced by transcriptions of films from the United States (Ushihara, foreword to the scenario for *Souls on the Road,* in *Nihon eiga shinario koten zenshū,* 1: 22. See also Kishi, "Kaisetsu: shinario tanjō izen," p. 797.

43. A special supplement dedicated to the Japanese opening of *Cabiria,* which was imported by the enterprising Kobayashi Kisaburō, appears in the June 1916 issue of *Katsudō no sekai.* See also the playwright Tsubouchi Shikō's article "*Cabiria* inshōki" in the same issue (pp. 2–3). The previous issue of *Katsudō no sekai* featured a special section on writing for film, "Katsudōgeki kyakuhon ni tsuite" ["On Scripts for Moving Picture Drama"], (May 1916): 24–55, which I discuss in detail in chapter 5.

44. Hollywood's flush economy was an object of considerable comment and envy. See also Anon., "Kyakuhon o eiga ni suru made," *Katsudō gahō* (September 1917): pp. 76–79.

45. The literal meaning of the word *serifugeki* is "line play (drama)" or "dialogue play (drama)," although in the latter definition the word "monologue" would be more appropriate. Pure film advocates used this word to refer to scripts for commercial films in a derogatory manner.

46. See Komatsu, "From Natural Colour to the Pure Motion Picture Drama," pp. 69–81 for a detailed account of Tenkatsu, including a good picture of what else was being made by the company while Kaeriyama was employed there.

47. Ōmori Masaru, "Sōsōki no kameraman," interview in Imamura et al., eds., *Nihon eiga no tanjō,* pp. 229–230.

48. Shibata [Ōmori] Masaru, "Jun'eigageki to kouta eiga," p. 18.

49. I discuss Tanaka's synopsis below. In an article written to commemorate one decade since the production of *The Glory of Life,* Kaeriyama included an excerpt of the scenario that corresponds to the published version translated here. See "Jūnen mae no hanashi," *Eiga jidai* 5 (October 1928): p. 109.

50. This excerpt of the script appears in Tanaka, "Onoe Matsunosuke-geki *Bingo Saburō,*" pp. 27–29. The translation of this excerpt in the appendix is from the original script as published in *Katsudō no sekai* 3 (June 1918): pp. 133–161.

51. See Kaeriyama's chapter on the scenario and the scenario writer, *Katsudō shashingeki no sōsaku to satsuei hō,* pp. 41–88.

52. For a discussion on the functions of expository titles, see Chisholm, "Reading Intertitles."

53. A review of *The Girl in the Mountain* describes the poetic effect of silhouette lighting in an exterior scene. Sōkyū Tominosuke, "Senkūsha no kage," *Katsudō kurabu* (November 1919): p. 44. Accounts of the film often mention Kaeriyama's attempt to experiment with new kinds of artificial lighting. For example, see Kaeriyama, "Jūnen mae no hanashi," p. 111.

54. Kyōbashi Shunbisei, "Miyama no otome kokuhyōki," *Kinema junpō* (11 October 1919): p. 8. Tanaka Jun'ichirō attributes the first use of art titles to Tanaka Eizō.

55. Kaeriyama, "Jūnen mae no hanashi," pp. 108–110. There is an undeniable hint of dogmatism to the written language of the script, and the punctuation is atrocious. I'm indebted to my colleague Mariko Tamate for helping me with a few of the murkier spots.

56. Kondō Iyokichi, "Yukeru eiga geijutsu kyōkai," in Okabe, ed., *Kaeriyama Norimasa to Tōmasu Kurihara,* p. 63. The amount and kind of attention given to the Bluebird films (a special attraction at Tokyo's Teikoku theater) is interesting in that descriptions of the films often reveal a perceived affinity with the *shinpa* film. The Bluebird films were also admired for their use of natural locations, which is notable in view of the attention given to the natural landscape in *The Glory of Life.* Hollywood's popularity in Japan after 1916 owed much to the success of the Bluebird films. T. D. Cochrane, the Tokyo representative of Universal (the first American studio to open a branch office in Tokyo in 1916), helped sponsor the film magazine *Katsudō hyōron* (later *Katsudō kurabu*), which featured numerous reviews and transcriptions of Bluebird films. For a

discussion of the Bluebird film in Japan, see also Komatsu Hiroshi, "Beru epokku no shūen," in Makino, ed., *Fukkokuban Kinema rekōdo II,* 1: 19–22, 25.

57. Ōmori suggests the regular production crew at Tenkatsu resented the fact that the company seemed to be favoring him over more experienced people like Edamasa Yoshirō. Edamasa's pure film, *Song of Sadness,* was made shortly after *The Glory of Life,* but was also held from release for about a year. See Ōmori, "Jun'eigageki to kouta eiga," pp. 18–19.

58. Tanaka, *Nihon eiga hattatsu shi,* pp. 284–285.

59. Kondō, "Yukeru eiga geijutsu kyōkai," p. 38.

60. See Kaeriyama, "Eiga seisaku no omoide,"in Okabe, ed., *Kaeriyama Norimasa to Tōmasu Kurihara,* p. 35, and Yoshida, *Mō hitotsu no eigashi,* pp. 93–96.

61. Kaeriyama Norimasa, "Aru hi aru hito no hanashi" *Katsudō kurabu* (September 1919): pp. 148–151.

CHAPTER 3

1. Ōmori, "Sōsōki no kameraman," p. 231.

2. *Kinema junpō* started the tradition of listing the ten best movies of the year (chosen by a jury of critics) in 1924; except for 1943–1945, this tradition has continued to this day. In 1924 and 1925 only foreign films were considered, rated separately as "artistic" films and "entertainment" films, but in 1926 foreign and Japanese films were both rated (separately) for the first time. Abe Yutaka's contemporary drama, *Ashi ni sawatta onna (The Woman Who Touched Legs),* was the first Japanese film to be chosen best film of the year in 1926, but the coveted position went to period dramas for the next three years: Itō Daisuke's *Chūji tabi nikki (Chūji's Travels II,* 1927), Makino Masahiro's *Rōningai, daiichiwa (The Street of Masterless Samurai,* 1928), and *Kubi no za (Beheading Place,* 1929). In 1930 contemporary drama and period films were judged separately for the first and only time, and in the foreign film category silent and sound films were judged separately. Since 1931 contemporary drama films have consistently been preferred for the top ratings, and the choice for best period film in 1930, Itō Daisuke's *Zoku Ōoka Seidan, mazōhen daiichi (Ōoka's Trial Continued, Part I)* was the last period film to achieve best film status (with the exception of Kinoshita Keisuke's 1958 *Narayama Bushiko [The Ballad of Narayama]*) until the genre's revitalization in the 1960s. For a listing of the Best Ten ratings through 1985, see Ishihara, ed., *Eigashō eigasai daizenshū,* pp. 154–155. In English, see Stuart Galbraith IV, *The Japanese Filmography: 1900 through 1994* (Jefferson, N.C.: McFarland & Company, 1996), pp. 479–486.

3. Satō Tadao, "Eizō hyōgen no kakuritsu," in Imamura et al., eds., *Musei eiga no kansei,* pp. 5–6.

4. For an overview of foreign film imports in Japan by country of origin, see Komatsu, "Kioku no mokuroku," in Makino, ed., *Fukkokuban Kinema rekōdo,* 1: 19–28 (introduction to the reprint edition of *Kinema Record*).

5. An example is Nakajima Iwajirō, known as the "Japanese Charlie Chaplin." Nakajima starred in Thomas Kurihara's comedy *Narikin (Sanji Gotō/The Upstart).* A print of the surviving fragment of this film is available for rental through general distribution in the United States. The production date is unclear (see note 39 below). It opened in Japan in August 1921.

6. An early multireel import, *Quo Vadis?* (Enrico Guazzoni, 1912) opened at the Astor Theater in New York City with an admission fee ten times the current going rate.

7. Tanaka, "Eigakan nyūjōryō," in *Nedan no fūzokushi,* 1: 488–489. After its run at the Teikoku Theater, *Intolerance* was shown in Osaka, Kobe, Kyoto, and Nagoya with a ten-yen admission price before a second run in a reedited version at Tokyo's Teikokukan, a movie theater in Asakusa specializing in foreign films, where admission was a more modest one to two yen.

Kobayashi made a personal profit of close to 400,000 yen from the film's distribution, and invested this in the establishment of Kokkatsu (established with a capital of 10,000,000 yen), which quickly absorbed his former company, Tenkatsu. See Okabe, ed., *Kaeriyama Norimasa to Tōmasu Kurihara*, pp. 11–12. According to Mori Iwao (Mori and Tomonari, *Katsudō shashin taikan,* 2: 29–30, 40), the 20,000 yen Kobayashi paid for the rights to the film was compensated for within a few days after the film opened. Taguchi Ōson, the Shōchiku executive who engaged Kaeriyama's Film Art Association in 1920, has been credited with inspiring the promotional tactics for *Intolerance*. He was working for the *Tōkyō maiyū* newspaper at the time. See Tanaka Jun'ichirō, *Nihon eiga hattatsu shi,* 1: 328.

8. Ushihara, "Kamata modanizumu no gunzō," pp. 111, 114; Shindō Kaneto, *Aru eiga kantoku no shōgai,* p. 116, interview with Itō Daisuke. Ushihara and Itō were both screenwriters at Osanai Kaoru's Shōchiku Cinema Institute in the early twenties. Itō comments that he found Italian movies much more instructional than the various imported "How to Write . . ." books. Ushihara, on the other hand, mentions collaborating with Itō on a script based on a story in an American film magazine, and claims he was subscribing to a dozen American film publications at the time.

9. See Kishi, "Kaisetsu *Rojō no reikon,*" in *Nihon shinario taikei,* 1: 797. According to Kishi, transcriptions of American continuity scripts in *Katsudō no sekai* were particularly helpful to Ushihara Kiyohiko, who used them as reference in writing the screenplay for *Souls on the Road.*

10. Azlant, "Theory, History, and Practice of Screenwriting," p. 138.

11. Ibid., pp. 127–128, 131, 135. The well-known Palmer Photoplay Corporation, which offered correspondence courses in screenwriting in the United States in the 1920s, was evidently known in Japan. See the entry on the Palmer method in Shigeno Nobuhiko, "Shinario yōgo," p. 289, in Iijima Tadashi, ed., *Shinario taikei* (Tokyo: Kawade shobō, 1937), vol. 1 of *Shinario bungaku zenshū.* For more on the Palmer Photoplay Corporation, see Anne Morey, "'Have You the Power?': The Palmer Photoplay Corporation and the Film Viewer/Author in the 1920s," in *Film History* 9, no. 3 (1997): pp. 300–319.

12. Henry Kotani (Kotani Kuraichi, 1887–1964) was born in Hiroshima and emigrated to the United States with his family when he was a child. His family settled in Hawaii and eventually moved to San Francisco, where he graduated from high school. He then enrolled in a dramatic college against the wishes of his father, a physician, and stayed for one year. After a brief try at college, he left school to pursue a career in the theater. In 1913 he joined the staff at Thomas H. Ince's 20,000 acre studio, "Inceville," where he met Thomas Kurihara and Sessue Hayakawa. He continued acting in films and on the stage until 1917, when he left Ince and acting behind as his interests shifted to camera work. He was already considered a promising young cameraman in Hollywood circles when he was invited back to Japan in 1920 by the executives of the newly established Shōchiku studio. He is attributed with having introduced Hollywood lighting techniques to the Japanese industry, and was apparently the best-paid staff member at Shōchiku and perhaps in the industry. Before Kotani left America, Cecil B. DeMille, who was fond of him, drew up a contract for him to present to his new employers, guaranteeing him a monthly salary of 1,500 yen at a time when the usual rate was sixty yen a month.

13. Abe Yutaka (known in Hollywood as Jackie (or Jack) Abbe, 1895–1977) was born into a farming family in Miyagi prefecture. In 1912 he went to the United States with a younger brother to visit an uncle in Los Angeles. He enrolled in an acting school in Los Angeles, and when he heard Ince was looking for Japanese extras to work at his studio, Abe applied and was accepted into the company in 1914, where he joined Henry Kotani, Sessue Hayakawa and his wife, Aoki Tsuruko, and Thomas Kurihara. After his debut in *The Wrath of the Gods* (1914), in which he played alongside Hayakawa, he decided to devote himself to a career in the movies and took a job as Hayakawa's secretary. He continued to act for various directors including Frank

Lloyd, Frank Borzage, and Cecil B. DeMille (he played Hayakawa's valet in DeMille's 1915 *The Cheat*), all the while writing scripts under Hayakawa's tutelage. In 1925 he returned to Japan and entered the Nikkatsu Taishōgun studio in Kyoto. His particular style of witty and sophisticated humor immediately became popular with the public, and his 1926 *Ashi ni sawatta onna* (*The Woman Who Touched Legs*) marked the beginning of the ascendancy of the contemporary drama film. While in Hollywood, Abe used the name "Jack" or "Jackie" Abbe, but unlike Henry Kotani, Frank Tokunaga, and Thomas Kurihara he is better known in Japan by his real name.

Frank Tokunaga (born Tokunaga Bunroku but better known as Tokunaga Furaanku, 1887–1975) crossed over to the United States as a child. His first job was as an errand boy at the Metro and Goldwyn studios, where he occasionally appeared in bit parts. He reportedly studied both acting and directing while abroad, but after returning to Japan in 1924, his first attempts at directing were not well received. He entered the Nikkatsu Taishōgun studio in Kyoto and worked as an assistant director on Murata's *Machi no tejinashi* (*The Street Juggler,* 1925), but he is better remembered for his peculiar style of using English phrases when directing than he is for any of his work. He directed his last film in 1932, and his final involvement in films was an appearance in MGM's *The Teahouse of the August Moon* in 1956.

Ushihara Kiyohiko (1897–1985) entered Osanai's Shōchiku Cinema Institute in July 1920, the same month he graduated from the English literature department of Tokyo Imperial University. He went to the United States in 1926 to study with Chaplin for nine months, after which he returned to a successful and varied career as both a screenwriter and director. In 1930 he made another trip abroad to observe the new sound studios in France, England, and the United States.

14. Mizutani Yaeko, one of the first film actresses and star of this film, came from a good family and appeared here under the stage name Fukumen reijō, the "Masked Miss." Two versions of the film are part of the collection of the National Film Center, the Museum of Modern Art, Tokyo.

15. Ushihara, "Kamata modanizumu no gunzō," p. 103.

16. Tanaka, *Katsudō shashin ga yatte kita,* p. 186. Accounts vary, but Tanizaki's monthly salary was a considerable 250–350 yen.

17. See Tanizaki Jun'ichirō, "Sono yorokobi o kansha sezaru o enai," *Katsudō kurabu* (December 1920), in *Tanizaki Jun'ichirō zenshū* (1966–1970), 22: 96–97. (Unless otherwise stated, Tanizaki Jun'ichirō is quoted hereafter from two editions of his collected works, referred to as *TJZ*). In this article, written shortly after the completion of *Amateur Club,* Tanizaki writes that he intends to learn to write continuity-style screenplays himself in the future: "If I don't, my involvement in film will have been meaningless."

18. Yoda, "Mizoguchi Kenji izen," p. 242. Yoda specifically refers to the *shingeki* actress Matsui Sumako.

19. Okabe, ed., *Nihon no haiyū gakkō,* pp. 59–60, 66. Murata Minoru, Ushihara Kiyohiko, Thomas Kurihara, and Henry Kotani were also mentioned in an advertisement for the school, but their names do not appear in the actual curriculum for the opening semester.

20. Iijima, "Nihon eiga no reimei," pp. 122–123.

21. For the 1917 restriction, see Yanai Yoshio, *Katsudō shashin no hogo to torishimaru,* in Okudaira Yasuhiro, ed., *Genron tōsei bunken shiryō shūsei* (Tokyo: Nihon tosho sentaa, 1991).

22. Okudaira Yasuhiro, "Eiga to ken'etsu," in *Musei eiga no kansei,* pp. 303–304, 307–309. For the 1925 edict, see Ichikawa Aya, ed., *Nihon eiga hōki ruishū,* in Okudaira, ed., *Genron tōsei bunken.* Makino Mamoru gives a detailed summation of the edict in Makino, *Kaisetsu: Fukkokuban, eiga ken'etsu jihō* (Tokyo: Fuji shuppan, 1986), pp. 29–30, 37–39. In brief, this law required the official authorization of *benshi* scripts, remakes, and film length, and contained a section on theater regulations. Restrictions on film content were divided into two categories: regulations pertaining to public peace (for example, issues related to the imperial

family, national honor, diplomatic relations, and social order) and public decency (for example, ancestor worship, religious belief, violence, offensive material, nudity, kissing, sexual innuendo, and prostitution).

23. Makino, *Kaisetsu: Fukkokuban Eiga ken'etsu jihō,* p. 5.

24. Silent Japanese films are generally believed to have been lost for several reasons: the lack of copyright procedures that might ensure the survival of film prints; official preservation policies; censorship considerations; overuse or attrition; destruction by fire; and, perhaps most significantly, the fact that as a rule Japanese production companies at the time made as few prints of a film as possible in the first place. A surviving partial print of the Osaka-based Teikoku Kinema (Teikine) production *What Made Her Do It?* was purchased from the Gosfilmofond archive in Moscow in 1993 by the grandson of the film's original producer. A reconstructed version (the missing scenes at the beginning and ending of the film were replaced by titlecards summarizing the missing footage and new intertitles were created throughout),supervised by Ōta Yoneo, debuted at the 1997 Tokyo International Film Festival/Kyoto Film Festival held in Kyoto, with live orchestral accompaniment by the Romanian Symphony Orchestra (of an original score by Günter Buchwald). The reconstructed film was also a feature at the 1999 Pordenone Silent Film Festival in Sacile, Italy (accompanied by Buchwald on the piano and violin).

25. Anderson and Richie, *Japanese Film,* p. 69. Richie notes that screenings of both Eisenstein's *Battleship Potemkin* (1925) and Pudovkin's *Mother* (1926) were forbidden in Japan. By late 1930, when the Japanese were allowed their first glimpse of the films of the Soviet revolution (films like Pudovkin's 1928 *Storm over Asia* and Viktor Turin's 1929 documentary, *Turksib*), the tendency movement was already almost over. According to Yamamoto Kikuo, between 1927, when the first Soviet films were imported to Japan, and 1931 approximately fourteen Soviet films had been shown in Japan; among these, films such as *Storm over Asia, Turksib, General Line/Old and New* (Eisenstein/Grigori Alexandrov, 1929), *Earth* (Alexander Dovzhenko, 1930), and *Man with a Movie Camera* (Dziga Vertov, 1929) were likely to have been censored. See Yamamoto, *Nihon eiga ni okeru gaikoku eiga no eikyō,* p. 180.

26. Tanaka, *Eiga nandemo kojiten,* p. 221. Tanaka singles out the case of Tasaka Tomotaka's 1930 *Kono haha o miyo (Behold This Mother),* a treatment of women's liberation. One-fourth of the film's total footage, including the title, was cut.

27. Iwasaki, "An Outline History of the Japanese Cinema," *Japan Cinema Yearbook* (1936), p. 8.

28. Personal interview with Yoda Yoshikata, 20 April 1985.

29. Anon., *"Tabakoya no musume* ken'etsu to kokutetsu senden eiga sono hoka," *Katsudō zasshi* (October 1921), in Okabe, ed., *Kaeriyama Norimasa to Tōmasu Kurihara,* p. 89.

30. Mori and Tomonari, *Katsudō shashin taikan.* See Mori's preface to vol. 1, and editor's note, p. 105. According to Mori, his friend Tomonari Yōzō assisted him in collecting information.

31. Ibid., preface to vol. 1. Citations from this source hereafter appear in the text.

32. Lindsay, *Art of the Moving Picture,* pp. 289, 208.

33. Rimer describes intellectuals involved in the *shingeki* theater movement in this way in *Toward a Modern Japanese Theatre,* p. 83.

34. Iijima, *Nihon eiga shi,* 1: 23.

35. The reference to Victor Freeburg reads "Free Burg."

36. Freeburg, *Art of Photoplay Making,* p. 29.

37. *Tōkyō asahi shinbun,* 24 February 1920; *Ōsaka mainichi,* 17 February 1920, evening edition.

38. Okabe, editor's note, *Kaeriyama Norimasa to Tōmasu Kurihara,* p. 110; Anon., "Jin-

318

butsu gettan: Tamasu Kurihara Kisaburō [*sic*]," *Kinema junpō* (May 1922); Okabe, ed., *Kaeriyama Norimasa to Tōmasu Kurihara,* pp. 101–102.

39. Approximately the first twenty-two minutes of *Sanji Goto,* "the story of a Japanese Enoch Arden," was discovered in the United States, and donated to the Tokyo Museum of Modern Art National Film Center by the Museum of Modern Art in New York. Codirected by Harry Williams, it is the only work by Kurihara known to survive. A print of this fragment is available for rental through general distribution in the United States. Together with *Tōyō no yume* (*A Dream of the Orient*), it is believed to have been made sometime between 1918 and 1919, but it is not clear where it was filmed. Kurihara was in Japan from April to November 1918 (when he left again for the United States), and he could have made these films at that time. Kurihara has written, however, that his trip to the United States in November 1918 was for the purpose of studying the New York market, editing, and art titles, and it would seem reasonable to believe he made these films after he returned to Japan in April 1919 (the surviving segment of *Sanji Goto,* for example, features illustrated art titles), then brought them to the United States that December. On the other hand, Kurihara also referred to being in Los Angeles "because of the production of *Sanji Goto,*" during which time he did a favor for his friend, the director George Loane Tucker, by playing an "Oriental" in Tucker's 1919 *The Miracle Man* with Lon Chaney. See "Eigageki kansō danpenroku," *Katsudō zasshi* 7 (October 1921): pp. 66–67. For Kurihara's account of his trips back and forth between the United States and Japan during this period, see Kurihara, "Katsudō shashin to boku," *Katsudō kurabu* 3 (June 1920): pp. 168–169.

40. Quoted from the company's prospectus, *Katsudō kurabu* 3 (June 1920): p. 170.

41. For background on this period, when several future influential members of the Japanese film world emigrated to the United States, see Tsurutani, *America Bound,* pp. 173–175. According to Tsurutani, the increase in the number of Japanese in America from 1880 to around 1908 reflects an increase in the number of Japanese who (like Kurihara) left home in search of temporary employment. This flow of emigrants reached its peak in 1905 to 1908, and was finally stemmed by increasing anti-Japanese sentiment and the conclusion of the Gentlemen's Agreement in 1908. This was a restriction enforced by the Japanese government itself, limiting direct Japanese emigration to the American mainland and marking the end of a period of free immigration that had begun in the late 1860s.

42. Satō Tadao, "Hollywood no Nihonjin-tachi," in Imamura et al., eds., *Nihon eiga no tanjō,* p. 261.

43. Ibid.

44. Kurihara, "Katsudō shashin to boku," pp. 168–169.

45. Bowser, *Transformation of Cinema,* p. 157.

46. For reference to Ince's use of the continuity script to supervise and control production, see Azlant, "Theory, History, and Practice of Screenwriting," pp. 160–175; Richard Koszarski, *An Evening's Entertainment: The Age of the Silent Feature Picture, 1915–1928,* vol. 3 of *History of the American Cinema* (Berkeley: University of California Press, 1990), pp. 216–217; and Janet Staiger, "Dividing Labor for Production Control: Thomas Ince and the Rise of the Studio System," in Gorham Kindhem, ed., *The American Movie Industry* (Carbondale: Southern Illinois University Press, 1982), pp. 94–103. Azlant points out that the organizational use of the silent script existed in rudimentary form at Biograph as early as 1898 (with the work of Roy McCardell), and to an extent had been employed even earlier by Georges Méliès and Edwin S. Porter.

47. Bowser, *Transformation of Cinema,* p. 222.

48. For C. Gardner Sullivan, see also Azlant, "Theory, History, and Practice of Screenwriting," pp. 172–175 (Azlant discusses in detail Sullivan's *Keys of the Righteous*).

49. For Tanizaki's own descriptions of his desire to master the craft and his indebtedness to

Kurihara for his patient instruction and guidance, see in particular his articles: "Katsudō shashin no genzai to shōrai" (*Shinshōsetsu,* September 1917), in *TJZ* (1966–1970), 20: 11–21; "Sono yorokobi o kansha sezaru o enai" (*Katsudō kurabu,* December 1920), in *TJZ* (1966–1970),14: 185–187; "Ko Kurihara Tōmasu shi tsuitō roku: Kurihara Tōmasu kun no koto," *Eiga jidai* 1 (November 1926): pp. 88–90; and "Eiga no koto nado" *Shinchō* (April 1955): pp. 345–347. Although Tanizaki's relations with Kurihara were eventually strained by the director's failing health and worsening financial conditions at Taikatsu after the completion of *The Lust of the White Serpent,* Tanizaki continued to praise Kurihara's expertise and dedication to his work long after he himself had left the studio.

50. According to Mori, although this film (*Omichi-san* in Japanese) was not successful, it did prove that "Japanese can act, too," a realization that encouraged Ince's staff to continue with vehicles for Aoki, Hayakawa, and their Japanese colleagues.

51. A print of *The Wrath of the Gods* is housed at the George Eastman House archive in Rochester, along with a restored version of the original script.

52. Satō, "Hollywood no Nihonjin-tachi," pp. 265–266. Satō implies that when Hayakawa returned to Japan in 1922 he received a much warmer welcome than might have been expected. Satō attributes this to respect for Hayakawa both for the success he had achieved abroad and his ability to "make Yankee girls swoon." According to Tanaka Jun'ichirō, Hayakawa was forgiven with the explanation that because of the "mechanical nature" of the American production system, the actor actually had no idea of the content of the films in which he appeared. See Tanaka, *Nihon eiga hattatsu shi,* 1: 324–325. It is worth noting, however, that prior to returning to Japan, Hayakawa (along with Frank Tokunaga) was a leading figure in the Japanese Photoplayers' Club of Los Angeles, which was organized in October 1917. The purpose of the club was to ascertain that its members did not appear in films portraying the Japanese in a derogatory manner; members were also expected to use their influence in the industry to promote more dignified portrayals of the Japanese.

53. The George Eastman House also holds Cecil B. DeMille's personal copy of the 1918 version of the film. I thank Paolo Cherchi Usai, senior curator of motion pictures at the George Eastman House, for informing me about the archive's restoration of the pre-1918 cut based on a 1915 copy of the continuity script among the archive holdings (originally from the DeMille fund at Brigham Young University in Provo, Utah), and for sending me a copy of GEH's comparison between the original shooting script and the GEH print of the 1918 release. It is important to note that in the original script Hayakawa's character's name is Hishuru Tori (he is first introduced, by titlecard, simply as "Tori—One of Long Island's Smart Set") because the seal that figures so importantly in the film carries the image of a *torii,* which commonly marks the entrance to the grounds of a Shinto shrine. In the 1918 version, this titlecard was replaced with one reading "Haka Arakau, a Burmese ivory king to whom the Long Island Smart-set is paying social tribute. Sessue Hayakawa."

54. Kurihara, "Katsudō shashin to boku," p. 168.

55. Satō, "Hollywood no Nihonjin-tachi," pp. 264–265; Mori and Tomonari, *Katsudō shashin taikan,* 2: 18. According to Tanaka Jun'ichirō, *The Wrath of the Gods* closed in Tokyo one week after it opened. See Tanaka, *Nihon eiga hattatsu shi,* 1: 325.

56. Kurihara, "Katsudō shashin to boku," p. 169.

57. Ibid.

58. Iijima, "Nihon eiga no reimei," p. 121. Iijima, a teenager when the pure film movement began, recalls that the often critical reactions to individual films were eclipsed by the general excitement the films collectively inspired.

59. Kurihara, "Katsudō shashin to boku," p. 169.

60. Kanasashi Eiichi, "Taikatsu zenshi: Tōyō kisen to Taishō katsuei," in Okabe, ed., *Kaeriyama Norimasa to Tōmasu Kurihara,* p. 60.

61. Ibid.

62. Kurihara, "Katsudō shashin to boku," p. 169. Kristin Thompson notes that Triangle was one of the first companies in Hollywood to introduce art titles (illustrated titlecards); the studio even had a separate department for painting these cards. See Thompson, "The Formulation of the Classical Style," in Bordwell, Staiger, and Thompson, *Classical Hollywood Cinema,* p. 187. Art titles appear in the Tōyō Film production *Gotō Sanji,* but there are no indications for art titles in the script for the comedy *Amateur Club;* Tanizaki used them sparingly in the script for the 1921 *The Lust of the White Serpent,* the only extant Taikatsu script in which they appear.

63. Kanasashi, "Taikatsu zenshi," p. 61.

64. Tanaka, *Nihon eiga hattatsu shi,* 1: 296–297.

65. The U.S. dollar equivalents given are approximate figures. The yen equivalent for one dollar for these years is as follows: 2.019 yen (1912); 2.032 yen (1914); 1.973 yen (1919); and 2.014 yen (1920) (*Nihon ginkō hyakunen shi,* 7 vols. [Tokyo: Nihon ginkō, 1986].)

66. See Hazumi Tsuneo, *Eiga gojūnen shi* (Tokyo: Masu shobō, 1943), p. 137.

67. Kanasashi, "Taikatsu zenshi," pp. 60–61.

68. Ibid., p. 61.

69. *Katsudō kurabu* 3 (June 1920): p. 170.

70. Satō Kōroku, *Katsudō shashinkai,* no. 8 (April 1910): p. 1.

71. Kurihara Tōmasu, "Taishō katsudō shashin danjo haiyū yōseijo no sōritsu," *Katsudō kurabu* 3 (August 1920), in Okabe, ed., *Nihon no haiyū gakkō,* p. 32.

72. See Okabe, ed., *Nihon no haiyū gakkō* for a history of screen acting in Japan, including the development of studio-sponsored acting schools. Secondary sources imply that the Yoshizawa school did not accept women, but plans to solicit women interested in acting do appear early on in *Katsudō shashinkai.* See "Engei in yōseisho kiyaku," in *Katsudō shashinkai,* no. 5 (January 1910): p. 13.

73. Benisawa, "Tanizaki Jun'ichirō to Taishō katsuei," p. 83; idem, "Omoide modan na sakuhin," p. 46.

74. Tokita Eitarō, "Taikatsu juken kiroku," in Okabe, ed., *Nihon no haiyū gakkō,* pp. 33–34. Asked to pretend he was a robber breaking into a mansion, Tokita, a complete novice to screen acting, passed the test by reenacting his own experience having run away from home with a substantial amount of his parent's money two months earlier. (The credits for *Amateur Club* list Hanabusa Takeshi, possibly Tokita's stage name at the time, as a robber in the film. Tokita later wrote the 1924 screen version of Tanizaki's play *Honmoku yawa,* directed by Suzuki Kensaku.) Benisawa recalls her screen test, which consisted of changing her expression and acting out various situations according to the instructions that Kurihara called out from his director's chair, as being easy enough "for anyone to pass." See Benisawa, "Tanizaki Jun'ichirō to Taishō katsuei," p. 83.

75. Benisawa Yōko, "Taikatsu no omoide ni sasaerarete," in Okabe, ed., *Kaeriyama Norimasa to Tōmasu Kurihara,* p. 98. According to Benisawa, Kurihara believed his actors should be amateurs, but preferred actresses who had some experience, and this might explain the actresses' higher salaries; or perhaps it was because actresses were such a rarity at the time. Benisawa was an exception among the group of amateurs Tanizaki and Kurihara assembled, as she had experience in the "Asakusa opera." (This term was used to describe the various types of popular musical entertainment featured in Asakusa theaters at the time. See chapter 6.)

76. Anon., "Jinbutsu gettan," p. 101.

77. Anon., "*Ryūboku to Kisen hōshi* no satsuei," *Katsudō kurabu* (June 1921), in Okabe, ed., *Kaeriyama Norimasa to Tōmasu Kurihara,* p. 88.

78. Tanaka, *Nihon eiga hattatsu shi,* 1: 302. Tanaka describes an incident that occurred during the filming of *Katsushika sunago* (*The Sands of Katsushika,* 1920). His description of Kurihara's directing technique calls to mind that of another perfectionist, Mizoguchi Kenji.

79. Anon., "Jinbutsu gettan," p. 101.
80. Benisawa, "Tanizaki Jun'ichirō to Taishō katsuei," pp. 84–86, 90–91.
81. Ōmori, "Sōsōki no kameraman," p. 232.
82. Ibid., p. 235.
83. Anon., "*Gen'ei no onna* no shikisha o miru," *Katsudō zasshi* (June 1920), in Okabe, ed., *Kaeriyama Norimasa to Tōmasu Kurihara,* p. 25.
84. Lindsay, *Art of the Moving Picture,* pp. 36–37.
85. Ibid., p. 53.
86. Ibid., pp. 36, 51–52.
87. Kurihara, "Katsudō shashin to boku," p. 168–169.
88. Kurihara Kisaburō, "Eigageki to kansō danpen roku," *Katsudō zasshi* (October 1920): p. 67.
89. Gerow, *Writing a Pure Cinema,* pp. 313, 315.
90. David Bordwell and Kristin Thompson, *Film Art: An Introduction* (New York: McGraw-Hill, 1997), pp. 77–78.

CHAPTER 4

1. Ramsaye, *A Million and One Nights,* p. 370; Azlant, "Theory, History, and Practice of Screenwriting," pp. 61–64; Stempel, *Framework,* pp. 3–4.
2. Azlant, "Theory, History, and Practice of Screenwriting," pp. 135–136. Although Taikatsu was not as directly influenced by developments in Europe as it was by American production practices (those who remember the studio never fail to comment on its "Yankee" appeal), it should be noted that a movement to attract a bourgeois audience with films written by well-known authors was also visible in Europe (the *film d'art* in France, for example, and authors like Max Reinhardt in Germany) from the early 1910s.
3. Ibid., p. 174. To emphasize just how well paid screenwriters were at the time, Azlant quotes Louella Parsons, who wrote in 1917 that Sullivan's salary, reported to be at least 52,000 dollars a year, equaled that of the president of the United States.
4. Excerpts from Osanai's diary appear in Maeda Ai, "Sakariba ni eigakan ga dekita," in Imamura et al., eds., *Nihon eiga no tanjō,* pp. 339–342.
5. Mori and Tomonari, *Katsudō shashin taikan,* 2: p. 30; Tanaka, *Nihon eiga hattatsu shi,* 1: 191–192. According to Ushihara Kiyohiko ("Kamata modanizumu no gunzō," p. 104), Osanai was in such demand as a commentator for films based on classic works of Western literature that his presence was taken for granted at all such screenings. Ushihara recalls that because these adaptations were extremely popular at the time, by the end of the decade the word "film" had come to be equated with Osanai's name among the members of literary and theatrical circles.
6. *Yōshō jidai,* in *TJZ* (1957–1959), 29: 111–112. This work has been translated into English by Paul McCarthy as *Childhood Years: A Memoir* (Tokyo: Kodansha International, 1988). The references to film are on pages 97–98.
7. Chiba, *Eiga to Tanizaki,* pp. 79–83. Chiba compares Tanizaki's descriptions in *Yōshō jidai* with the original promotional material for the first imported Edison films appearing in the appendix to Tsuruta, *Nihon eiga shi no kenkyū: Katsudō shashin torai zengo no jijō,* pp. 288–306.
8. *Yōshō jidai,* p. 112.
9. Keene, *Dawn to the West,* 1: 746–747. As Keene points out, the *kōjin* was a mythical creature originating in China. It resembled a merman and was believed to live in southern seas, where it wove cloth on a loom and wept tears that were pearls.
10. See Tanizaki, "Tōkyō o omou," in *TJZ* (1966–1970), 21: 9.

11. Iijima, "Nihon eiga no reimei," p. 115.

12. Chiba, *Eiga to Tanizaki,* pp. 60–61. For a description of this story see Keene, *Dawn to the West,* 1: 744–746. Keene comments that "there could hardly be a more wholehearted affirmation of the West than Tanizaki professed in 'The German Spy'" (p. 746).

13. "Jinmenso," in *TJZ* (1966–1970), 5: 281–305. Two years later Tanizaki wrote that he had been told this story had an inherent cinematic quality and remarked that he would like to make it into a film, shooting the Hollywood scenes on location in the United States (*Yomiuri shinbun,* 9 May 1920). Tanizaki seems to have been serious about this project: at one point *Kinema junpō* reported that the film was in the planning stage at Taikatsu (see Okabe, ed., *Kaeriyama Norimasa to Tōmasu Kurihara,* p. 78). Plans to adapt the story at Taikatsu were never realized. It was finally made into a film, *Oiran,* in 1982 by the director Takechi Tetsuji, based on Takechi's own screenplay.

14. "Jinmenso" (1966–1970), 5: 302.

15. "*Karigari hakase* o miru," in *TJZ* (1966–1970), 22: 107–112.

16. "Eiga zakkan," in *TJZ* (1966–1970), 22: 100.

17. "Eiga e no kansō: *Shunkinshō* eigaka ni saishite," in *TJZ* (1957–1959), 30: 69–73.

18. The original story, "Jasei no in" ("The Lust of the White Serpent"), appears in Ueda Akinari's eighteenth-century collection of ghost stories, *Ugetsu monogatari.* Akinari's story is based on *Bai niangzi yong zhen Leifeng ta* (*Eternal Prisoner under the Thunder Peak Pagoda*), a Chinese tale with origins dating as far back as the T'ang Dynasty. "Jasei no in" has been adapted for film several times. In 1953 Mizoguchi Kenji and Yoda Yoshikata used it with another story from Akinari's collection, "Asaji ga yado" ("The House among the Thickets"), and Maupassant's short story, "Decoré" ("Decorated!"/"How He Got the Legion of Honor"), as source material for the well-known Kyoto Daiei production, *Ugetsu monogatari* (1953).

19. *Nikkai,* in *TJZ* (1966–1970), 9: 40–41.

20. "Tōkyō o omou," p. 149.

21. Ibid., pp. 148–149. Iijima Tadashi (*Jidenteki essei,* p. 38) remembers the Teikokukan as a movie theater specializing in Bluebird films and serials. The Odeonza, the first movie theater to specialize in foreign films, opened in Yokohama in October 1911. According to Tanaka Jun'ichirō ("Eigakan nyūjōryō," p. 486), it was a "first run" theater, and showed the newest imports even before they were released in Tokyo.

22. Ozaki et al., "Zadankai," *Yūrin* 220 (10 March 1986): p. 2.

23. "Shina shumi to iu koto," in *TJZ* (1966–1970), 22: 122–123.

24. "Tōkyō o omou," p. 23.

25. Tanizaki moved to Kansai on 20 September 1923, nearly three weeks after the earthquake. He and his family were accompanied by Osanai Kaoru and his sister. See Yokozeki Aizō, "Daishinsai koro no sakka-tachi," in the supplement to vol. 9 of *TJZ* (1966–1970), p. 5.

26. Ibid., p. 164. See also Keene, *Dawn to the West,* p. 752.

27. Chiba, *Eiga to Tanizaki,* pp. 168, 176.

28. "Eiga e no kansō," p. 72.

29. Tanaka, *Katsudō shashin ga yatte kita,* pp. 177–178.

30. Yanagisawa et al., "Shinjidai ryūkō no shōchō toshite mitaru 'jidōsha' to 'katsudō shashin' to 'kafe' no inshō," p. 96. The article consists of fourteen contributions; in addition to Tanizaki and Osanai, the contributors included Tanizaki's friend, the novelist and poet Satō Haruo, and playwright and author Kubota Mantarō, who later directed Tanizaki's play *Honmoku yawa.*

31. "Katsudō shashin no genzai to shōrai," in *TJZ* (1966–1970), 20: 11–21.

32. "Keikoba to butai no aida," in *TJZ* (1966–1970), 22: 147.

33. "Eigaka sareta *Honmoku yawa,*" in *TJZ* (1966–1970), 22: 168. The film *Honmoku*

yawa was directed by Suzuki Kensaku in 1924, and starred Hayama Michiko. See Chiba, *Eiga to Tanizaki,* p. 134.

34. "*Kōjin* no genkō ni tsuite," in *TJZ* (1966–1970), 23: 54.

35. "Shōsetsu mo kaki, katsudō shashin ni mo chikara o sosogu," in *TJZ* (1957–1959), 14: 214.

36. "Sono yorokobi o kansha sezaru o enai," in *TJZ* (1966–1970), 22: 96–97.

37. Ibid.

38. Both *The Radiance of the Moon* and *The Lust of the White Serpent* are included in *TJZ* (1957–1959), 11: 133–182 and 183–232 respectively. *The Night of the Doll Festival* is included in *TJZ* (1966–1970), 9: 409–426. See also *Shinengei* 9 (September 1924): pp. 118–124. In both the 1924 *Shinengei* version and the version in *TJZ,* the narrative seems to come to an abrupt end at scene 79 and does not include scenes described in a review of the film written by Noda Kōgō under the pen name "Midori no Hoshi" ("Green Star"). (See Noda Kōgō, "*Hinamatsuri no yoru:* Taikatsu dai san kai sakuhin," *Katsudō kurabu* 4 (June 1921): pp. 22–23. Either Kurihara and Tanizaki improvised considerably during the shooting of the film, or the final scenes (according to Noda's description, probably about a fourth of the film) were omitted by *Shinengei* and were subsequently lost.

39. Itō Daisuke, "*Kōbō Shinsengumi* no shinario ni tsuite," in *Nihon shinario taikei,* 1: 792; Itō Daisuke, Mimura Shintarō, Kishi Matsuo, and Kobayashi Masaru, "Nihon eiga shinario dangi," pp. 15–16. Itō states that rush prints were not commonly used for editing until the sound period; during the silent period the negative itself was cut by the director with the assistance of the cameraman (according to Shibata Masaru and Kaeriyama Norimasa, this was apparently the case with *The Glory of Life*). According to Tanizaki, however, Kurihara edited his films using a positive print instead of the negative, which took considerably more time. See Tanizaki, "Kurihara Tōmasu kun no koto," p. 89.

40. Itō, "*Kōbō Shinsengumi* no shinario," p. 792; Itō et al., "Nihon eiga shinario dangi," p. 16.

41. See, for example, Iijima, *Nihon eiga shi,* 1: 33; Tanaka, *Nihon eiga hattatsu shi,* 1: 302; Shindō, "Shinario tanjō zengo," p. 185. The chronology here is unclear. Tanaka implies that *Katsushika sunago* (*The Sands of Katsushika*) was made after Tanizaki had already completed the script for *The Radiance of the Moon,* which had originally been planned as the second Taikatsu production after *Amateur Club. Amateur Club* opened on 11 November 1920, *The Sands of Katsushika* opened on 28 December, and "I Must Be Grateful for that Happiness," in which Tanizaki describes working on *The Radiance of the Moon,* appeared in the December edition of *Katsudō kurabu. Gendai* began serializing the script the following month. In view of the very short time lapse between all three projects, Tanizaki conceivably worked on *The Sands of Katsushika* and *The Radiance of the Moon* at the same time.

42. Tanizaki, "Kurihara Tōmasu kun no koto" in *TJZ* (1966–1970), 22: 194.

43. "Eiga e no kansō," p.72.

44. Tanaka Eizō, "*Katsushika sunago* to kare no shukumei," *Eiga no tomo* (September 1941), in Okabe, ed., *Kaeriyama Norimasa to Tōmasu Kurihara,* p. 99. Tanaka was particularly impressed with the extent to which the titles were faithful to Kyōka's original work.

45. Editor's note, in *TJZ* (1957–1959), 11: 237.

46. Like Kurihara in his continuity for *Amateur Club,* Tanizaki also used the Japanese term for "close-up," or "close shot," "*ōutsushi*" (the term Kaeriyama used exclusively in *The Glory of Life*). Japanese technical terms have virtually disappeared from the modern Japanese screenplay, which rarely features any technical terms at all, but the alternate use of both Western and Japanese technical terms is not unusual in other stages of the production process.

47. Yasumi Toshio, "Shinario shi josetsu 6," *Shinario* 37 (October 1981): pp. 63–64.

48. Ibid., p. 64.

49. Ibid., pp. 63–64.
50. *Tsuki no kagayaki,* p. 157.
51. Ibid., p. 140.
52. Ibid., p. 165.
53. Ibid., p. 155.
54. Ibid., p. 164.
55. Ibid., p. 139.
56. Noda, *"Hinamatsuri no yoru,"* p. 413.
57. Ibid., p. 424.
58. Ibid., pp. 442–443.
59. Ibid., pp. 424, 442–443.
60. "Eiga e no kansō," p. 72; "Keikoba to butai no aida," p. 230.
61. Tanaka, *Nihon eiga hattatsu shi,* 1: 302.
62. Noda, *"Hinamatsuri no yoru,"* p. 23. Noda felt Tanizaki's handling of the dolls was unsatisfactory. Noda was critical of the film in general, reserving his praise for the acting talent of Tanizaki's daughter.
63. "Jasei no in," in *TJZ* (1957–1959), 11: 194. The painters of the native Japanese style Tosa school of painting (early fifteenth to late nineteenth centuries) were primarily employed by the imperial court. Accordingly, they specialized in painting courtly scenes, often drawing inspiration from classical literature. Their work was characterized by a flat, decorative composition; it was also colorful, delicate, and refined, with much care given to detail.
64. Ibid., p. 208.
65. Ibid., p. 215.
66. Ibid., p. 213.
67. Ibid., p. 189.
68. Iijima, "Nihon eiga no reimei," p. 117.
69. Tanaka, *Nihon eiga hattatsu shi,* 1: 304; Iijima, *Nihon eiga shi,* 1: 34. Iijima quotes from the 21 November 1921 entry in his diary:

> However you look at it, ten reels is too long. Six would have been better. The first half of the film drags. The sixth, seventh, and eighth reels in the second half of the film were good. . . . Really mediocre compared to a Shōchiku film. In general, unpolished. Can't seem to escape the amateurish style of Kaeriyama's films. . . . Many scenes were so long they didn't appear to have been edited at all. If the cutting were a bit livelier, the film would double in quality. At any rate, a poor job. Really shabby. They used real snakes, but the actresses didn't seem the least bit concerned.

70. Tanaka, *Nihon eiga hattatsu shi,* 1: 304.
71. See, for example, Benisawa, "Omoide: modan na sakuhin," p. 46. Benisawa notes in particular that Tanizaki, rather than return to his own home after a day's work, often stayed the night at the home of another staff member.
72. See Tanizaki, "Eiga no koto nado," p. 346. Tanizaki wrote that although he was often given credit for directing the film together with Kurihara, he only gave advice on the customs and manners of the period in which the film is set.
73. "Jasei no in," p. 185.
74. Ibid., p. 186.
75. Iijima, *Nihon eiga shi,* 1: 24–25.
76. Shindō, "Shinario tanjō zengo," p. 195.
77. "Eiga no koto nado," p. 346.
78. "Taikatsu, Kurihara sakuhin kiroku" ("Taikatsu/Kurihara Filmography"), in Okabe, ed., *Kaeriyama Norimasa to Tōmasu Kurihara,* p. 109. The film is listed in the *Nihon eiga sakuhin jiten* (2: 1085) as having been produced by Henry Kotani and directed by Kurihara, and featured Kotani, Kurihara, Seki Misao, and Hayama Michiko.

79. "Eiga e no kansō," p. 320. See also "Eiga no koto nado," p. 295. After Kurihara died in 1926, Tanizaki wrote that he was so concerned about the director's health during his last days at Taikatsu that the studio's rapid demise took him completely by surprise. See "Kurihara Tōmasu kun no koto," p. 103.

80. Eiga e no kansō, p. 320.

81. Ibid.

82. Yasumi Toshio, "Shinario shi josetsu," 37(October 1981): p. 82.

83. "*Akatsuki no dassō* o miru," in *TJZ* (1966–1970), 22: 386–391. Tanizaki's reference to these two Marlene Dietrich vehicles by Josef von Sternberg is predictable: the director had a tremendous following among Japanese film viewers in the 1920s and 1930s, and his work was an important influence on one of the leading directors of the contemporary genre during the silent period, Murata Minoru.

84. Ibid., pp. 249–250.

85. Ibid., p. 252.

86. Chiba, *Eiga to Tanizaki*, pp. 170–171.

87. Iijima Tadashi makes this point in his *Nihon eiga shi*, 1: 126.

88. Shōchiku remains a major production company, but as this manuscript went to press what is left of the historic Shōchiku Ōfuna studio was scheduled to be acquired in June 2000 by Kamakura Women's College (which was reported to have paid nearly 11 billion yen for the site). Shōchiku's financial difficulties were exacerbated by the death, in 1996, of Atsumi Kiyoshi, the star of the popular series *Otoko wa tsuraiyo* (*It's Tough Being a Man*).

89. Although the screenplay for *A Page of Madness* (based on the story "A Page out of Order") is usually attributed to Kawabata, it was a collaborative effort by the group of writers. Yokomitsu apparently provided the connection between the writers and Kinugasa: the director had just made a controversial screen adaptation of Yokomitsu's *Nichirin* (*The Sun*) in 1925. For a detailed discussion of *A Page of Madness,* including its resemblance to *The Cabinet of Dr. Caligari,* see Burch, "Kinugasa Teinosuke," in *To the Distant Observer,* pp. 123–139.

90. "Eiga no koto nado," p. 346.

91. "Kurihara Tōmasu kun no koto," p. 89.

CHAPTER 5

1. Quotations and passages cited are from Makino, ed., *Nihon eiga shoki shiryō shūsei* (*NES*).

2. Iijima, *Jidenteki essei*, pp. 34–35.

3. Ibid., p. 35. See also Anderson, "Second and Third Thoughts," p. 442. Anderson's description of these programs implies that by the 1920s they had become "elaborate, printed programs," with "credits, star portraits . . . gossip . . . and "complete, ending-revealing synopses and commentaries." The Namikiza, a theater in Tokyo specializing in reruns of classic Japanese films (it announced plans to close in early 1999), put out a small program the size of a handbill that featured black and white photographs and information on the films being featured as well as articles written by the theater management and contributions by members of the audience. Such small programs, almost more like fan newsletters, are not unusual at small revival houses, and movie theaters located outside major metropolitan areas. According to Iijima (p. 36), the *eiga zakkan* also stocked "bromide portraits" (publicity shots) of film stars, particularly foreign actors and actresses, and single frames of film. Collecting frames was popular among moving picture fans at the time; Osanai Kaoru was particularly proud of his collection, which he mentions in his contribution to the *Chūō kōron* questionnaire "Cars, Moving Pictures, and Cafes," p. 93 (see chapter 5, note 30). Iijima remarks that he rarely bought photos of film stars because he

and his colleagues discovered that writing fan letter requests to each individual star was more economical.

4. According to Makino Mamoru, the prototype *chirashi* was issued at the Denkikan the week of 3 January 1907; it was put together by the Denkikan resident *benshi* Somei Saburō. See Makino, "Meijiki no bunmeikaika to zasshi *Katsudō shashinkai,*" p. 31. In Hazumi, *Eiga gojūnen shi,* there is a picture of the Asakusa Teikokukan's *Daiichi shinbun,* which was first printed in 1915. The caption describes this program as Japan's first (p. 63). According to Iijima (see note 2 to this chapter), many of the names of these programs included the words *shinbun* ("newspaper") or "news."

5. Makino, "Eizō bunkengaku no seiritsu," p. 101; Makino, "Meijiki no bunmeikaika to zasshi *Katsudō shashinkai,* pp. 29–30.

6. Komatsu, "Yume no tekusuto," pp. 18–19. For more on the publication history of other studio-sponsored publications of this period, as well as more detail on *Katsudō shashinkai*'s background, see the introductions by Iwamoto Kenji, Komatsu Hiroshi, and Makino Mamoru in Makino, ed., *Fukkokuban Katsudō shashinkai,* pp. 7–33.

7. Komatsu, "Yume no tekusuto," pp. 16, 21.

8. Iwamoto, "Ōbei eiga o kagami toshite," p. 13.

9. Komatsu, "Kioku no mokuroku," pp. 15–16; Makino, "Eiga jyanarizumu no genryū, *Firumu rekōdo* to *Kinema rekōdo* no wakaki gunzō," p. 30.

10. Makino quotes Imamura Miyoo's description of this process in "Ametsuchi no maji-warishi koro," introduction to *NES,* 1 (5): 1–2. See Imamura, *Nihon eiga bunkenshi,* p. 183. According to Imamura, after the transcription was completed, the transcriber often obtained sin-gle frames of the film from the projectionist to illustrate the transcription in place of drawings or production stills. (Publicity shots, production stills, and signed bromides apparently came into regular use in fan magazines after 1915; the transcriptions in the early issues of *Katsudō shashin zasshi,* for example, the earliest of the magazines discussed here, are unusual in that they are almost exclusively illustrated by hand.) See also "Ametsuchi no majiwarishi koro," p. 11, for Makino's description of the influence these transcriptions had on various forms of film-gener-ated popular literature that first appeared at the time, such as *Kinema bunko, Eiga kōdan, Kinema kōdan,* and *Eiga setsumei zenshū.* According to Makino, these publications were written in a style imitating *benshi* narration, with dialogue that resembled dialogue intertitles. They also featured titles listing the production company, staff members, and cast of characters, and were generously illustrated either by hand or with actual frame enlargements.

11. *Katsudō gahō* (January 1917), in *NES,* 6: 17.

12. Makino, "Ametsuchi no majiwarishi koro," p. 10.

13. Makino Mamoru points out that *Katsudō shashin zasshi* in particular actively encour-aged readership participation, and the amount of space allotted to such outside contributions vis-ibly increased during the magazine's first year of publication. See ibid., p. 11.

14. Kōda Rohan, "Kokorozashi aru tōgyōsha wa dare ka," in *NES,* 3: 312.

15. Ibid., pp. 312–313.

16. Kōda Rohan, "Kyakuhon sakusha ni tsuite," in *NES,* 5: 241.

17. Ibid., p. 242.

18. *Cabiria* was in fact based on the director Giovanni Pastrone's adaptation of a novel by Emilio Salgari, *Il romanzo delle fiamme.* For a filmography of all works adapted from D'Annunzio's writings, as well as those films to which he contributed (titles, captions, etc.), see Martinelli, "D'Annunziana," pp. 44–49. D'Annunzio received 50,000 gold lire to allow his sig-nature to be put on *Cabiria,* and has been credited with adding his inimitable touch to the titles and suggesting the names of the characters and the film's title (the name of the protagonist of the film). Martinelli is of the opinion that other than such "practical contribution[s]," authorship of the film belongs entirely to Giovanni Pastrone. In a 1931 reissue of the film, the composer

Ildebrando Pizzetti (who composed the film's "Sinfonia del fuoco") was erroneously credited as the scriptwriter (Paolo Cherchi Usai, "Cabiria, an Incomplete Masterpiece: The Quest for the Original 1914 Version," *Film History* 2 [1988]: p. 163). For a study of D'Annunzio's contribution to film intertitles, including those of *Cabiria,* see Sergio Raffaelli, "Il D'Annunzio prosatore nelle didascalie dei suoi film," *D'Annunzio e il cinema,* Quaderni del Vittoriale (August 1977): pp. 45–53.

19. Tsubouchi Shikō, "*Cabiria* inshōki," *Katsudō no sekai* (July 1916), in *NES,* 4: 446. The special supplement that appeared in the June issue of *Katsudō no sekai,* "Furoku, *Cabiria* kōhen zenbu kanketsu," was an appendix to "Dai shigeki, *Cabiria,*" in the same issue.

20. Anon., "Beikoku kashū katsudō shashin hattatsu shi," in *NES,* 9: 558–563.

21. Nakura Bun'ichi, "Katsudōgeki no kyakuhon no kakikata," in *NES,* 3: 314–321.

22. Tsubouchi Shikō, Ikeda Daigo, and Matsui Shōyō, "Katsudōgeki kyakuhonka ni tsuite," in *NES,* 4: 48–56.

23. Tsubouchi Shikō, "Kyakuhonka no kushin subeki ten," pp.48–52 (after the first citation of each, subsequent references to all three articles in this segment are cited in the text).

24. Ikeda Daigo, "Katsudō shashin to Chikamatsu no fukkatsu," pp. 52–54.

25. Matsui Shōyō, "Tensai no shutsugen o matsu," pp. 54–56.

26. Kōda, "Kyakuhon sakusha ni tsuite," pp. 240–241.

27. Anon., "Kyakuhon o eiga ni suru made, Beikoku sho kaisha no Ōjiikake no satsuei furi," in *NES,* 8: 650–651, 653.

28. Ibid., p. 651.

29. Kaeriyama Norimasa, *Katsudō gahō* (September 1917), "Katsudō shashingeki no kyakushoku hō oyobi torikku," in *NES,* 8: 753.

30. "Kenshō katsudō shashin kyakuhon kōgai dai boshū," *Katsudō gahō* (October 1917), in *NES,* 9: 226–227.

31. Kaeriyama Norimasa, "Katsudō shashin kōgyō ni tsuite," in *NES,* 8: 619–621. Kaeriyama gives the title of the *Kinema Record* article as "Katsudō shashin no shakaiteki chii oyobi sekimu."

32. Chiba, "Modanaizeeshyon jokyoku," pp. 32–34. Gonda's association with film and his subsequent influence on journalistic discourse in this respect is addressed in Gerow, "Writing a Pure Cinema."

33. Kaeriyama, "Katsudō shashin kōgyō," p. 619.

34. Mukai Shunkō, "Katsudō shashinkai no shin keikō: kigeki no zensei jidai kuru," *Katsudō gahō* (March 1917), in *NES,* 6: 596. *Yamato damashii,* a phrase dating back to the Heian period (794–1185), has been used in various ways to refer to cultural or spiritual qualities regarded as unique to the Japanese people. The meaning of the word has changed over the years: in the Heian period, for example, it was used to distinguish native culture from that of the Chinese, which was highly admired by Heian nobility, who adopted or imitated many qualities of this foreign culture at that time. In modern years, particularly in the period of military aggression that began in the 1930s and continued until the end of World War II, the term was used to describe absolute loyalty and devotion to the Japanese emperor and the nation.

35. Taguchi Ōson, "Mo me no sameru toki darō, Nihon no katsudō shashin jūgyōsha ni nozomu," in *NES,* 6: 346–351; Bokutei Inshi, "Nihonsei firumu no ketten to sono jissaiteki kenkyū," in *NES,* 6: 628–632; Matsumoto Ryūkotsu, "Nihon eiga no shinro," in *NES,* 9: 548–557. "Bokutei Inshi," or "hermit of the banks of the Sumida River," is one of the more colorful pen names used in these articles.

36. Bokutei, "Nihonsei firumu no ketten," p. 630.

37. See, for example, Matsumoto, "Nihon eiga no shinro," pp. 555–557, and Azusagawa Hōchō, "Geijutsugan yori mitaru Beikokusei eiga" *Katsudō gahō* (December 1917), in *NES,* 9: 3.

38. Azusagawa, "Geijutsugan yori," p. 299.

39. For example, see Mukai, "Katsudō shashinkai no shin keikō." Comedy was also a popular subject during the first year of publication (1916) of *Katsudō no sekai.* See Tsubouchi Shikō, "Kyakuhonka no kushin subeki ten," in which Tsubouchi declares that Japan conceivably could make even better comedies than Keystone (p. 51); and idem, "Katsudō shashin no honryō wa kigeki ni ari," (June 1916) in *NES,* 4: 243–247 (this issue of the magazine was a special issue on comedy). Articles on Chaplin appear regularly in *Katsudō no sekai* after June 1916, and in the first three issues of *Katsudō gahō.*

40. Gerow sees the interest in film on the part of literary giants from a very specific perspective, as "an attempt to control a more ambiguous and threatening medium through inscribing it within the familiar boundaries of literary construction." See Gerow, "Writing a Pure Cinema," p. 296.

41. Ogasawara Takeo, "*Katsudō no sekai* sōkan no toshi ni tsuite," introduction to *NES,* 3: 2.

42. Ibid., p. 3.

43. Takata Sanae, "Kōki aru nihon no katsudō shashin," *Katsudō no sekai* (March 1917), in *NES,* 3: 432–433. Takata was one of the founding fathers of Waseda University.

44. Tsubouchi Shōyō, "Katsudō shashin to kusazōshi," in *NES,* 3: 634–636.

45. Shimamura Hōgetsu, "Katsudō shashin no shin ni sakanna jidai," in *NES,* 4: 42–43.

46. Shimazaki Tōson, "Pari kara kaette kite," in *NES,* 5: 405.

47. Bokutei, "Nihonsei firumu no ketten," p. 632.

48. All "Katsudō shashin no genzai to shōrai" citations in the text are from *TJZ* (1966–1970), 20: 11–21.

49. The word "Photoplay" appears in English.

50. In the script, the Kamakura Amateur Club stages a performance of the *yukashita* (under the floor) scene of *Sendaihagi* (the full name of the play is *Meiboku Sendaihagi*), a play based on the rivalry between different factions of the powerful Date clan of Sendai in northern Japan, and the tenth act of *Taikōki,* drawn from the events surrounding the assassination of Oda Nobunaga by one of his generals, Akechi Mitsuhide, in June 1583.

51. There is an abridged translation of *Journey to the West* by Arthur Waley titled *Monkey,* and a full translation by Anthony Yu in four volumes, titled *Journey to the West.* A screen version directed by Yoshino Jirō was released in Japan in 1917. See Shibata [Ōmori], "Jun'eigageki to kouta eiga," pp. 9–10 for a description of the trick photography used in this film. Tanizaki was probably not familiar with the Italian director Giuseppe De Liguoro's 1909 five-reel screen adaptation of Dante's *Inferno,* which was not released in Japan.

52. See Chiba, *Eiga to Tanizaki* (pp. 102–105), for a list of screen adaptations from 1910 to 1983 of Izumi Kyōka's works. More recently, the actor Bandō Tamasaburō directed a short (fifty-minute) film for commercial release based on one of Kyōka's most popular stories, "Gekashitsu" ("The Operating Room"). It opened in Japan in February 1992.

53. Tanizaki, "Kurihara Tōmasu kun no koto," pp. 194–195. Kyōka's novel, serialized in *Shinshōsetsu* in 1890, is set in the mid-1800s in an area known from ancient times as Katsushika. Katsushika was formerly a country that straddled part of Tokyo and what are now the prefectures of Chiba and Saitaima. Kyōka had trouble naming the piece once it was written and thought of the title, which can also be read as a woman's name, only as he was delivering the manuscript to the publisher.

54. The word *Crystallization* appears in English.

55. *Ono ga tsumi (One's Own Sin,* 1899–1900), a best-selling melodramatic novel by Kikuchi Yūhō, was the source for the *shinpa* play of the same name. The first screen version was made in 1908; it proved to be popular and subsequently was made into a film several times in the early years of the industry, most notably by Tanaka Eizō in 1919. Tanizaki, who admitted his

preference for foreign films, apparently did not know a screen version already existed. The stage version of *Konjiki yasha* (*The Demon Gold,* 1905)—Ozaki Kōyō's last, unfinished novel—was also a staple of the *shinpa* repertory; Tanaka Eizō directed a screen version of the play in 1918.

56. *Yomiuri shinbun,* 20 May 1920.

57. Ibid. *Kōdan* is a genre of oral storytelling. *Kibyōshi* is a subgenre of *kusazōshi,* popular illustrated fiction of the Edo period (1600–1868).

CHAPTER 6

1. Chiba, *Eiga to Tanizaki,* pp. 11–12.

2. See, for example, Uchida Tomu, "Taishō katsuei jidai," in Okabe, ed., *Kaeriyama Norimasa to Tōmasu Kurihara,* p. 94. Uchida was one of several Taikatsu recruits who went on to important careers in the industry. Uchida's career as a director lasted from the late 1920s until his death in 1970. Among his better-known films outside of Japan are the three-part *Dai Bosatsu tōge* (*The Great Bodhisattva Pass,* 1958–1960), and *Kiga kaikyō* (*Hunger Straits,* 1965). Kurihara apparently considered building a larger studio, or at least enlarging the studio on the Yamate bluff, shortly before production was terminated altogether in 1922. See Kurihara Kisaburō, "Eiga seisakusha o dokuritsu seshimeyo," *Katsudō zasshi* (June 1922), in *Kaeriyama Norimasa to Tōmasu Kurihara,* p. 71.

3. "Eiga zakkan," in *TJZ* (1966–70), 22: 101–102. Sankei Garden (Sankei-en) is a landscaped park in Yokohama with old villas, small tea arbors, temple halls, and a farmhouse; the elements of the park have been collected from different parts of Japan.

4. Suzuki, "Geijutsu toshite eigageki," *Katsudō gahō* (December 1917): p.11.

5. "Eiga no koto nado," pp. 292–293.

6. Satō Kiichirō, "Taikatsu no Yūrakuza kōgyō," *Katsudō gahō* (January 1921), in Okabe, ed., *Kaeriyama Norimasa to Tōmasu Kurihara,* p. 79.

7. Hazumi, *Eiga gojūnen shi,* p. 141.

8. Yoshimura Kōzaburō, "*Amachua Kurabu* o miru," in *Nihon eiga shinario koten zenshū,* supplementary volume, p. 10.

9. See, for example, Hazumi, *Eiga gojūnen shi,* p. 144; Iwasaki Akira, *Eiga to genjitsu,* p. 65; Iijima, *Nihon eiga shi,* 1:34–35.

10. Tanizaki, "Eiga no koto nado," p. 346.

11. Tanizaki, "Sono yorokobi," pp. 185–186.

12. Ibid., p. 186.

13. See *Kōjin,* in *TJZ,* 9: 89–256. One of the characters in this novel is believed to have been inspired in part by Tanizaki's friend Kamiyama Sōjin. (See Itō Hitoshi, "Kaisetsu," in *TJZ,* 9: 259.)

14. Yanagisawa et al., "'Jidōsha' to 'katsudō shashin' to 'kafe' no inshō," pp. 95–96.

15. For a description of Asakusa opera, see Seidensticker, *High City, Low City,* pp. 267–271.

16. Tanizaki, *Kōjin,* p. 145.

17. Tanizaki, "Tōkyō o omou," pp. 154–155. See also Keene, *Dawn to the West,* p. 751. As Keene notes, Tanizaki envisioned the emergence of "a new species of Japanese woman" with Western figures, eyes, and skin color resembling that of Westerners, and an accent that would make even the Japanese they spoke resemble a European language.

18. For examples of passages revealing Tanizaki's fondness for Japanese women in Western clothes, see his *Seven Japanese Tales,* trans. Howard Hibbett (New York: Knopf, 1963), pp. 191–192, 199.

19. Chiba, *Eiga to Tanizaki,* p. 37.

20. Tanizaki, "Eiga no koto nado," p. 345.

21. Interview with Hayama Michiko in Chiba, *Eiga to Tanizaki,* p. 34. Chiba interviewed Hayama in Yokohama in 1989. Hayama's last appearance on screen was in an adaptation of Kawabata Yasunari's *Asakusa kurenaidan* (*The Scarlet Gang of Asakusa*) in 1930, the year she married (p. 37). According to her interview with Chiba, her only recollection of *Amateur Club* itself was that it was "boring" (p. 35).

22. Tanizaki, "Eiga no koto nado," p. 345.

23. See Keene, *Dawn to the West,* pp. 744, 746–748; Kon Tōkō, *Jūnikai hōkai.* Written by one of Tanizaki's protégé at the time, the novelist Kon Tōkō, *Jūnikai hōkai* is a semi-fictionalized account of the author's relationship with Tanizaki (he was a self-styled, and by his own account, unpaid "personal secretary") as well as his observations of his mentor's personal life during his two years in Yokohama. The book contains several references to Tanizaki's work at Taikatsu and his relationship with Hayama (see in particular pp. 37–56), but Kon Tōkō himself had no interest in Tanizaki's films (he writes that he did not see *Amateur Club* when it opened), and in spite of Kon's association with the author at the time, there is a surprising lack of information about Taikatsu that is not available from other sources. There are more than a few anecdotes about Kon's exploits with aspiring actresses, however, which suggests that he was really more interested in telling a good story.

24. Tanizaki, *Chijin no ai,* in *TJZ,* vol. 15. See also Keene, *Dawn to the West,* for a discussion of the novel and a comparison of Hayama (referred to by her actual first name, Seiko) and Naomi, pp. 746, 753–754. The English translation of this novel is called *Naomi.*

25. See, for example, *Chijin no ai,* pp. 9–10, 29 for Naomi's resemblance to Mary Pickford; p. 19 for a description of Jōji's choice of decor (photographs of American movie actresses) for Naomi's room; and pp. 29–30 for references to "Mack Sennett's Bathing Beauties." In *Eiga to Tanizaki,* Chiba Nobuo lists all the references to foreign film actresses in the novel by order of appearance. In addition to Mary Pickford, the list includes Annette Kellerman, Geraldine Farrar, Gloria Swanson, and Pola Negri (pp. 52–54).

26. *Chijin no ai,* pp. 30–31. The champion swimmer and diver Annette Kellerman, known as "The Diving Venus," starred in a number of silent films (in addition to *Neptune's Daughter, A Daughter of the Gods,* 1916; *Queen of the Sea,* 1918; *Venus of the South Seas,* 1924; and others) that featured her swimming skills as the main attraction.

27. See Keene, *Dawn to the West,* p. 754.

28. See Chiba, *Eiga to Tanizaki,* p. 56, and Tachibana, ed. *Tanizaki Jun'ichirō sensei chosho sōmokuroku* for this photograph of Hayama. The cover of *Eiga to Tanizaki* features two photographs of Annette Kellerman, in *Neptune's Daughter,* in a similar pose. This photograph appears in *Kinema Record* (10 March 1917).

29. Sakai Hiroshi, "Watashi no gijutsu shi," *Eiga terebi gijutsu* (June 1970), in Okabe, ed., *Kaeriyama Norimasa to Tōmasu Kurihara,* p. 52. According to Sakai, much of the film was cut by the censors.

30. Tanizaki, "Sono yorokobi," pp. 185–186.

31. Tanizaki, "Eiga no koto nado," pp. 345–346.

32. Tanizaki, "Sono yorokobi," p. 186.

33. Tanizaki, *Amachua kurabu.* All subsequent citations appear in the text according to shot number. A version that coincides with all but the final installment of the serialized script (in other words, accurate through scene 251) appears in *Nihon eiga shinario koten zenshū,* supplementary volume, pp. 32–45. For some reason, the final installment was not included in this published version. It ends abruptly with Chizuko's father trying to convince the police that Shigeru is his daughter. The police have caught both the robbers and Shigeru, but Chizuko has gone off after the Rat and the precise whereabouts of the rest of the Amateur Club are unclear.

34. According to the cameraman for *The Glory of Life,* this was one of the few scenes changed in the film at the actors' request. See Shibata [Ōmori] Masaru, "Jun'eigageki to kouta eiga," p. 18.

35. Iijima, "Nihon eiga no reimei," pp. 116–117; idem, *Nihon eiga shi,* 1: 32–34; Hazumi, *Eiga gojūnen shi,* pp. 138–139.

36. Ōmori, "Sōsōki no kameraman," p. 235.

37. Tanizaki, "Sono yorokobi," p. 186.

38. Satō, "Taikatsu no Yūrakuza kōgyō," pp. 79–80.

39. At least one viewer at the time, however, found the dialogue stilted. See Hazumi, *Eiga gojūnen shi,* pp. 140–141. Hazumi quotes "a fan" who saw the film at the Chiyoda theater, where it opened approximately a month after its initial release at the Yūrakuza. (Hazumi is apparently quoting from a theater program).

40. Shigeru and Chizuko's parents are introduced with close-up shots in addition to intertitles; Chizuko and Shigeru's father are introduced by intertitles only.

41. "Eiga kyakuhon *Amachua kurabu* no keisai ni tsuite," *Katsudō zasshi* (June 1921): 148–149.

42. The character, Nikki Danjō, is the villain of the play, and he appears here in his transformed disguise. A master of occult arts, he can assume the form of a rat at will.

43. "*Amachua kurabu* kanketsu ni tsuite, *Katsudō zasshi* 7 (October 1921): p. 108.

44. For a translation of the preface to *The Lust of the White Serpent,* see chapter 5.

45. "Eiga kyakuhon *Amachua kurabu* no keisai ni tsuite," pp. 148–149.

46. Benisawa, "Omoide modan na sakuhin," p. 46.

47. Tanizaki, "Sono yorokobi," p. 187.

48. Chiba, *Eiga to Tanizaki,* pp. 62–63.

49. Iijima, *Nihon eiga shi,* 1: 24–25; excerpts from Iijima's journals can be found in Iijima Tadashi, "Musei jidai no eiga nikki 1," pp. 37–38.

50. Ōmori, "Sōsōki no kameraman," p. 232; Shibata [Ōmori], "Jun'eigageki to kouta eiga," p. 21.

51. Satō, "Taikatsu no Yūrakuza kōgyō," p. 79. Few recollections of the film fail to mention the opening credits. See, for example, Uchida Tomu, "Taishō katsuei jidai," p. 94; Benisawa, "Tanizaki Jun'ichirō to Taishō katsuei," p. 86; Hazumi, *Eiga gojūnen shi,* p. 139; Tanizaki, "Eiga no koto nado," p. 293.

52. See for example, Hazumi, *Eiga gojūnen shi,* pp. 140–141, for a comparison with *Shinsei,* a Shōchiku film shot by Henry Kotani. Kurihara's technical expertise is praised, although Kotani's film is judged the photographically superior of the two films. On the other hand, the acting in *Amateur Club* is described as better than the performances given in *Shinsei.*

53. Iijima, "Nihon eiga no reimei," p. 117.

54. Satō, "Taikatsu no Yūrakuza kōgyō," p. 80; Hazumi, *Eiga gojūnen shi,* pp. 138–139; Yoshimura, "*Amachua kurabu* o miru," pp. 9–10. Hazumi notes that Kurihara was well known as a character actor in Hollywood, and was "a genius" with makeup and costumes. He was apparently so skilled in the application of moustaches and hair pieces that he was known as the "clip-hair King."

55. Kotani did not decide to go to Shōchiku until the last minute. An article giving a brief biographical sketch of Kotani and announcing that he would join Taikatsu along with Kurihara appeared in the May 1920 issue of *Katsudō kurabu.* See Okabe, ed., *Kaeriyama Norimasa to Tōmasu Kurihara,* p. 67.

56. See in particular Kondō Iyokichi, "*Amachua kurabu* o mite," *Kinema junpō* (November 1920), in Okabe, ed., *Kaeriyama Norimasa to Tōmasu Kurihara,* p. 81; and Anon., "Jinbutsu gettan," p. 101.

57. Satō, "Taikatsu no Yūrakuza kōgyō," p. 80. See also Iijima, "Nihon eiga no reimei," p. 117.

58. Iijima, *Nihon eiga shi,* 1: 34.

59. Yodogawa Nagaharu, "Taishō katsuei no sakuhin," in Tachibana, ed., *Tanizaki Jun'ichirō sensei chosho sōmokuroku,* p. 58.

60. Mukai, "Katsudō shashin no shin keikō," *Katsudō gahō* (February 1917), in *NES,* 6: 43.

61. Iijima, "Nihon eiga no reimei," p. 117.

62. Hazumi, *Eiga gojūnen shi,* p. 143.

63. Even Shōchiku's first film, *Island Woman,* which opened a few weeks before *Amateur Club,* featured performers who had been trained on the traditional stage.

64. Satō, "Taikatsu no Yūrakuza kōgyō," p. 80.

65. Iijima, "Nihon eiga no reimei," pp. 116–117.

66. For Kurihara's filmography, see his entry in *Nihon eiga kantoku zenshū,* p. 156; and "Taikatsu/Kurihara sakuhin kiroku," in Okabe, ed., *Kaeriyama Norimasa to Tōmasu Kurihara,* pp. 107–109.

67. Tanaka, *Nihon eiga hattatsu shi,* 1: 296.

68. Chiba, *Eiga to Tanizaki,* p. 153.

69. Ibid.

70. See the promotional advertisement for Taikatsu that appeared in *Katsudō kurabu* (December 1921), in Okabe, ed., *Kaeriyama Norimasa to Tōmasu Kurihara,* p. 66. Masumura Yasuzō also makes this point in his "Profilo storico del cinema giapponese," pp. 193–194.

71. Nakatani Giichirō, conversation quoted in Tanaka, *Nihon eiga hattatsu shi,* p. 304. Nakatani was employed by Taikatsu at the time.

72. Benisawa, "Omoide modan na sakuhin," p. 46; idem, "Taikatsu no omoide ni sasaerarete," p. 98.

73. Nakatani, in Tanaka, *Nihon eiga hattatsu shi,* pp. 304–305.

74. Anon., "Kokutetsu senden eiga sono hoka," p. 89.

75. Ibid.

76. Chiba, *Eiga to Tanizaki,* pp. 153–154.

77. Anon., "Jinbutsu gettan," p. 102. According to Tanizaki, Kurihara was constantly at odds with the studio management, particularly with the managing director himself, Shimo Nariyasu. See Tanizaki, "Kurihara Tōmasu kun no koto," p. 89, and "Eiga no koto nado," p. 345.

78. Tanaka, *Nihon eiga hattatsu shi,* p. 306.

79. See, for example, the company's promotional advertisement in *Katsudō zasshi,* December 1921. The announcement states that Kurihara and Tanizaki will collaborate on "special productions."

80. Tanizaki, "Shōsetsu mo kaki," p. 214.

81. Ozaki et al., "Zadankai," p. 2.

82. Iijima, "Nihon eiga no reimei," p. 116.

83. Tanaka, *Nihon eiga hattatsu shi,* 1: 302.

84. See "Eiga no koto nado," p. 347, and "Kurihara Tōmasu kun no koto," pp. 89–90.

85. Tanizaki Shūhei, "Yokohama kara Kansai e," *Kaisō no ani Tanizaki Jun'ichirō,* no. 8, supplement to *TJZ,* 9: 7.

86. Anon., "Jinbutsu gettan," p. 102.

87. Ogasawara Meihō, "Ko Kurihara Tōmasu shi tsuitō roku: Kurihara Tōmasu sensei no shi," *Eiga jidai* 1 (November 1926): p. 92.

88. Tanizaki, "Kurihara Tōmasu kun no koto," p. 90.

APPENDIX: *THE GLORY OF LIFE*

1. Dialogue not included in an intertitle was not unusual in silent film scripts; it heightened the sense of continuity and helped the actors remain in character.

2. The term used here is *tozu* ("shut" or "close") rather than Kaeriyama's usual choice, *shiboru* (fade). This is possibly because the term follows the use of a "vision" scene.

3. Here I have interpreted "F" as fade. Although there is no indication of such, it could also be meant to indicate "full shot."

4. This is the most elusive of Kaeriyama's terminology, appearing as "C.F." [*sic*]. I am grateful to Ōta Yoneo for suggesting the possible interpretation of "quick fade."

APPENDIX: *A FATHER'S TEARS*

This translation of the first five scenes of *A Father's Tears* (*Chichi no namida*) is from the original published version of the script in *Katsudō no sekai* 3 (June 1918): pp. 133–161 (up to and including scene 23). Tanaka Jun'ichirō also includes the first three scenes (with relevant commentary) in his article, "Onoe Matsunosuke-geki *Bingo Saburō*," pp. 27–29. Tanaka does not include the prologue to the script, and there are minor discrepancies between the original version in *Katsudō no sekai* and Tanaka's rendering of the opening scenes. I mention the most notable of these below.

1. Ide Shōichi was the editor in chief of *Katsudō no sekai*.

2. This phrase is only identifiable as a title because of the following reference to it as a title. Throughout the script, potential titles are not regularly designated as such, making it difficult to distinguish them with any certainty.

3. The use of technical terms to describe the transition from one shot (title) to the next here is very vague: the coupling of *kieru to* and *bokashi ni natte* alternatively could be interpreted as describing a fade-out and fade-in, fade-out and iris-in, or a dissolve (perhaps an overlapping fade-out and fade-in) transition. This is another example of the lack of consistency in the phrasing and application of terminology during this period.

4. A *shakuhachi* is a five-holed bamboo wind instrument resembling a clarinet.

5. In the original, "Related, Unrelated" appears on a single line as if it might be a title, followed by the next sentence, also on a single line. Tanaka more clearly designates "Related, Unrelated" as a title by enclosing it in brackets, as he does with the earlier title, "A Wanderer." He moves the following line ("The foot of a bridge . . .") so that it appears as part of the exposition. Because of what is known of the nature of *shinpa* titlecards (they were similar to the chapter titles of a book) and Tanaka's presumed familiarity with the film, it is plausible that Tanaka is correct in his designation of how much text actually appeared on each titlecard in these opening scenes. These are the only two titles included in his transcription. I have tried to remain consistent with this "chapter title" style of titling throughout, designating as titlecard text only those phrases that appear at the beginning of a scene on a single line.

6. I enclose in parentheses all expository text that is clearly designated as *togaki* (expository text set apart by the katakana character *to* in a smaller font).

7. The word used for close-up or close shot here and throughout is *ōutsushi*.

8. *Taifuun geki*. *Taifuun* appears in katakana (phonetic syllabary, rather than Chinese characters). This possibly refers to a specific type of drama, or simply a drama about a typhoon.

9. This sentence is presumably also *togaki,* but it is not set apart from the main text (*to* appears in hiragana, and in the same font as the main text).

APPENDIX: *AMATEUR CLUB*

This translation is made from the original imprint serialized in *Katsudō zasshi* 7 (June–October 1921). Other than the difference in the number of scenes, with the exception of typographical discrepancies, this version is essentially the same as the later version in *Horidasareta meisakusen,* supplement to *Nihon eiga shinario koten zenshū.*

1. The term used in the original imprint in *Katsudō zasshi* is *butai shūnin.*

2. The actors playing the roles of Chizuko's mother and the second thief are not identified here.

3. In the kabuki drama *Ehon Taikōki,* the tenth act of which is performed by the Amateur Club, the name of the character based on the historical figure Toyotomi Hideyoshi is conventionally called Mashiba Hisayoshi.

4. This practice of airing articles in the summer, known as *doyōboshi,* evolved as a means of protecting valuables and other rarely used objects against mildew and insects. The focus on the airing of family heirlooms here provides an additional satirical touch. Kabuki dramas often feature the loss of or search for such precious family treasures (garments, swords, cups, bowls, painted scrolls, calligraphy, etc.) as a key element of the narrative.

5. This is presumably Katō Kenzō. His name also appears with alternative characters in a subsequent scene.

6. This line is missing from the 1966 version of the script.

7. Here "playhouse" is a translation of the pejorative *shibai koya,* a more likely choice than "theater" for someone like Shigeru's father.

8. Such iron-ribbed fans were a common samurai accoutrement, used to signal troops on the battlefield. They often appear in historical kabuki plays, sometimes being used to strike enemies on the forehead.

9. Although Tanizaki and Kurihara's desire to write a modern comedy makes it tempting to translate *kuruma* as automobile or motorcar, the word more likely signifies a jinrikisha here because of the period.

10. *Hiroma* is an awkward word to translate in this context. It is equivalent to a kind of living room, or a fairly large room in which guests could be entertained ("salon" is another common translation).

11. Here "out" appears in English.

12. The overlapping plates in Japanese armor are laced together with colored silk braid or strips of leather. The colors are important, as armor is classified according to the both the color and pattern of the laces. Here it is important that the set of armor that fascinates Chizuko has scarlet laces. In act 10 of the *Taikōki,* presented later in the script by the Amateur Club, the character played by Muraoka Shigeru, Takechi Jūjirō, also conventionally wears scarlet-laced armor.

13. This is the usual dress for such performers. A *kataginu* is a kind of stiff, sleeveless robe or cape that exaggerates the breadth of the shoulders. *Hakama* are wide, pleated "trousers" resembling a divided skirt. Such formal dress is worn by actors, singers, and instrumentalists in the kabuki theater.

14. The drama being performed, act 10 of *Ehon Taikōki* (1799), also known as *Amagasaki no ba* (*At Amagasaki*), is the only surviving act of the original thirteen. The entire thirteen-act drama was based on the thirteen days between Akechi Mitsuhide's (Takechi Mitsuhide in the drama) murder of Oda Nobunaga (Harunaga) and Akechi's own death confronting the forces of Toyotomi Hideyoshi (Mashiba Hisayoshi). The setting for the scene performed here is a summer evening, a lowly cottage in the midst of bamboo and a trellis of gourd vines. Satsuki (Mitsuhide's mother), Misao (Mitsuhide's wife), and Hatsugiku (Mitsuhide's betrothed) are taking refuge in the cottage. Presumably, the Amateur Club's performance here has begun at the point

where the scene often starts. Hatsugiku overhears her betrothed, Mitsuyoshi, say aloud that he wishes her to marry another if he is killed in battle, now that he must join forces with his father against Hisayoshi. Hatsugiku reveals herself, weeping, and the two decide to be married right away. Satsuki and Misao assist with the ceremonial cups of sake, and with Mitsuyoshi in full armor, the two pledge themselves to each other. Mitsuyoshi immediately leaves for the battle-field, leaving the women alone in their sorrow.

15. In the kabuki theater, it is customary for spectators to shout the actor's title (the *yago* of his acting family) in order to show appreciation and encouragement, particularly during a notably effective pose or after the delivery of a well-known line. Each acting family has its own *yago*. Here, Narikomaya is the *yago* of the Nakamura family, and Suketakaya is the *yago* of the Suketakaya family.

16. After the wedding ceremony and Mitsuyoshi's departure, Mitsuyoshi's father, Mit-suhide, emerges from the bamboo thickets surrounding the cottage dressed as a farmer. Here, "strikes a pose" is the translation of *mie o kiru* (strike a *mie*). Such poses (*mie*) are an integral part of kabuki drama. While the principal actors take such poses, all other movement onstage "freezes," coming to a halt.

17. In the *Katsudō zasshi* imprint, scenes #251–253 were rewritten in the final installment (which included #251–#265). The 1966 version of the script does not include the rewritten scenes. In the 1966 version, #251 is the same with the exception of the title, which was added in the rewrite only. After #251, the first version of the script before being rewritten is as follows:

#252. Exterior. A street with a hedge (street corner)
Shigeru runs smack into a policeman at the street corner and is caught.
#253. Exterior. Street.
A continuation of #251. Watching from a distance, Mr. Miura shouts, "Hey, that's my daughter. She's no criminal!"

APPENDIX: *THE LUST OF THE WHITE SERPENT*

1. Tanizaki specifically calls for "costume and scenery resembling that of the Ōchō era"— the year 1311, during the reign of Emperor Hanazono (1308–1318) in the late Kamakura period. For an English translation of Ueda Akinari's original story, see "The Lust of the White Serpent," in Leon M. Zolbrod, trans. and ed., *Ugetsu Monogatari: Tales of Moonlight and Rain* (Vancouver: University of British Columbia Press, 1974): pp. 161–184.

2. Tanizaki retains the archaic names, as used by Akinari, for present-day Nara (Yamato) and Wakayama (Kii).

3. I have translated the term *yōmei* as "fade," although in his introduction to the script Tanizaki gives the term the corresponding English word "dissolve."

4. Cape Miwa, at the southern tip of the Kii Peninsula, is now part of the city of Shingū. Akinari reads Takesuke's family name as "Ōya."

5. An alternate name for the Kumano Hayatama Shrine in Shingū, one of the three holy places of Kumano, the old name of this area.

6. This title borrows a poem by Naga Okimaro from the *Man'yōshū* (*Kokka taikan,* no. 265): "Kurushikumo furikuru ame ka Miwagasaki / Sanu no Watari ni ie mo aranaku ni."

SELECT BIBLIOGRAPHY

As this manuscript went to press, Matsuda Film Productions released *Masterpieces of Japanese Silent Cinema,* a bilingual (Japanese-English) DVD-ROM for Windows database that is a particularly valuable reference for *benshi* history and style.

Abel, Richard. "The 'Blank Screen of Reception' in Early French Cinema." *IRIS* 11 (summer 1990): pp. 27–47.

Anderson, Joseph L., and Donald Richie. *The Japanese Film: Art and Industry.* 1959. Reprint, New York: Grove Press, 1960. Expanded edition, Princeton: Princeton University Press, 1982.

Azlant, Edward. "Screenwriting for the Early Silent Film: Forgotten Pioneers, 1897–1911." *Film History* 9, no. 3 (1997): pp. 228–256.

———. The Theory, History, and Practice of Screenwriting, 1897–1920. Ph.D. diss., University of Wisconsin, 1980.

Benisawa Yōko. "Omoide modan na sakuhin" ("Recollections of a Modern Film"). In *Horidasareta meisaku sen* (*Recovered Masterpieces*), p. 46. Supplement to *Nihon eiga shinario koten zenshū* (*Classic Japanese Screenplays/Scenario Classics Collection*). Tokyo: Kinema junpō, 1966.

———. "Tanizaki Jun'ichirō to Taishō Katsuei" ("Interview: Tanizaki Jun'ichirō and Taishō Katsuei"). In *Kikigaki kinema no seishun* (*Interviews: Japanese Cinema in Its Youth*), edited by Iwamoto Kenji and Saiki Tomonori, pp. 77–100. Tokyo: Libroport, 1988.

Bernardi, Joanne. The Early Development of the Gendaigeki Screenplay: Kaeriyama Norimasa, Kurihara Tomas, Tanizaki Jun'ichirō and the Pure Film Movement. Ph.D. diss., Columbia University, 1992.

———. "Genre Distinctions in the Japanese Contemporary Drama Film." In *La nascita dei generi cinematografici* (*The Birth of Film Genres*), edited by Leonardo Quaresima et al., pp. 407–421. Udine: Forum, 1999.

———. "The Literary Link: Tanizaki and the Pure Film Movement." In *A Tanizaki Feast: The International Symposium in Venice,* edited by Adriana Boscaro and Anthony Hood Chambers, pp. 75–92. Ann Arbor: Center for Japanese Studies, The University of Michigan, 1998.

———. "Norimasa Kaeriyama and *The Glory of Life. Film History* 9, no. 4 (1997): pp. 365–387.

337

———. "The Pure Film Movement and the Contemporary Drama Genre in Japan." In *Film and the First World War,* edited by Karel Dibbets and Bert Hogenkamp, pp. 50–61. Amsterdam: Amsterdam University Press, 1995.

———. "Tanizaki Jun'ichirō's 'The Present and Future of the Moving Pictures.'" In *Currents in Japanese Culture: Translations and Transformations,* edited by Amy Vladeck Heinrich, pp. 291–308. New York: Columbia University Press, 1997.

Bordwell, David. "Visual Style in Japanese Cinema, 1925–1945." *Film History* 7, no. 1 (1995): pp. 5–31.

Bordwell, David, Janet Staiger, and Kristin Thompson. *The Classical Hollywood Cinema: Film Style and Mode of Production to 1960.* New York: Columbia University Press, 1985.

Bowser, Eileen. *The Transformation of Cinema: 1907–1915.* Vol. 2 of *History of the American Cinema.* Berkeley: University of California Press, 1990.

Burch, Noël. *To the Distant Observer: Form and Meaning in the Japanese Cinema.* Berkeley: University of California Press, 1979.

Cherchi Usai, Paolo. *Burning Passions: An Introduction to the Study of Silent Cinema.* London: BFI Publishing, 1994.

Chiba Nobuo. *Eiga to Tanizaki (Film and Tanizaki).* Tokyo: Seiabō, 1989.

———. "Modanaizeeshyon jokyoku eiga ron 1914–1918" ("A Prelude to Modernism: Film Theory, 1914–1918"). In *Nihon eiga to modanizumu, 1920–1930 (The Japanese Cinema and Modernism, 1920–1930),* edited by Iwamoto Kenji, pp. 32–49. Tokyo: Libroport, 1991.

Chiba Nobuo et al. *Nihon eiga shi jitsusha kara seichō, konmei no jidai made (History of the Japanese Film).* Vol. 31 of *Sekai no eiga sakka (Directors of the World).* Tokyo: Kinema junpō, 1976.

Chisholm, Brad. "Reading Intertitles." *Journal of Popular Film and Television* 15 (fall 1987): pp. 137–142.

Eisner, Lotte H. *The Haunted Screen.* Berkeley: University of California Press, 1973.

Elsaesser, Thomas, ed. *Early Cinema: Space, Frame, Narrative.* London: British Film Institute, 1990.

Freeburg, Victor O. *The Art of Photoplay Making.* New York: The Macmillan Company, 1918.

Futaba Jūzaburō. *Eiga no rekishi (The History of Film).* Vol. 1 of *Eiga no kōza (Film Symposium).* Tokyo: Mikasa shobō, 1952.

Gerow, Aaron. Writing a Pure Cinema: Articulations of Early Japanese Film. Ph.D. diss., University of Iowa, 1996.

Hakurai kinema sakuhin jiten (Complete Dictionary of Imported Movies up to August 1945). 4 vols. Tokyo: Kagaku shoin, 1997.

Hannon, William Morgan. *The Photodrama: Its Place among the Fine Arts.* New Orleans: Ruskin Press, 1915.

Hayashi, Jōji. *Joyūji hajime Kurishima Sumiko, Okada Yoshiko, Natsukawa Shizue. (The First Actresses: Kurishima Sumiko, Okada Yoshiko, Natsukawa Shizue).* Tokyo: Heibonsha, 1986.

Hazumi Tsuneo. *Eiga gojūnen shi (Fifty-Year History of Film).* Tokyo: Masu shobō, 1943.

High, Peter B. "The Dawn of Cinema in Japan." *Journal of Contemporary History* 19 (1984): pp. 23–57.

Iijima Tadashi. *Jidenteki essei boku no Meiji, Taishō, Shōwa (Autobiographical Essays: My Meiji, Taishō, and Shōwa Periods).* Tokyo: Seiabō, 1991.

———. "Musei jidai no eiga nikki 1: 1921–1923" ("Diary of the Silent Era, 1: 1921–1923"). *Eigashi kenkyū (Studies in Film History)* 8 (1976): pp. 31–41.

———. *Nihon eiga shi (A History of the Japanese Film).* Vol. 1. Tokyo: Hakusuisha, 1955.

Imamura Miyoo. *Nihon eiga bunkenshi (A History of Japanese Film Publications)*. Tokyo: Kagamiura shobō, 1967.

Imamura Shōhei et al., eds. *Musei eiga no kansei (The Perfection of the Silent Film)*. Vol. 2 of *Kōza nihon eiga*. Tokyo: Iwanami shoten, 1986.

———. *Nihon eiga no tanjō (The Birth of the Japanese Film)*. Vol. 1 of *Kōza nihon eiga (Symposium: Japanese Film)*. Tokyo: Iwanami shoten, 1985.

Ishihara Ryota, ed. *Eiga shō eiga sai daizenshū (A Dictionary of Film Awards and Film Festivals)*. Tokyo: Kaga shoten, 1985.

Itō Daisuke. "Sairento jidai no shinario *Kōbō Shinsengumi* no shinario ni tsuite" ("The Age of the Silent Screenplay: The *Kōbō Shinsengumi* Screenplay"). In *Nihon shinario taikei (A Historical Collection of Japanese Screenplays)*, edited by the Shinario sakka kyōkai, pp. 792–793. Vol. 1. Tokyo: Eijinsha, 1973.

Itō Daisuke et al. "Tokubetsu zadankai: Nihon eiga shinario dangi" ("A Discussion of the Japanese Screenplay"). In *Horidasareta meisaku sen,* pp. 15–24. Supplement to *Nihon eiga shinario koten zenshū*. Tokyo: Kinema junpō, 1966.

Iwamoto Kenji. "Japanese Movie Narrators (Benshi) and Montage." Unpublished lecture, May 1973.

———, ed. *Nihon eiga to modanizumu 1920–1930 (Japanese Cinema and Modernism, 1920–1930)*. Tokyo: Libroport, 1991.

Iwamoto Kenji and Makino Mamoru, eds. *Fukkokuban Kinema junpō*. Reprint edition of *Kinema junpō*. 19 vols. Tokyo: Yūshōdō, 1994–1996.

Iwamoto Kenji and Saiki Tomonori, eds. *Kikigaki kinema no seishun*. Tokyo: Libroport, 1988.

Iwasaki Akira. *Eiga ga wakakatta toki Meiji, Taishō, Shōwa no kioku (When Film Was Young: My Memories of Meiji, Taishō, and Shōwa)*. Tokyo: Heibonsha, 1980.

———. *Eigashi (Film History)*. Tokyo: Tōyō keizai shinpōsha, 1961.

———. *Eiga to genjitsu (Film and Reality)*. Tokyo: Shunyōdō shoten, 1939.

———. "Nihon eiga shi I" ("Japanese Film History"). In *Eiga no rekishi (History of Film)*, edited by Yamada Kazuo, pp. 5–55. Vol. 2 of *Eigaron kōza (A Symposium on Film Theory)*. Tokyo: Gōdō shuppan, 1977.

Japan Times Weekly and Mail, July–September 1919.

Kaeriyama Norimasa. *Katsudō shashingeki no sōsaku to satsuei hō (The Production and Photography of Moving Picture Drama)*. Tokyo: Hikōsha, 1917. 2d ed., Tokyo: Seikōsha, 1921.

———. *Kogata eiga no satsuei to eisha (The Photography and Projection of Amateur Movies)*. Tokyo: Seibundō jussen bunko, 1930.

———. Mizusawa Takehiko [pseud.]. *Sei no kagayaki (The Glory of Life)*. In *Nihon shinario taikei,* edited by the Shinario sakka kyōkai, pp. 7–17. Vol. 1. Tokyo: Eijinsha, 1973.

Katsudō gahō (1917–1923).

Katsudō kurabu [originally *Katsudō hyōron*] (1918–1924).

Katsudō no sekai (1916–1918).

Katsudō shashinkai (1909–1911).

Katsudō shashin zasshi (1915–1918).

Kawatake Shigetoshi. *Nihon engeki zenshi (A Complete History of the Japanese Theater)*. Tokyo: Iwanami shoten, 1959.

Keene, Donald. *Dawn to the West: Japanese Literature in the Modern Era.* 2 vols. New York: Holt, Rinehart and Winston, 1984.

———. *World within Walls: Japanese Literature of the Pre-Modern Era, 1600–1867.* New York: Grove Press, 1976.

Kern, Stephen. *The Culture of Time and Space, 1880–1918*. Cambridge: Harvard University Press, 1983.

Kinema junpō (1919–1925).

Kinema Record [originally *Film Record*] (1913–1917).

Kinugasa Teinosuke. *Waga eiga no seishun* (*My Youth in Films*). Tokyo: Chūō kōronsha, 1977.

Kirihara, Donald. "A Reconsideration of the Institution of the Benshi." *Film Reader* 6 (1985): pp. 42–45.

Kishi Matsuo. *Jinbutsu nihon eiga shi 1* (*Personalities: A History of the Japanese Film 1*). Tokyo: Dabiddosha, 1970.

———. "Kaisetsu: Shinario tanjō izen" ("Commentary: Before the Birth of the Screenplay"). In *Nihon shinario taikei,* edited by the Shinario sakka kyōkai, pp. 794–801. Vol. 1. Tokyo: Eijinsha, 1973.

Komatsu Hiroshi. "From Natural Colour to the Pure Motion Picture Drama: The Meaning of Tenkatsu Company in the 1910s of Japanese Film History." *Film History* 7, no. 1 (1995): pp. 81–86.

———. "The Fundamental Change: Japanese Cinema before and after the Earthquake of 1923." *Griffithiana* 38/39 (October 1990): pp. 186–193.

———. "Japan: Before the Great Kanto Earthquake." In *The Oxford History of World Cinema,* edited by Geoffrey Nowell-Smith, pp. 177–182. New York: Oxford University Press, 1996.

Kon Tōkō. *Jūnikai hōkai* (*Collapse of the Twelve-Story Tower*). Tokyo: Chūō kōronsha, 1978.

Lacasse, Alain. Introduction to "On the Notion of Genre in Cinema/Sur la notion de genre au cinéma." *IRIS* 20 (autumn 1995).

Lindsay, Vachel. *The Art of the Moving Picture.* 1915. Reprint, New York: MacMillan Company, 1916.

Loughney, Patrick. "From *Rip Van Winkle* to *Jesus of Nazareth:* Thoughts on the Origins of the American Screenplay." *Film History* 9, no. 3 (1997): pp. 277–389.

Makino Mamoru. "Eizō bunkengaku no seiritsu (A Way to the Image- Philology)" [a compilation of research on literature pertaining to the visual image]. *Kawasaki-shi shimin museum kiyō* (*Bulletin of the Kawasaki City Museum*) 3 (1990): pp. 98–145.

———, ed. *Fukkokuban Katsudō shashinkai.* 3 vols. Facsimile edition of *Katsudō shashinkai* (June 1909–May 1911), nos. 1–21; (November 1911), no. 26. Tokyo: Kokusho kankō, 1999.

———. *Fukkokuban Kinema rekōdo I.* 3 vols. Facsimile edition of *Film Record* (1 October 1913–11 November 1913), vol. 1, nos. 1–4; *Kinema Record* (10 December 1913–10 May 1915), vol. 1, no.5–vol. 4, no. 23. Tokyo: Kokusho kankō, 1999.

———. *Fukkokuban Kinema rekōdo II.* 3 vols. Facsimile edition of *Kinema Record* (10 January 1916–10 December 1916), vol. 4, nos. 31–42; (10 January 1917–1 December 1917), vol. 5, nos. 43–51. Tokyo: Kokusho kankō, 2000.

———, ed. *Nihon eiga shoki shiryō shūsei* (*A Collection of Research Material from the Early Days of Japanese Film*). Vols. 1–9. Facsimile edition of *Katsudō shashin zasshi* (June–December 1915), vols. 1–2; *Katsudō no sekai* (January–December 1916), vols. 3–5; *Katsudō gahō* (January–December 1917), vols. 6–9. Tokyo: Sanichi shobō, 1990–1991.

———. *Nihon eiga shoki shiryō shūsei* (*A Collection of Research Material from the Early Days of Japanese Film*). Vols. 10–14. Facsimile edition of *Katsudō hyōron* (December 1918–August 1919), vols. 10-11; *Katsudō kurabu* (September 1919–December 1920), vols. 11-14. Tokyo: Sanichi shobō, 1992.

Manvell, Roger. "Screenwriting." In *The International Encyclopedia of Film,* pp. 446–451. New York: Bonanza Books, 1975.

Marion, Frances. *Off with Their Heads: A Serio-Comic Tale of Hollywood.* New York: Macmillan, 1972.

Martinelli, Vittorio. "D'Annunziana." *Griffithiana*, no. 64 (October 1998): pp. 27–49.

Masumoto Kiyoshi."Shinsaku kyakuhon *Chichi no namida*" ("*A Father's Tears*"). *Katsudō no sekai* 3 (June 1918): pp. 133–161.

Masumura Yasuzō. "Profilo storico del cinema giapponese" ("Historical Outline of the Japanese Film"). In *La finzione e il sentimento* (*Fiction and Sentiment*), edited by Mostra Internazionale del Nuovo Cinema, pp. 189–251. Vol. 2 of *Schermi giapponese* (*The Japanese Screen*). Venezia: Marsilio Editori, 1984,

Matsuura Kōzō. *Nihon eiga shi taikan* (*A Chronological History of the Japanese Cinema*). Tokyo: Bunka shuppan kyoku, 1982.

McDonald, Keiko I. *From Book to Screen: Modern Japanese Literature in Film.* Armonk, N.Y.: M. E. Sharpe, 2000.

Meadow, Arnold. "An Analysis of Japanese Character Structure Based on Japanese Film Plots and Thematic Apperception Tests on Japanese Americans." Unpublished document. New York: Institute for Intercultural Studies, 1944.

Misono Kyōhei, ed. *Kaisō Makino eiga* (*Reminiscences: Makino Films*). Kyoto: Makino Shōzō sensei kenshō kai, 1971.

———. *Katsuben jidai* (*The Age of Katsuben*). Tokyo: Iwanami shoten, 1990.

Mori Iwao and Tomonari Yōzō. *Katsudō shashin taikan* (*A Survey of the Moving Pictures*). 4 vols. Supplement to *Nihon eiga shi sōkō* (*Notes on Japanese Film History*). Edited by Okabe Ryū. Tokyo: Tokyo Film Library Council, 1976–1978.

Münsterberg, Hugo. *The Film: A Psychological Study* (*The Silent Photoplay in 1916*). New York: Dover Publications, Inc., 1970. Reprint of *The Photoplay: A Psychological Study.* New York: D. Appleton and Company, 1916.

Murata Minoru and Ushihara Kiyohiko, eds. *Eiga kagaku kenkyū* (*Scientific Film Research.* Vols. 1, 3–5. Tokyo: Eiga kagaku kenkyū kai, 1928–1929.

Nihon eiga daihyō shinario zenshū (*Representative Japanese Screenplays Collection*). Tokyo: Kinema junpō, 1959.

Nihon eiga sakuhin jiten senzenhen (*Complete Dictionary of Japanese Movies from 1896 to August 1945*). 5 vols. Tokyo: Kagaku shoin, 1996.

Nihon eiga shinario koten zenshū (*Classic Japanese Screenplays/Scenario Classics Collection*). Vol. 1. Tokyo: Kinema junpō, 1965.

Nihon eiga shinario koten zenshū horidasareta meisakusen (*Classic Japanese Screenplays/ Scenario Classics Collection: Recovered Masterpieces*). Supplement. Tokyo: Kinema junpō, 1966.

Nihon shinario sakka kyōkai, ed. *Nihon shinario taikei* (*A Historical Collection of Japanese Screenplays*). Vol. 1. Tokyo: Eijinsha, 1973.

Nolletti, Arthur, and David Desser, eds. *Reframing Japanese Cinema: Authorship, Genre, History.* Bloomington: Indiana University Press, 1992.

Okabe Ryū, ed. *Kaeriyama Norimasa to Tōmasu Kurihara no gyōseki* (*A Collection of Material on Kaeriyama Norimasa and Thomas Kurihara*). Nihon eiga shi sōkō, no. 8. Tokyo: Film Library Council, 1973.

———. *Nihon no haiyū gakkō* (*Acting Schools in Japan*). Nihon eiga shi sōkō, no.7. Tokyo: Film Library Council, 1972.

Okada Susumu. *Nihon eiga no rekishi* (*History of Japanese Cinema*). Tokyo: Dabiddosha, 1967.

Ottaviani, Gioia. "The Shingeki Movement until 1930: Its Experience in Western Approach." In *Rethinking Japan,* edited by Adriana Boscaro, Franco Gatti, and Massimo Raveri. Vol. 1, pp. 178–183. New York: St. Martins Press, 1991.

Ozaki Hotsuki et al. "Zadankai Tanizaki Jun'ichirō to Yokohama—Nihon eiga shijō ni mo jūyō na kakawari" ("Discussion: Tanizaki Jun'ichirō and Yokohama: A Relationship Important to the History of Japanese Film"). *Yūrin*,10 March 1986.

Pollack, David. *Reading against Culture*. Ithaca: Cornell University Press, 1992.

Ramsaye, Terry. *A Million and One Nights: A History of the Motion Picture*. New York: Simon and Schuster, 1926.

Reynauld, Isabelle. "Written Scenarios of Early French Cinema: Screenwriting Practices in the First Twenty Years." *Film History* 9, no. 3 (1997): pp. 257–268.

Rimer, J. Thomas. *Toward a Modern Japanese Theatre: Kishida Kunio*. New Jersey: Princeton University Press, 1974.

Sargent, Epes Winthrop. *Technique of the Photoplay*. 1912. 2d ed., New York: Chalmers, 1913; 3rd ed., New York: Chalmers, 1916.

Satō Tadao. *Nihon eiga shi* (*History of Japanese Cinema*). Vol. 1. Tokyo: Iwanami shoten, 1995.

Scrittura e immagine: La didascalia nel cinema muto (*Writing and Image: Titles in Silent Cinema*). Edited by Francesco Pitassio and Leonardo Quaresima. Udine: Forum, 1998.

Seidensticker, Edward. *High City, Low City: Tokyo from Edo to the Earthquake*. New York: Knopf, 1983.

———. *Tokyo Rising: The City since the Great Earthquake*. New York: Knopf: 1990.

Shibata Masaru [Ōmori Masaru]. "Jun'eigageki to kouta eiga" ("Interview: Pure Films and Musical Films"). In *Kikigaki kinema no seishun,* edited by Iwamoto Kenji and Saiki Tomonori, pp. 7–46. Tokyo: Libroport, 1988.

Shimaji Takamaro, ed. *Nihon eiga kantoku zenshū* (*A Dictionary of Japanese Film Directors*). Tokyo: Kinema junpō, 1976.

Shindō Kaneto. *Aru eiga kantoku no shogai Mizoguchi Kenji no kiroku* (*The Life of a Film Director: Records of Mizoguchi Kenji*). 1975. Reprint, Tokyo: Eijinsha, 1984.

Shōchiku kyūjūnen shi (*A Ninety-Year History of Shōchiku*). Tokyo: Shōchiku kabushiki kaisha, 1985.

Stempel, Tom. *Framework: A History of Screenwriting in the American Film*. New York: The Continuum Publishing Company, 1988.

Tachibana Kōichirō, ed. *Tanizaki Jun'ichirō sensei chosho sōmokuroku* (*A Catalogue of Works by Tanizaki Jun'ichirō*). Supplementary vol. Tokyo: Gyararii gohachi, 1966.

Tanaka Jun'ichirō. "Eigakan nyūjōryō" ("Movie Theater Admission Fees"). In *Nedan no fūzokushi* (*A Popular History of Prices*), pp. 485–490. Vol. 1. Tokyo: Asahi shinbunsha, 1988.

———. *Katsudō shashin ga yatte kita* (*When the Moving Pictures Came Along*). Tokyo: Chūō kōronsha, 1985.

———. *Nihon eiga hattatsu shi* (*A History of the Development of Japanese Cinema*). 5 vols. Tokyo; Chūō kōronsha, 1975–1976.

———. "Onoe Matsunosuke-geki *Bingo Saburō,* Mukōjima shinpageki, *Chichi no namida,* Yamazaki Naganosuke rensageki *Utashigure,* Sawamura Shirogorō-geki, *Josō ninjutsu*" ("Scripts for an Onoe Matsunosuke film, *Bingo Saburō;* a Mukōjima *shinpageki, Chichi no namida;* a Yamazaki Naganosuke chain drama, *Utashigure;* a Sawamura Shirogorō film, *Josō ninjutsu*"). In *Horidasareta meisakusen*, pp. 25–31. Supplement to *Nihon eiga shinario koten zenshū*. Tokyo: Kinema junpō, 1966.

Tanizaki Jun'ichirō. *Amachua kurabu* (*Amateur Club*). In *Horidasareta meisakusen,* pp. 32–45. Supplement to *Nihon eiga shinario koten zenshū*. Tokyo: Kinema junpō, 1966.

———. *Amachua kurabu*. *Katsudō zasshi* 7, nos. 6–10 (June–October 1921): no. 6, pp. 150–155; no. 7, pp. 140–147; no. 8, pp. 134–138; no. 9, pp. 136–140; no. 10, pp. 108–109.

———. "Eiga no koto nado" ("On Film"). *Shinchō* (April 1955): pp. 345–348.

342

———. "Otogigeki *Hinamatsuri no yoru*" (*The Night of the Doll Festival*). *Shinengei* 9 (September 1924).

Tanizaki Jun'ichirō. Shinchō Nihon bungaku arubamu. Vol. 7. Tokyo: Shinchōsha, 1985.

Tanizaki Jun'ichirō zenshū (*Collected Works of Tanizaki Jun'ichirō*). Tokyo: Chūō kōronsha, 1957–1959.

Tanizaki Jun'ichirō zenshū (*Collected Works of Tanizaki Jun'ichirō*). Tokyo: Chūō kōronsha, 1966–1970.

Tessier, Max, ed. *Cinéma et littérature au Japon: De l'ère Meiji à nos jours* (*Cinema and Literature in Japan: From Meiji to Today*). Paris: Editions du Centre Pompidou, 1986.

Tsivian, Yuri. "Spoken Titles in Russian Films." *Scrittura e immagine: La didascalia nel cinema muto*, edited by Francesco Pitassio and Leonardo Quaresima, pp. 247–254. Udine: Forum, 1998.

Tsuruta Yoshinobu. *Nihon eiga shi no kenkyū katsudō shashin torai zengo no jijō* (*A Study of Japanese Film History: The Introduction of Moving Pictures*). Tokyo: Kōbunsha, 1980.

Tsurutani Hisashi. *America Bound: The Japanese and the Opening of the American West.* Translated by Betsey Scheiner with the assistance of Yamamura Mariko. Tokyo: The Japan Times, 1989.

Ushihara Kiyohiko. "Kamata modanizumu no gunzō" ("Interview: The Kamata Modernism Group"). In *Kikigaki kinema no seishun,* edited by Iwamoto Kenji and Saiki Tomonori, pp. 101–140. Tokyo: Libroport, 1988.

Welsh, Robert E. *A.B.C. of Motion Pictures.* New York: Harper & Brothers Publishers, 1916.

Weston, Harold. *The Art of Photo-Play Writing.* London: McBride, Nast and Company, 1916.

Yamamoto Kajirō. *Katsudōya suiro* (*"Katsudōya" Waterway: Memoirs of a Movie Man*). Tokyo: Chikuma shobō, 1965.

Yamamoto Kikuo. "Bluebird eiga ni tsuite" ("Bluebird Films"). *FC,* no. 12 (February 1963).

———. *Nihon eiga ni okeru gaikoku eiga no eikyō hikaku eiga kenkyū* (*A Comparative Study of the Influence of Foreign Films on the Japanese Cinema*). Tokyo: Waseda daigaku shuppanbu, 1983.

Yanagisawa Ken et al. "Shinjidai ryūkō no shōchō toshite mitaru 'jidōsha' to 'katsudō shashin' to 'kafe' no inshō" ("Cars, Moving Pictures, Cafes as Symbols of the New Age"). *Chūō kōron* (September 1918): pp. 67–96.

Yasumi Toshio. "Shinario shi josetsu" ("An Introduction to the History of Screenwriting") nos. 1–7. *Shinario* 37, nos. 5–11 (1981).

Yoda Yoshikata. "Mizoguchi Kenji izen" ("Interview: Before Mizoguchi Kenji"). In *Kikigaki kinema no seishun,* edited by Iwamoto Kenji and Saiki Tomonori, pp. 233–258. Tokyo: Libroport, 1988.

———. *Mizoguchi Kenji no hito to geijutsu* (*Mizoguchi Kenji: The Man and His Art*). Tokyo: Tabata shoten, 1970.

Yoshida Chieo. *Mō hitotsu no eigashi* (*One More Film History*). Tokyo: Jiji tsūshinsha, 1978.

INDEX

(page numbers in italics refer to
    illustrations)

Abe Kōbō, 165
Abel, Richard, 39
Abe Yutaka (Jack "Jackie" Abbe), 102, 120,
    133, 315 n. 2, 316–317 n. 13
Akatsuki no dassō (*Escape at Dawn,*
    Taniguchi Senkichi, 1950), 163
Akimoto Kikuya, *40*
Alien Land Law: California (1913), 123; —,
    (1920), 135
Amachua kurabu. See *Amateur Club*
Amateur Club (Thomas Kurihara, 1920),
    263; acting in, 129; cast and crew,
    Yuigahama location, during production
    of, *224;* censorship of, 109, 222–223;
    Hayama Michiko in, *211, 213;* parody
    of kabuki in, 196; mentioned, 14,
    18–20; 26, 105, 119, 157, 158,
    160–165; 239–240
American-Japan Film Co., 131
Anderson, Joseph L., 17, 326 n. 3, 236
Aoki Tsuru(ko) (Mrs. Sessue Hayakawa),
    105, 120, *121,* 316 n. 13
Aoyama Sugisaku, *81, 94*
art, cinema as, 20, 22, 124, 236; literary
    writers and, 141; Tanizaki's reference
    to (1917), 196–197
Art of the Moving Picture, The (Vachel

Lindsay, 1915), 111, 135. *See also*
    Lindsay, Vachel
Art of Photoplay Making, The (Victor
    Freeburg, 1918), 113. *See also*
    Freeburg, Victor
art titles. *See* intertitles
Asakusa, 208, *209*
Asakusa opera, 321 n. 75, 209
Asano Yoshizō, 116, 124–125, 164, 187,
    207, 230
Ashi ni sawatta onna (*The Woman Who
    Touched Legs,* Abe Yutaka, 1926),
    315 n. 2, 317 n. 13
Aware no kyoku. See *Song of Sadness*
Azlant, Edward, 141
Azuma Teru(ko), *94, 95,* 213, *214*

Barker, Reginald, 124
Belasco, David, 141
Benisawa Yōko, 129, 130, 223, *224,* 230,
    233, *300,* 321 n. 74
bensetsu (benshi narration, delivery), 35,
    258; *serifugeki* and, 112;
    transcriptions, synopses and, 178
benshi, 34, 308 n. 40; *Amateur Club* and,
    207; censorship and, 195; 107;
    endurability, popularity of, 27, 77–78;
    export and, 85; *Glory of Life, The* and,
    89; institution of, 33–37; intertitles
    and, 13, 35–36, 237; *kuchidate* and,

345

Books in the Contemporary Film and Television Series

Mythologies of Violence in Postmodern Media, edited by Christopher Sharrett, 1999

Feminist Hollywood: From Born in Flames *to* Blue Steel, by Christina Lane, 2000

Reading Cavell's The World Viewed: *A Philosophical Perspective on Film,* by William Rothman and Marian Keane, 2000

Writing in Light: The Silent Scenario and the Japanese Pure Film Movement, by Joanne Bernardi, 2001